Grand Blue Dreaming

PRESENTED BY KENJI INOUE & KIMITAKE YOSHIOKA

Ch. 66: Sakurako's Journey 003

Ch. 67: Shit! 057

Ch. 68: Who Likes Who? 097

Ch. 69: Two Returning 149

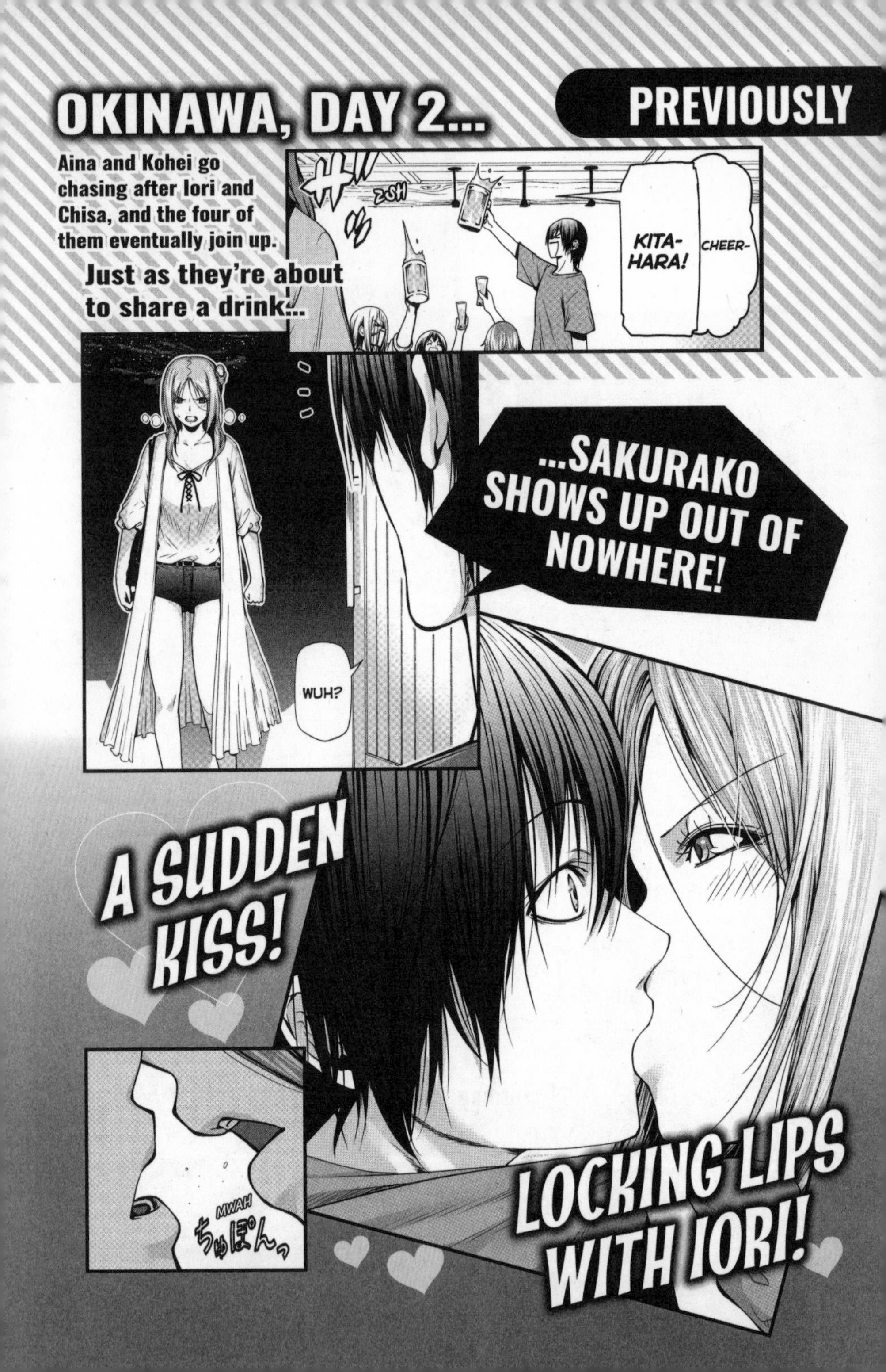
PREVIOUSLY
OKINAWA, DAY 2...
Aina and Kohei go chasing after Iori and Chisa, and the four of them eventually join up.
CHEER-
KITA-HARA!
ZSH
Just as they're about to share a drink...
...SAKURAKO SHOWS UP OUT OF NOWHERE!
WUH?
A SUDDEN KISS!
LOCKING LIPS WITH IORI!
MWAH
ちゅぽんっ

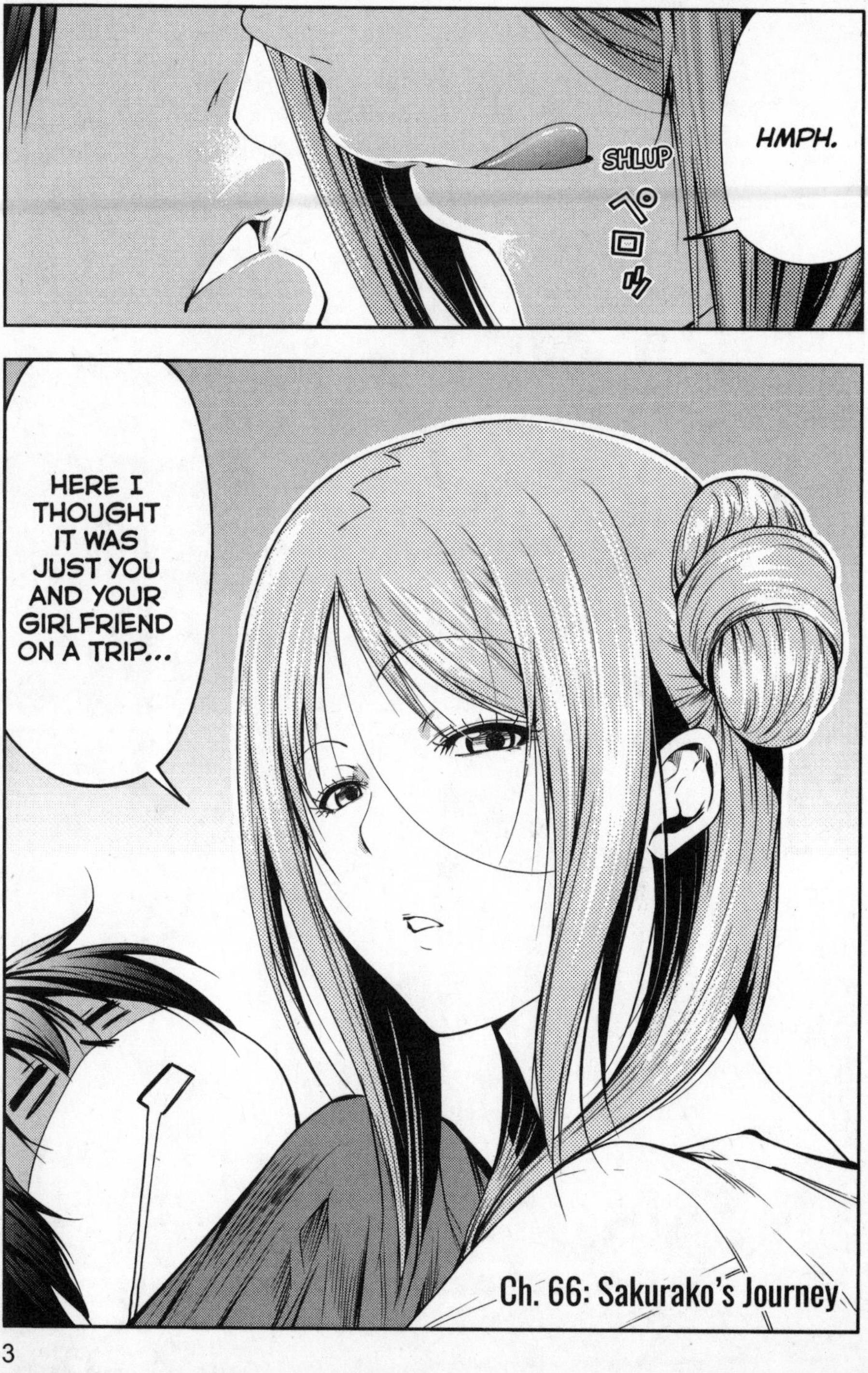
HMPH.
SHLUP
ペロッ
HERE I THOUGHT IT WAS JUST YOU AND YOUR GIRLFRIEND ON A TRIP...
Ch. 66: Sakurako's Journey

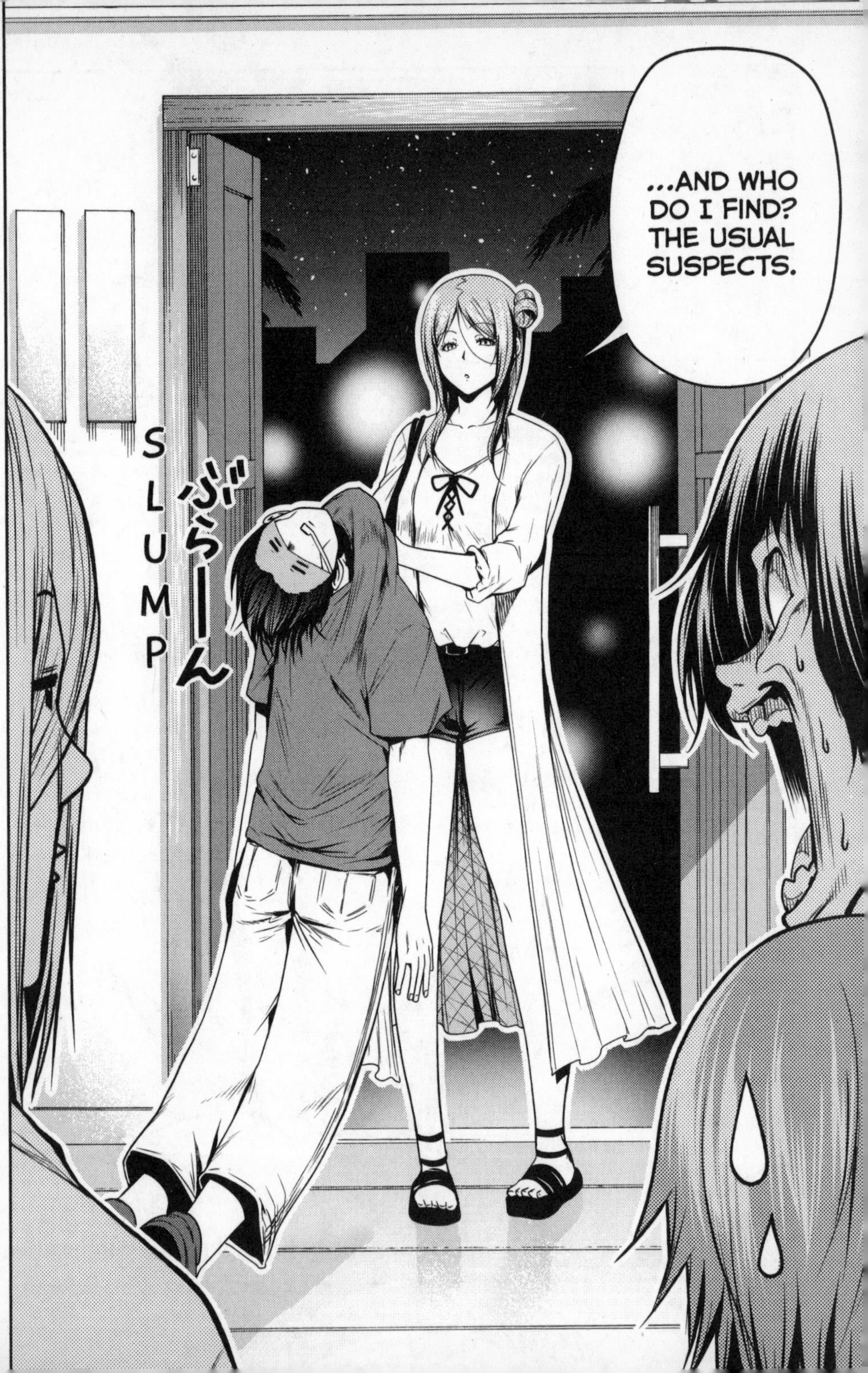
...AND WHO DO I FIND? THE USUAL SUSPECTS.
ぶら〜ん
SLUMP

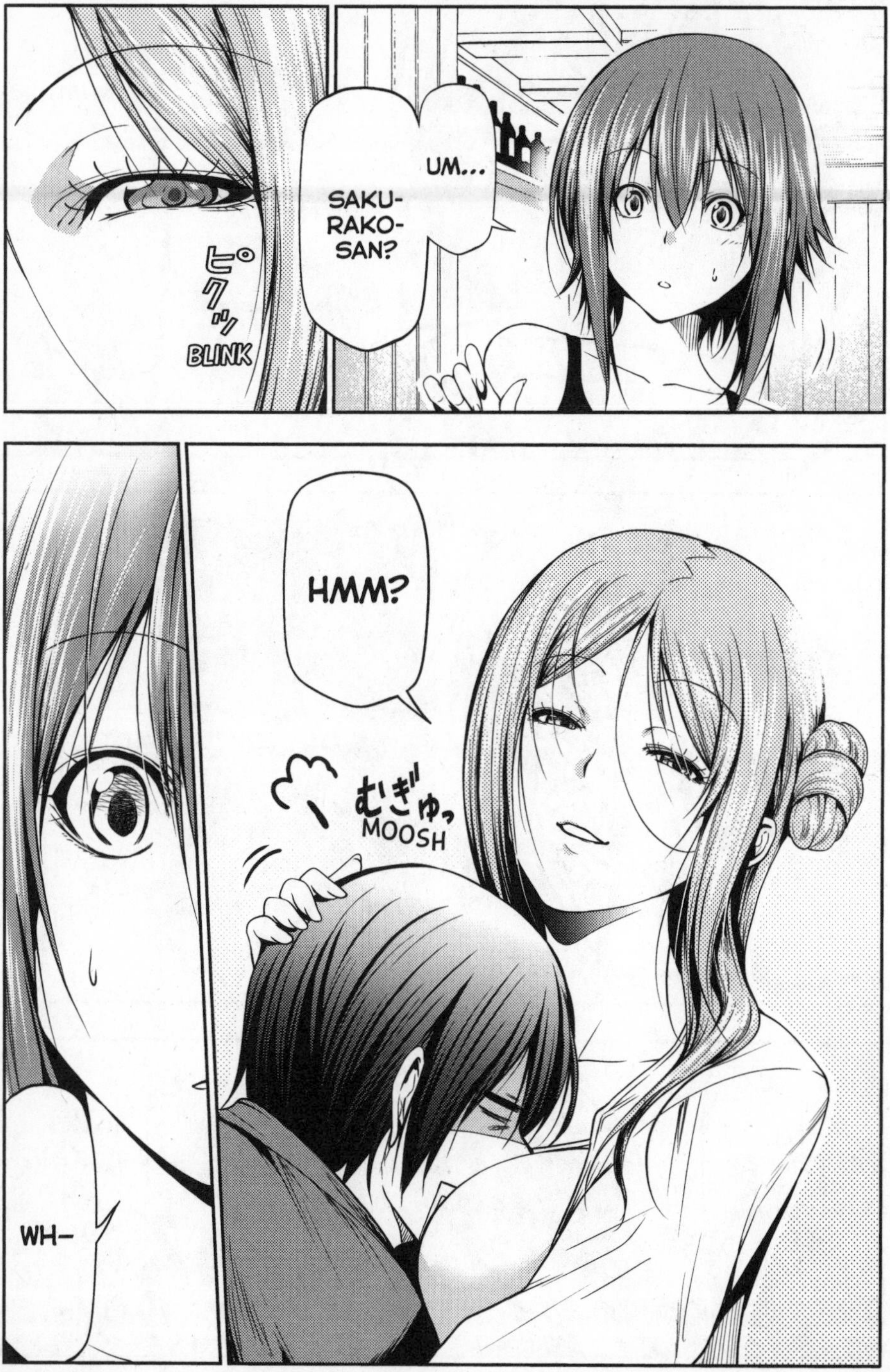
UM...
SAKU-RAKO-SAN?
ピクッ
BLINK
HMM?
むぎゅっ
MOOSH
WH-

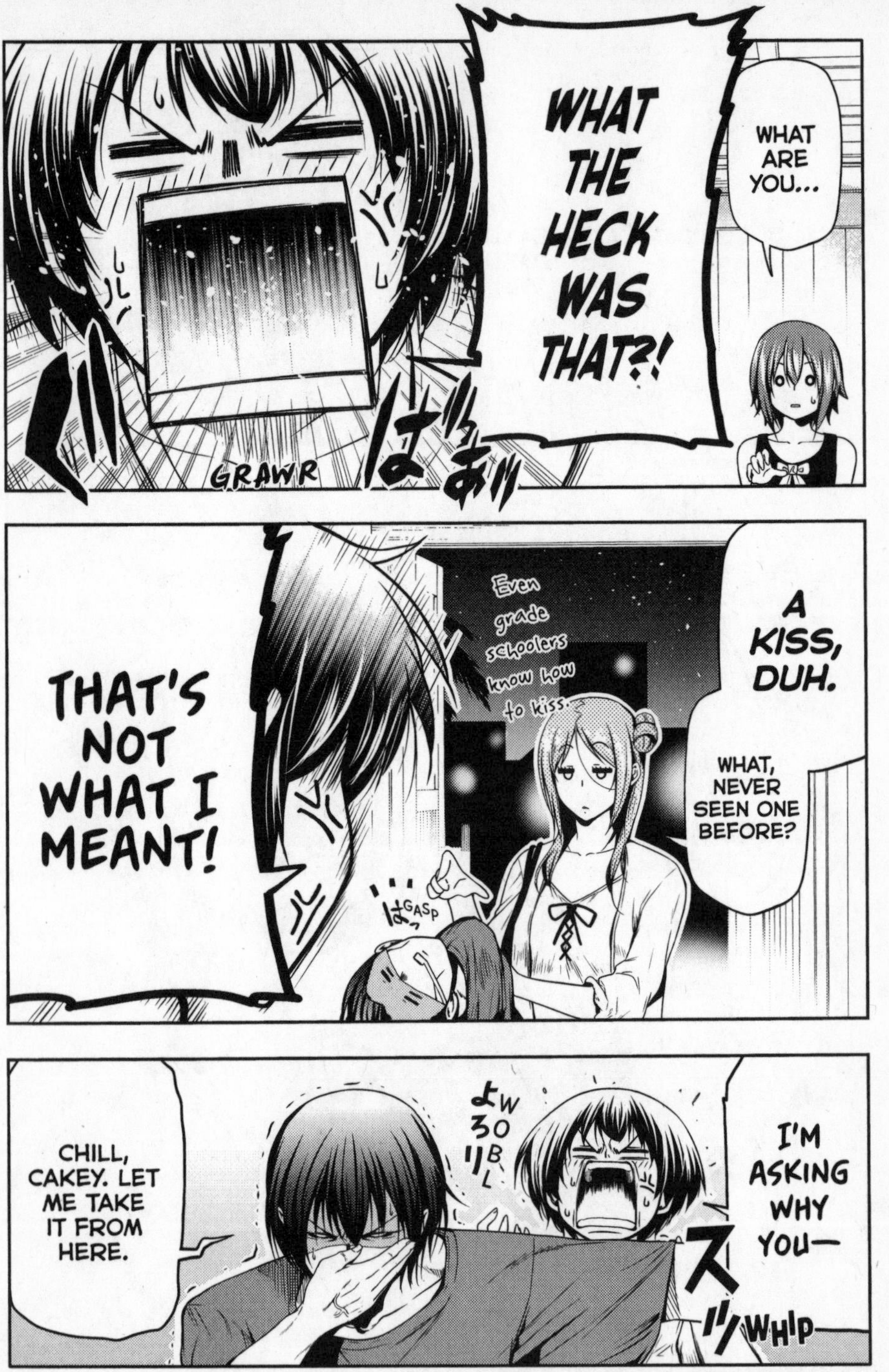
WHAT ARE YOU...
WHAT THE HECK WAS THAT?!
GRAWR
A KISS, DUH.
WHAT, NEVER SEEN ONE BEFORE?
Even grade schoolers know how to kiss.
THAT'S NOT WHAT I MEANT!
GASP
I'M ASKING WHY YOU—
WHIP
WOBBL
CHILL, CAKEY. LET ME TAKE IT FROM HERE.

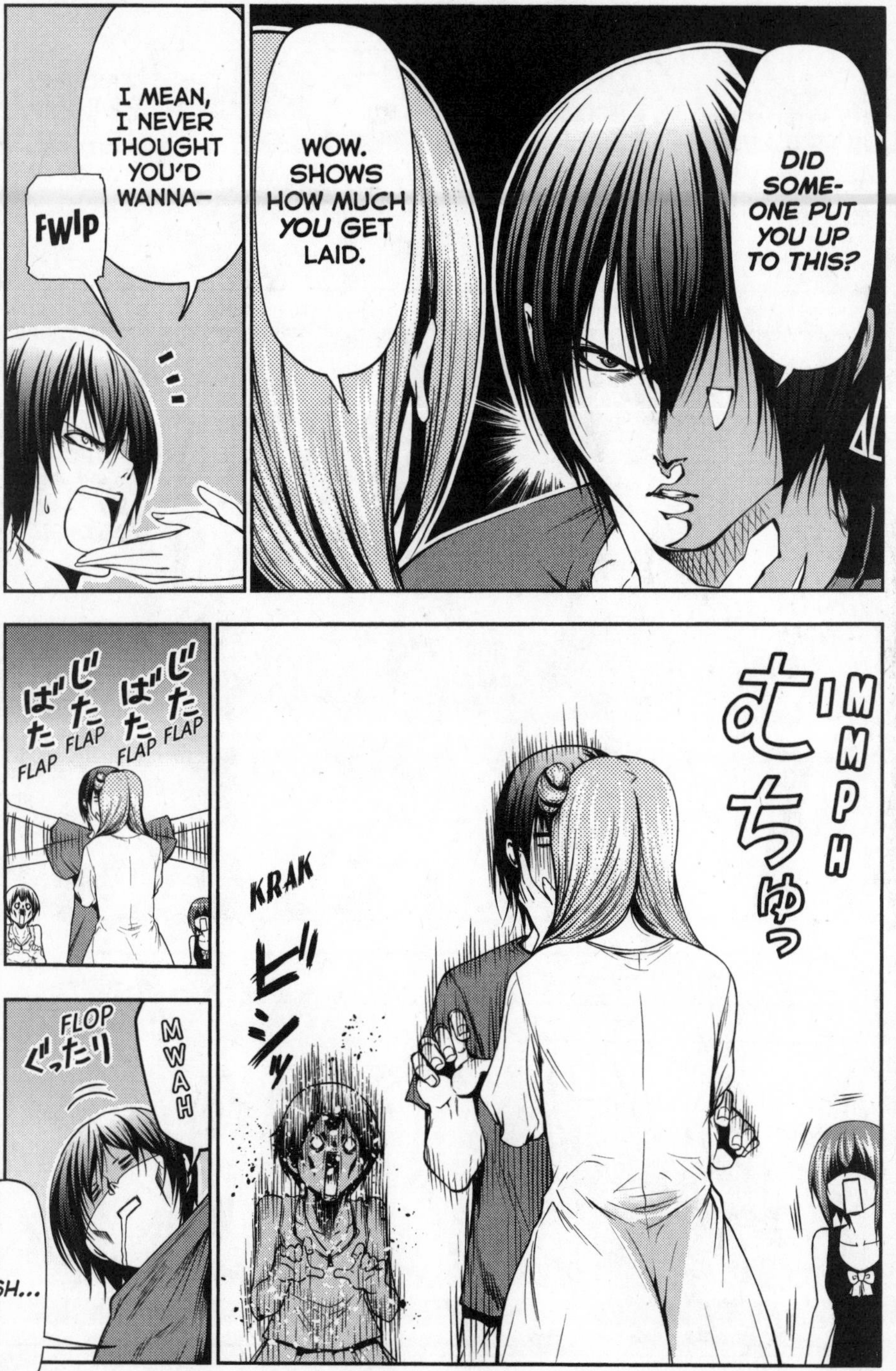
DID SOME-ONE PUT YOU UP TO THIS?
WOW. SHOWS HOW MUCH YOU GET LAID.
I MEAN, I NEVER THOUGHT YOU'D WANNA-
FWIP
...
MMMPH
むちゅっ
KRAK
ビシッ
じたばた FLAP FLAP
じたばた FLAP FLAP
FLOP
ぐったり
MWAH
UGH...

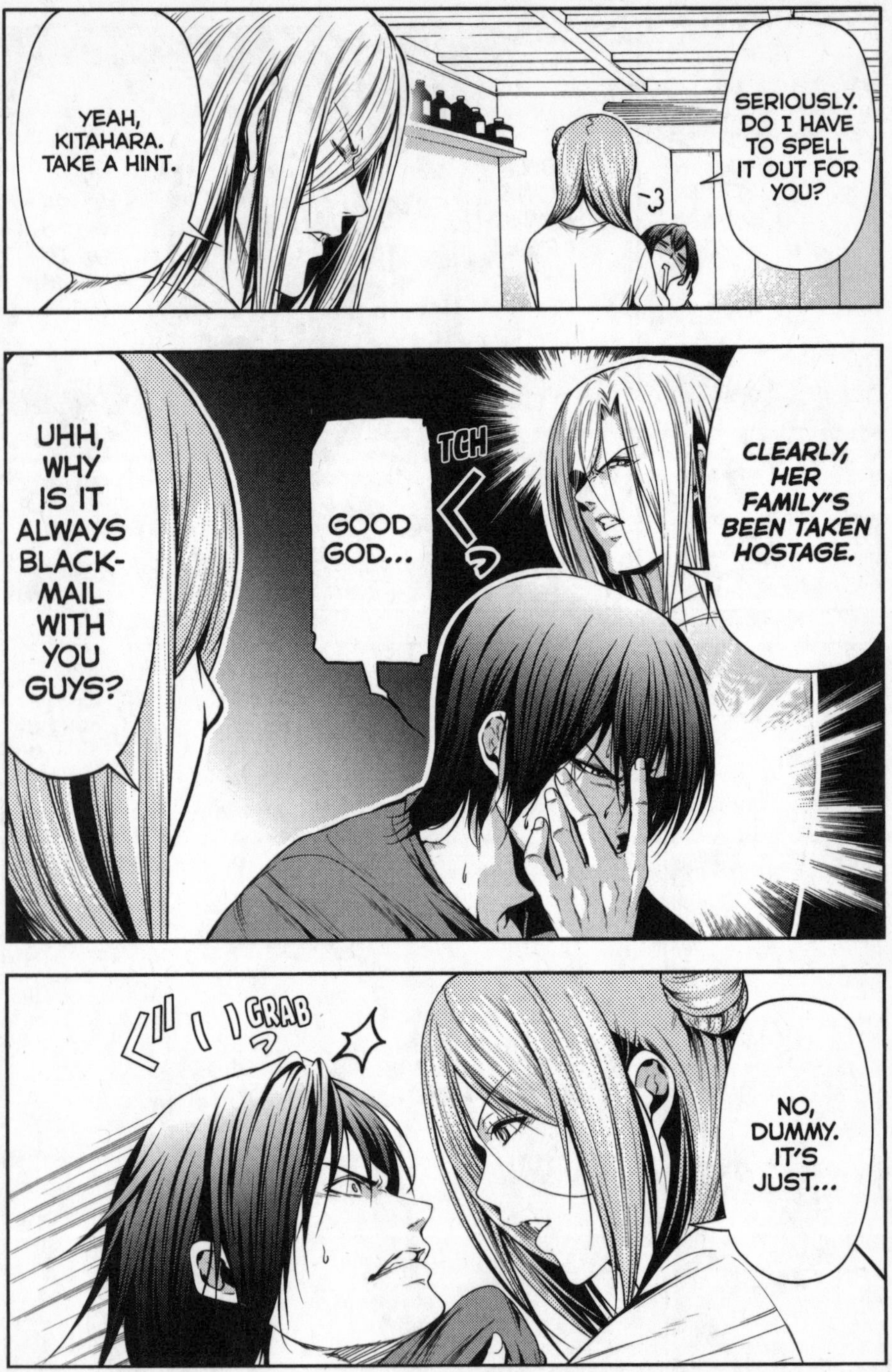
SERIOUSLY. DO I HAVE TO SPELL IT OUT FOR YOU?
YEAH, KITAHARA. TAKE A HINT.
CLEARLY, HER FAMILY'S BEEN TAKEN HOSTAGE.
TCH
GOOD GOD...
UHH, WHY IS IT ALWAYS BLACK-MAIL WITH YOU GUYS?
NO, DUMMY. IT'S JUST...
GRAB

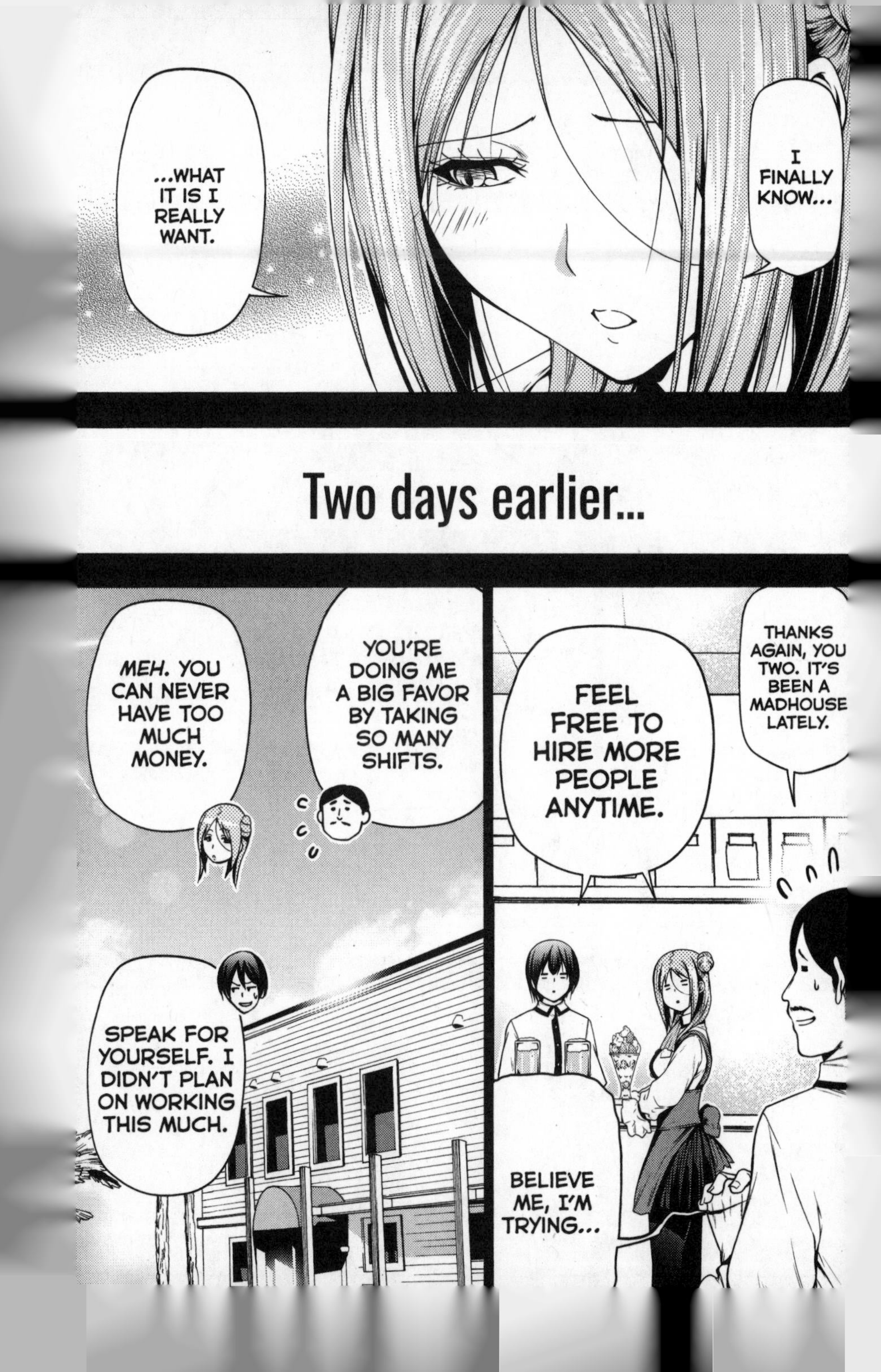
I FINALLY KNOW...
...WHAT IT IS I REALLY WANT.
Two days earlier...
THANKS AGAIN, YOU TWO. IT'S BEEN A MADHOUSE LATELY.
FEEL FREE TO HIRE MORE PEOPLE ANYTIME.
BELIEVE ME, I'M TRYING...
YOU'RE DOING ME A BIG FAVOR BY TAKING SO MANY SHIFTS.
MEH. YOU CAN NEVER HAVE TOO MUCH MONEY.
SPEAK FOR YOURSELF. I DIDN'T PLAN ON WORKING THIS MUCH.

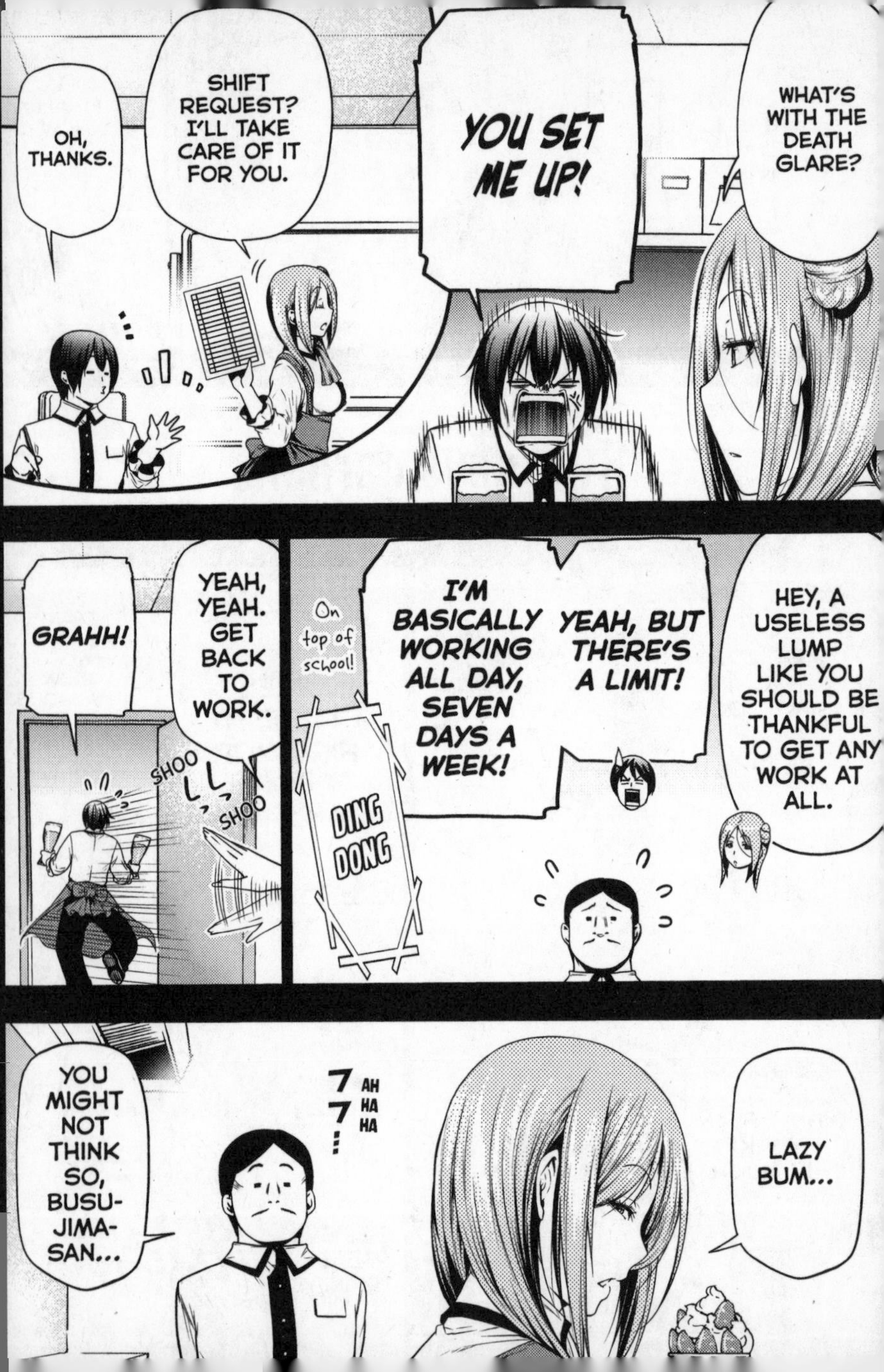
WHAT'S WITH THE DEATH GLARE?
YOU SET ME UP!
SHIFT REQUEST? I'LL TAKE CARE OF IT FOR YOU.
OH, THANKS.
HEY, A USELESS LUMP LIKE YOU SHOULD BE THANKFUL TO GET ANY WORK AT ALL.
YEAH, BUT THERE'S A LIMIT!
I'M BASICALLY WORKING ALL DAY, SEVEN DAYS A WEEK!
On top of school!
DING DONG
YEAH, YEAH. GET BACK TO WORK.
SHOO SHOO
GRAHH!
LAZY BUM...
AH HA HA
YOU MIGHT NOT THINK SO, BUSUJIMA-SAN...

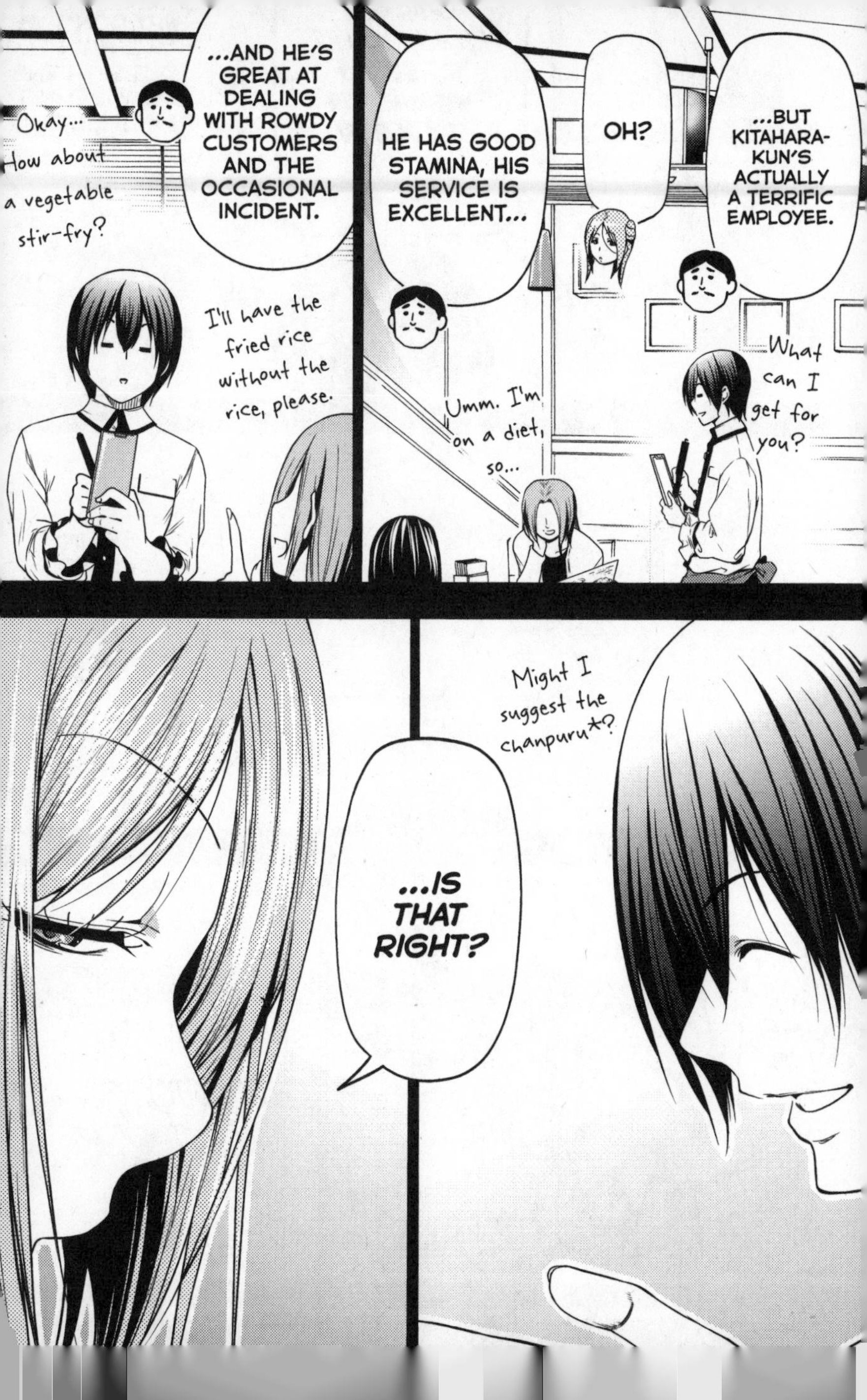
...BUT KITAHARA-KUN'S ACTUALLY A TERRIFIC EMPLOYEE.
OH?
HE HAS GOOD STAMINA, HIS SERVICE IS EXCELLENT...
What can I get for you?
Umm. I'm on a diet, so...
...AND HE'S GREAT AT DEALING WITH ROWDY CUSTOMERS AND THE OCCASIONAL INCIDENT.
I'll have the fried rice without the rice, please.
Okay... How about a vegetable stir-fry?
Might I suggest the chanpuru*?
...IS THAT RIGHT?

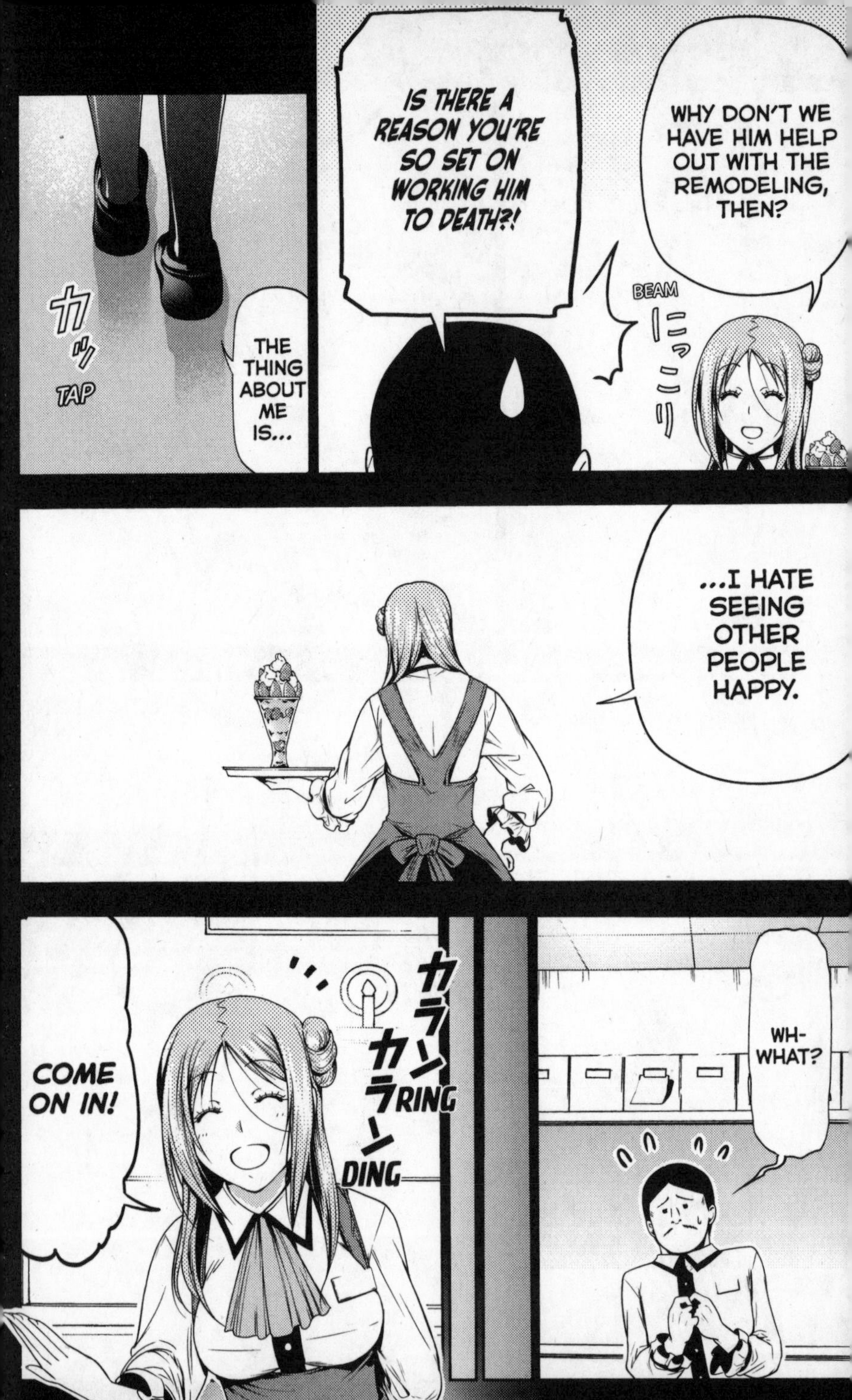
WHY DON'T WE HAVE HIM HELP OUT WITH THE REMODELING, THEN?
BEAM
にっこり
IS THERE A REASON YOU'RE SO SET ON WORKING HIM TO DEATH?!
THE THING ABOUT ME IS...
カッ
TAP
...I HATE SEEING OTHER PEOPLE HAPPY.
WH- WHAT?
カランカラン
RING
DING
COME ON IN!

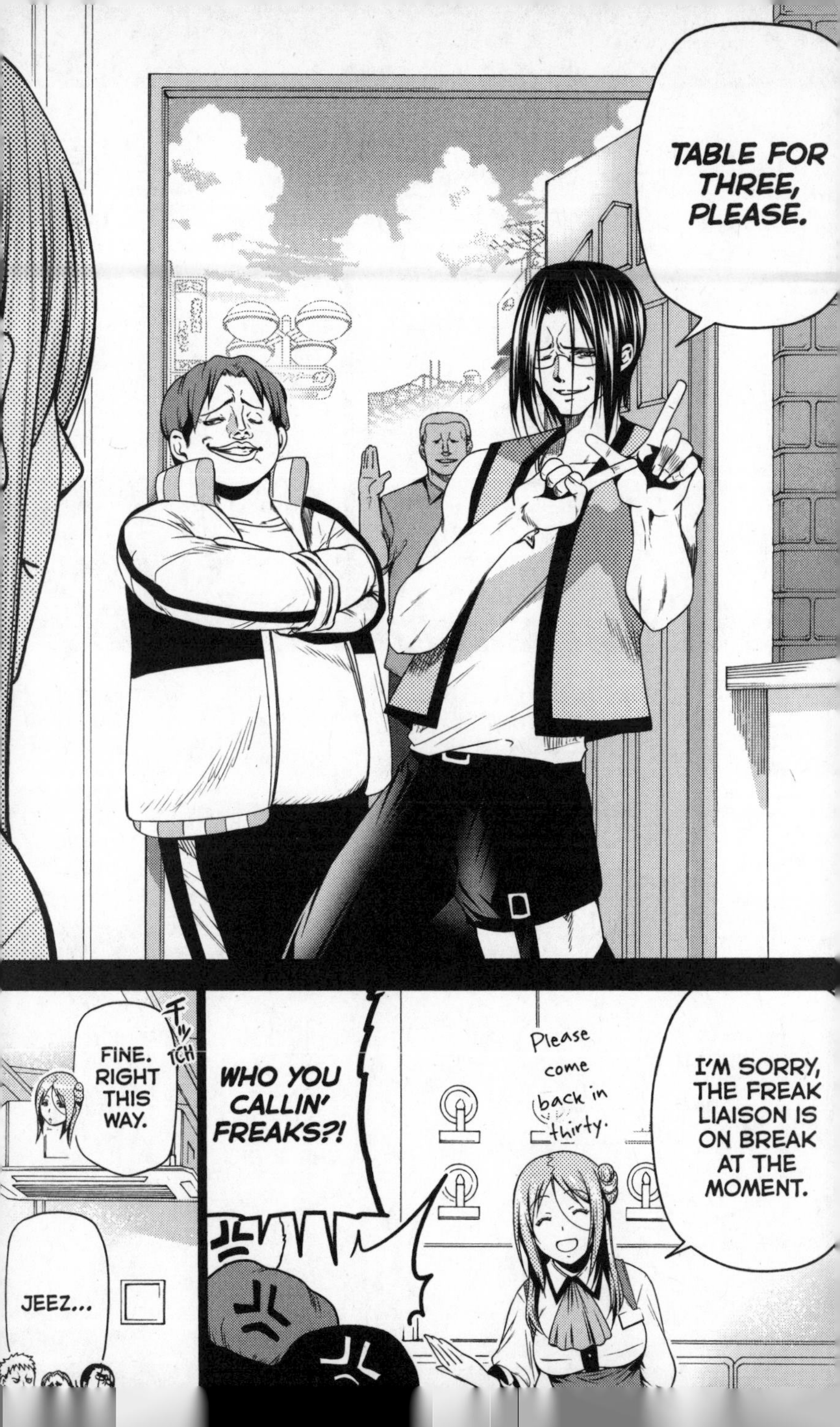
TABLE FOR THREE, PLEASE.
I'M SORRY, THE FREAK LIAISON IS ON BREAK AT THE MOMENT.
Please come back in thirty.
WHO YOU CALLIN' FREAKS?!
チッ TCH
FINE. RIGHT THIS WAY.
JEEZ...

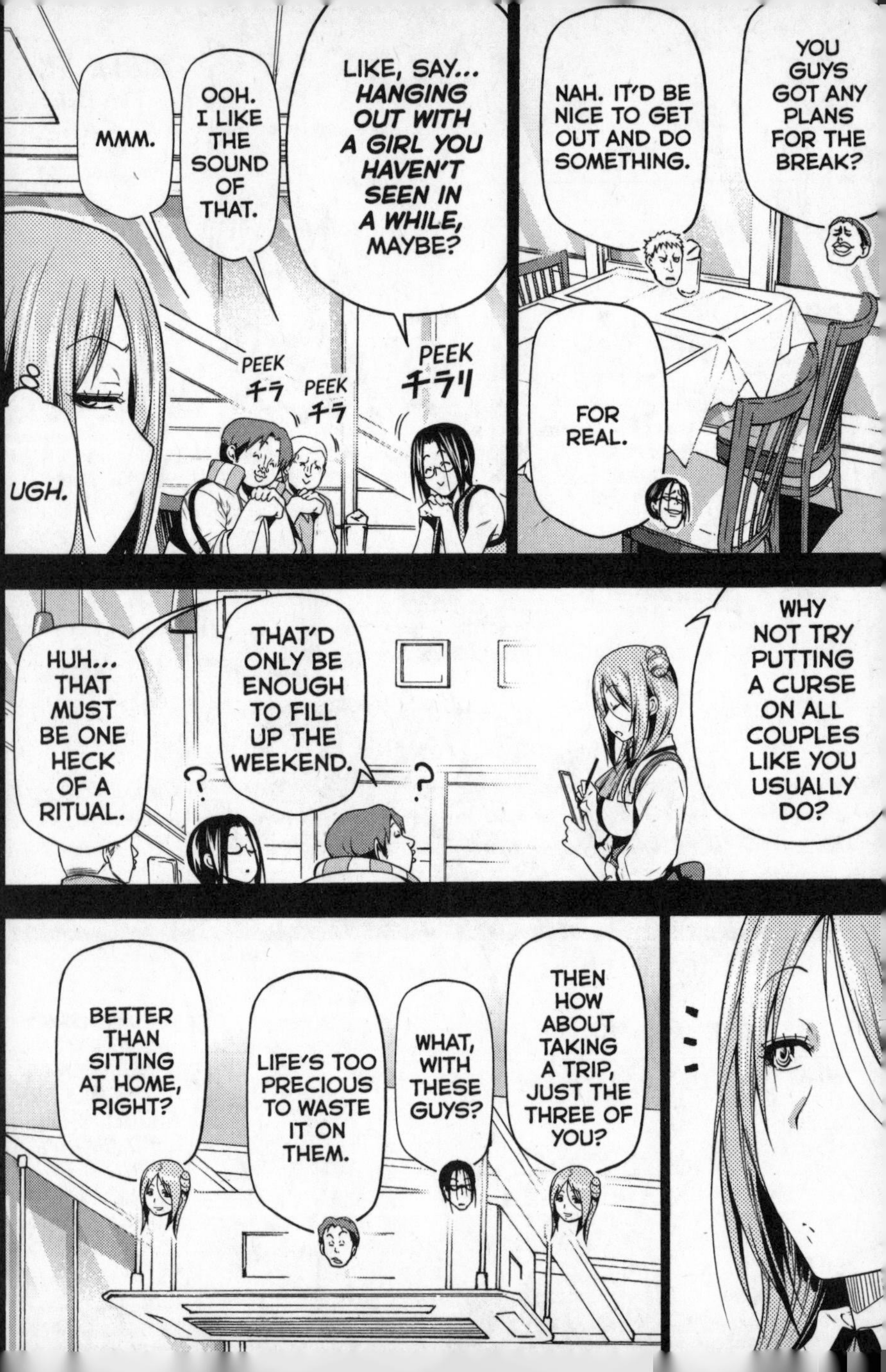
YOU GUYS GOT ANY PLANS FOR THE BREAK?
NAH. IT'D BE NICE TO GET OUT AND DO SOMETHING.
FOR REAL.
LIKE, SAY... *HANGING OUT WITH A GIRL YOU HAVEN'T SEEN IN A WHILE,* MAYBE?
PEEK チラリ
OOH. I LIKE THE SOUND OF THAT.
PEEK チラ
PEEK チラ
MMM.
UGH.
WHY NOT TRY PUTTING A CURSE ON ALL COUPLES LIKE YOU USUALLY DO?
THAT'D ONLY BE ENOUGH TO FILL UP THE WEEKEND.
HUH... THAT MUST BE ONE HECK OF A RITUAL.
...
THEN HOW ABOUT TAKING A TRIP, JUST THE THREE OF YOU?
WHAT, WITH THESE GUYS?
LIFE'S TOO PRECIOUS TO WASTE IT ON THEM.
BETTER THAN SITTING AT HOME, RIGHT?

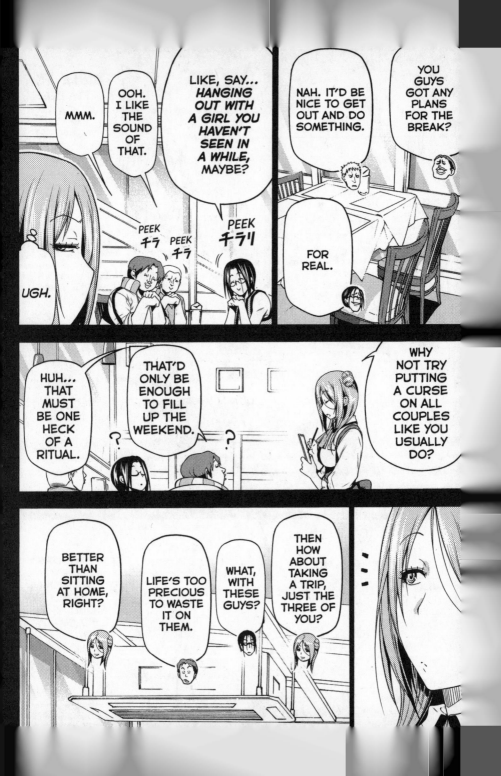

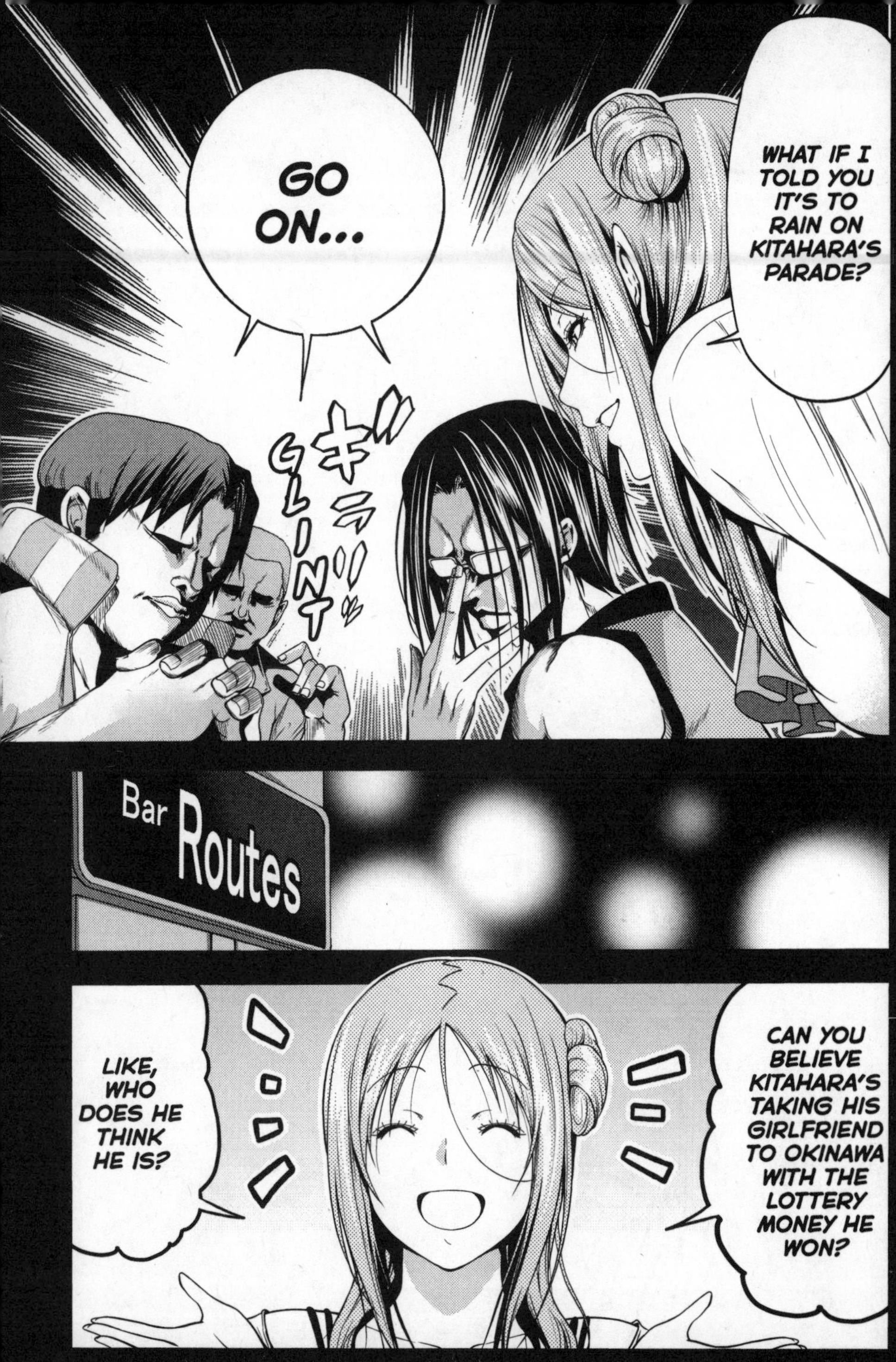
WHAT IF I TOLD YOU IT'S TO RAIN ON KITAHARA'S PARADE?
GO ON...
GLINT
Bar Routes
CAN YOU BELIEVE KITAHARA'S TAKING HIS GIRLFRIEND TO OKINAWA WITH THE LOTTERY MONEY HE WON?
LIKE, WHO DOES HE THINK HE IS?

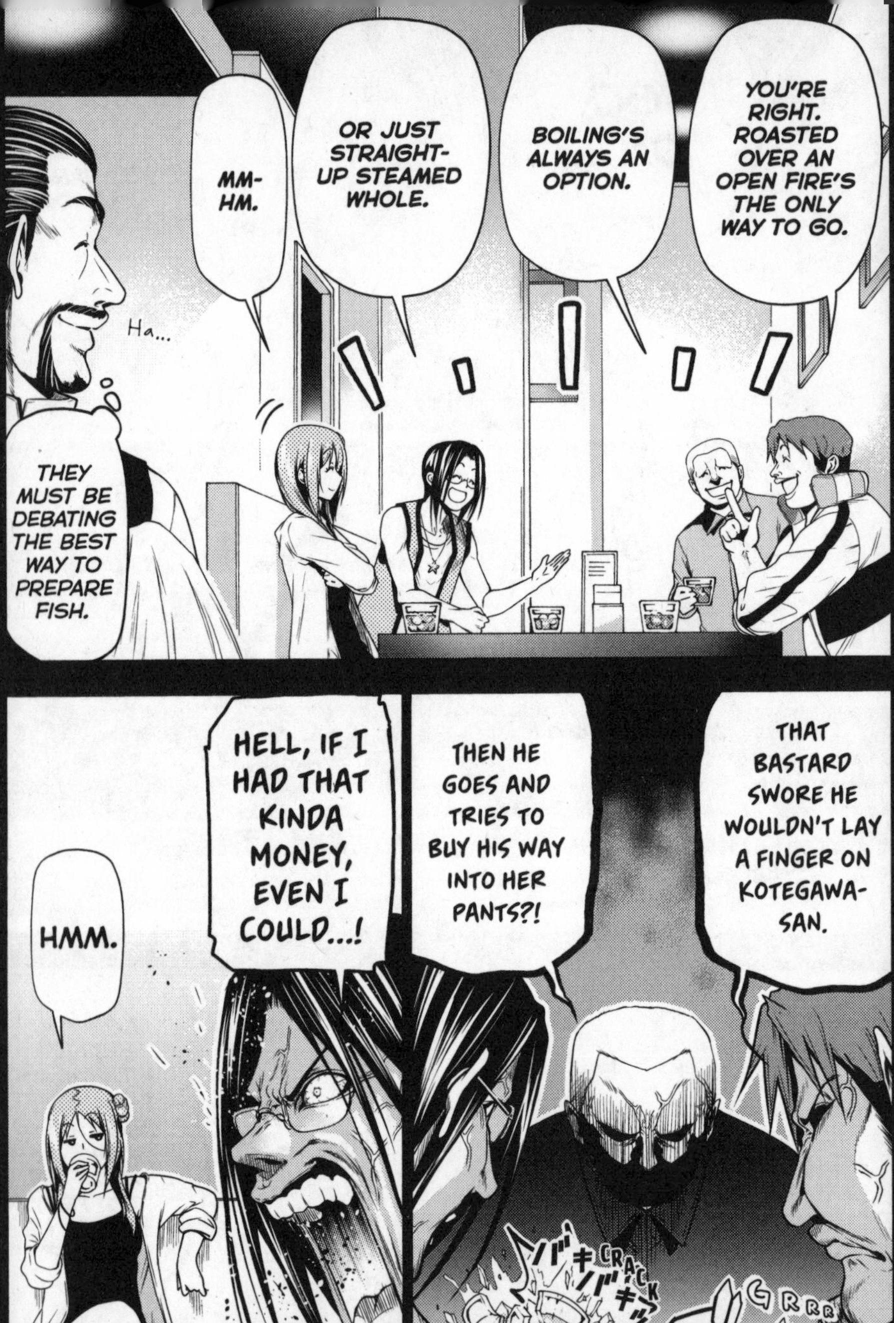
YOU'RE RIGHT. ROASTED OVER AN OPEN FIRE'S THE ONLY WAY TO GO.
BOILING'S ALWAYS AN OPTION.
OR JUST STRAIGHT-UP STEAMED WHOLE.
MM-HM.
Ha...
THEY MUST BE DEBATING THE BEST WAY TO PREPARE FISH.
THAT BASTARD SWORE HE WOULDN'T LAY A FINGER ON KOTEGAWA-SAN.
THEN HE GOES AND TRIES TO BUY HIS WAY INTO HER PANTS?!
GRRR
CRACK
HELL, IF I HAD THAT KINDA MONEY, EVEN I COULD...!
HMM.

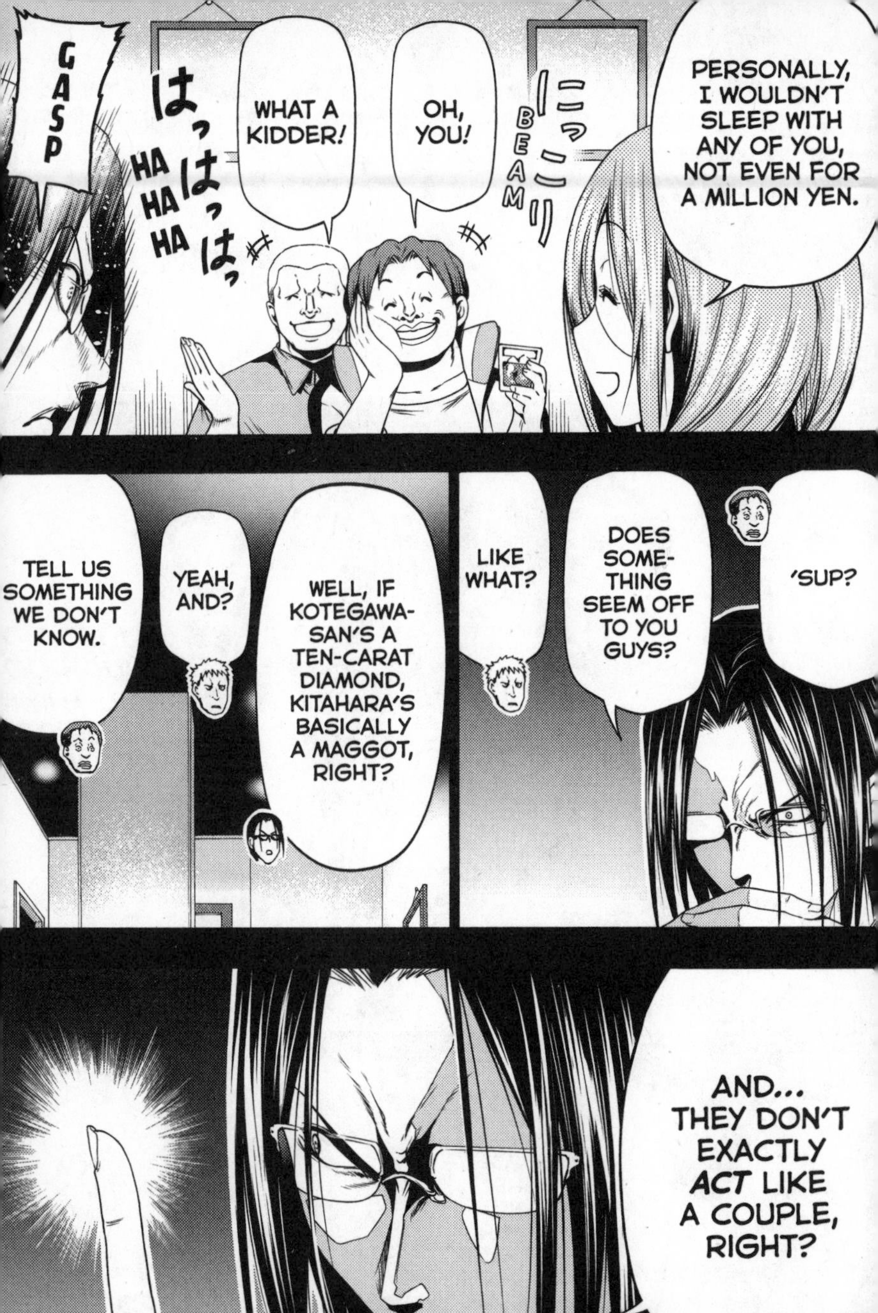
PERSONALLY, I WOULDN'T SLEEP WITH ANY OF YOU, NOT EVEN FOR A MILLION YEN.
BEAM
にっこり
OH, YOU!
WHAT A KIDDER!
HA HA HA
はっはっはっ
GASP
'SUP?
DOES SOME-THING SEEM OFF TO YOU GUYS?
LIKE WHAT?
WELL, IF KOTEGAWA-SAN'S A TEN-CARAT DIAMOND, KITAHARA'S BASICALLY A MAGGOT, RIGHT?
YEAH, AND?
TELL US SOMETHING WE DON'T KNOW.
AND... THEY DON'T EXACTLY *ACT* LIKE A COUPLE, RIGHT?

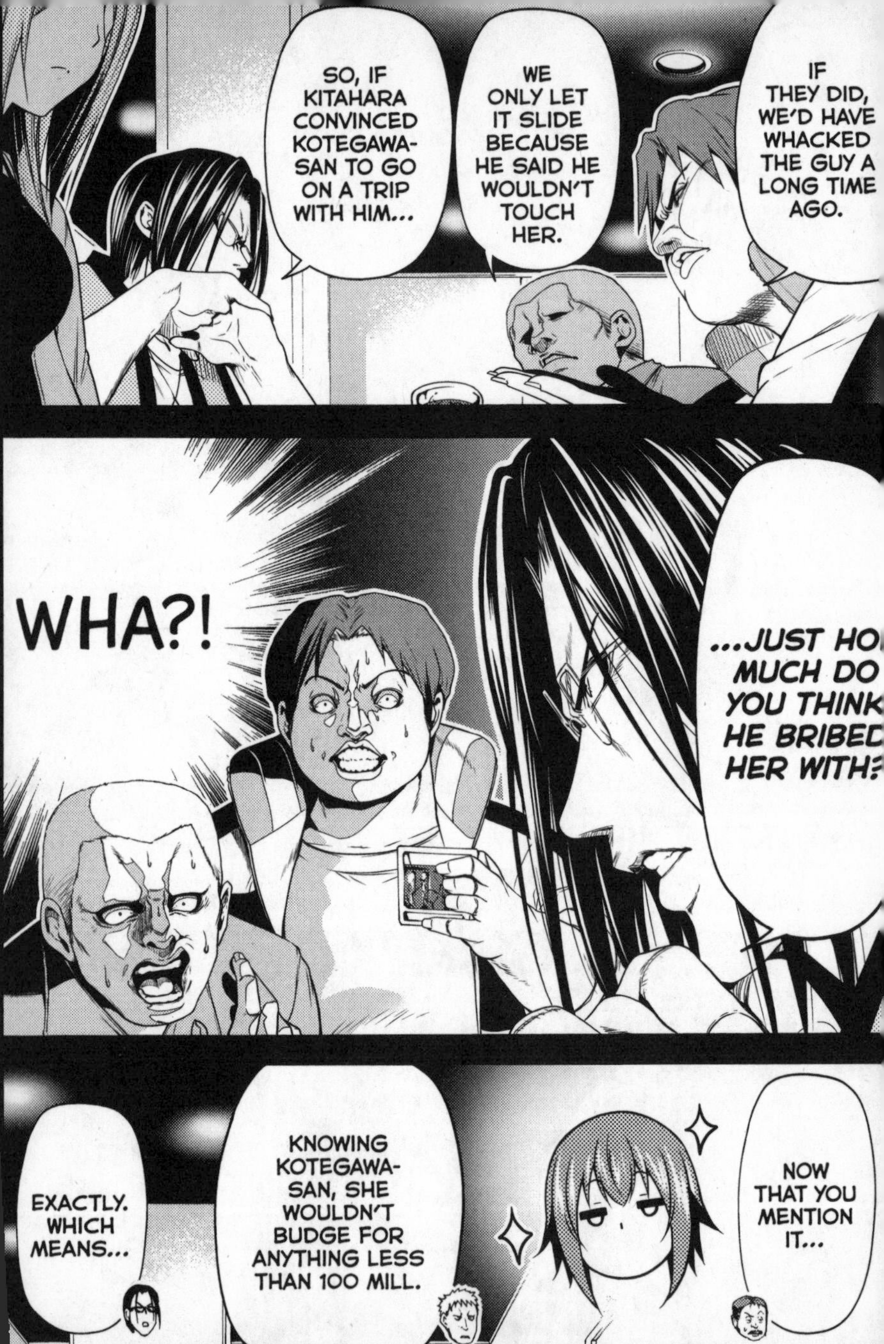
IF THEY DID, WE'D HAVE WHACKED THE GUY A LONG TIME AGO.
WE ONLY LET IT SLIDE BECAUSE HE SAID HE WOULDN'T TOUCH HER.
SO, IF KITAHARA CONVINCED KOTEGAWA-SAN TO GO ON A TRIP WITH HIM...
...JUST HO MUCH DO YOU THINK HE BRIBED HER WITH?
WHA?!
NOW THAT YOU MENTION IT...
KNOWING KOTEGAWA-SAN, SHE WOULDN'T BUDGE FOR ANYTHING LESS THAN 100 MILL.
EXACTLY. WHICH MEANS...

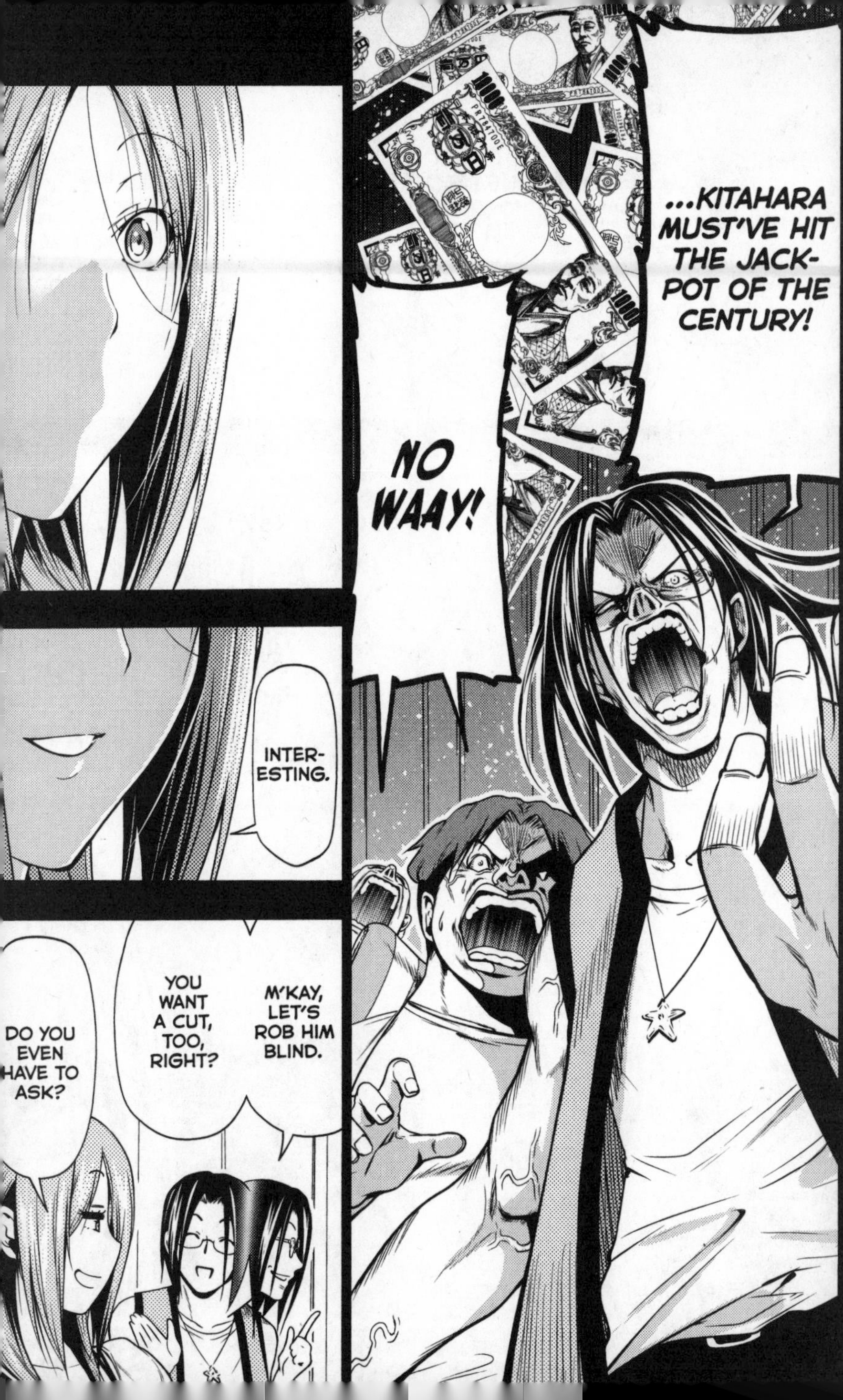
...KITAHARA MUST'VE HIT THE JACK-POT OF THE CENTURY!
NO WAAY!
INTER-ESTING.
M'KAY, LET'S ROB HIM BLIND.
YOU WANT A CUT, TOO, RIGHT?
DO YOU EVEN HAVE TO ASK?

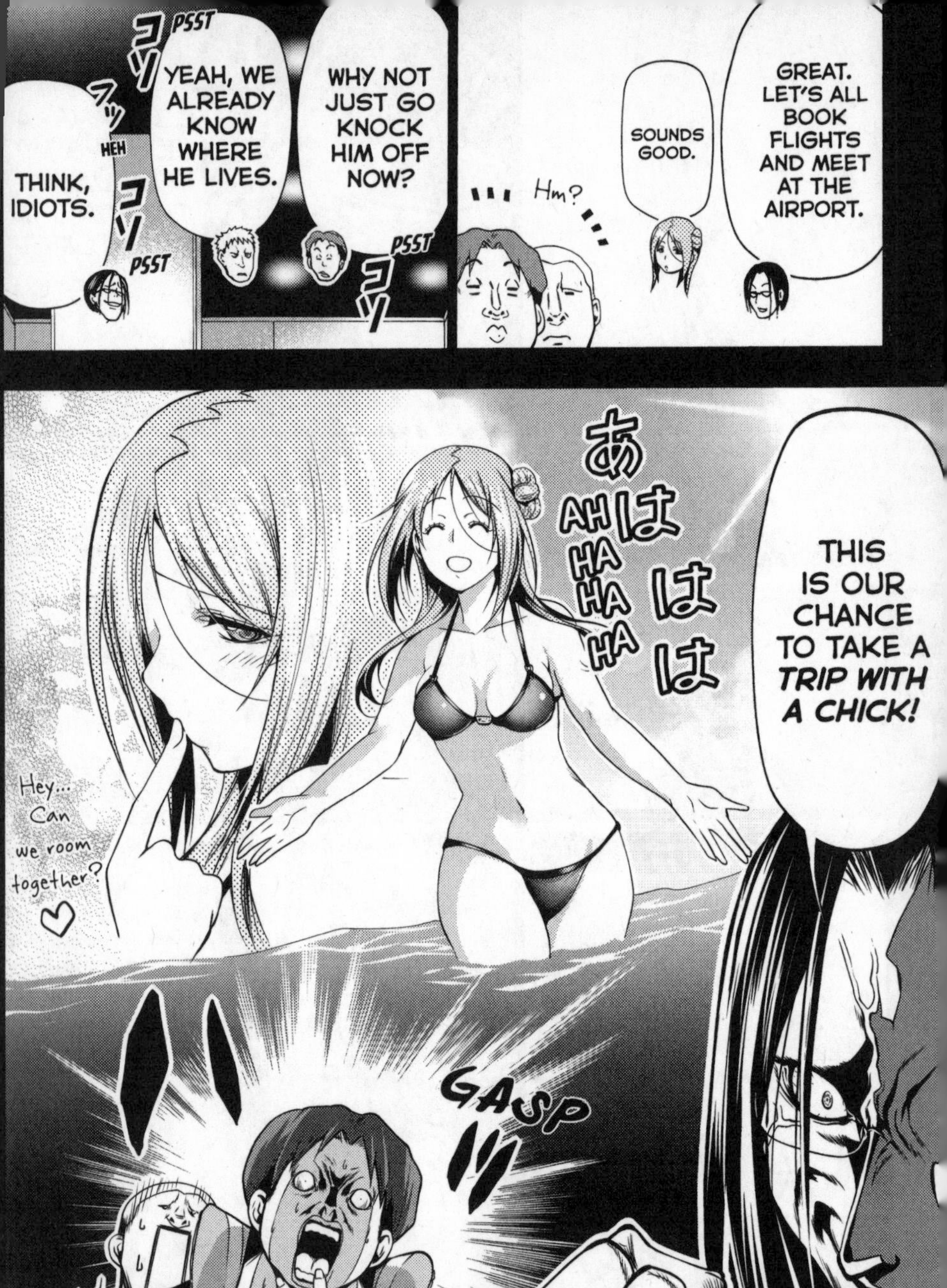
GREAT. LET'S ALL BOOK FLIGHTS AND MEET AT THE AIRPORT.
SOUNDS GOOD.
Hm?
WHY NOT JUST GO KNOCK HIM OFF NOW?
コソ PSST
YEAH, WE ALREADY KNOW WHERE HE LIVES.
コソ PSST
フッ HEH
THINK, IDIOTS.
コソ PSST
THIS IS OUR CHANCE TO TAKE A *TRIP WITH A CHICK!*
あははは
AH HA HA HA
Hey... Can we room together? ♡
GASP!!

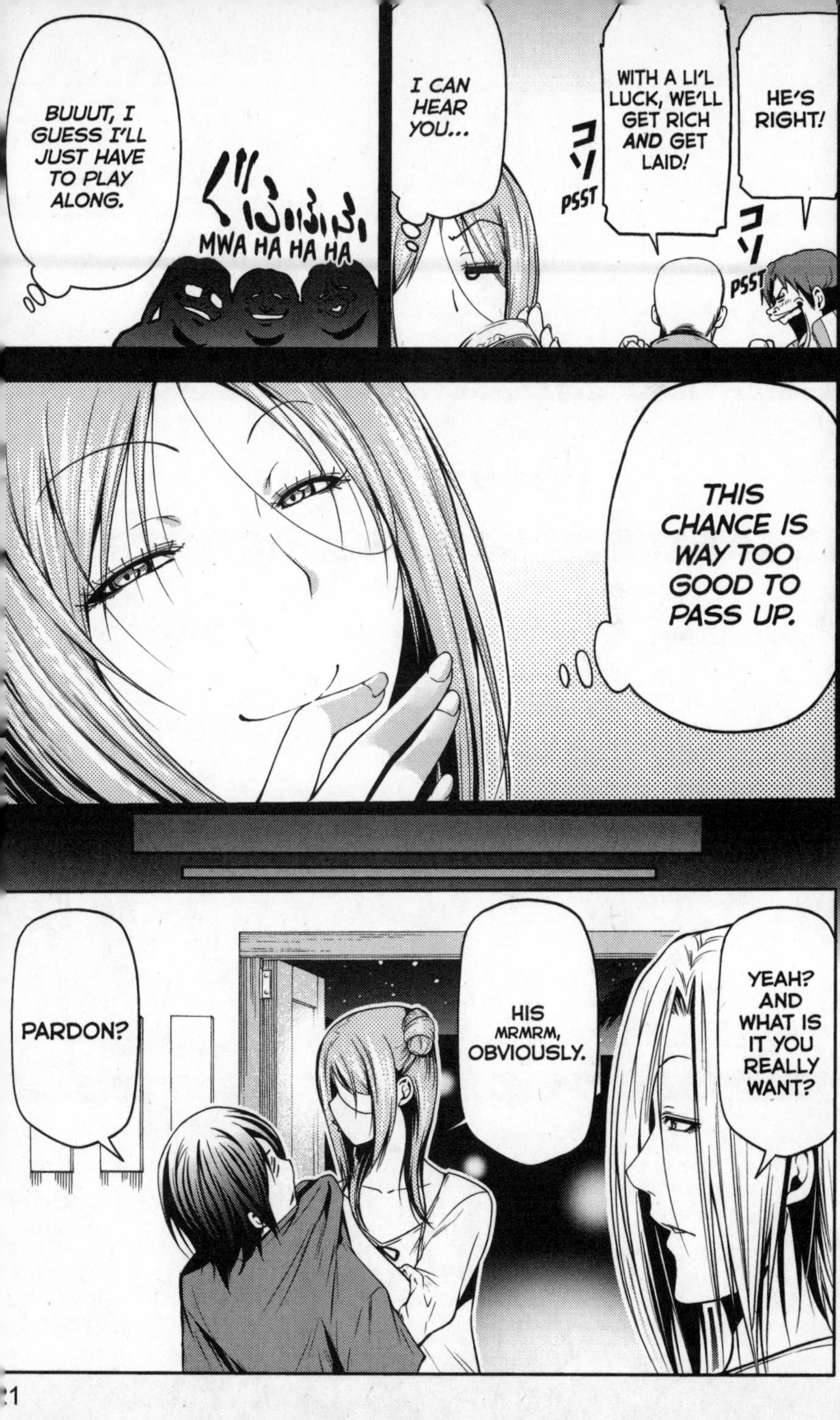
HE'S RIGHT!
コソ
PSST
WITH A LI'L LUCK, WE'LL GET RICH AND GET LAID!
コソ
PSST
I CAN HEAR YOU...
BUUUT, I GUESS I'LL JUST HAVE TO PLAY ALONG.
MWA HA HA HA
THIS CHANCE IS WAY TOO GOOD TO PASS UP.
YEAH? AND WHAT IS IT YOU REALLY WANT?
HIS MRMRM, OBVIOUSLY.
PARDON?

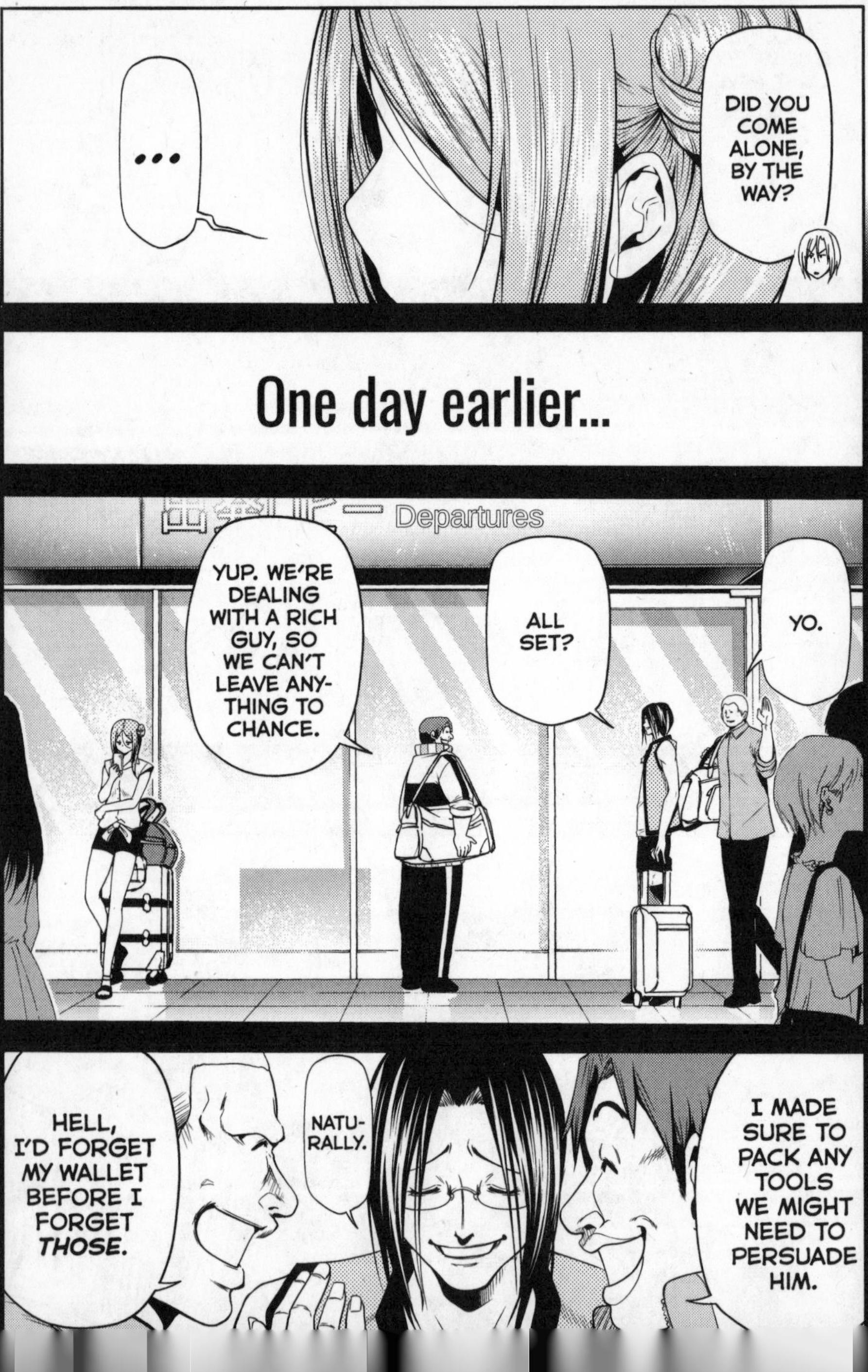
DID YOU COME ALONE, BY THE WAY?
...
One day earlier...
Departures
YO.
ALL SET?
YUP. WE'RE DEALING WITH A RICH GUY, SO WE CAN'T LEAVE ANYTHING TO CHANCE.
I MADE SURE TO PACK ANY TOOLS WE MIGHT NEED TO PERSUADE HIM.
NATURALLY.
HELL, I'D FORGET MY WALLET BEFORE I FORGET *THOSE*.

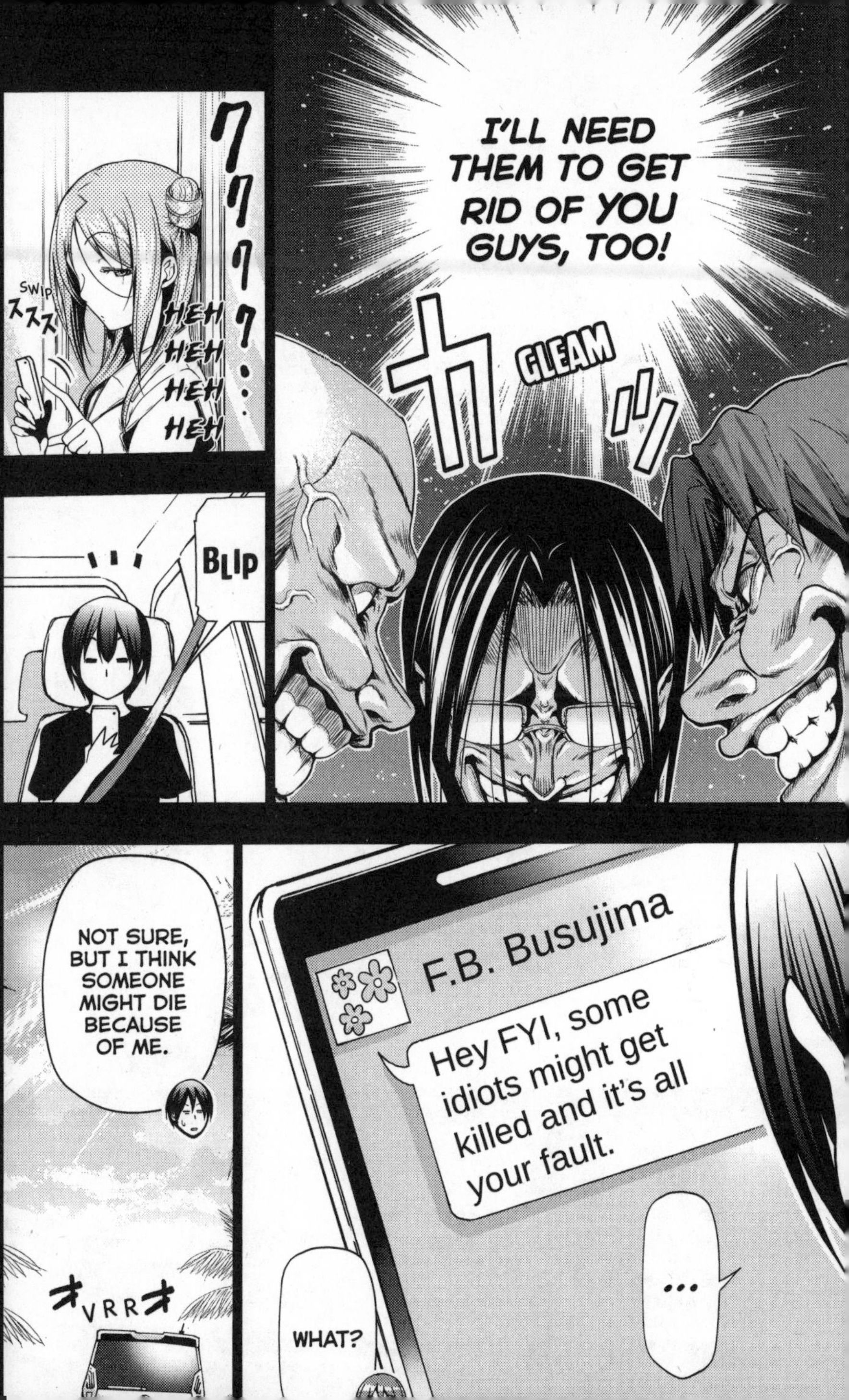
I'LL NEED THEM TO GET RID OF YOU GUYS, TOO!
GLEAM
HEH HEH HEH HEH
SWIP
BLIP
F.B. Busujima
Hey FYI, some idiots might get killed and it's all your fault.
...
WHAT?
NOT SURE, BUT I THINK SOMEONE MIGHT DIE BECAUSE OF ME.
VRRR

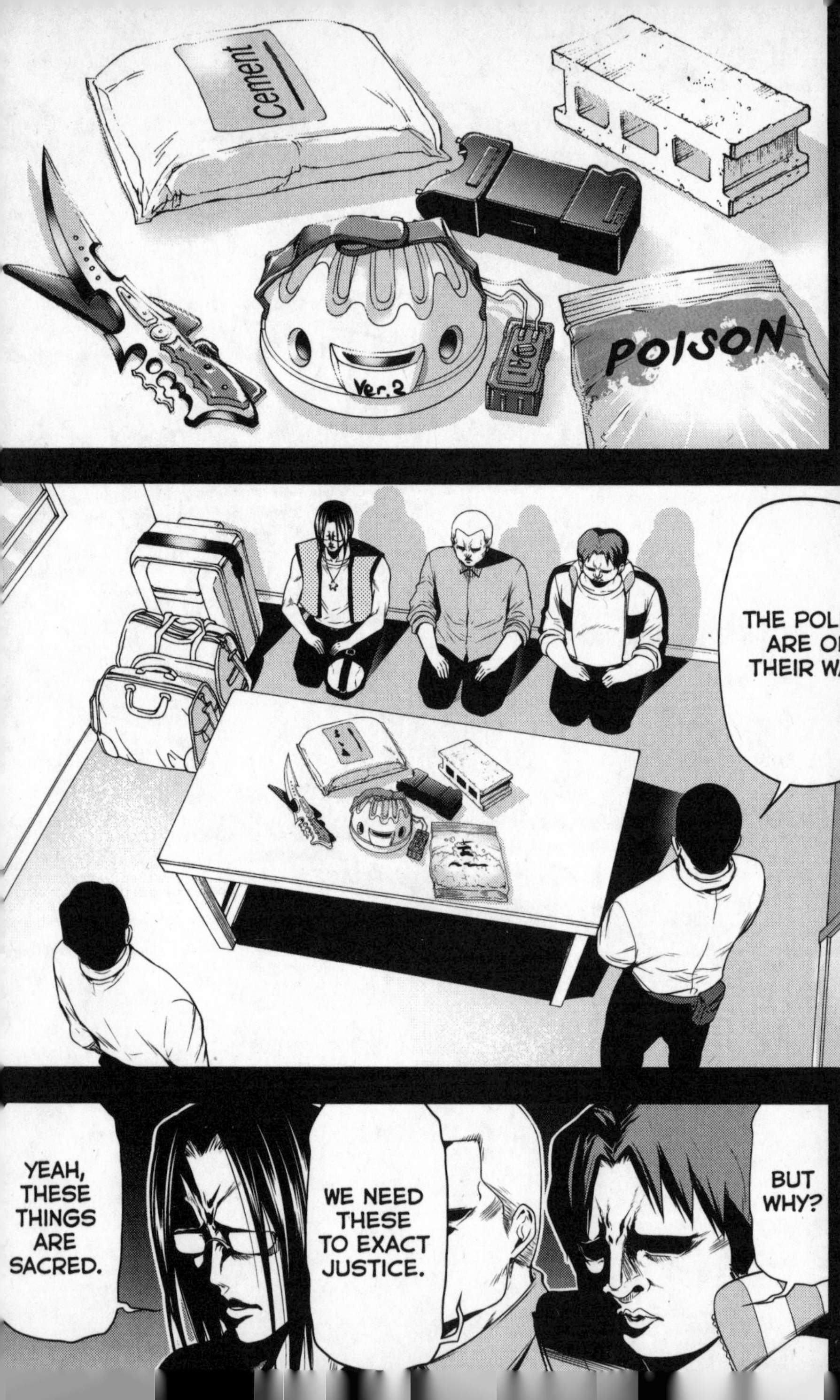
Cement
POISON
Ver.2
THE POLIC ARE ON THEIR WA
BUT WHY?
WE NEED THESE TO EXACT JUSTICE.
YEAH, THESE THINGS ARE SACRED.

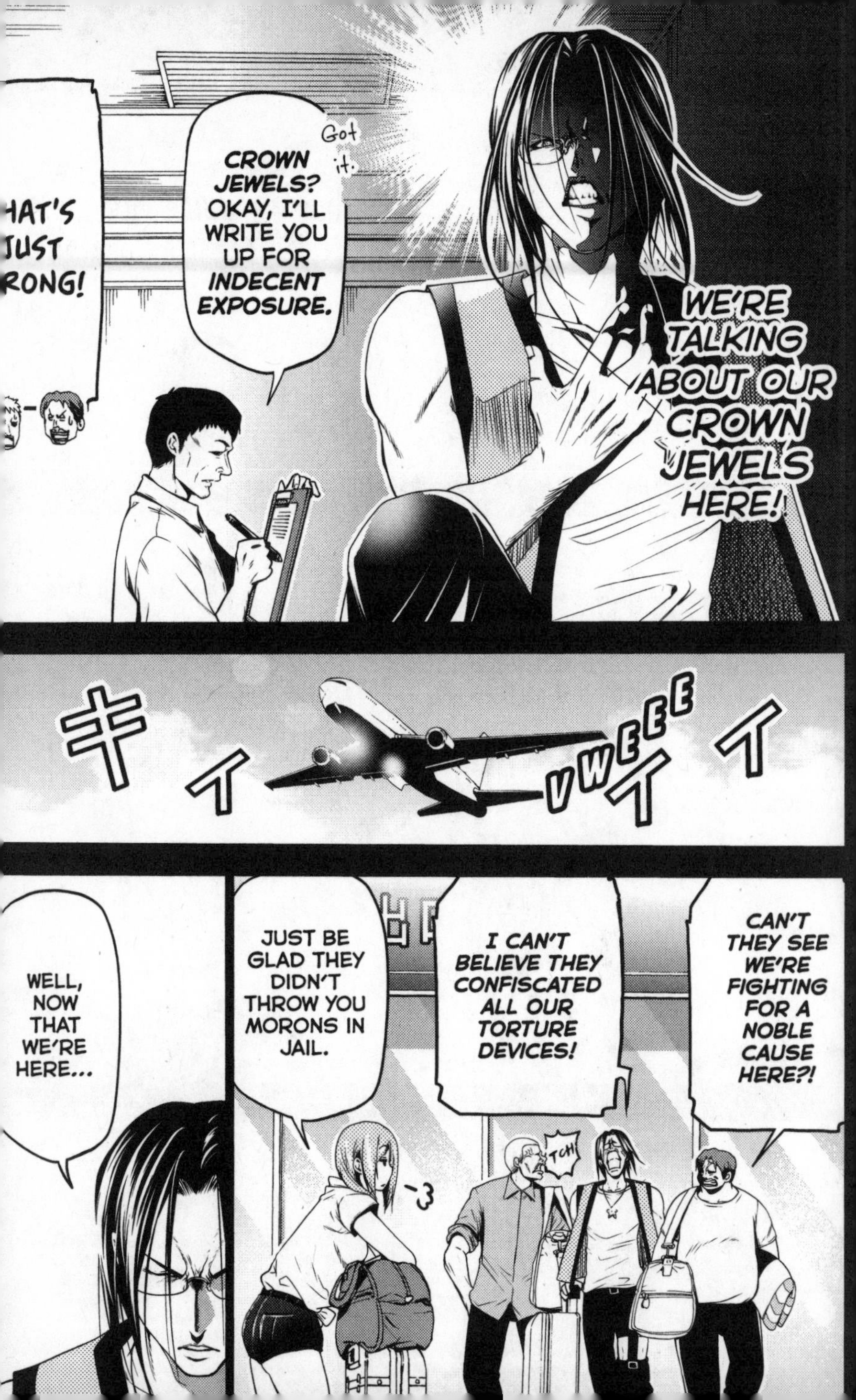
WE'RE TALKING ABOUT OUR CROWN JEWELS HERE!
Got it.
CROWN JEWELS? OKAY, I'LL WRITE YOU UP FOR INDECENT EXPOSURE.
HAT'S JUST RONG!
キイイイ
VWEEE
CAN'T THEY SEE WE'RE FIGHTING FOR A NOBLE CAUSE HERE?!
I CAN'T BELIEVE THEY CONFISCATED ALL OUR TORTURE DEVICES!
TCH!
JUST BE GLAD THEY DIDN'T THROW YOU MORONS IN JAIL.
WELL, NOW THAT WE'RE HERE...

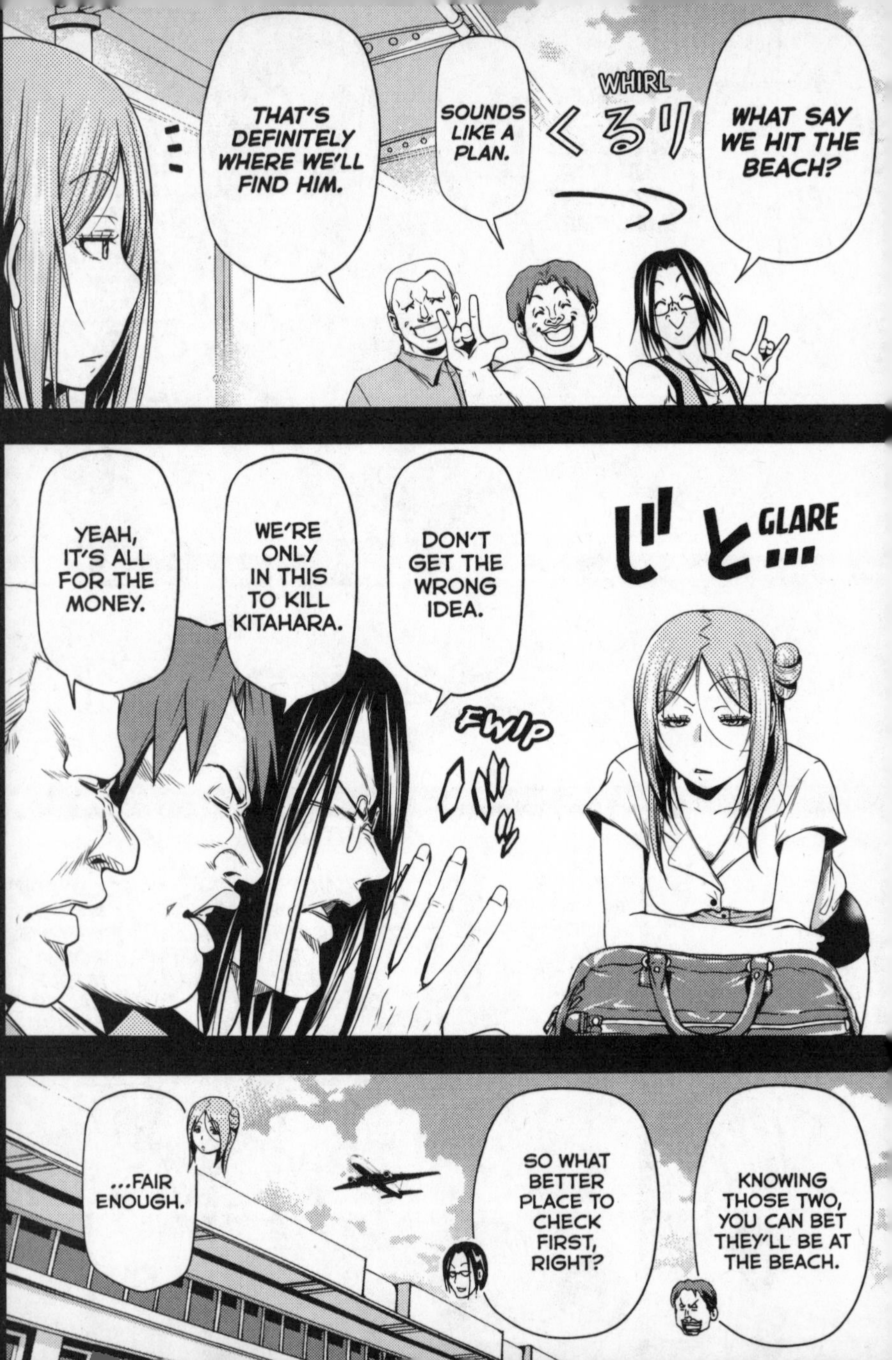
WHAT SAY WE HIT THE BEACH?
WHIRL
くるり
SOUNDS LIKE A PLAN.
THAT'S DEFINITELY WHERE WE'LL FIND HIM.
GLARE
じと…
DON'T GET THE WRONG IDEA.
WE'RE ONLY IN THIS TO KILL KITAHARA.
YEAH, IT'S ALL FOR THE MONEY.
FWIP
KNOWING THOSE TWO, YOU CAN BET THEY'LL BE AT THE BEACH.
SO WHAT BETTER PLACE TO CHECK FIRST, RIGHT?
...FAIR ENOUGH.

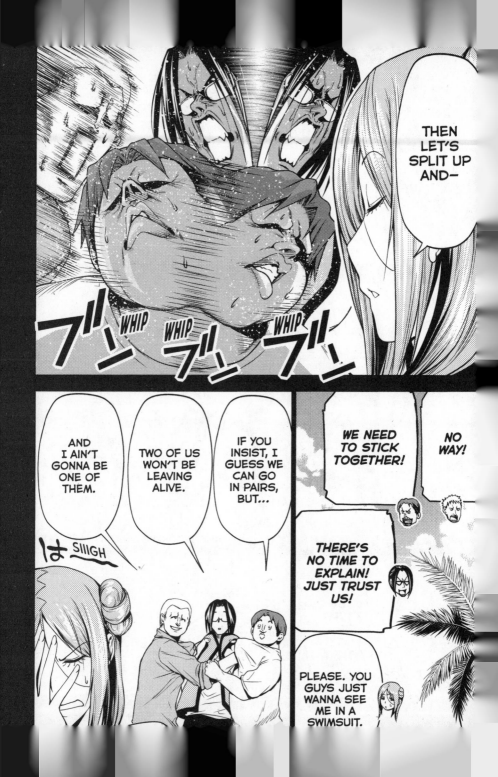

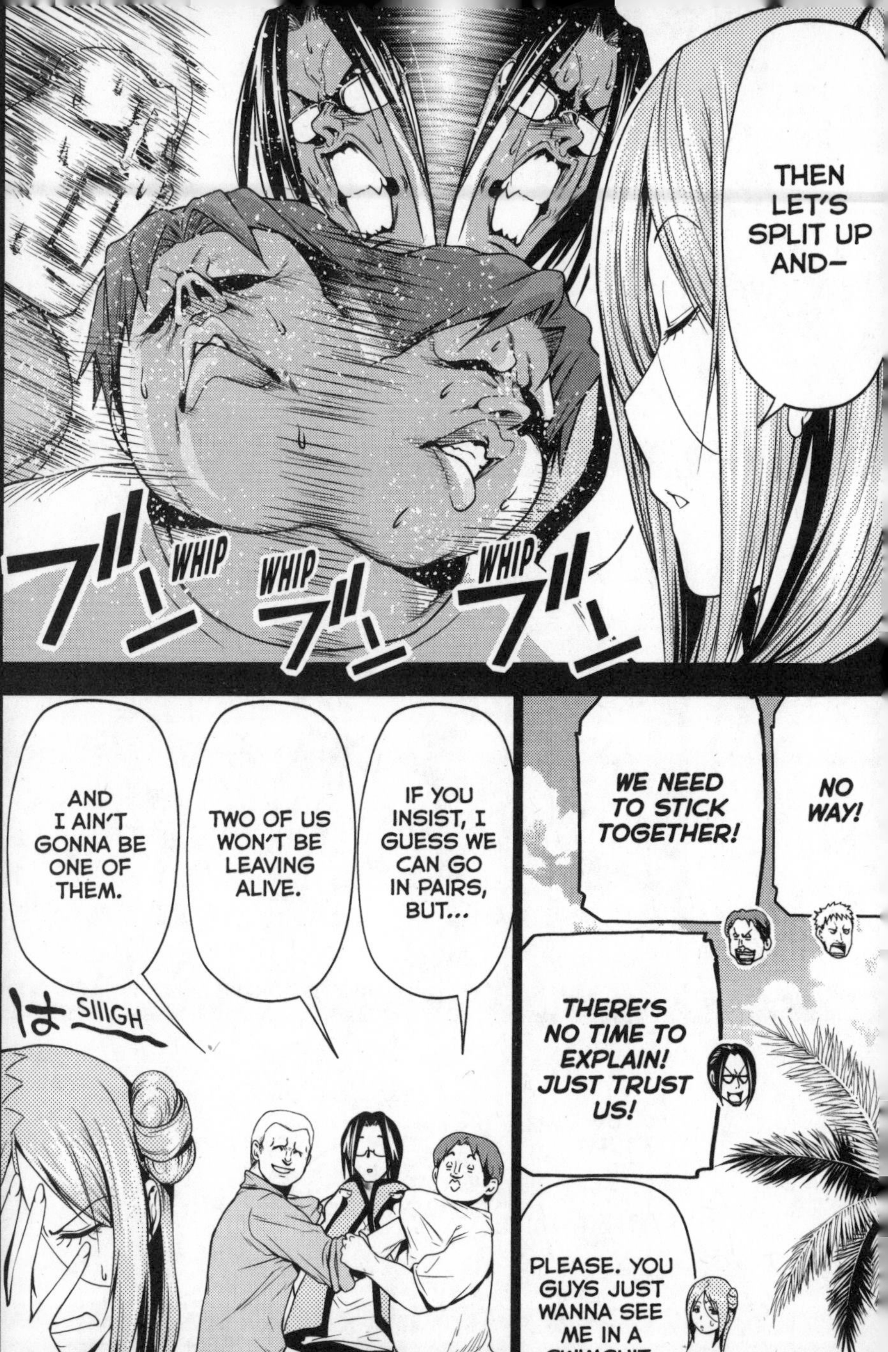
THEN LET'S SPLIT UP AND–
ブン WHIP
ブン WHIP
ブン WHIP
NO WAY!
WE NEED TO STICK TOGETHER!
THERE'S NO TIME TO EXPLAIN! JUST TRUST US!
PLEASE. YOU GUYS JUST WANNA SEE ME IN A SWIMSUIT.
IF YOU INSIST, I GUESS WE CAN GO IN PAIRS, BUT...
TWO OF US WON'T BE LEAVING ALIVE.
AND I AIN'T GONNA BE ONE OF THEM.
は SIIIGH

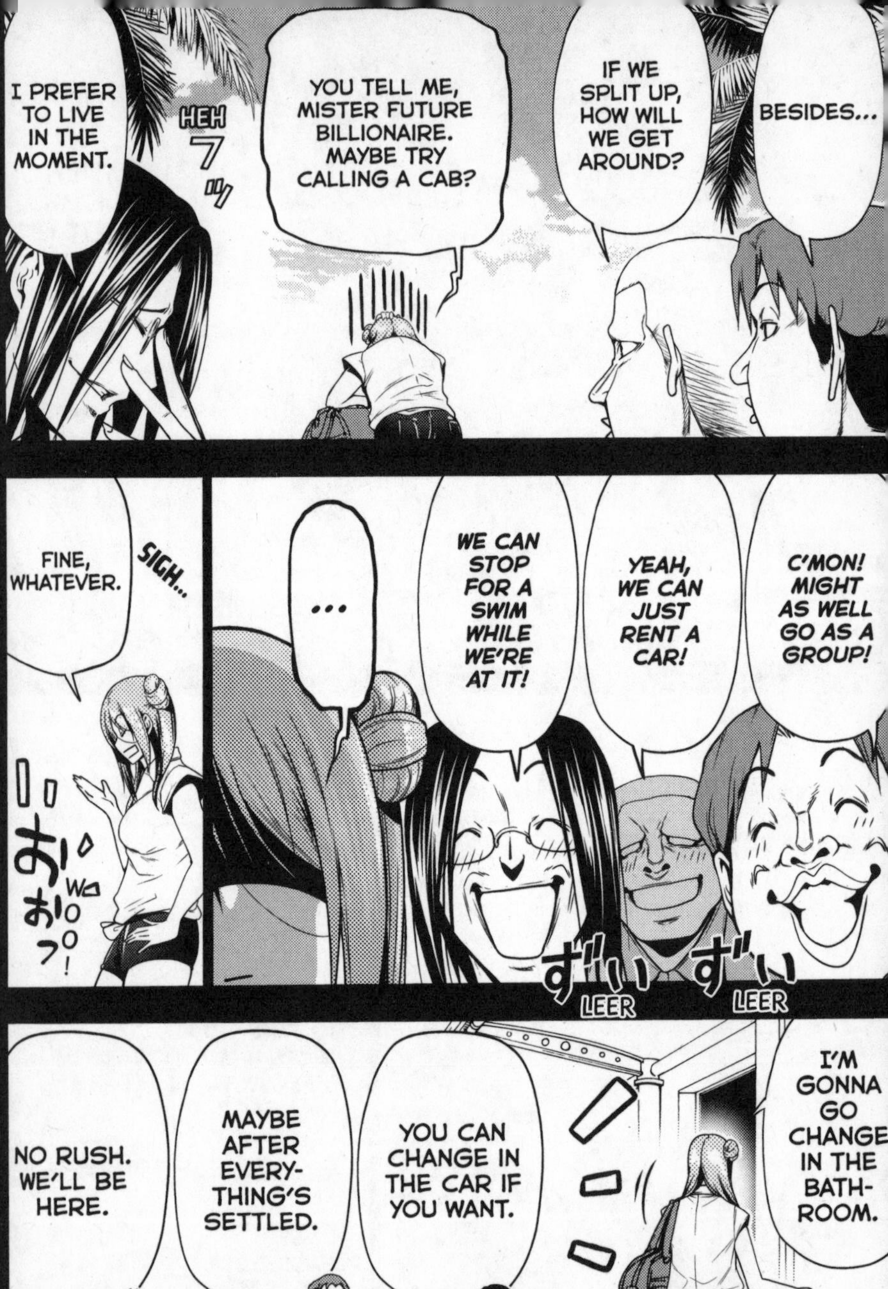
BESIDES...
IF WE SPLIT UP, HOW WILL WE GET AROUND?
YOU TELL ME, MISTER FUTURE BILLIONAIRE. MAYBE TRY CALLING A CAB?
HEH
I PREFER TO LIVE IN THE MOMENT.
C'MON! MIGHT AS WELL GO AS A GROUP!
YEAH, WE CAN JUST RENT A CAR!
WE CAN STOP FOR A SWIM WHILE WE'RE AT IT!
...
LEER
LEER
SIGH...
FINE, WHATEVER.
WOOO!
I'M GONNA GO CHANGE IN THE BATHROOM.
YOU CAN CHANGE IN THE CAR IF YOU WANT.
MAYBE AFTER EVERYTHING'S SETTLED.
NO RUSH. WE'LL BE HERE.

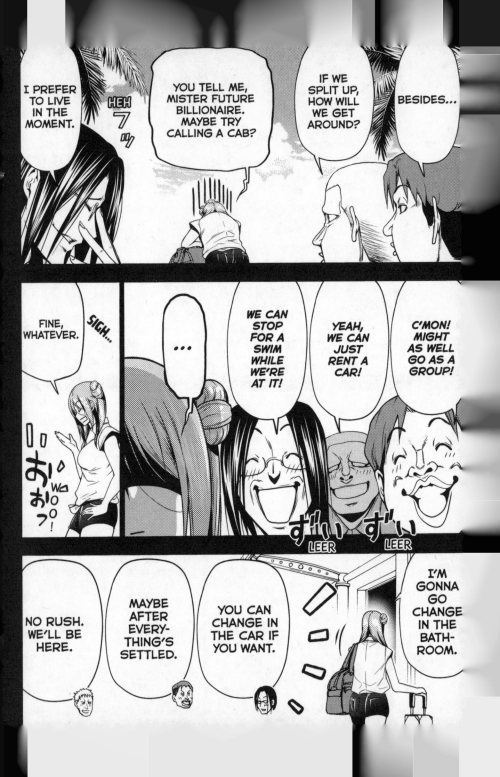

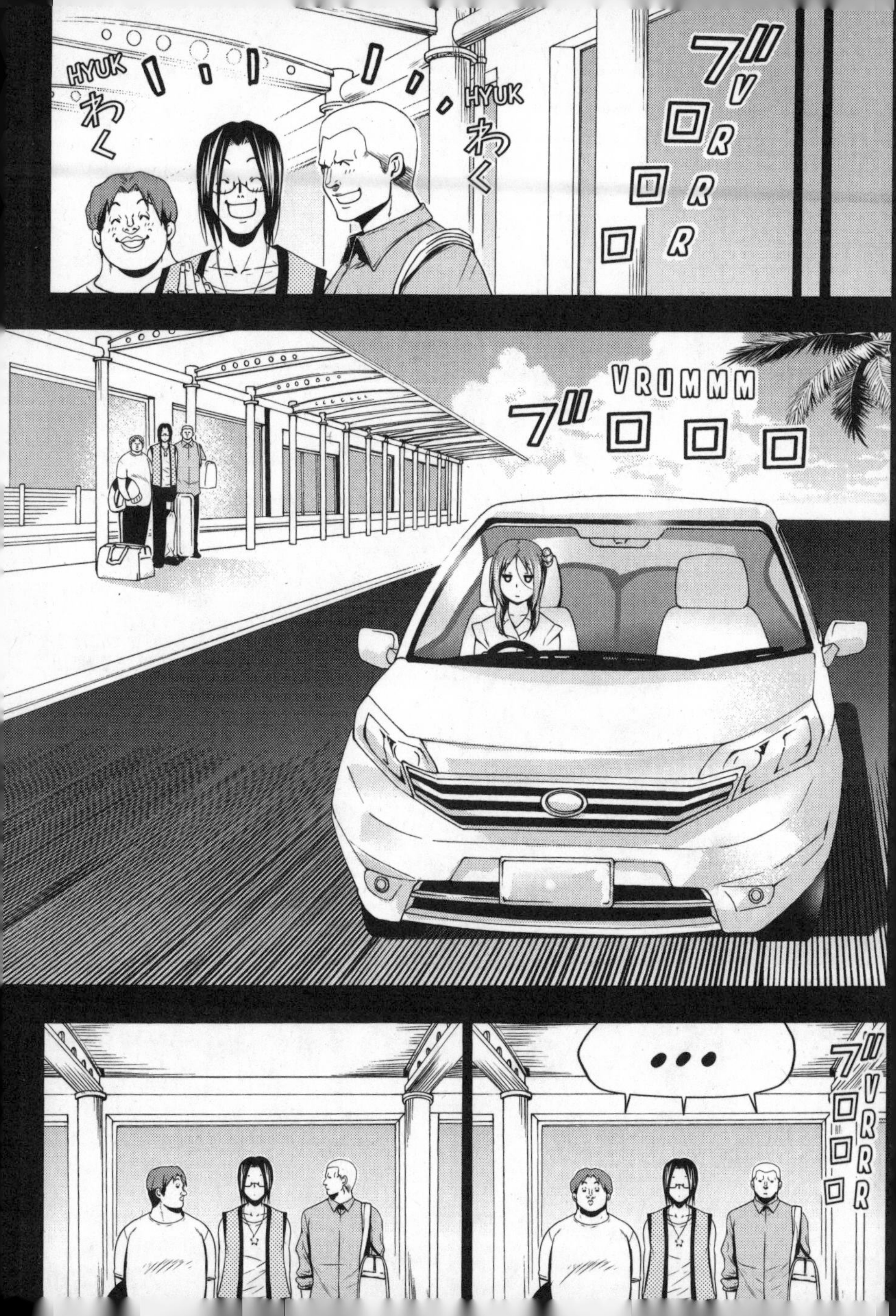
ブロロロ
VRRR
HYUK
わく
HYUK
わく
VRUMMM
ブロロロ
•••
ブロロロ
VRRR

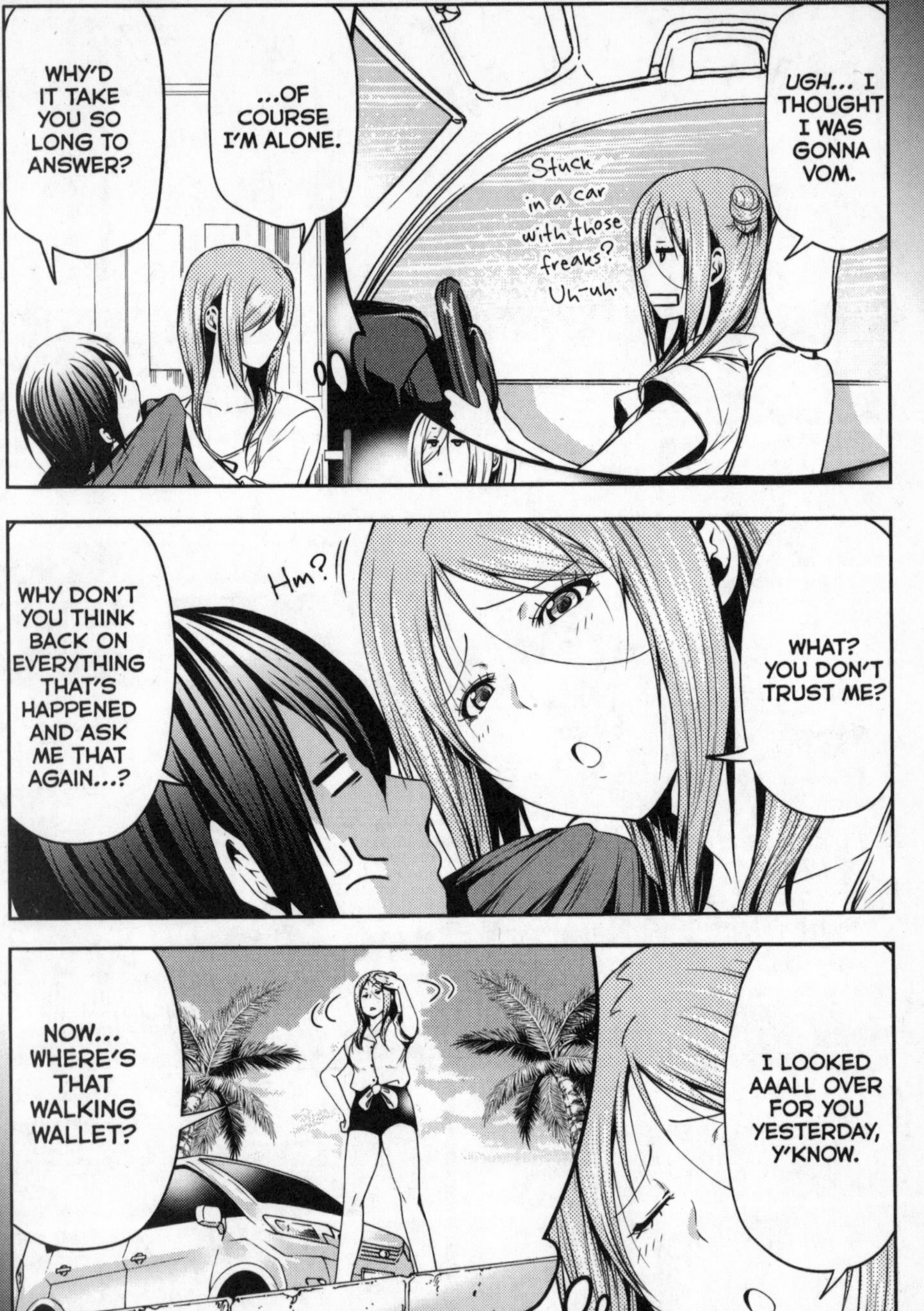
UGH... I THOUGHT I WAS GONNA VOM.
Stuck in a car with those freaks? Uh-uh
...OF COURSE I'M ALONE.
WHY'D IT TAKE YOU SO LONG TO ANSWER?
WHAT? YOU DON'T TRUST ME?
Hm?
WHY DON'T YOU THINK BACK ON EVERYTHING THAT'S HAPPENED AND ASK ME THAT AGAIN...?
I LOOKED AAALL OVER FOR YOU YESTERDAY, Y'KNOW.
NOW... WHERE'S THAT WALKING WALLET?

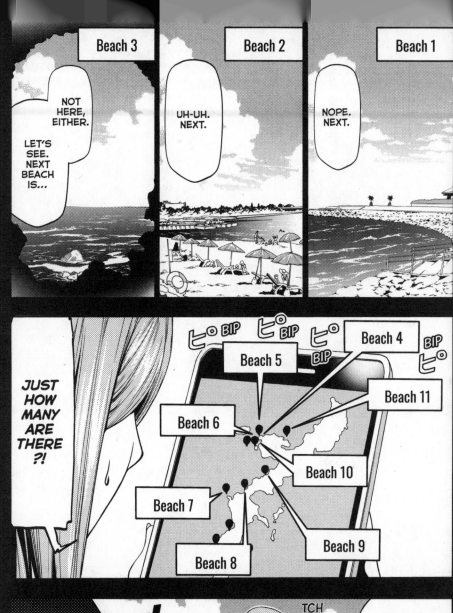

Beach 3

Beach 2

Beach 1

NOT HERE, EITHER.

LET'S SEE. NEXT BEACH IS...

UH-UH. NEXT.

NOPE. NEXT.

JUST HOW MANY ARE THERE ?!

Beach 5

Beach 4

Beach 11

Beach 6

Beach 10

Beach 7

Beach 9

Beach 8

ピ°BIP ピ°BIP ピ° BIP BIP ピ°

THUD

TCH

GUESS I'M GONNA NEED HELP, AFTER ALL.

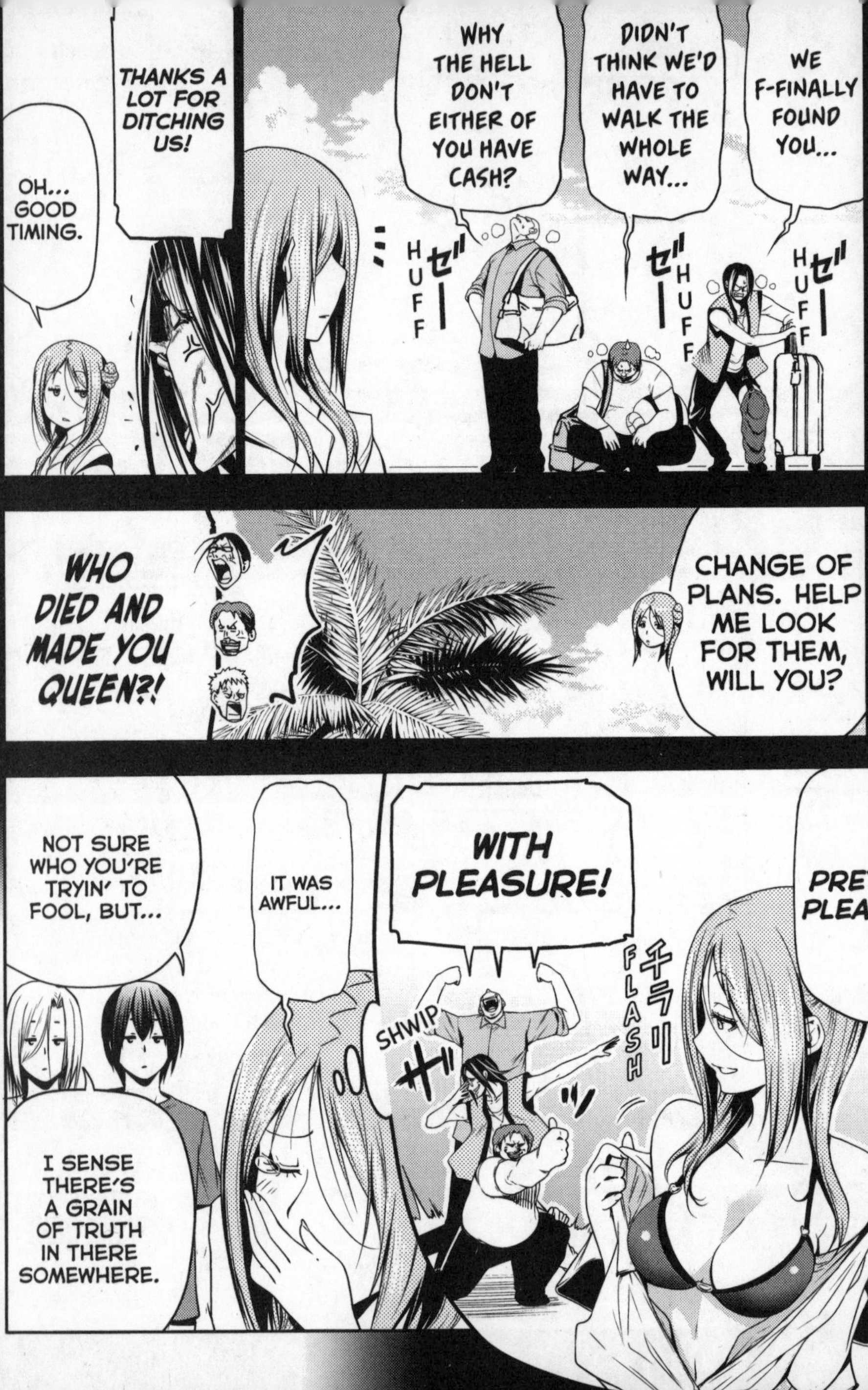
WE F-FINALLY FOUND YOU...
HUFF
ゼー
DIDN'T THINK WE'D HAVE TO WALK THE WHOLE WAY...
HUFF
ゼー
WHY THE HELL DON'T EITHER OF YOU HAVE CASH?
HUFF
ゼー
THANKS A LOT FOR DITCHING US!
OH... GOOD TIMING.
CHANGE OF PLANS. HELP ME LOOK FOR THEM, WILL YOU?
WHO DIED AND MADE YOU QUEEN?!
PRETTY PLEASE?
チラリ
FLASH
WITH PLEASURE!
SHWIP
IT WAS AWFUL...
NOT SURE WHO YOU'RE TRYIN' TO FOOL, BUT...
I SENSE THERE'S A GRAIN OF TRUTH IN THERE SOMEWHERE.

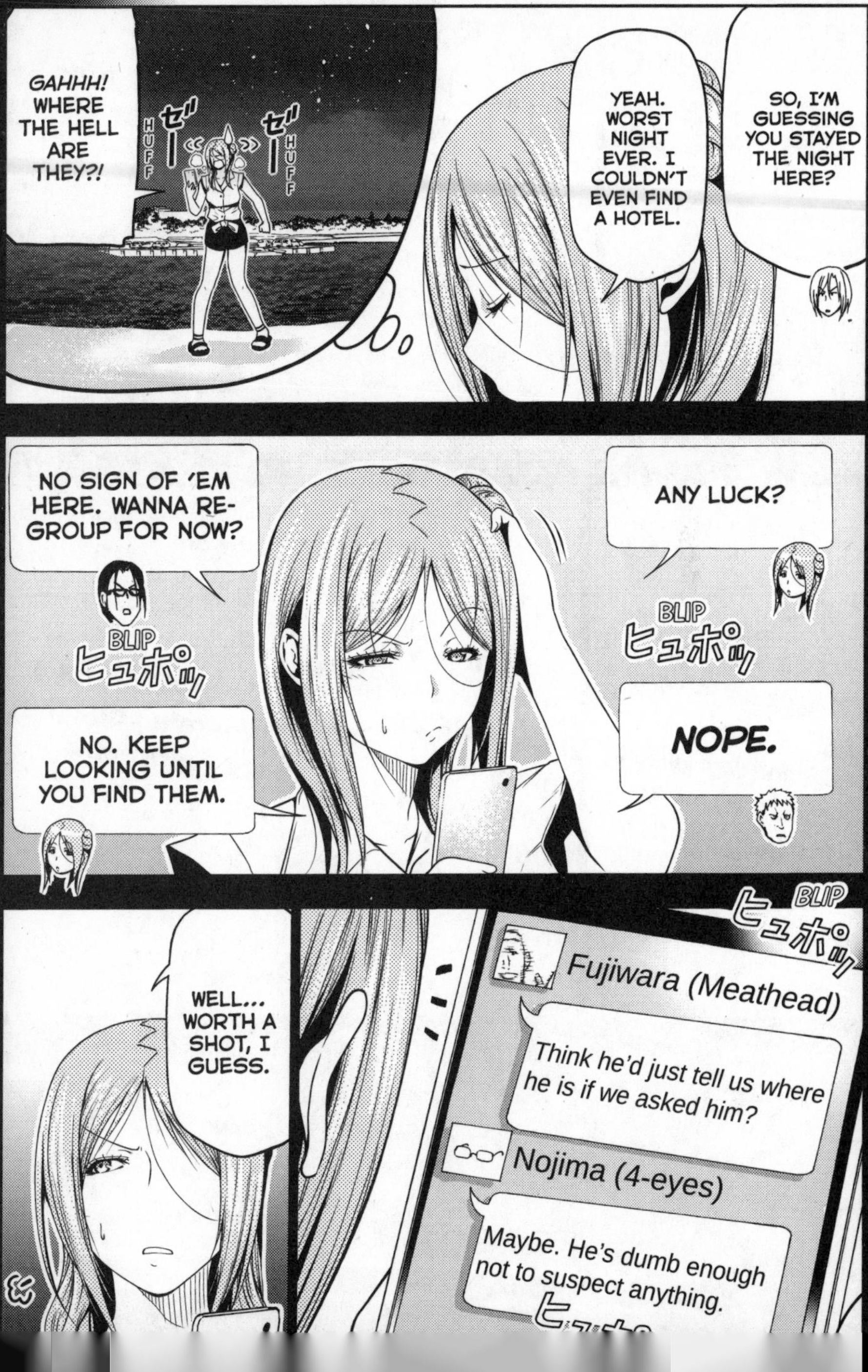
SO, I'M GUESSING YOU STAYED THE NIGHT HERE?
YEAH. WORST NIGHT EVER. I COULDN'T EVEN FIND A HOTEL.
GAHHH! WHERE THE HELL ARE THEY?!
HUFF ゼー
HUFF ゼー
ANY LUCK?
BLIP ヒュポッ
NO SIGN OF 'EM HERE. WANNA RE-GROUP FOR NOW?
BLIP ヒュポッ
NOPE.
NO. KEEP LOOKING UNTIL YOU FIND THEM.
BLIP ヒュポッ
Fujiwara (Meathead)
Think he'd just tell us where he is if we asked him?
Nojima (4-eyes)
Maybe. He's dumb enough not to suspect anything.
WELL... WORTH A SHOT, I GUESS.

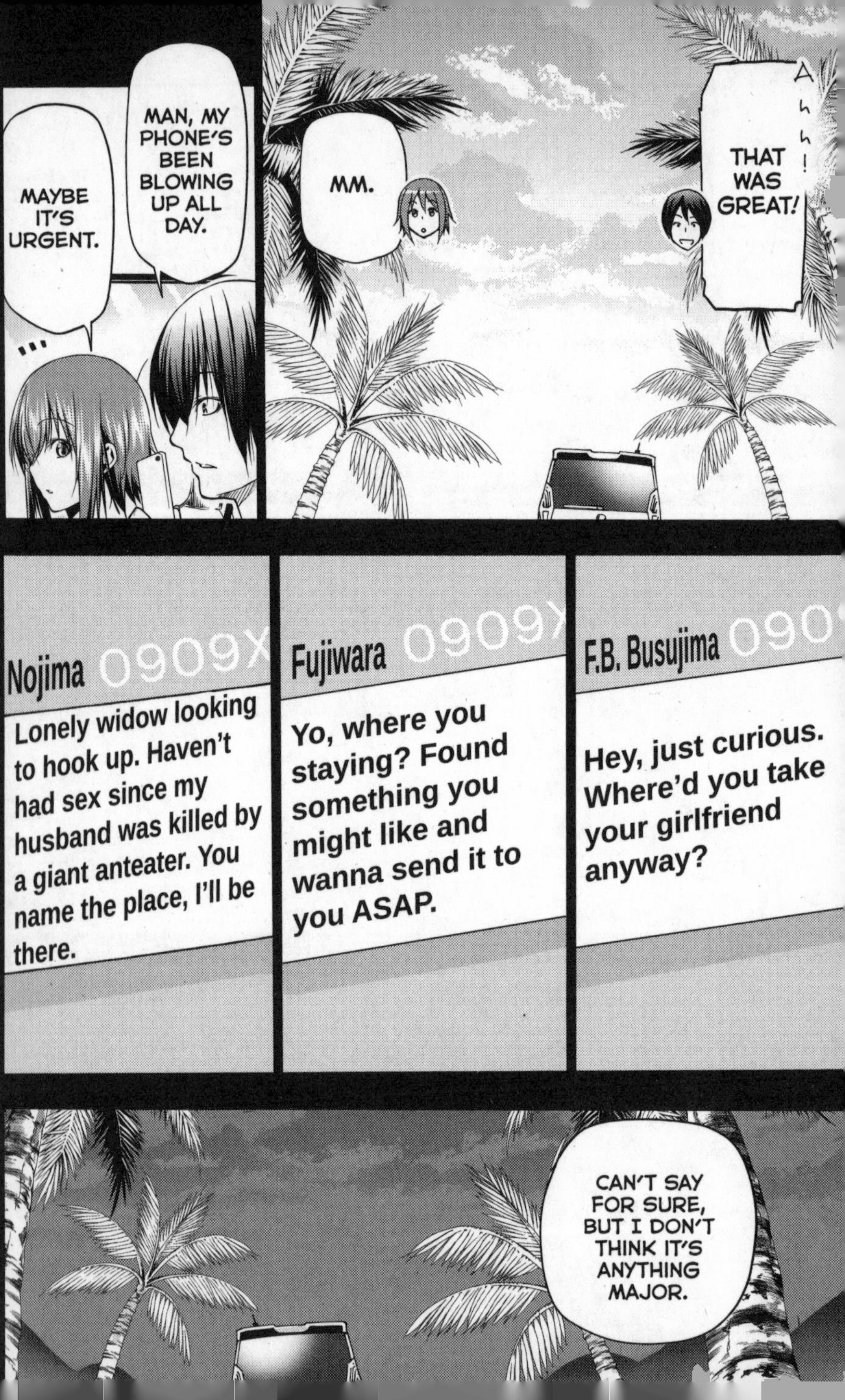
Ahh!
THAT WAS GREAT!
MM.
MAN, MY PHONE'S BEEN BLOWING UP ALL DAY.
MAYBE IT'S URGENT.
...
F.B. Busujima 090
Hey, just curious. Where'd you take your girlfriend anyway?
Fujiwara 0909X
Yo, where you staying? Found something you might like and wanna send it to you ASAP.
Nojima 0909X
Lonely widow looking to hook up. Haven't had sex since my husband was killed by a giant anteater. You name the place, I'll be there.
CAN'T SAY FOR SURE, BUT I DON'T THINK IT'S ANYTHING MAJOR.

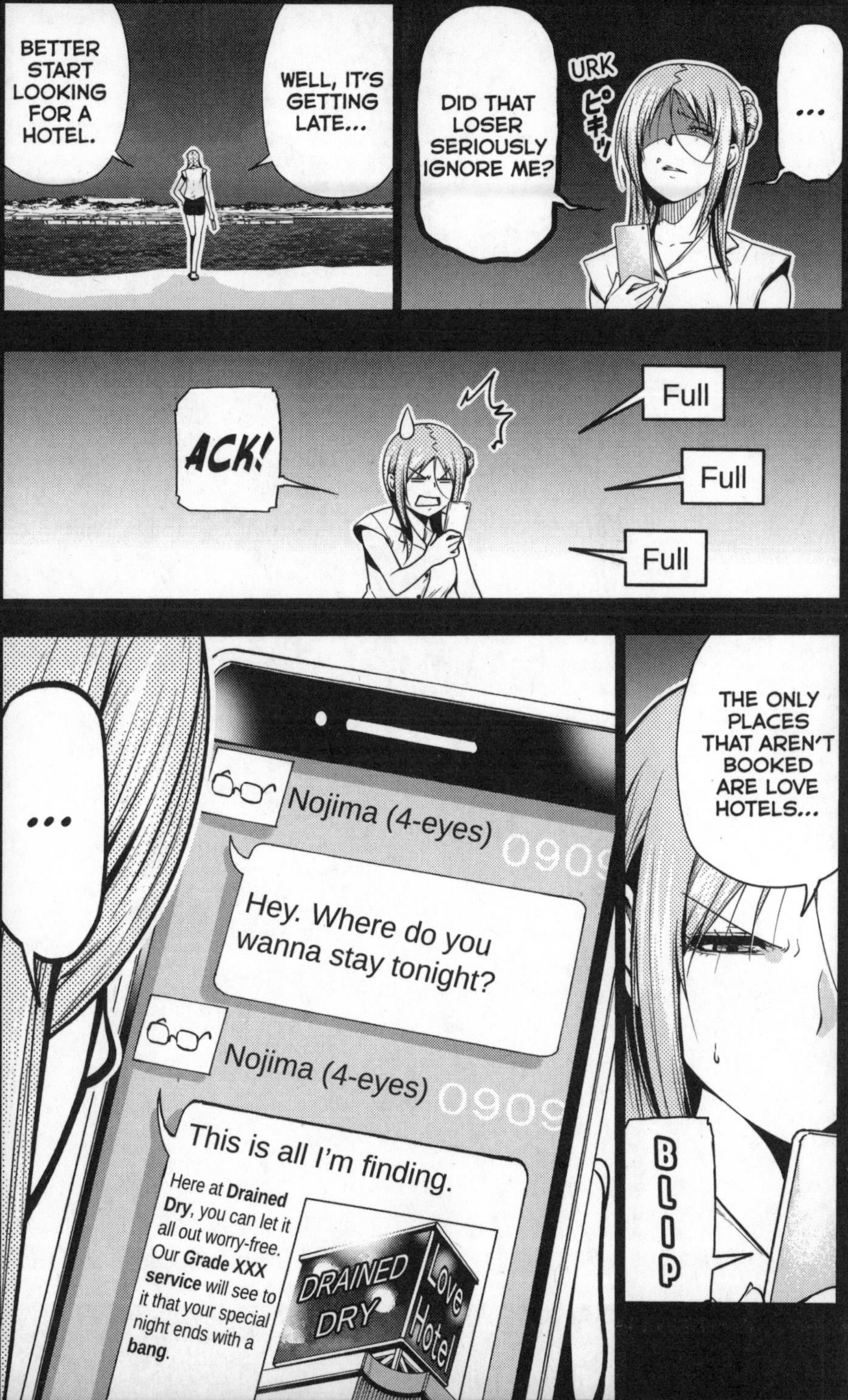
...
URK
ピキッ
DID THAT LOSER SERIOUSLY IGNORE ME?
WELL, IT'S GETTING LATE...
BETTER START LOOKING FOR A HOTEL.
Full
Full
Full
ACK!
THE ONLY PLACES THAT AREN'T BOOKED ARE LOVE HOTELS...
BLIP
...
Nojima (4-eyes)
0909
Hey. Where do you wanna stay tonight?
Nojima (4-eyes)
0909
This is all I'm finding.
Here at Drained Dry, you can let it all out worry-free. Our Grade XXX service will see to it that your special night ends with a bang.
DRAINED DRY
Love Hotel

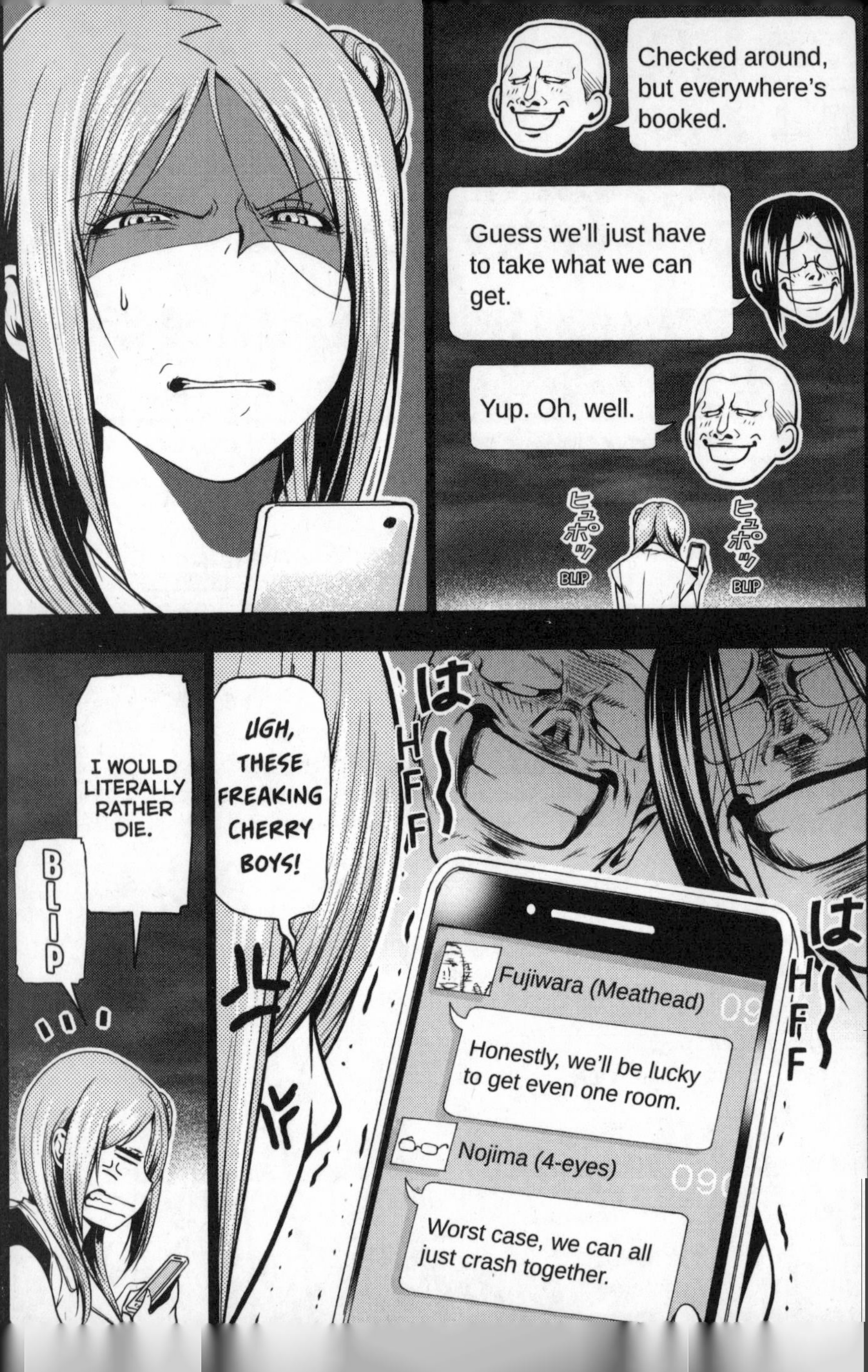
Checked around, but everywhere's booked.
Guess we'll just have to take what we can get.
Yup. Oh, well.
ヒュポッ
BLIP
ヒュポッ
BLIP
は HFF
は HFF
Fujiwara (Meathead)
Honestly, we'll be lucky to get even one room.
Nojima (4-eyes)
Worst case, we can all just crash together.
UGH, THESE FREAKING CHERRY BOYS!
I WOULD LITERALLY RATHER DIE.
BLIP

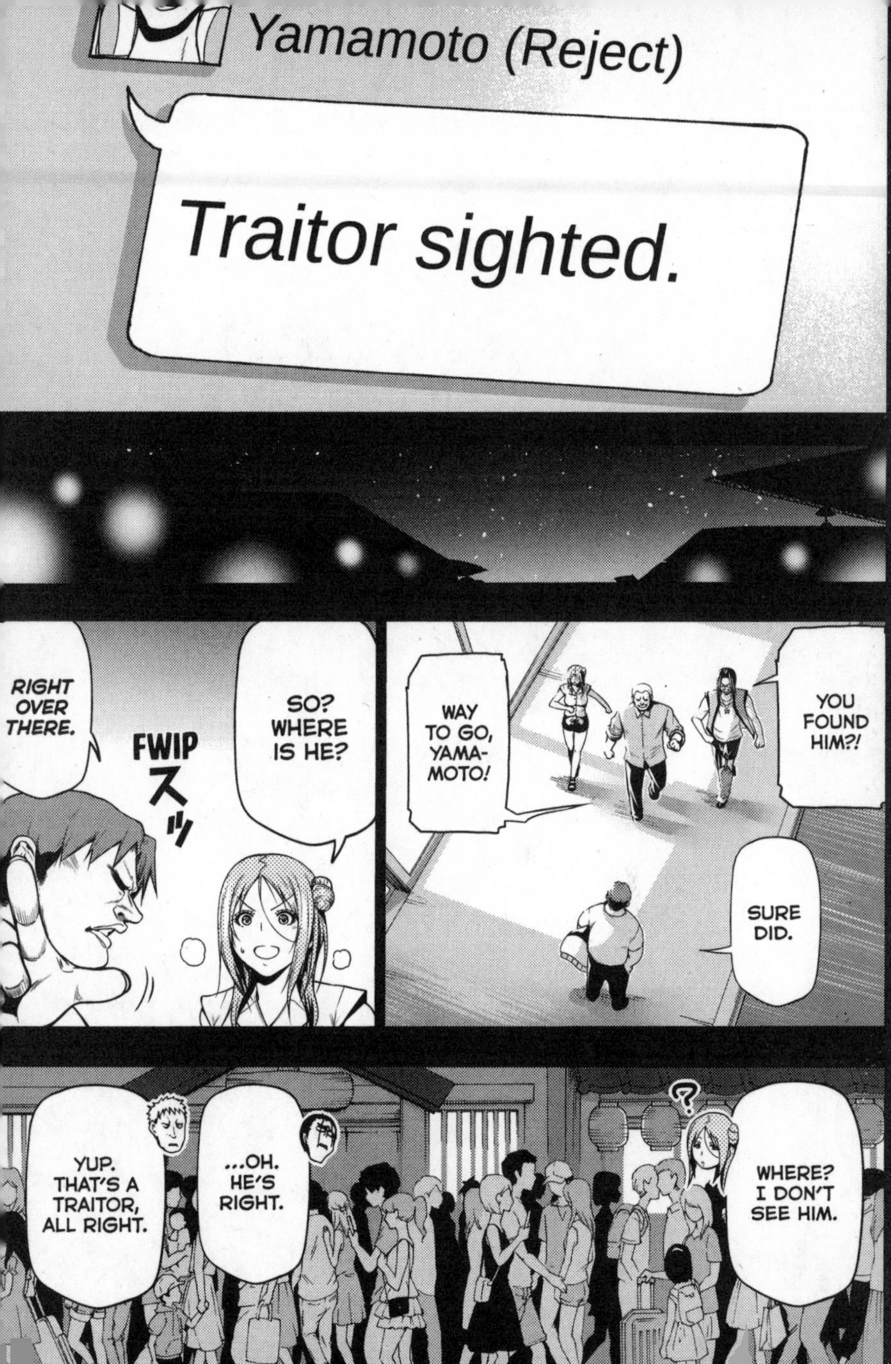
Yamamoto (Reject)
Traitor sighted.
YOU FOUND HIM?!
WAY TO GO, YAMAMOTO!
SURE DID.
SO? WHERE IS HE?
RIGHT OVER THERE.
FWIP スッ
?
WHERE? I DON'T SEE HIM.
...OH. HE'S RIGHT.
YUP. THAT'S A TRAITOR, ALL RIGHT.

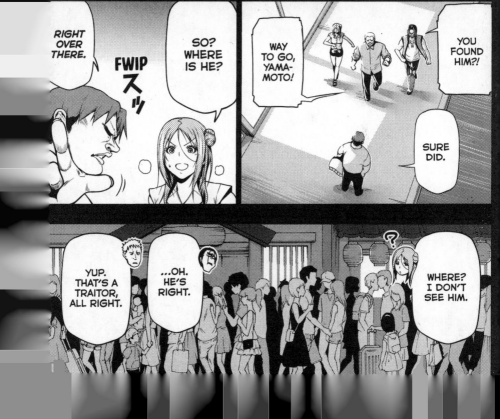

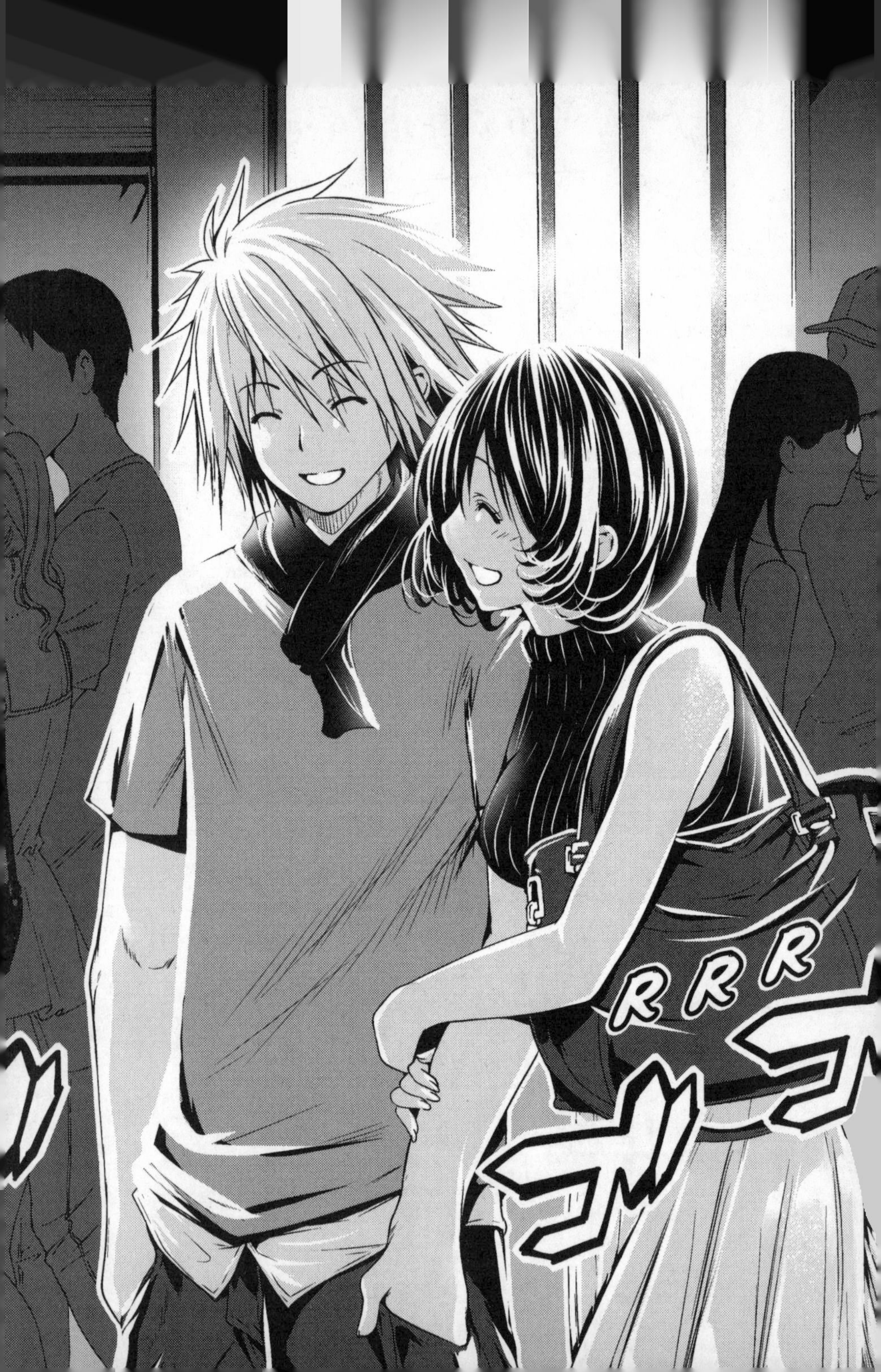
RRR

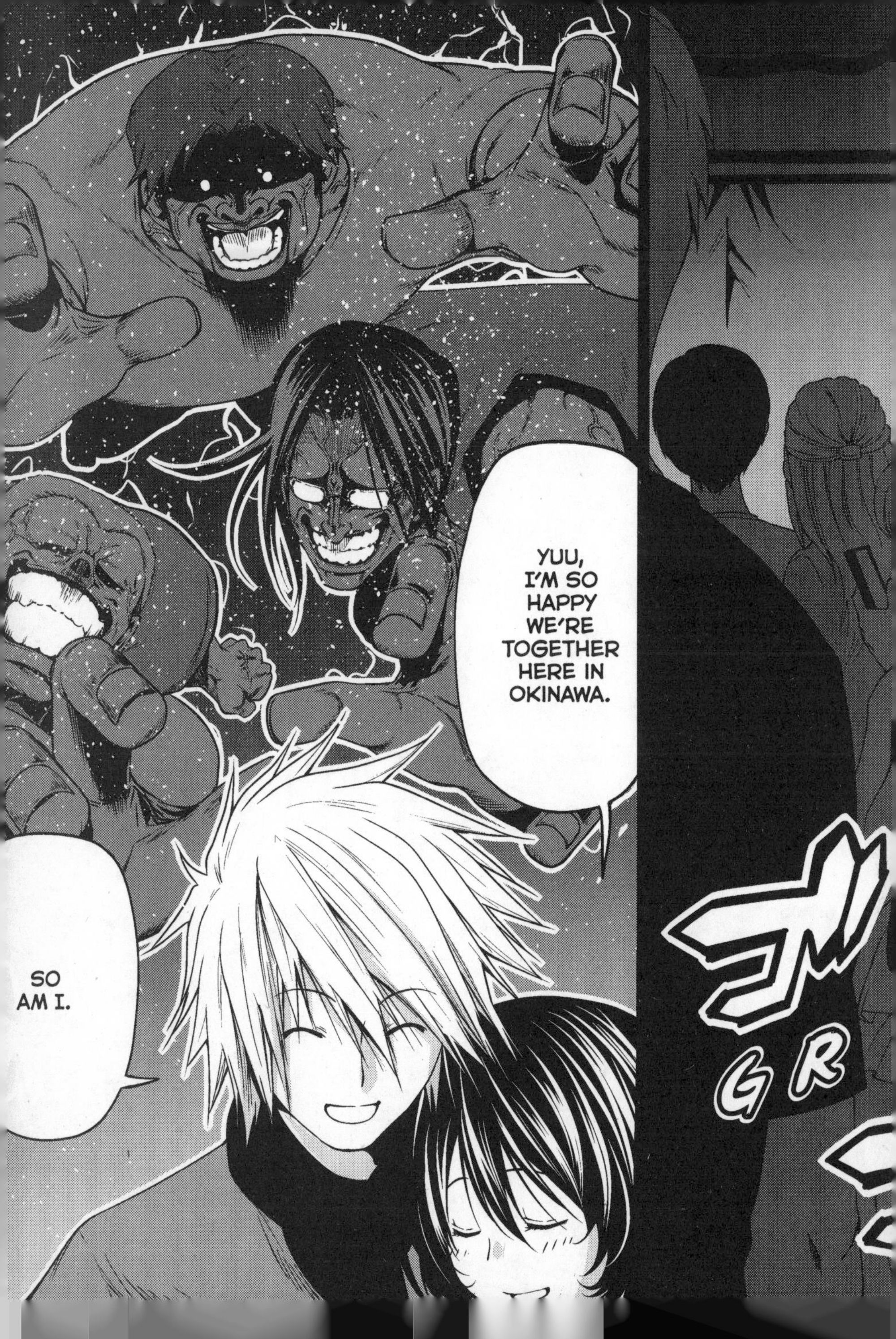
GR
YUU, I'M SO HAPPY WE'RE TOGETHER HERE IN OKINAWA.
SO AM I.

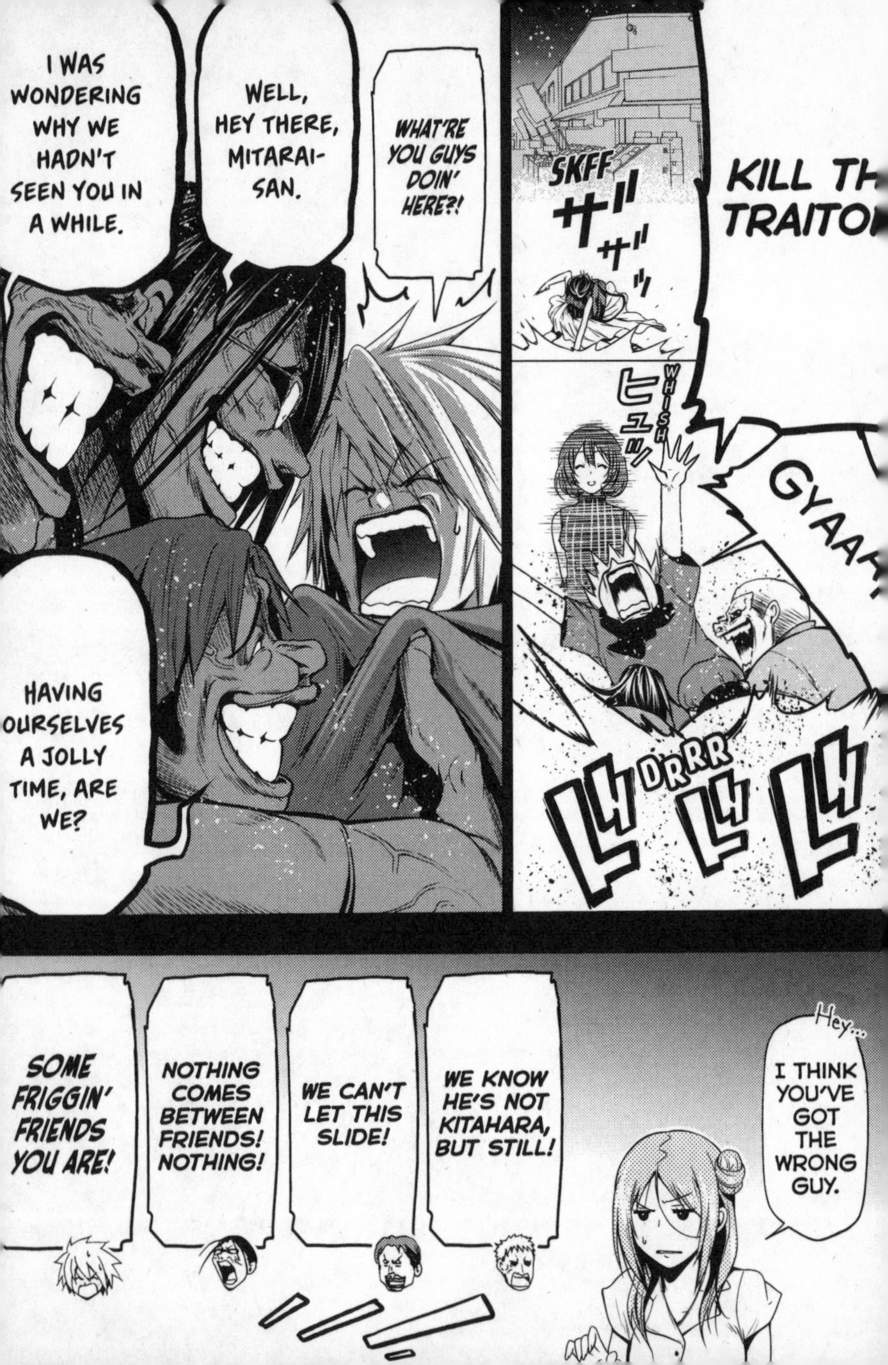
SKFF
サザザッ
KILL TH
TRAITO
WHISH
ヒュッ
GYAAA
DRRR
ドドド
WHAT'RE YOU GUYS DOIN' HERE?!
WELL, HEY THERE, MITARAI-SAN.
I WAS WONDERING WHY WE HADN'T SEEN YOU IN A WHILE.
HAVING OURSELVES A JOLLY TIME, ARE WE?
Hey...
I THINK YOU'VE GOT THE WRONG GUY.
WE KNOW HE'S NOT KITAHARA, BUT STILL!
WE CAN'T LET THIS SLIDE!
NOTHING COMES BETWEEN FRIENDS! NOTHING!
SOME FRIGGIN' FRIENDS YOU ARE!

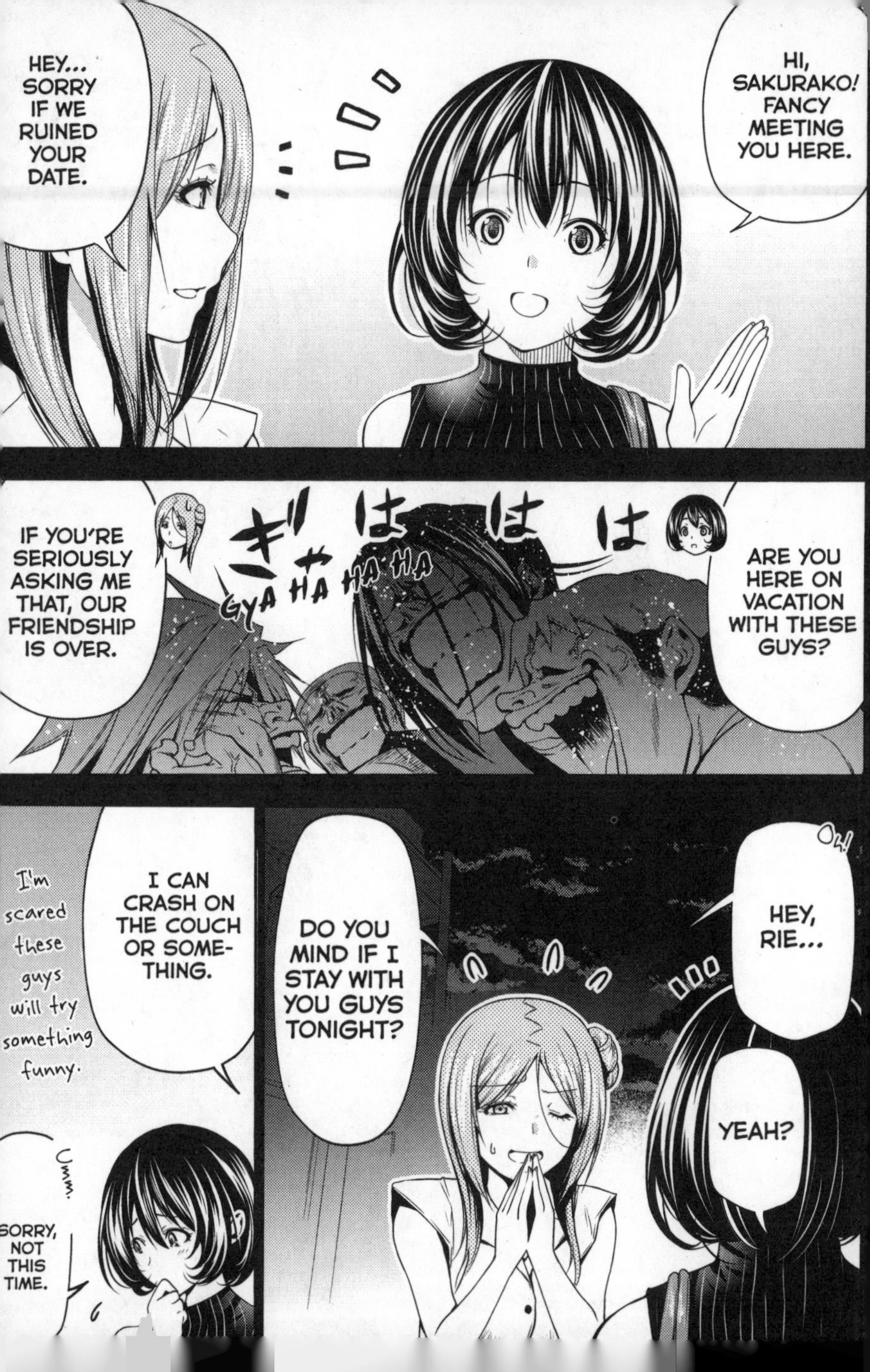
HI, SAKURAKO! FANCY MEETING YOU HERE.
HEY... SORRY IF WE RUINED YOUR DATE.
ARE YOU HERE ON VACATION WITH THESE GUYS?
ぎゃははは
GYA HA HA HA
IF YOU'RE SERIOUSLY ASKING ME THAT, OUR FRIENDSHIP IS OVER.
Oh!
HEY, RIE...
YEAH?
DO YOU MIND IF I STAY WITH YOU GUYS TONIGHT?
I CAN CRASH ON THE COUCH OR SOMETHING.
I'm scared these guys will try something funny.
Umm.
SORRY, NOT THIS TIME.

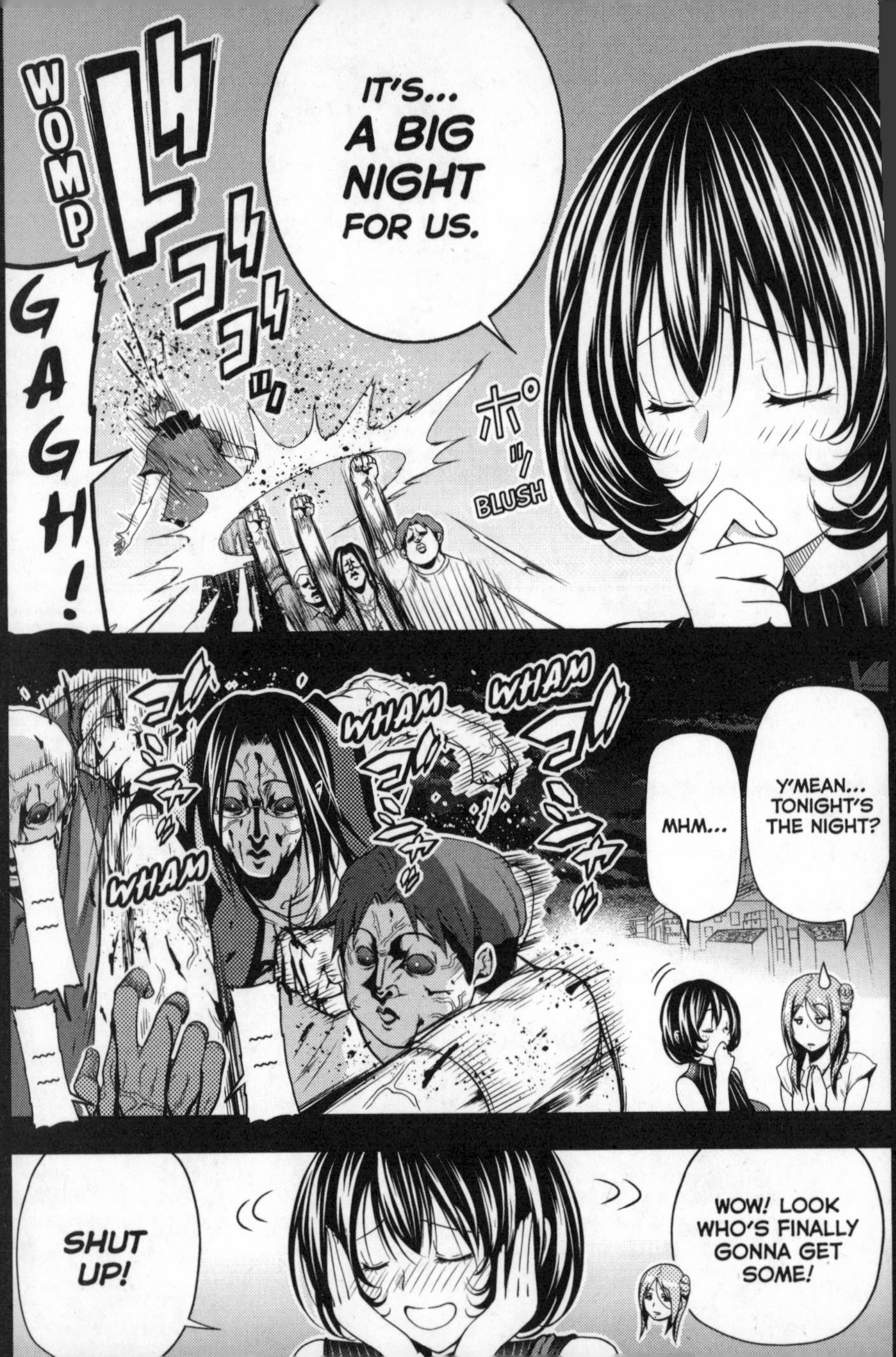
IT'S... A BIG NIGHT FOR US.
BLUSH
WOMP
GAGH!
Y'MEAN... TONIGHT'S THE NIGHT?
MHM...
WHAM
WHAM
WHAM
WOW! LOOK WHO'S FINALLY GONNA GET SOME!
SHUT UP!

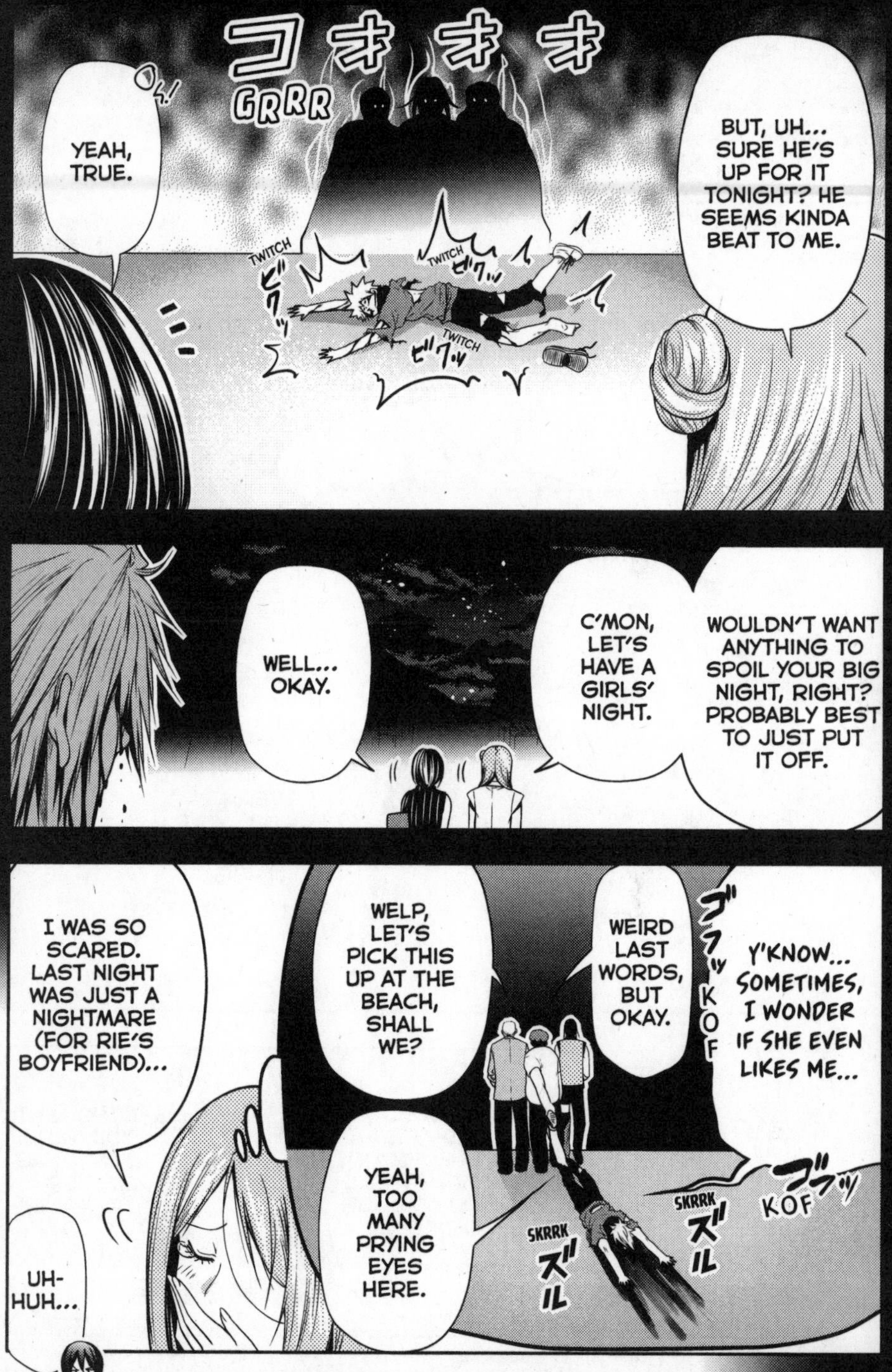
コオオオ
BUT, UH... SURE HE'S UP FOR IT TONIGHT? HE SEEMS KINDA BEAT TO ME.
GRRR
TWITCH
TWITCH
TWITCH
YEAH, TRUE.
WOULDN'T WANT ANYTHING TO SPOIL YOUR BIG NIGHT, RIGHT? PROBABLY BEST TO JUST PUT IT OFF.
C'MON, LET'S HAVE A GIRLS' NIGHT.
WELL... OKAY.
Y'KNOW... SOMETIMES, I WONDER IF SHE EVEN LIKES ME...
KOF
WEIRD LAST WORDS, BUT OKAY.
WELP, LET'S PICK THIS UP AT THE BEACH, SHALL WE?
KOF
SKRRK
YEAH, TOO MANY PRYING EYES HERE.
SKRRK
I WAS SO SCARED. LAST NIGHT WAS JUST A NIGHTMARE (FOR RIE'S BOYFRIEND)...
UH-HUH...

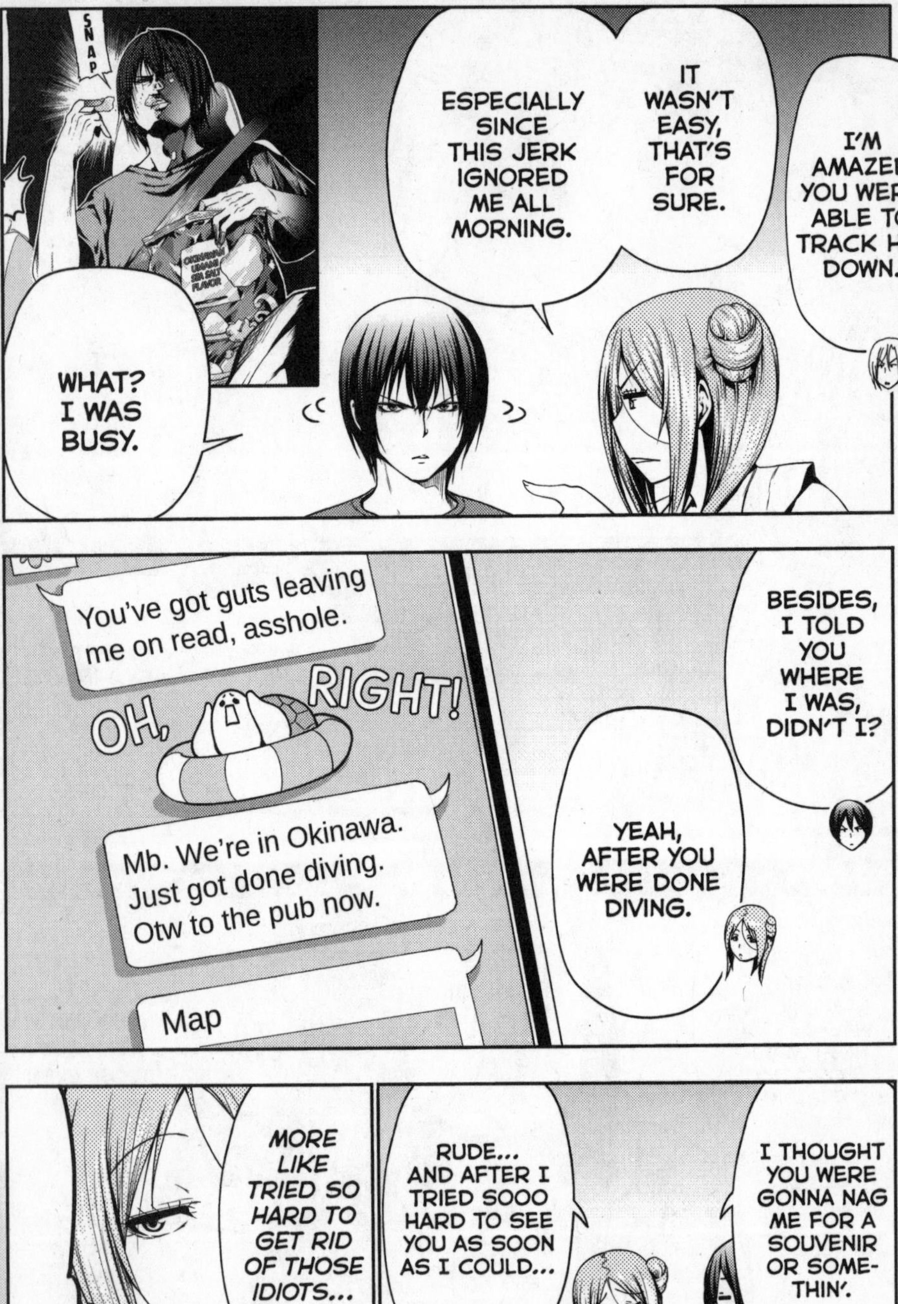
I'M AMAZED YOU WERE ABLE TO TRACK HIM DOWN.
IT WASN'T EASY, THAT'S FOR SURE.
ESPECIALLY SINCE THIS JERK IGNORED ME ALL MORNING.
SNAP
OKINAWAN UMAMI SEA SALT FLAVOR
WHAT? I WAS BUSY.
BESIDES, I TOLD YOU WHERE I WAS, DIDN'T I?
YEAH, AFTER YOU WERE DONE DIVING.
You've got guts leaving me on read, asshole.
OH, RIGHT!
Mb. We're in Okinawa. Just got done diving. Otw to the pub now.
Map
I THOUGHT YOU WERE GONNA NAG ME FOR A SOUVENIR OR SOME-THIN'.
RUDE... AND AFTER I TRIED SOOO HARD TO SEE YOU AS SOON AS I COULD...
MORE LIKE TRIED SO HARD TO GET RID OF THOSE IDIOTS...

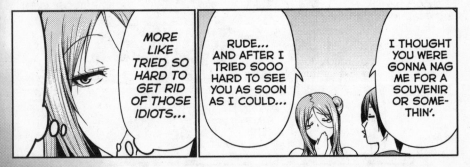

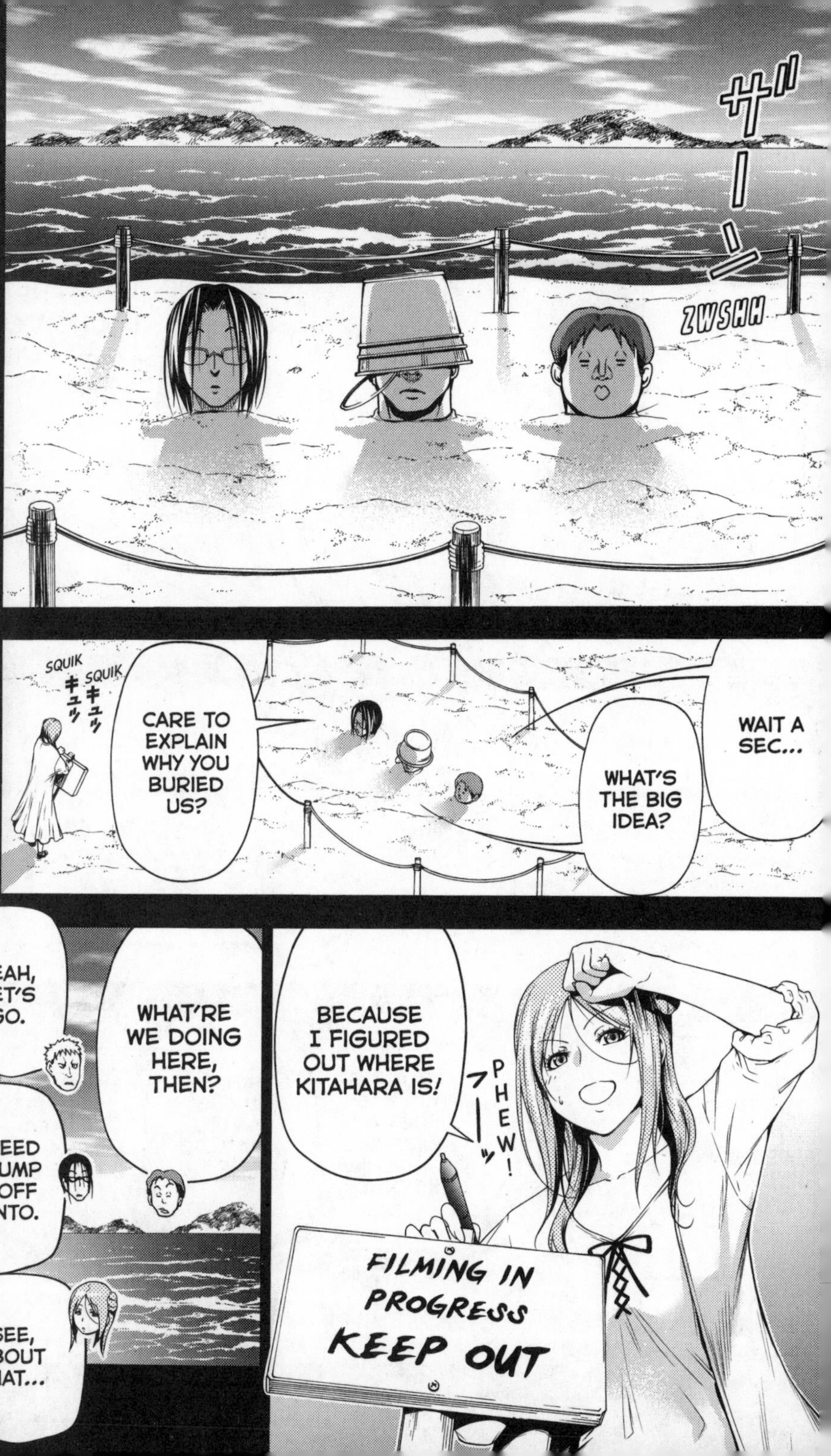
ZWSHH
WAIT A SEC...
WHAT'S THE BIG IDEA?
CARE TO EXPLAIN WHY YOU BURIED US?
SQUIK SQUIK
BECAUSE I FIGURED OUT WHERE KITAHARA IS!
PHEW!
FILMING IN PROGRESS
KEEP OUT
WHAT'RE WE DOING HERE, THEN?
YEAH, LET'S GO.
WE NEED TO BUMP HIM OFF PRONTO.
SEE, ABOUT THAT...

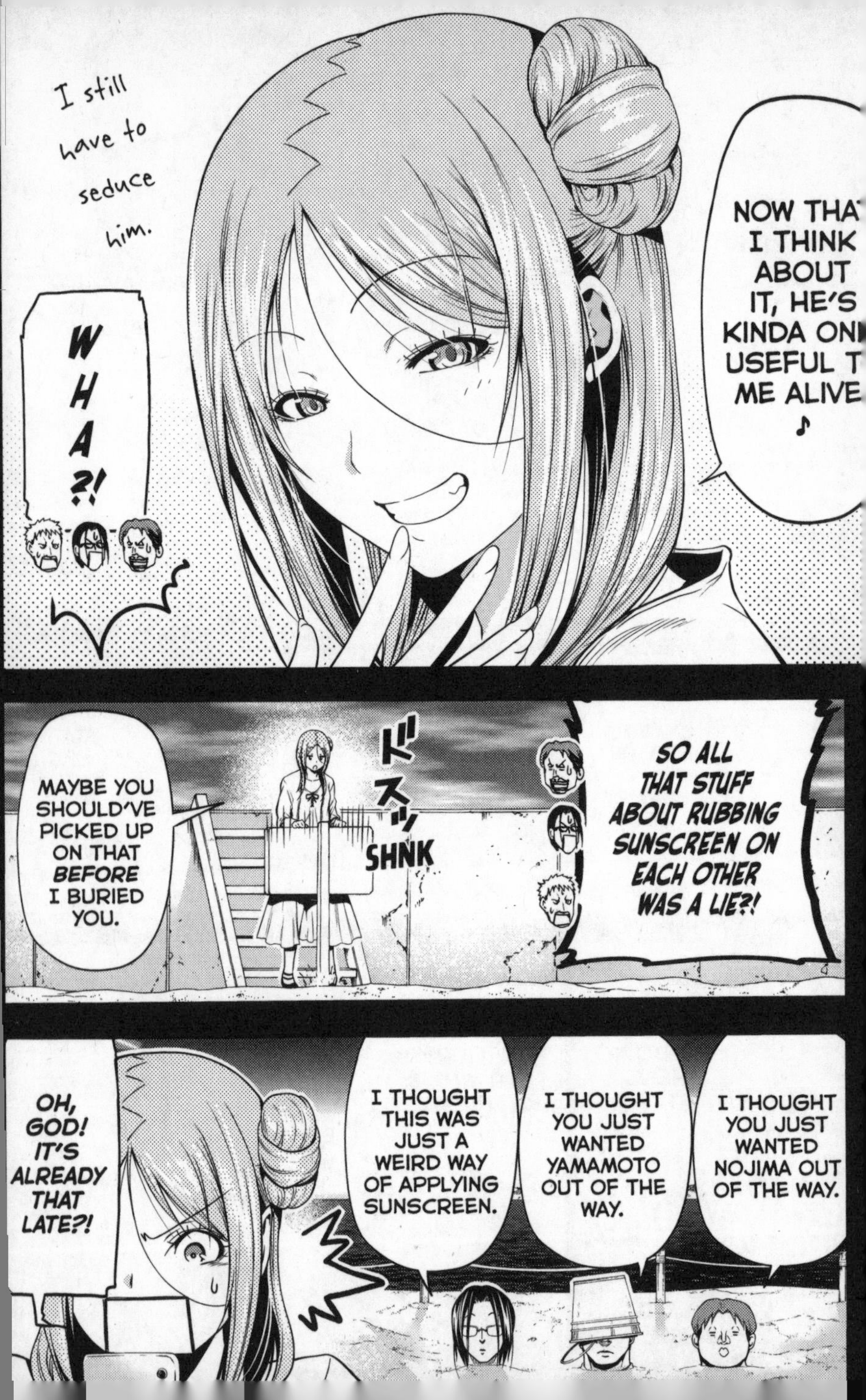
NOW THA I THINK ABOUT IT, HE'S KINDA ONI USEFUL T ME ALIVE ♪
I still have to seduce him.
WHA?!
SO ALL THAT STUFF ABOUT RUBBING SUNSCREEN ON EACH OTHER WAS A LIE?!
ドスッ
SHNK
MAYBE YOU SHOULD'VE PICKED UP ON THAT BEFORE I BURIED YOU.
I THOUGHT YOU JUST WANTED NOJIMA OUT OF THE WAY.
I THOUGHT YOU JUST WANTED YAMAMOTO OUT OF THE WAY.
I THOUGHT THIS WAS JUST A WEIRD WAY OF APPLYING SUNSCREEN.
OH, GOD! IT'S ALREADY THAT LATE?!

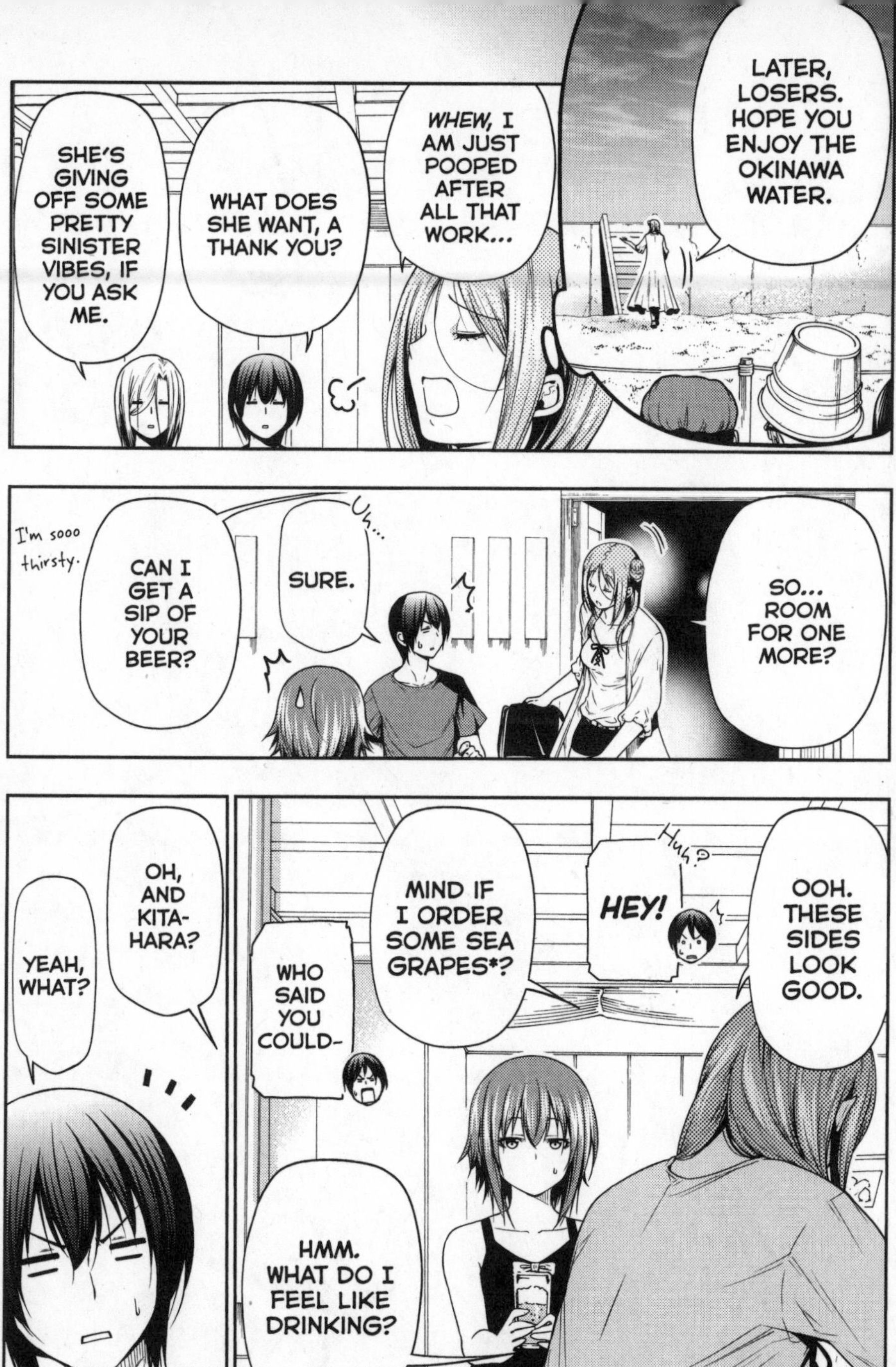
LATER, LOSERS. HOPE YOU ENJOY THE OKINAWA WATER.
WHEW, I AM JUST POOPED AFTER ALL THAT WORK...
WHAT DOES SHE WANT, A THANK YOU?
SHE'S GIVING OFF SOME PRETTY SINISTER VIBES, IF YOU ASK ME.
SO... ROOM FOR ONE MORE?
Uh...
SURE.
CAN I GET A SIP OF YOUR BEER?
I'm sooo thirsty.
OOH. THESE SIDES LOOK GOOD.
Huh?
HEY!
MIND IF I ORDER SOME SEA GRAPES*?
WHO SAID YOU COULD-
HMM. WHAT DO I FEEL LIKE DRINKING?
OH, AND KITA-HARA?
YEAH, WHAT?

*A type of seaweed.

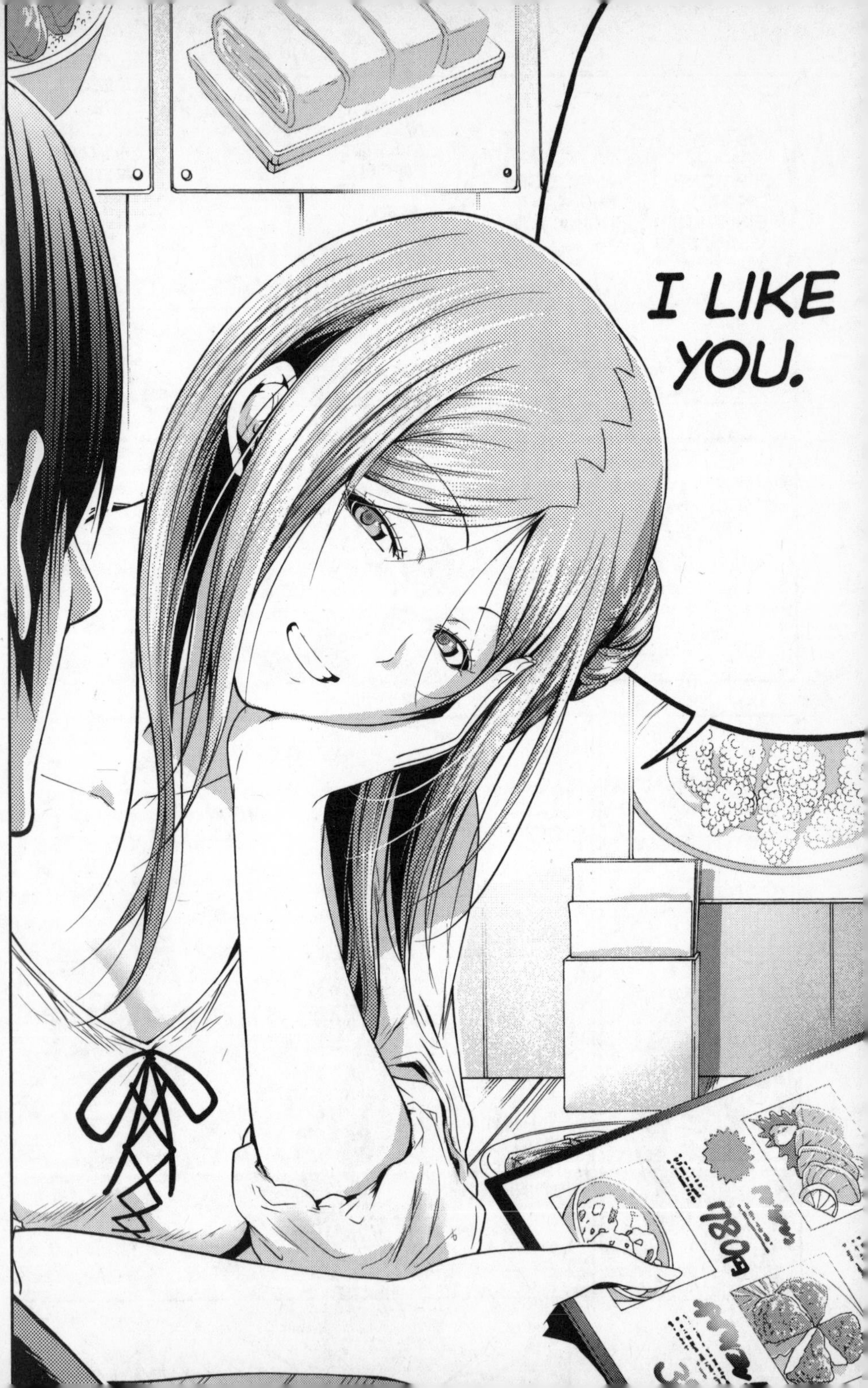
I LIKE YOU.
780円

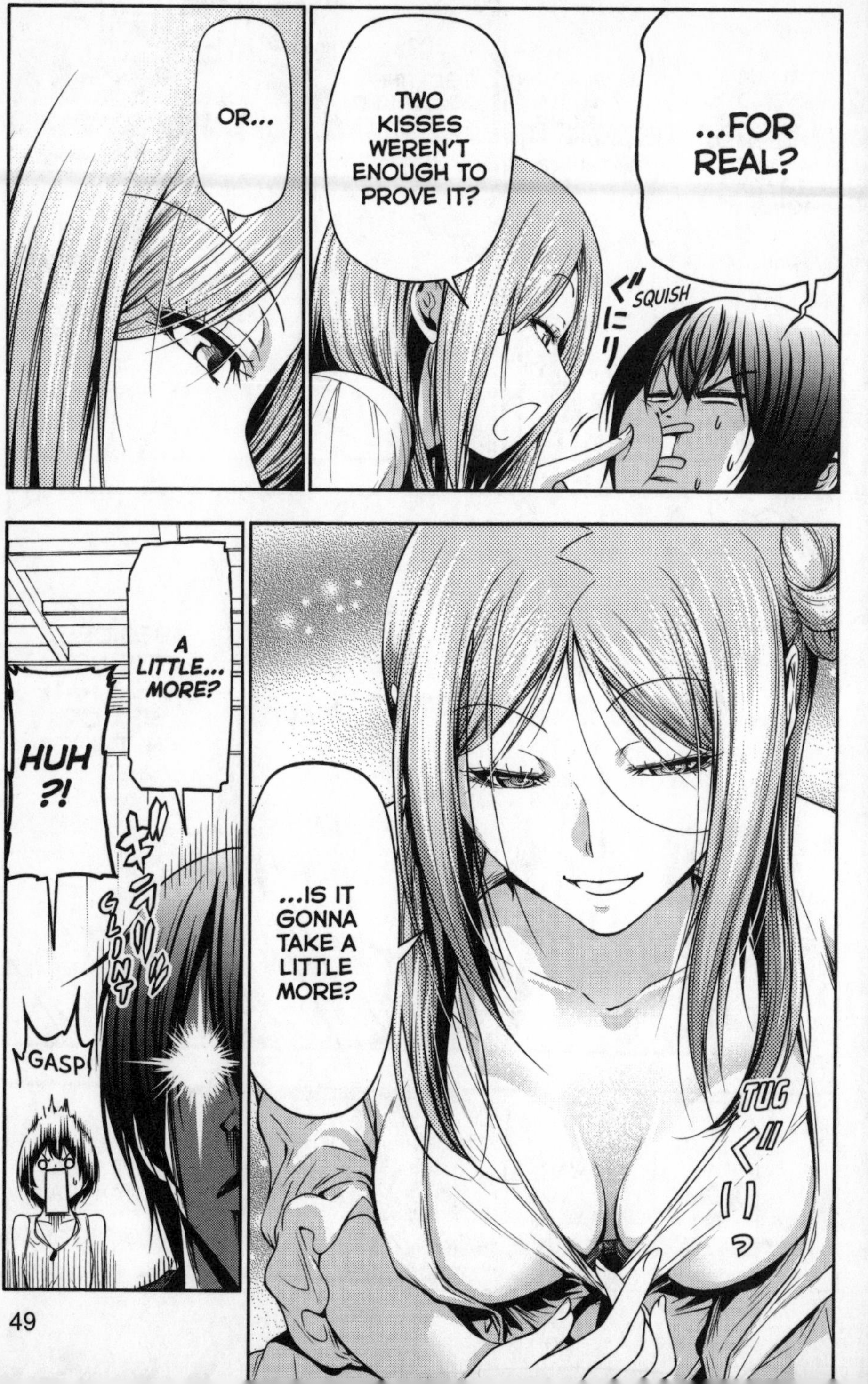
...FOR REAL?
TWO KISSES WEREN'T ENOUGH TO PROVE IT?
SQUISH
OR...
...IS IT GONNA TAKE A LITTLE MORE?
TUG
A LITTLE... MORE?
HUH?!
GLINT
GASP

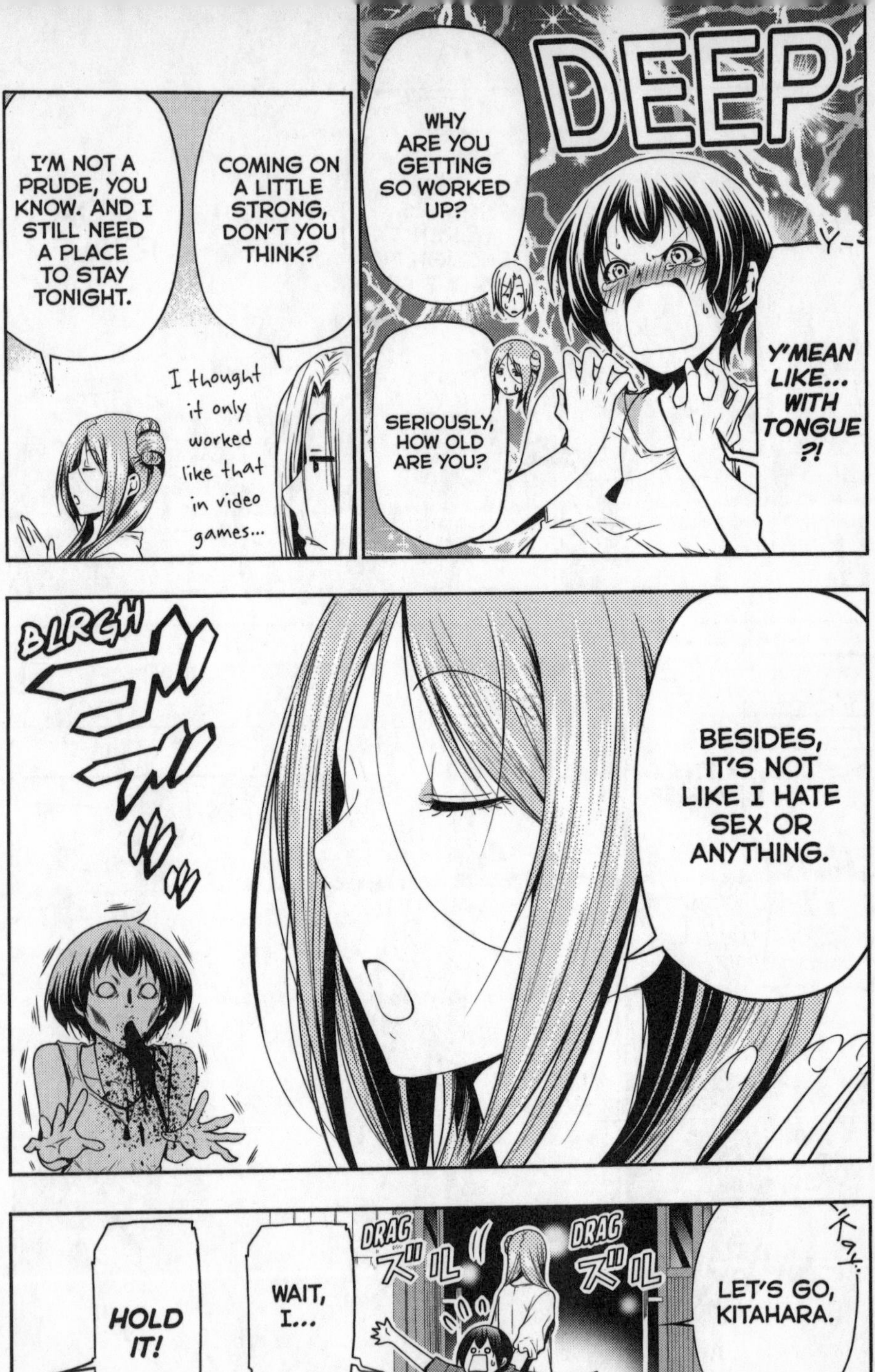
DEEP
Y—
WHY ARE YOU GETTING SO WORKED UP?
Y'MEAN LIKE... WITH TONGUE?!
SERIOUSLY, HOW OLD ARE YOU?
COMING ON A LITTLE STRONG, DON'T YOU THINK?
I'M NOT A PRUDE, YOU KNOW. AND I STILL NEED A PLACE TO STAY TONIGHT.
I thought it only worked like that in video games...
BESIDES, IT'S NOT LIKE I HATE SEX OR ANYTHING.
BLRGH
LET'S GO, KITAHARA.
DRAG
DRAG
WAIT, I...
HOLD IT!

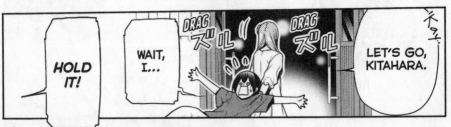

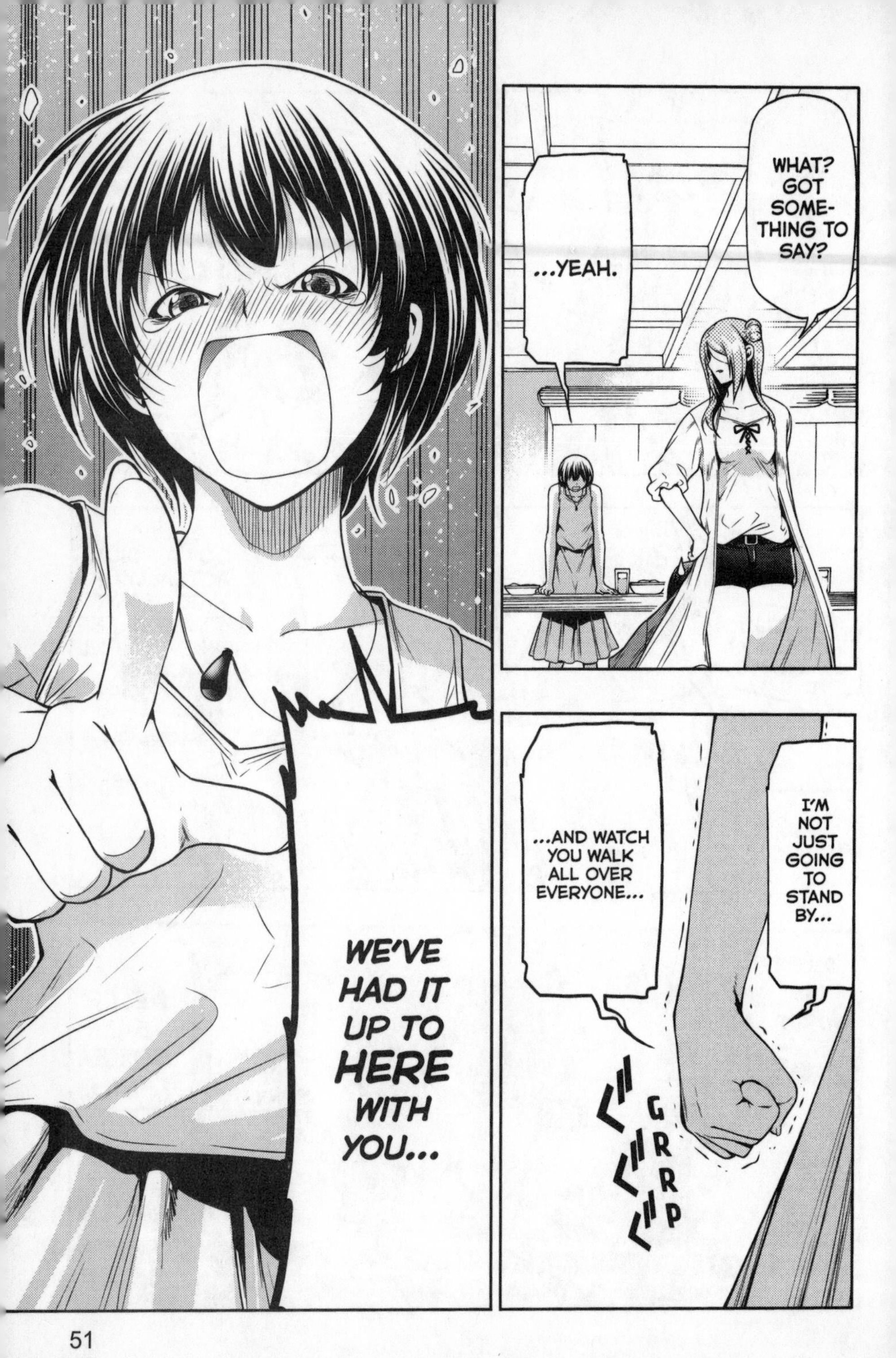
WHAT? GOT SOME-THING TO SAY?
...YEAH.
I'M NOT JUST GOING TO STAND BY...
...AND WATCH YOU WALK ALL OVER EVERYONE...
GRRP
WE'VE HAD IT UP TO HERE WITH YOU...

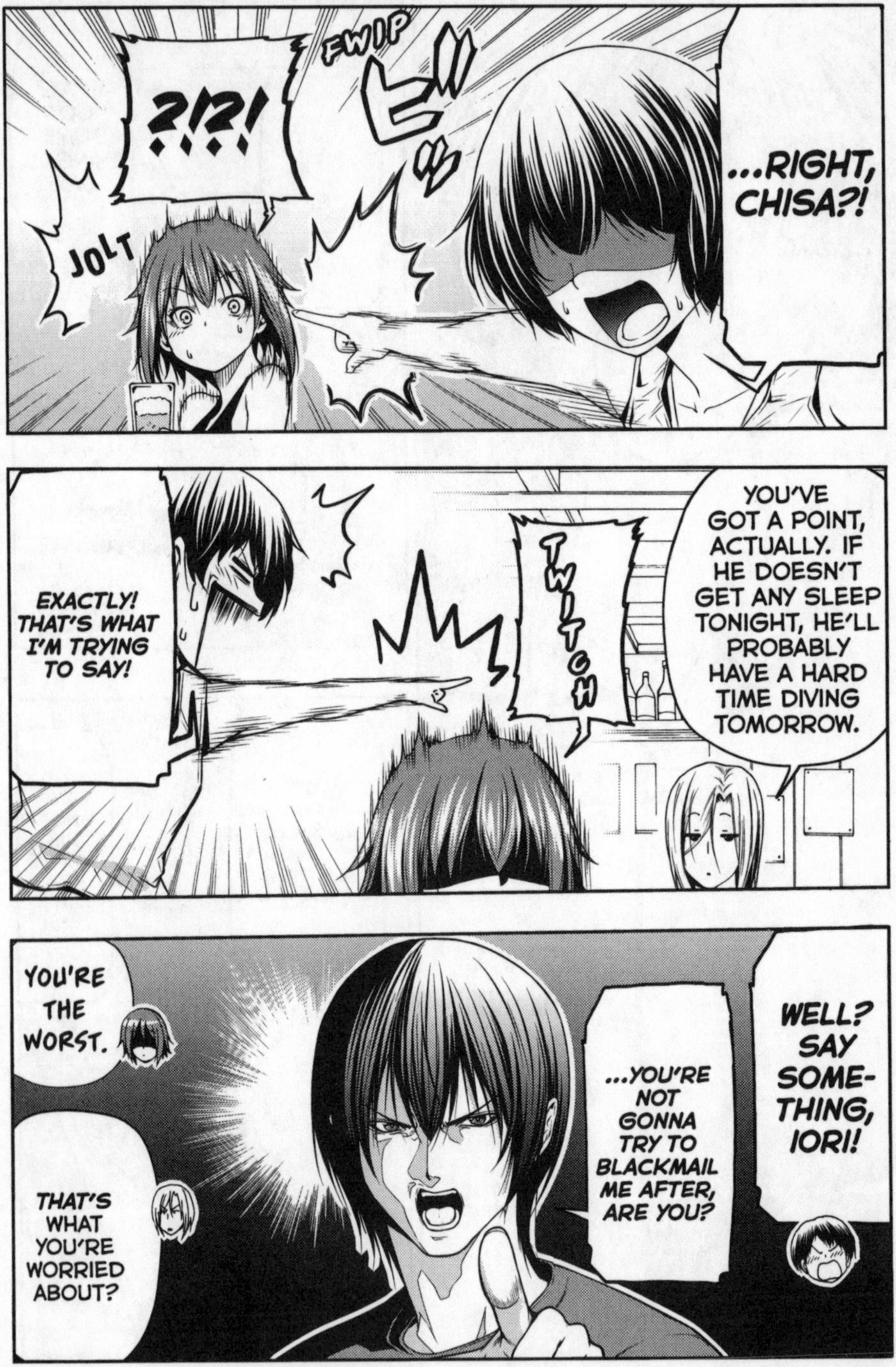
...RIGHT, CHISA?!
FWIP
?!?!
JOLT
YOU'VE GOT A POINT, ACTUALLY. IF HE DOESN'T GET ANY SLEEP TONIGHT, HE'LL PROBABLY HAVE A HARD TIME DIVING TOMORROW.
TWITCH
EXACTLY! THAT'S WHAT I'M TRYING TO SAY!
WELL? SAY SOME-THING, IORI!
...YOU'RE NOT GONNA TRY TO BLACKMAIL ME AFTER, ARE YOU?
YOU'RE THE WORST.
THAT'S WHAT YOU'RE WORRIED ABOUT?

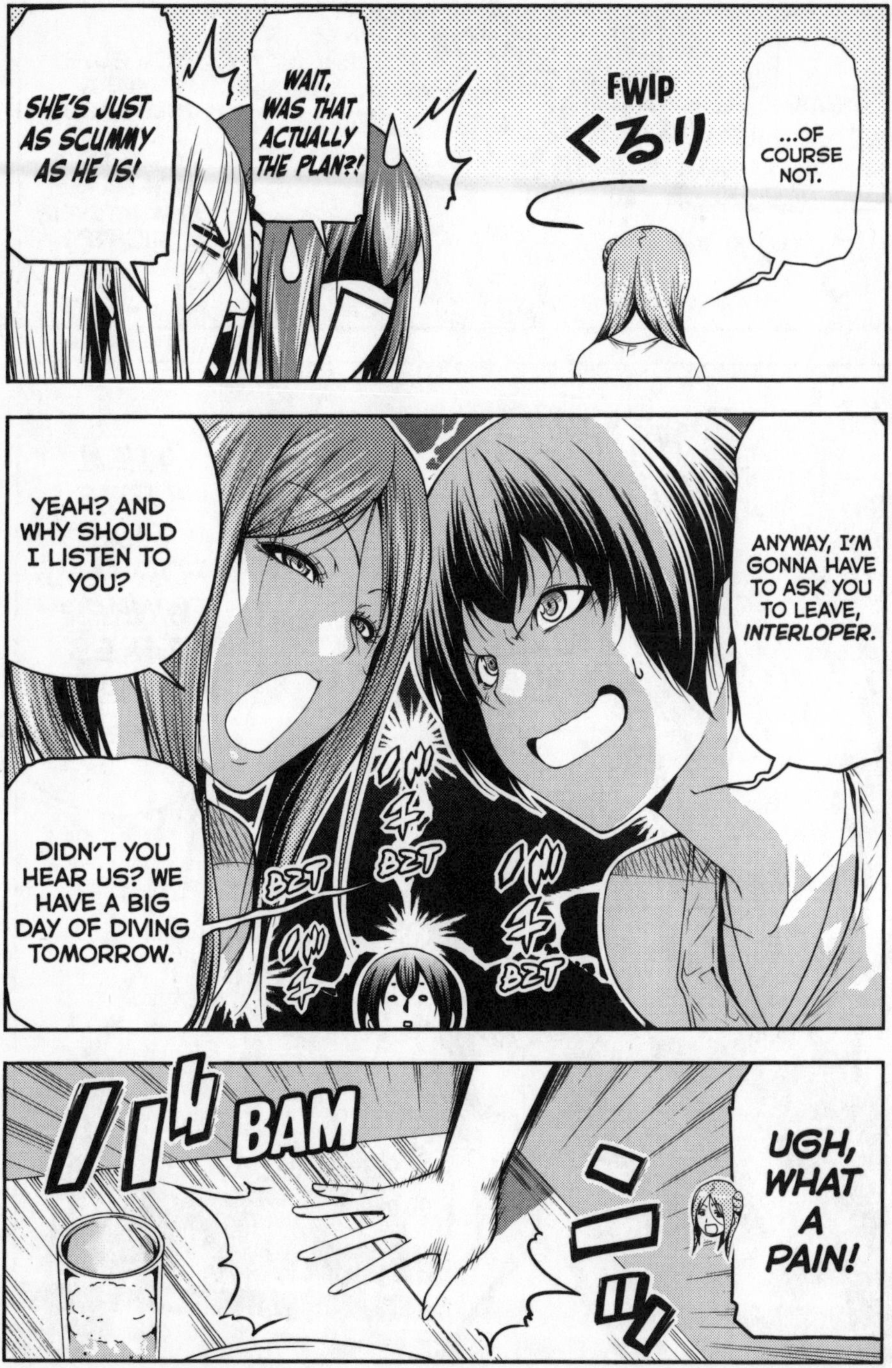
...OF COURSE NOT.
FWIP
くるり
WAIT, WAS THAT ACTUALLY THE PLAN?!
SHE'S JUST AS SCUMMY AS HE IS!
ANYWAY, I'M GONNA HAVE TO ASK YOU TO LEAVE, *INTERLOPER*.
YEAH? AND WHY SHOULD I LISTEN TO YOU?
BZT
BZT
BZT
BZT
DIDN'T YOU HEAR US? WE HAVE A BIG DAY OF DIVING TOMORROW.
UGH, WHAT A PAIN!
BAM

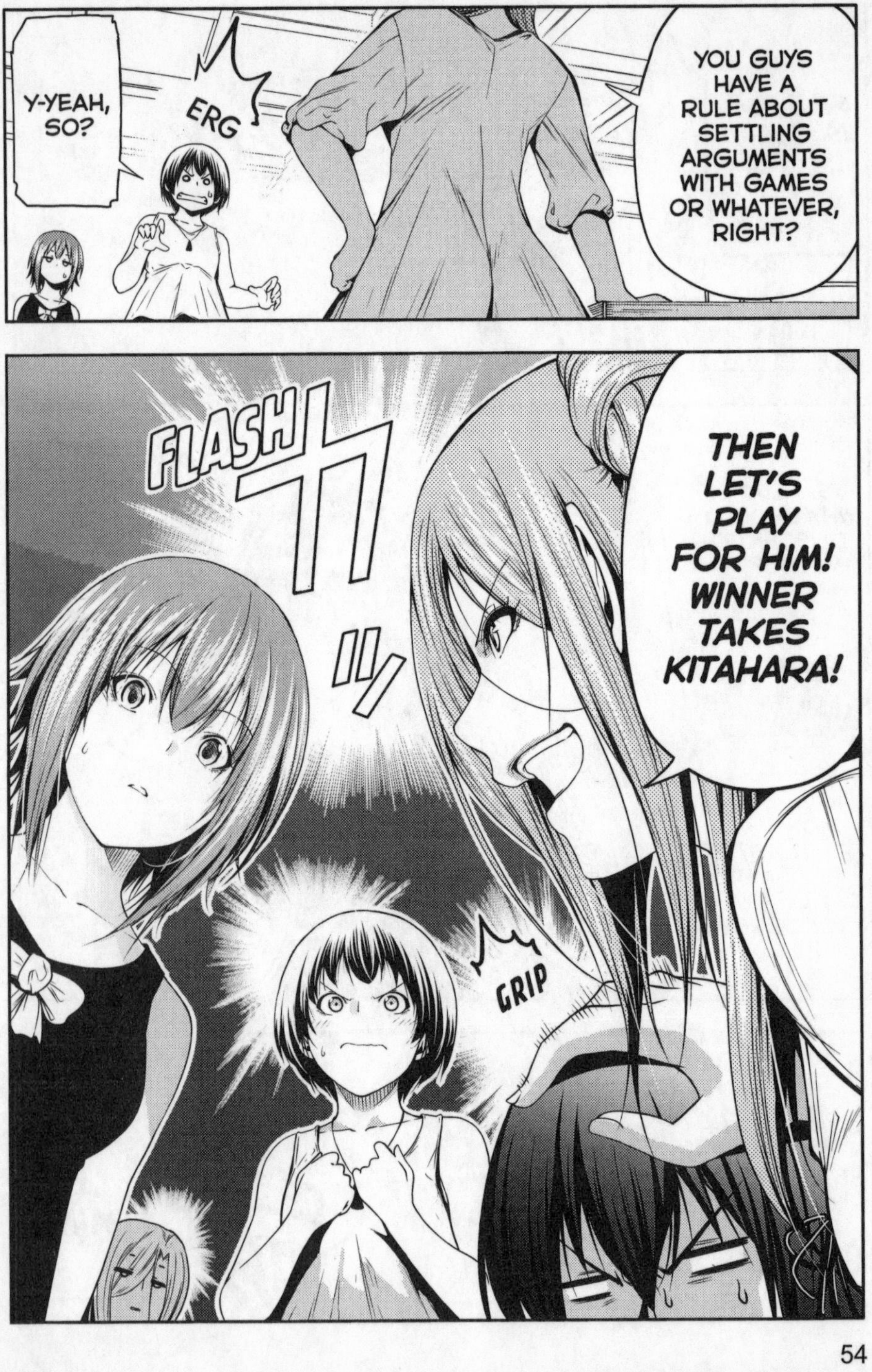
YOU GUYS HAVE A RULE ABOUT SETTLING ARGUMENTS WITH GAMES OR WHATEVER, RIGHT?
ERG
Y-YEAH, SO?
THEN LET'S PLAY FOR HIM! WINNER TAKES KITAHARA!
FLASH
GRIP

TIDE'S COMING IN...
ZSHHH
YEAH ...
FILMING IN PROGRESS KEEP OUT

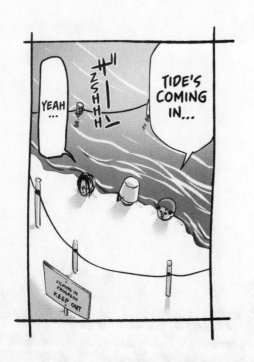

Grand Blue Dreaming

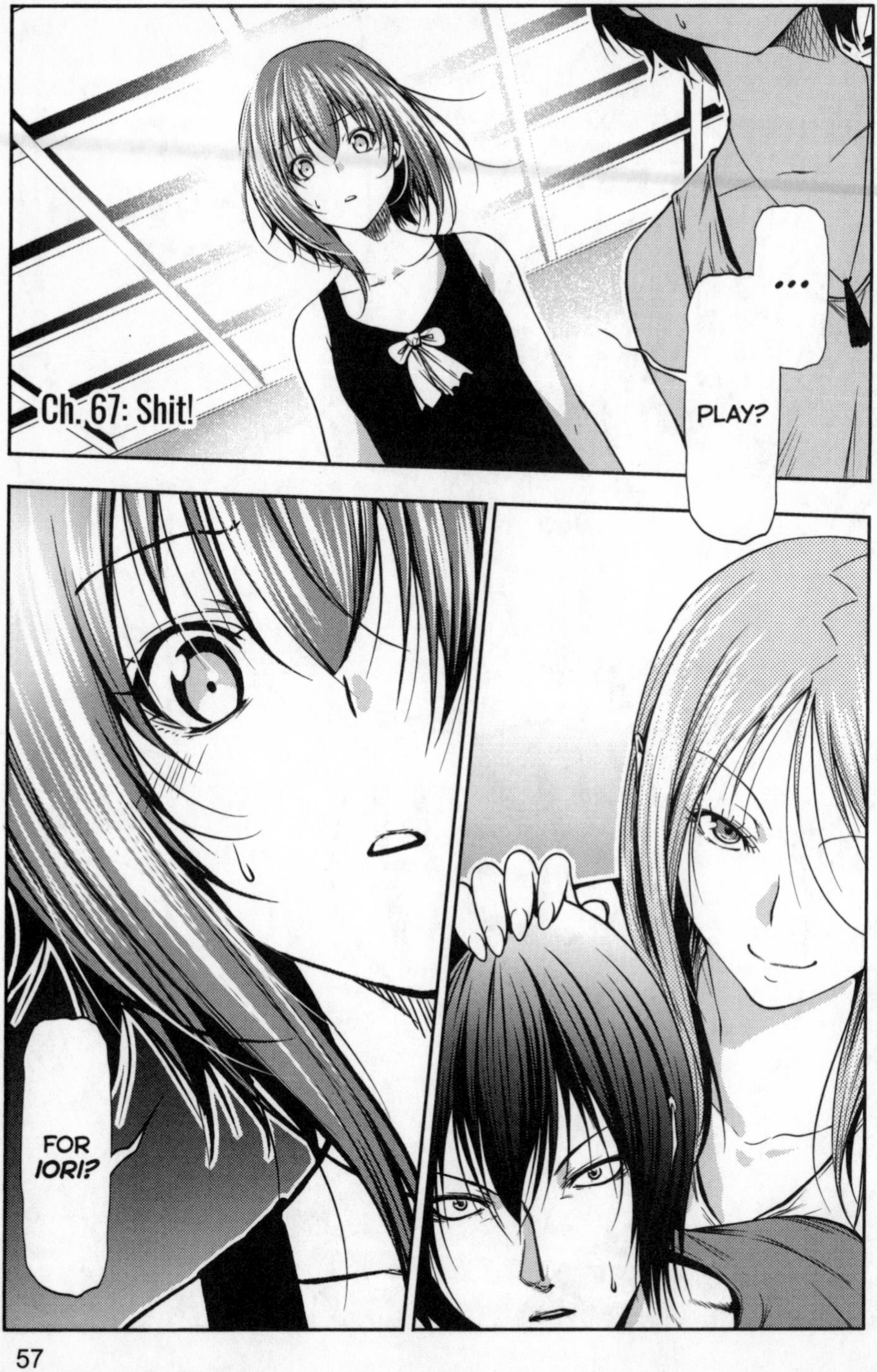
... PLAY?
Ch. 67: Shit!
FOR IORI?

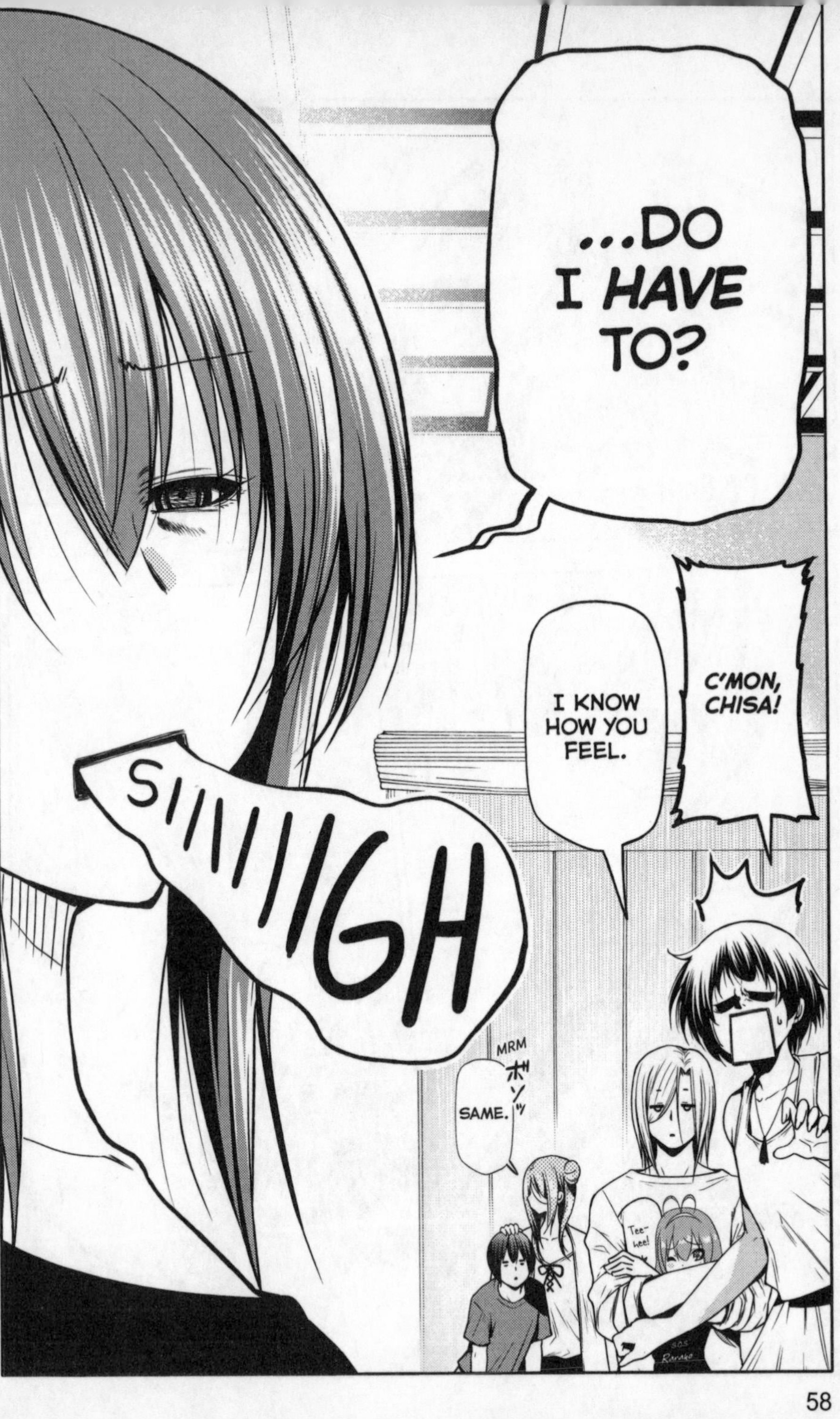
...DO I HAVE TO?
C'MON, CHISA!
I KNOW HOW YOU FEEL.
SIIIIIGH
Tee-hee!
MRM
ボソッ
SAME.

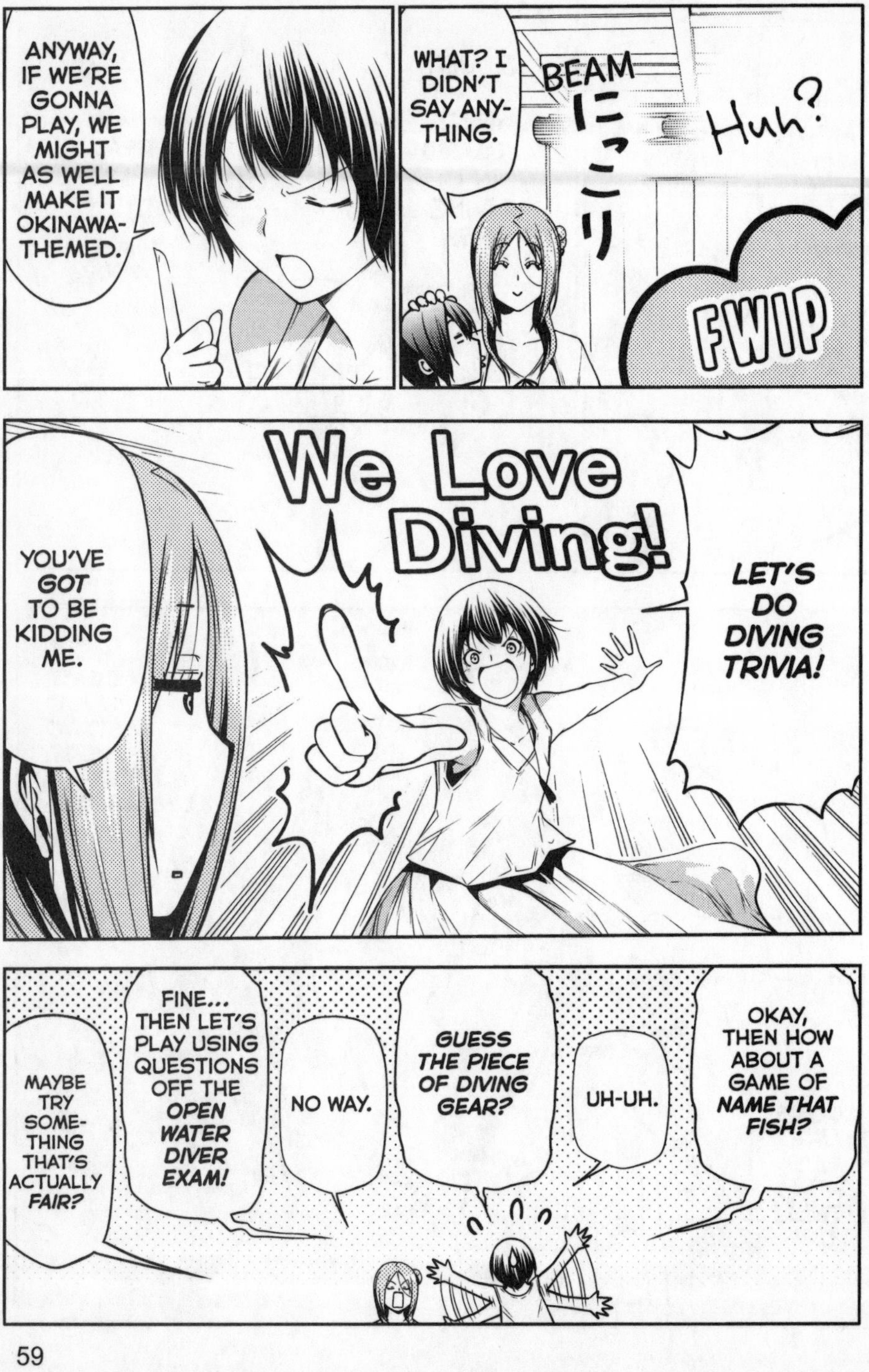

Huh?
BEAM にっこり
WHAT? I DIDN'T SAY ANYTHING.
FWIP
ANYWAY, IF WE'RE GONNA PLAY, WE MIGHT AS WELL MAKE IT OKINAWA-THEMED.
We Love Diving!
LET'S DO DIVING TRIVIA!
YOU'VE GOT TO BE KIDDING ME.
OKAY, THEN HOW ABOUT A GAME OF NAME THAT FISH?
UH-UH.
GUESS THE PIECE OF DIVING GEAR?
NO WAY.
FINE... THEN LET'S PLAY USING QUESTIONS OFF THE OPEN WATER DIVER EXAM!
MAYBE TRY SOMETHING THAT'S ACTUALLY FAIR?

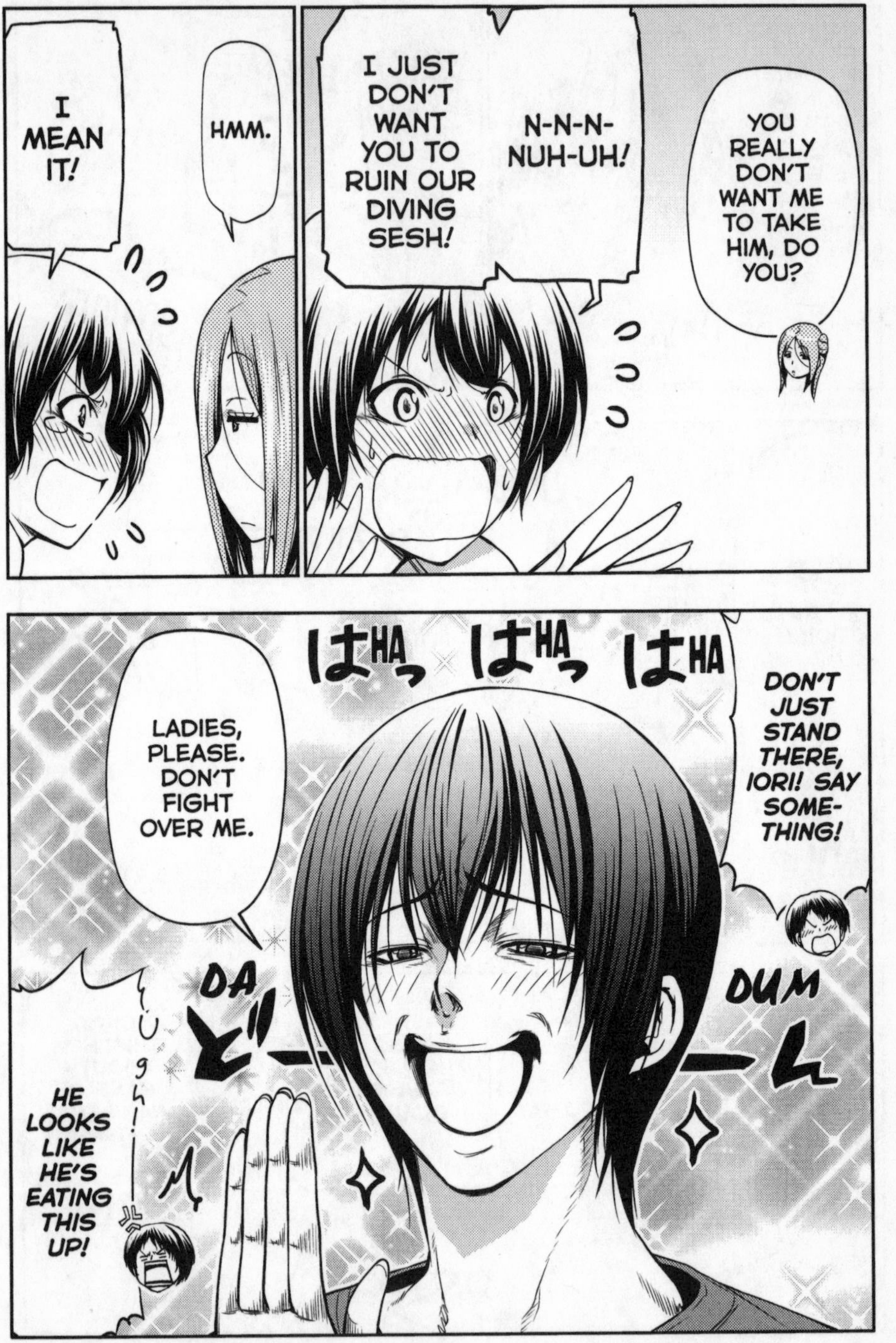
YOU REALLY DON'T WANT ME TO TAKE HIM, DO YOU?
N-N-N-NUH-UH!
I JUST DON'T WANT YOU TO RUIN OUR DIVING SESH!
HMM.
I MEAN IT!
DON'T JUST STAND THERE, IORI! SAY SOMETHING!
はHAっ はHAっ はHA
LADIES, PLEASE. DON'T FIGHT OVER ME.
DA どーー DUM ーん
HE LOOKS LIKE HE'S EATING THIS UP!

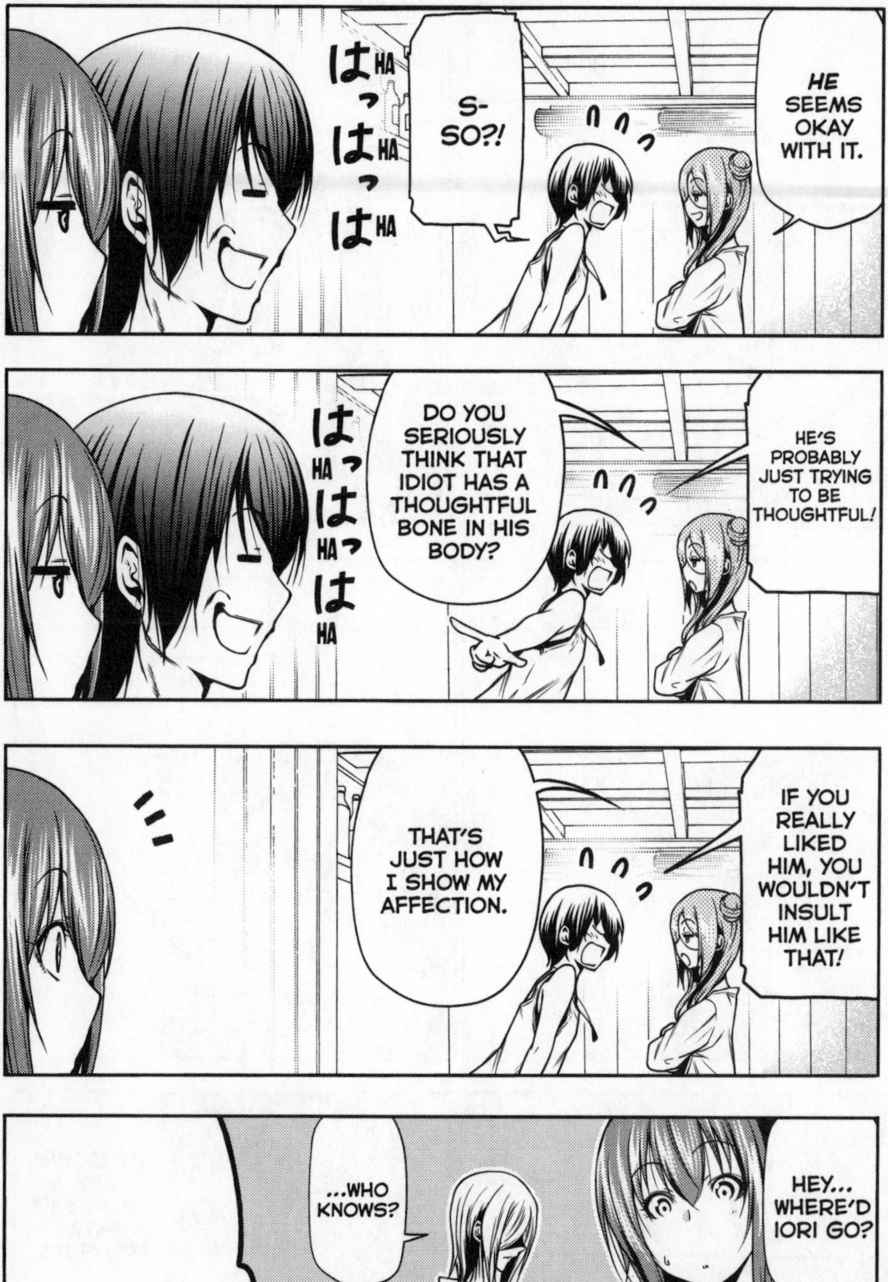
HE SEEMS OKAY WITH IT.
S-SO?!
はっはっは HA HA HA
HE'S PROBABLY JUST TRYING TO BE THOUGHTFUL!
DO YOU SERIOUSLY THINK THAT IDIOT HAS A THOUGHTFUL BONE IN HIS BODY?
はっはっは HA HA HA
IF YOU REALLY LIKED HIM, YOU WOULDN'T INSULT HIM LIKE THAT!
THAT'S JUST HOW I SHOW MY AFFECTION.
HEY... WHERE'D IORI GO?
...WHO KNOWS?

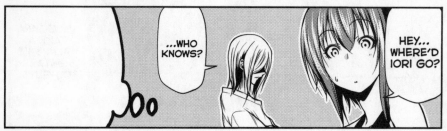

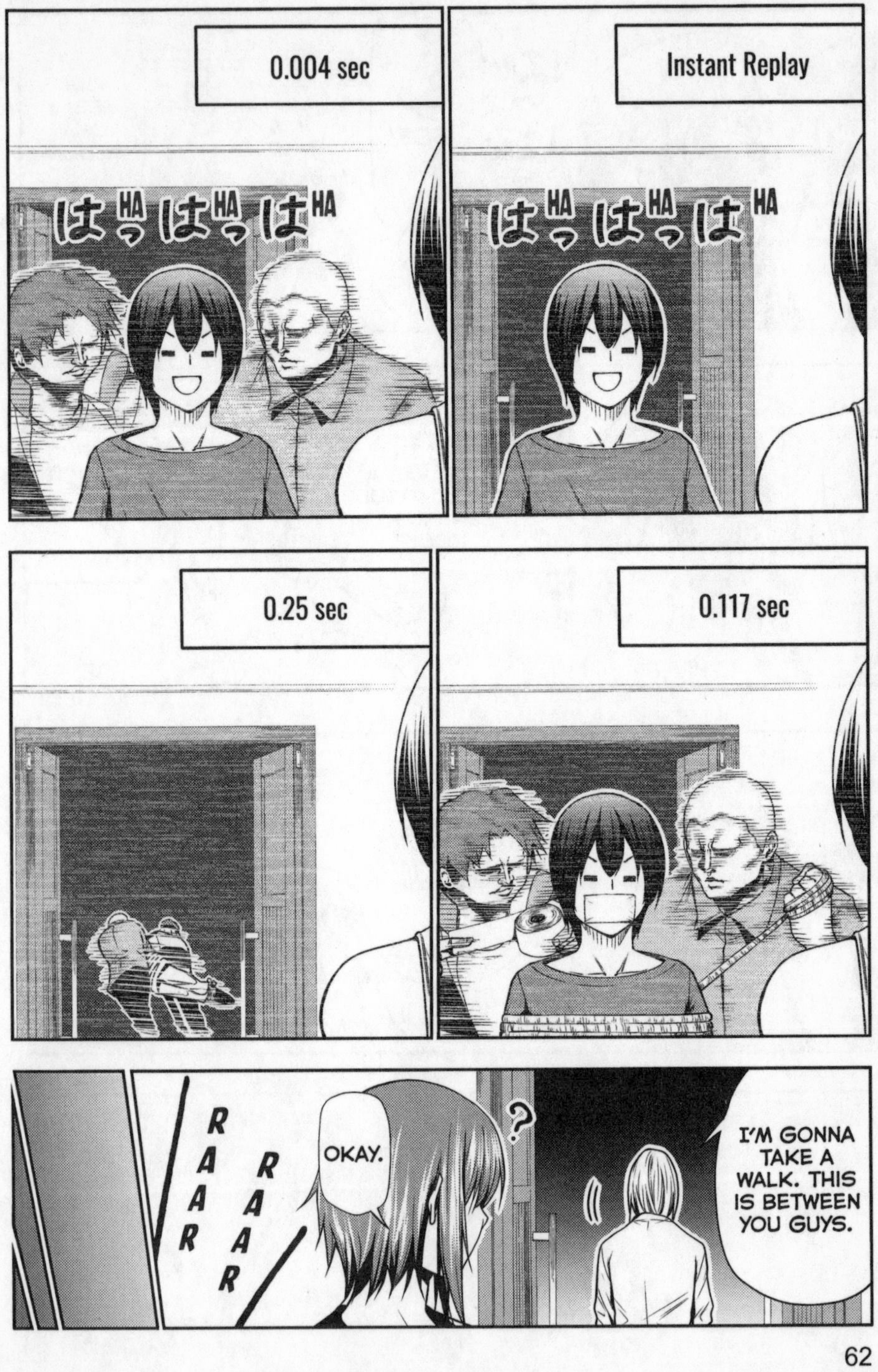
Instant Replay
はっはっは
HA HA HA
0.004 sec
はっはっは
HA HA HA
0.117 sec
0.25 sec
I'M GONNA TAKE A WALK. THIS IS BETWEEN YOU GUYS.
?
OKAY.
RAAR
RAAR

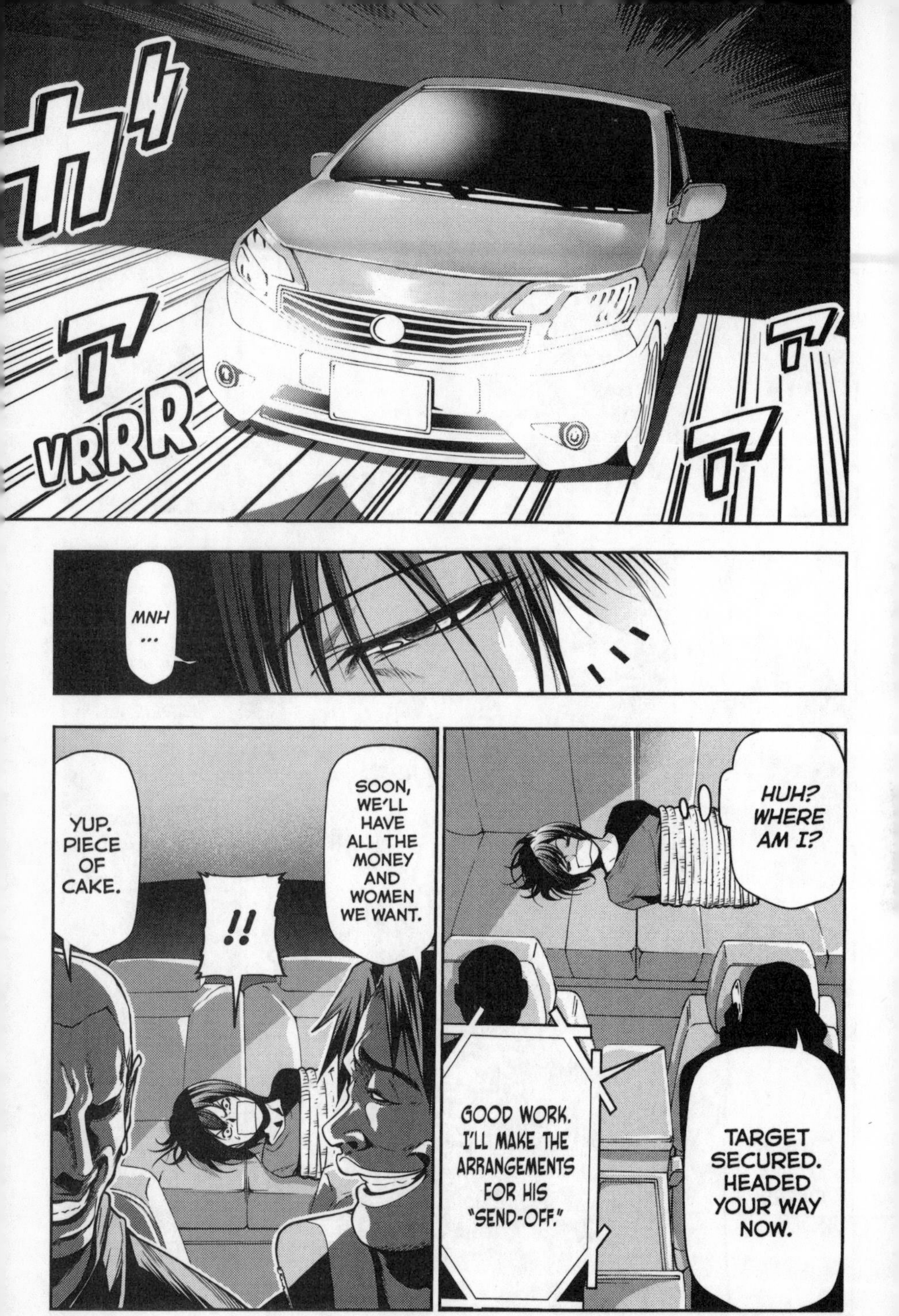
VRRR
MNH...
HUH? WHERE AM I?
TARGET SECURED. HEADED YOUR WAY NOW.
GOOD WORK. I'LL MAKE THE ARRANGEMENTS FOR HIS "SEND-OFF."
SOON, WE'LL HAVE ALL THE MONEY AND WOMEN WE WANT.
!!
YUP. PIECE OF CAKE.

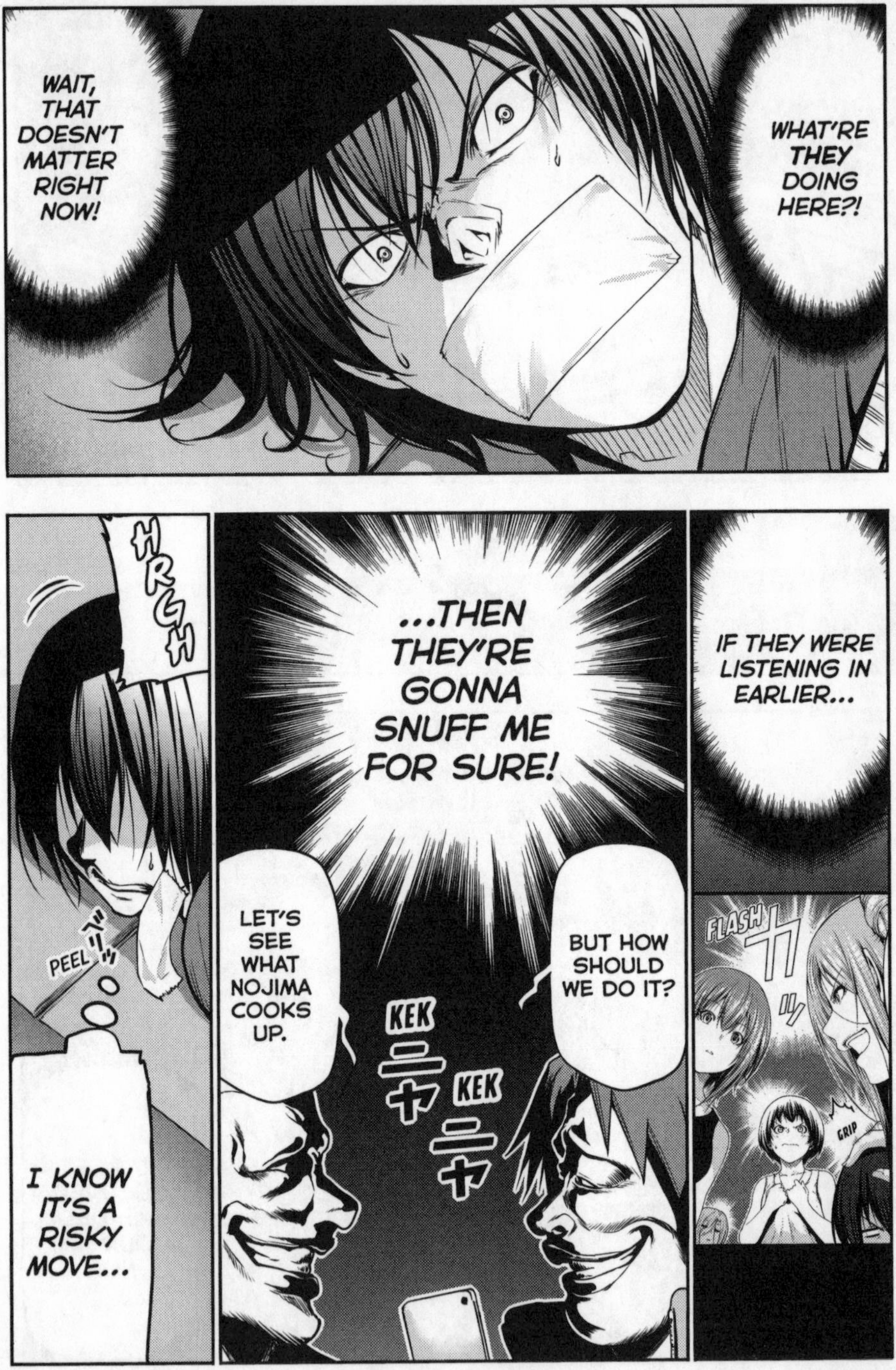
WHAT'RE THEY DOING HERE?!
WAIT, THAT DOESN'T MATTER RIGHT NOW!
IF THEY WERE LISTENING IN EARLIER...
FLASH
GRIP
...THEN THEY'RE GONNA SNUFF ME FOR SURE!
BUT HOW SHOULD WE DO IT?
LET'S SEE WHAT NOJIMA COOKS UP.
KEK
ニヤ
KEK
ニヤ
HRGH
PEEL
I KNOW IT'S A RISKY MOVE...

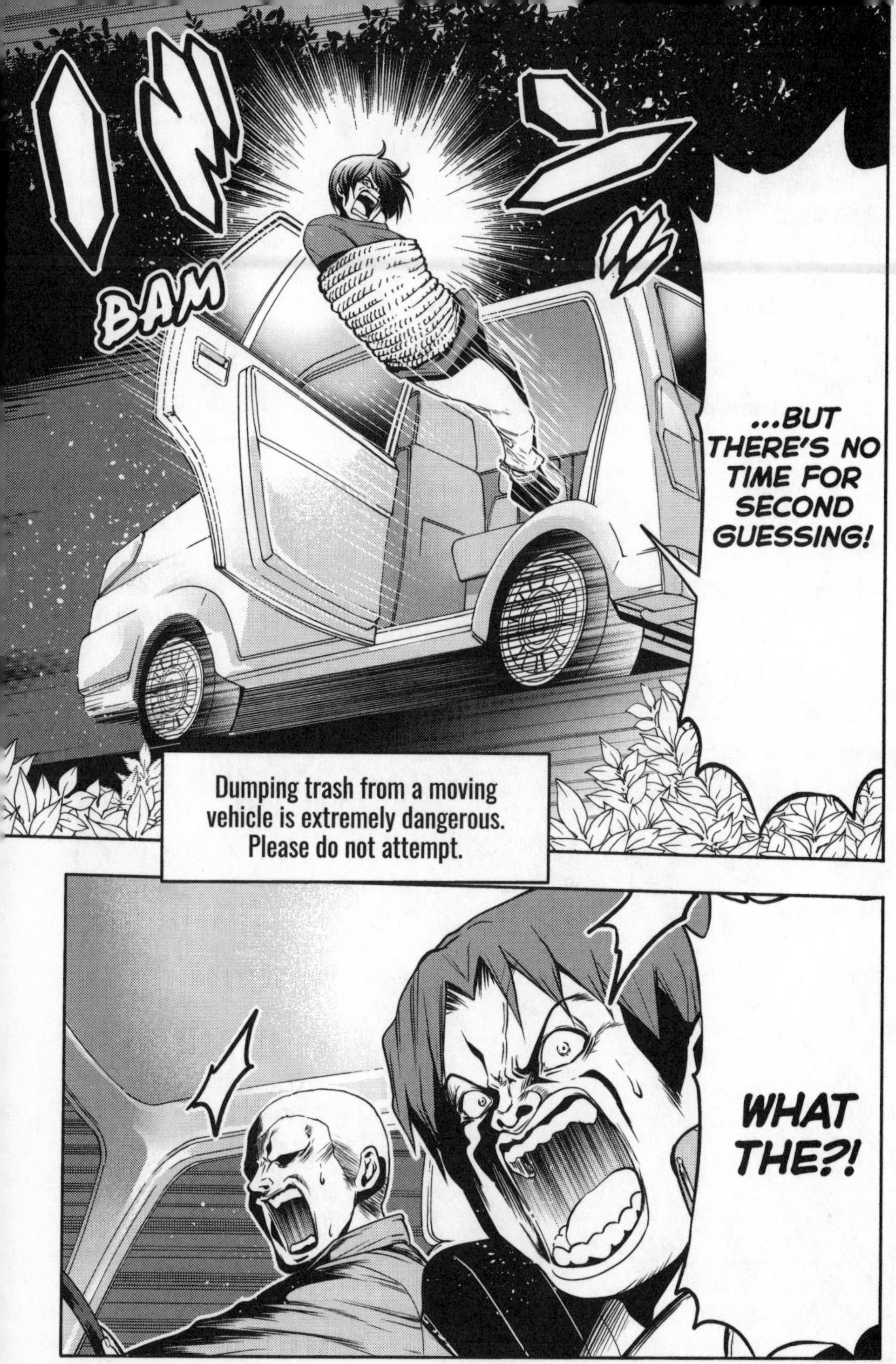
...BUT THERE'S NO TIME FOR SECOND GUESSING!
BAM
Dumping trash from a moving vehicle is extremely dangerous. Please do not attempt.
WHAT THE?!

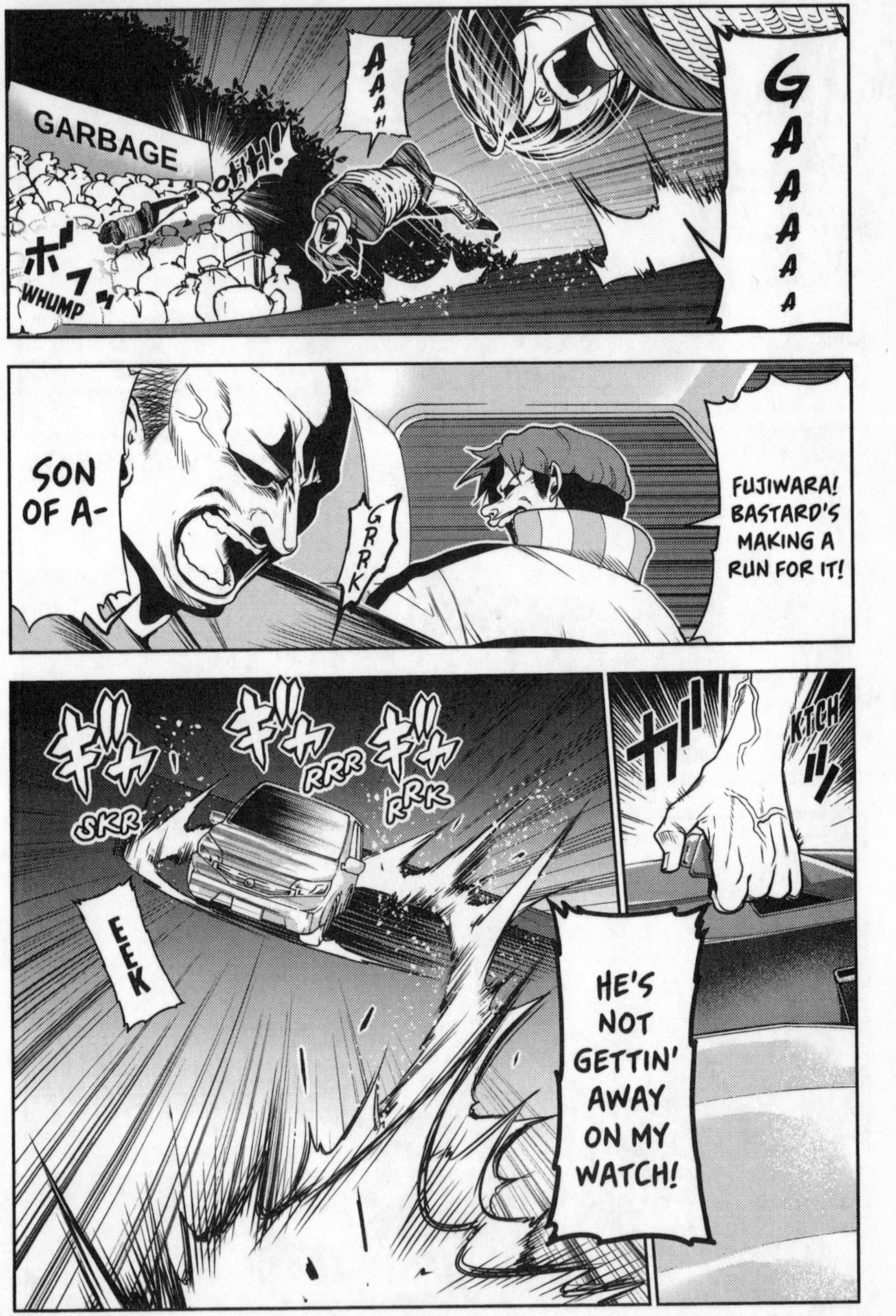
GAAAAAA
AAAAH
OHHH!
GARBAGE
ボフッ
WHUMP
FUJIWARA! BASTARD'S MAKING A RUN FOR IT!
GRRK
SON OF A-
カッ
KTCH
HE'S NOT GETTIN' AWAY ON MY WATCH!
ギャ
RRK
ギャ
RRR
ギャ
SKR
EEK

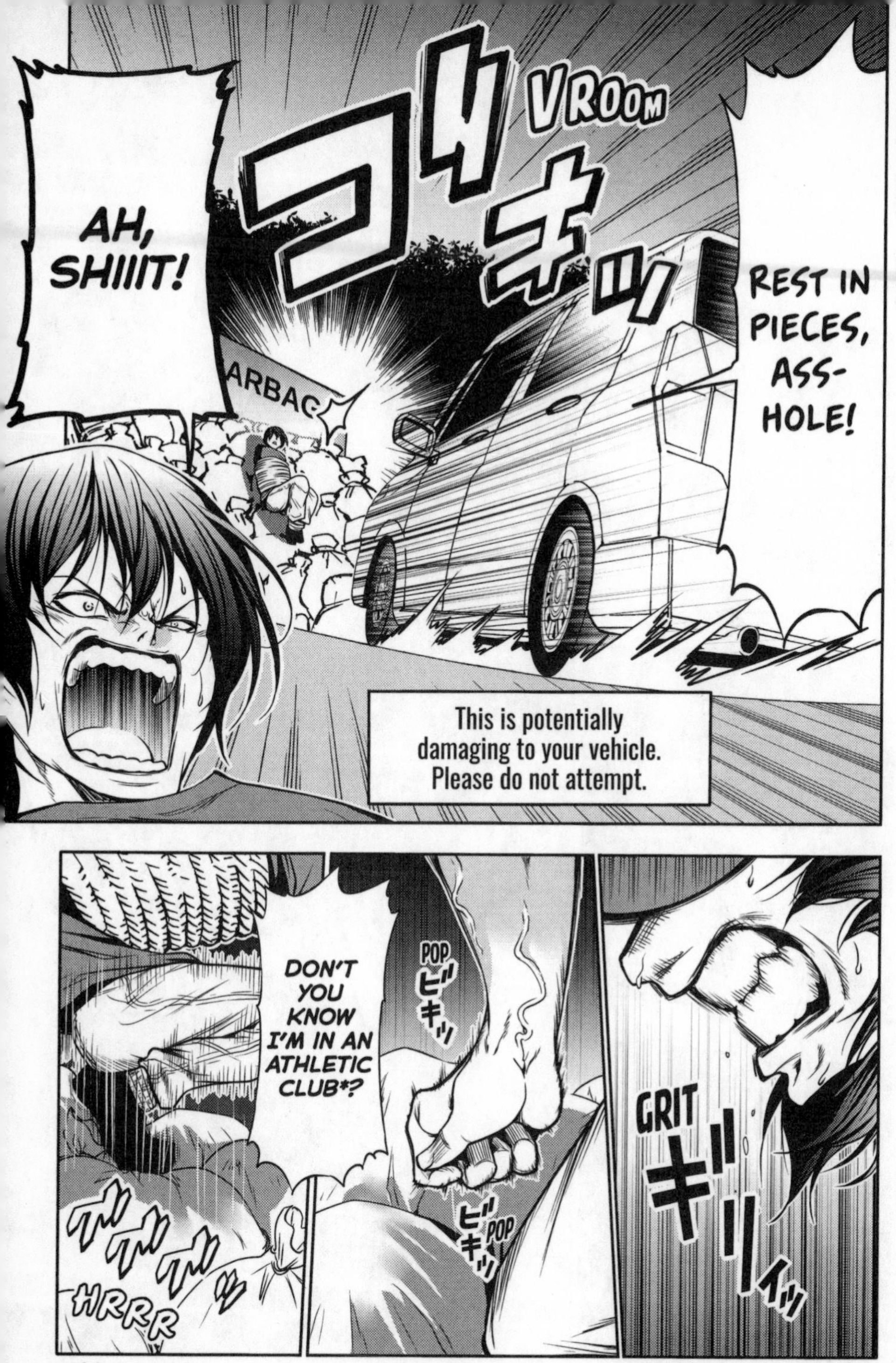
VROOM
REST IN PIECES, ASS-HOLE!
AH, SHIIIT!
ARBAG
This is potentially damaging to your vehicle. Please do not attempt.
GRIT
POP
DON'T YOU KNOW I'M IN AN ATHLETIC CLUB*?
POP
HRRR

*If diving counts.

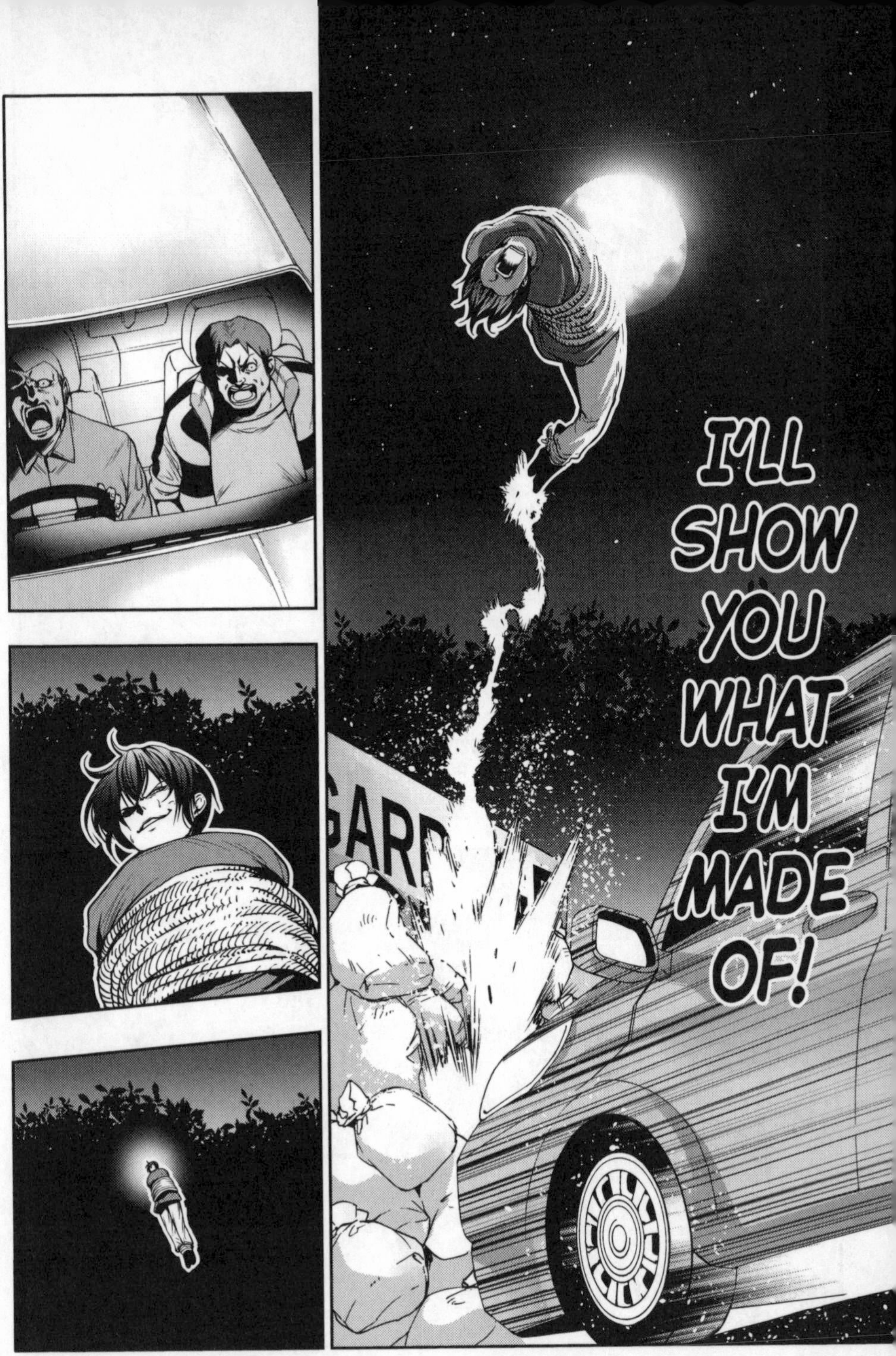
I'LL SHOW YOU WHAT I'M MADE OF!

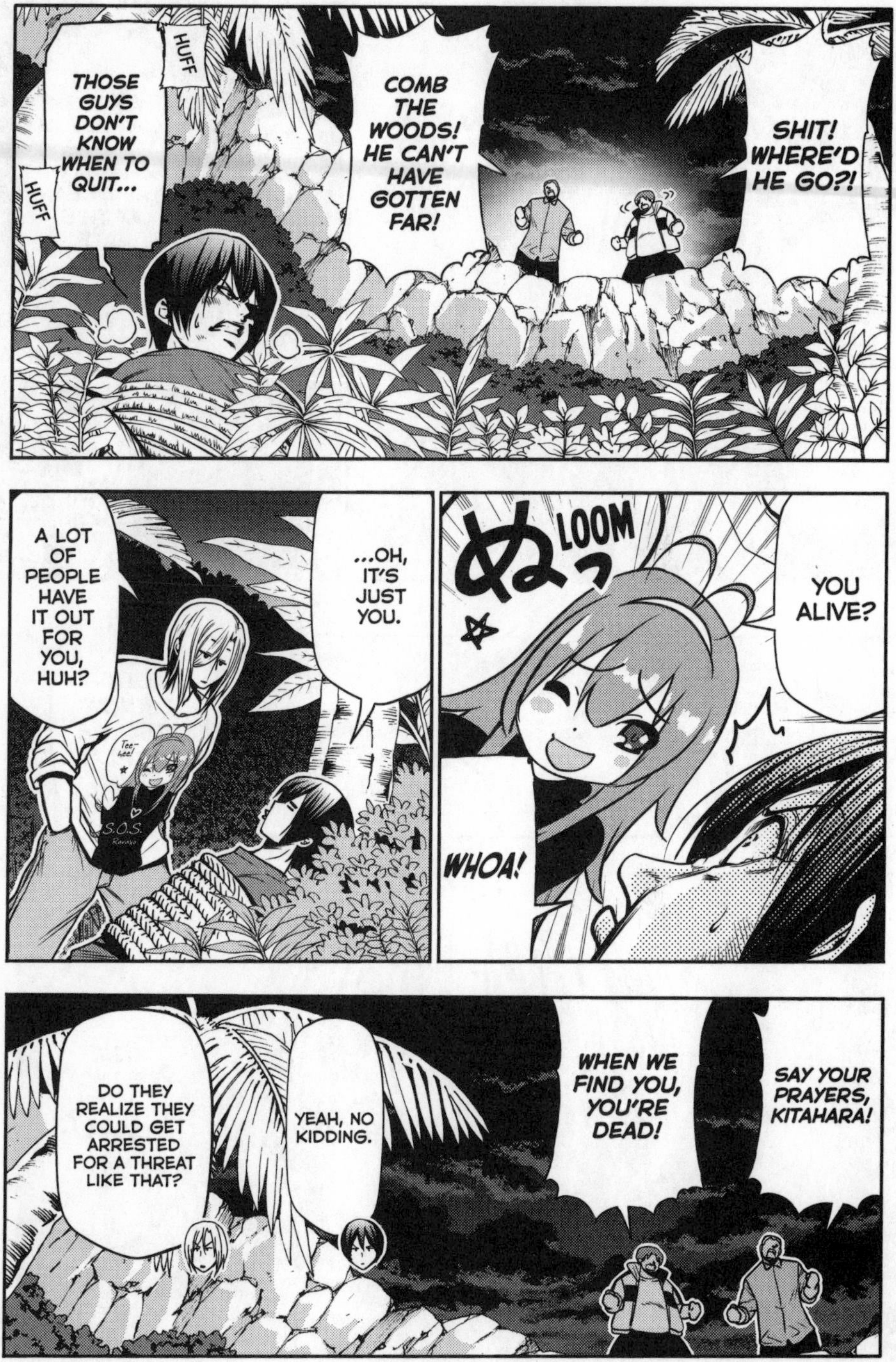
SHIT! WHERE'D HE GO?!
COMB THE WOODS! HE CAN'T HAVE GOTTEN FAR!
HUFF
THOSE GUYS DON'T KNOW WHEN TO QUIT...
HUFF
YOU ALIVE?
ぬっ LOOM
WHOA!
...OH, IT'S JUST YOU.
A LOT OF PEOPLE HAVE IT OUT FOR YOU, HUH?
Tee-hee!
S.O.S.
SAY YOUR PRAYERS, KITAHARA!
WHEN WE FIND YOU, YOU'RE DEAD!
YEAH, NO KIDDING.
DO THEY REALIZE THEY COULD GET ARRESTED FOR A THREAT LIKE THAT?

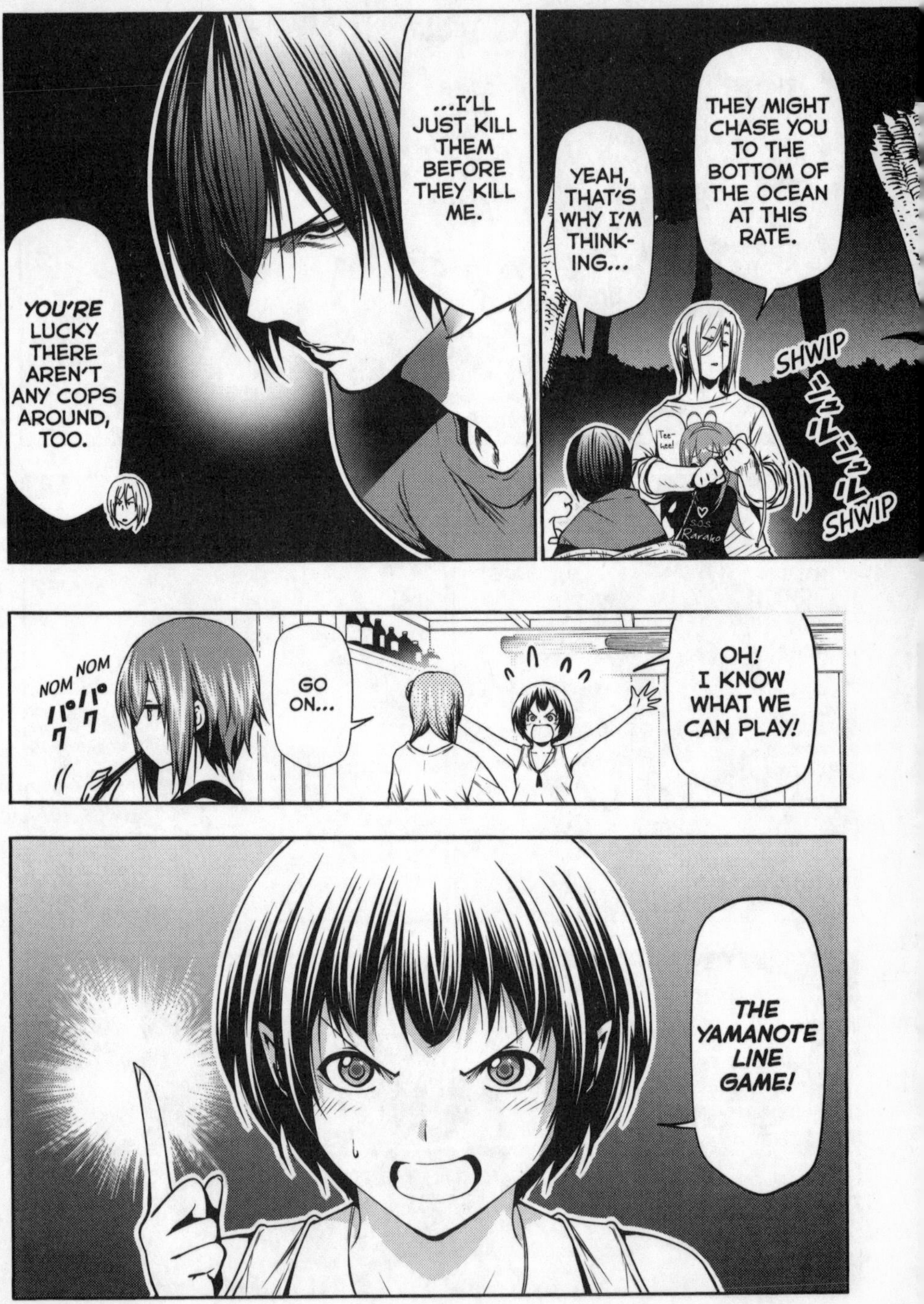
THEY MIGHT CHASE YOU TO THE BOTTOM OF THE OCEAN AT THIS RATE.
YEAH, THAT'S WHY I'M THINK-ING...
SHWIP SHWIP
Tee-hee!
S.O.S. Rarako
...I'LL JUST KILL THEM BEFORE THEY KILL ME.
YOU'RE LUCKY THERE AREN'T ANY COPS AROUND, TOO.
OH! I KNOW WHAT WE CAN PLAY!
GO ON...
NOM NOM
パクパク
THE YAMANOTE LINE GAME!

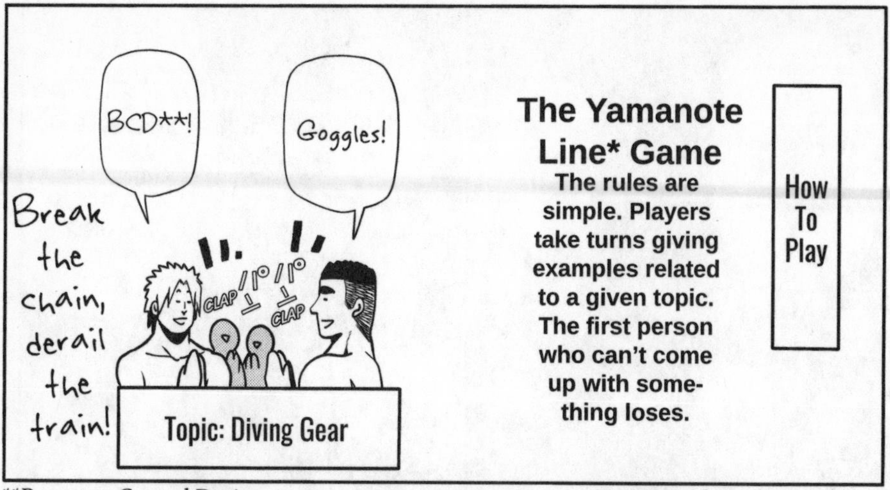
How To Play
The Yamanote Line* Game
The rules are simple. Players take turns giving examples related to a given topic. The first person who can't come up with something loses.
Goggles!
BCD**!
Break the chain, derail the train!
CLAP
CLAP
Topic: Diving Gear

*A major subway line in Tokyo.

**Buoyancy Control Device.

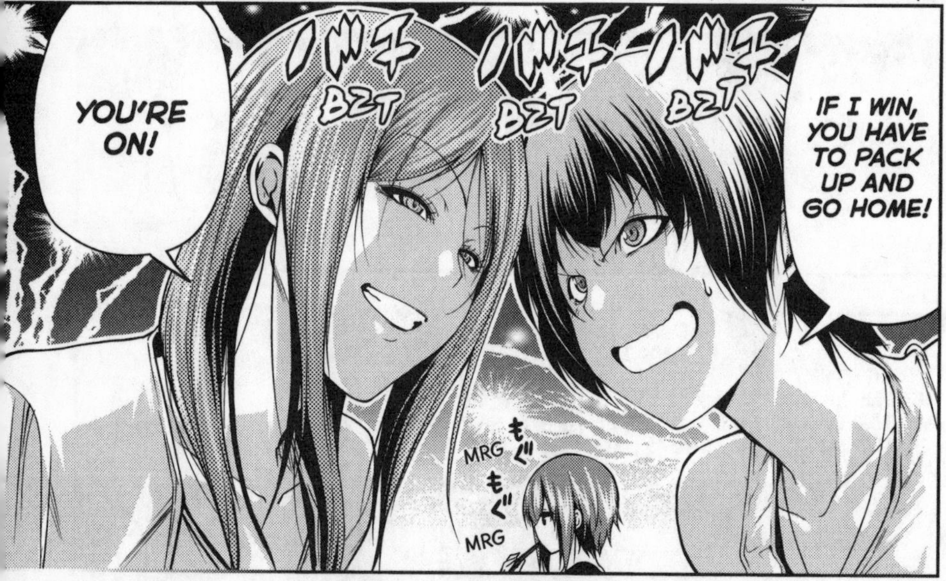
IF I WIN, YOU HAVE TO PACK UP AND GO HOME!
BZT
BZT
BZT
YOU'RE ON!
MRG
MRG

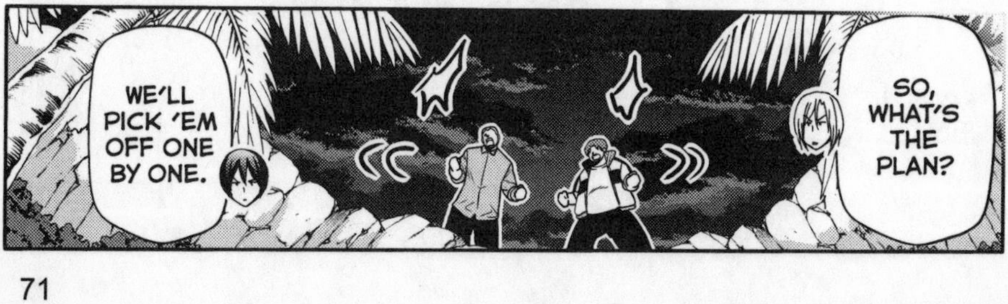
SO, WHAT'S THE PLAN?
WE'LL PICK 'EM OFF ONE BY ONE.

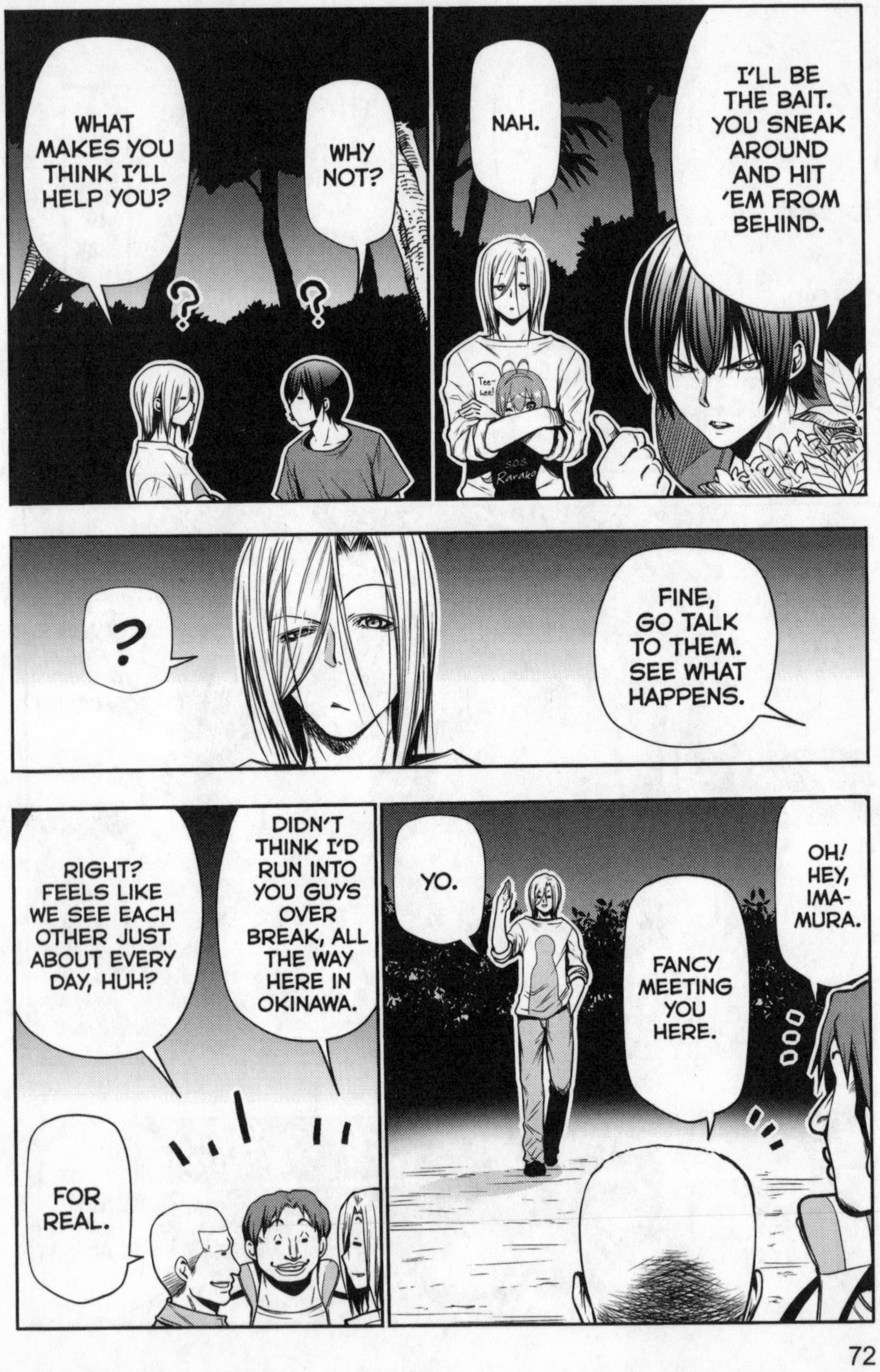
I'LL BE THE BAIT. YOU SNEAK AROUND AND HIT 'EM FROM BEHIND.
NAH.
Tee-hee!
S.O.S. Rarako
WHY NOT?
WHAT MAKES YOU THINK I'LL HELP YOU?
FINE, GO TALK TO THEM. SEE WHAT HAPPENS.
?
OH! HEY, IMA-MURA.
FANCY MEETING YOU HERE.
YO.
DIDN'T THINK I'D RUN INTO YOU GUYS OVER BREAK, ALL THE WAY HERE IN OKINAWA.
RIGHT? FEELS LIKE WE SEE EACH OTHER JUST ABOUT EVERY DAY, HUH?
FOR REAL.

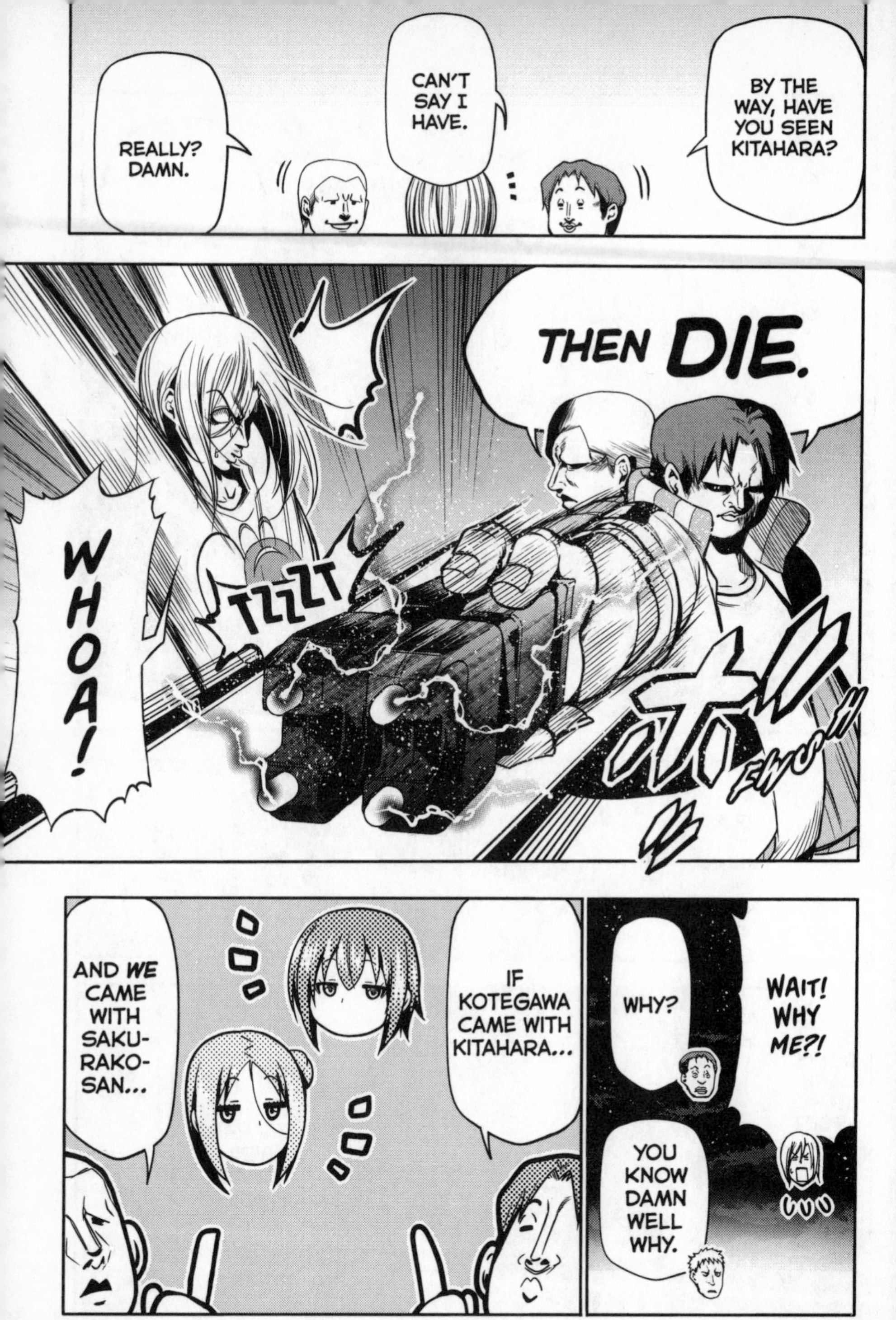
BY THE WAY, HAVE YOU SEEN KITAHARA?
CAN'T SAY I HAVE.
REALLY? DAMN.
THEN DIE.
TZZZT
WHOA!
WAIT! WHY ME?!
WHY?
YOU KNOW DAMN WELL WHY.
IF KOTEGAWA CAME WITH KITAHARA...
AND WE CAME WITH SAKU-RAKO-SAN...

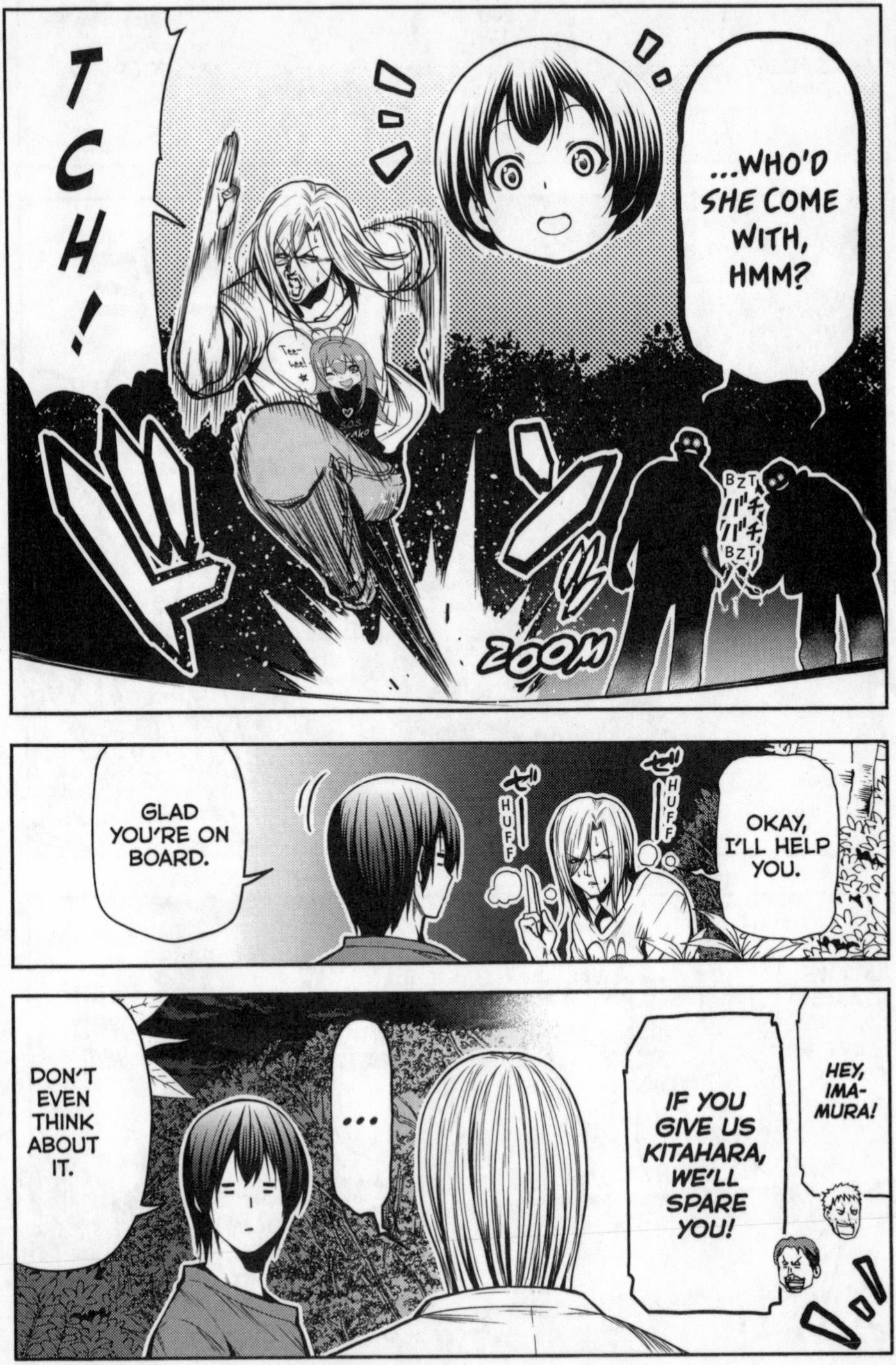
...WHO'D SHE COME WITH, HMM?
TCH!
BZT バチ バチ BZT
ZOOM
OKAY, I'LL HELP YOU.
ゼー HUFF
ゼー HUFF
GLAD YOU'RE ON BOARD.
HEY, IMA-MURA!
IF YOU GIVE US KITAHARA, WE'LL SPARE YOU!
...
DON'T EVEN THINK ABOUT IT.

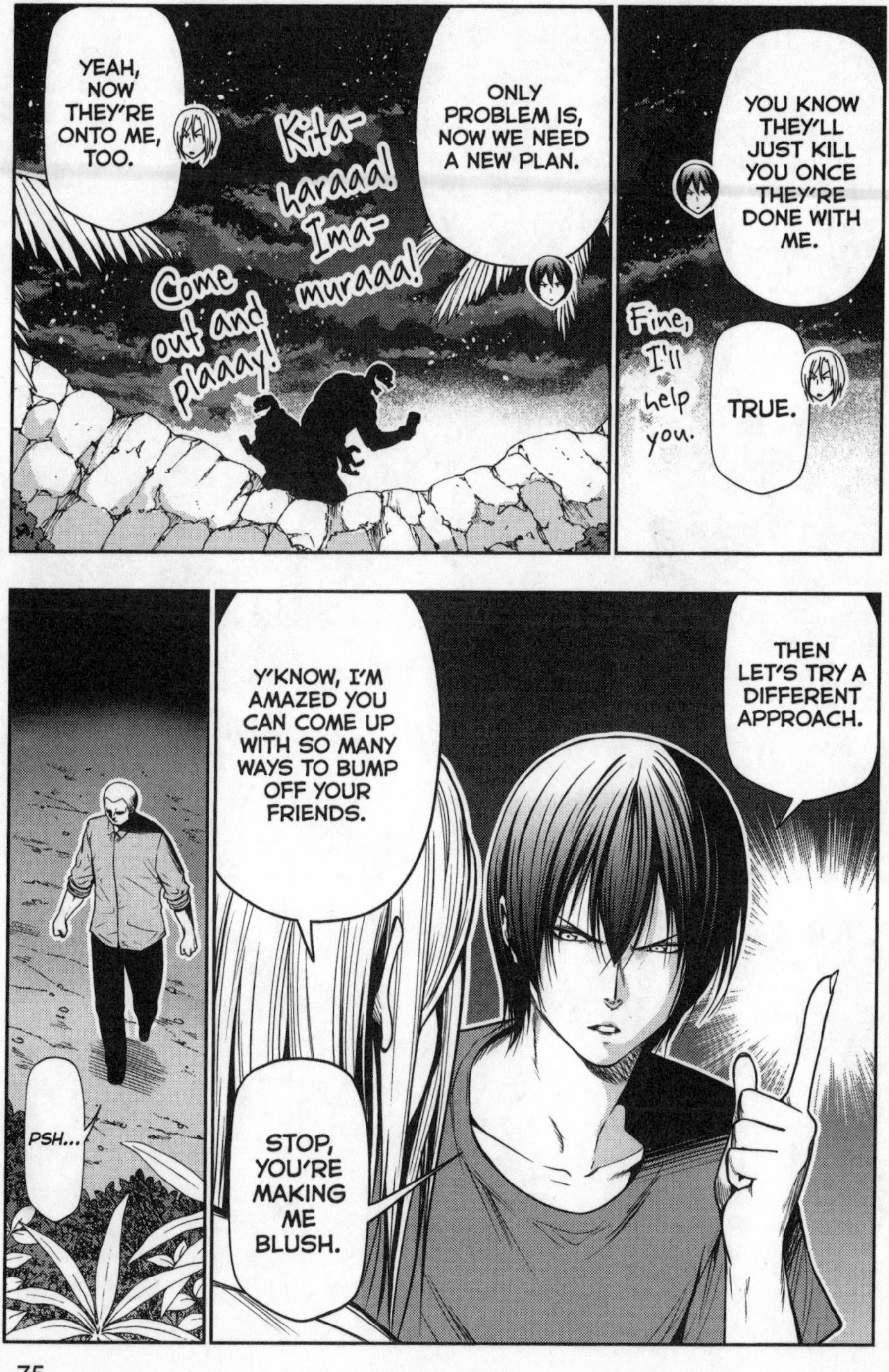
YOU KNOW THEY'LL JUST KILL YOU ONCE THEY'RE DONE WITH ME.
TRUE.
Fine, I'll help you.
ONLY PROBLEM IS, NOW WE NEED A NEW PLAN.
YEAH, NOW THEY'RE ONTO ME, TOO.
Kita-haraaa! Ima-muraaa!
Come out and plaaay!
THEN LET'S TRY A DIFFERENT APPROACH.
Y'KNOW, I'M AMAZED YOU CAN COME UP WITH SO MANY WAYS TO BUMP OFF YOUR FRIENDS.
STOP, YOU'RE MAKING ME BLUSH.
PSH...

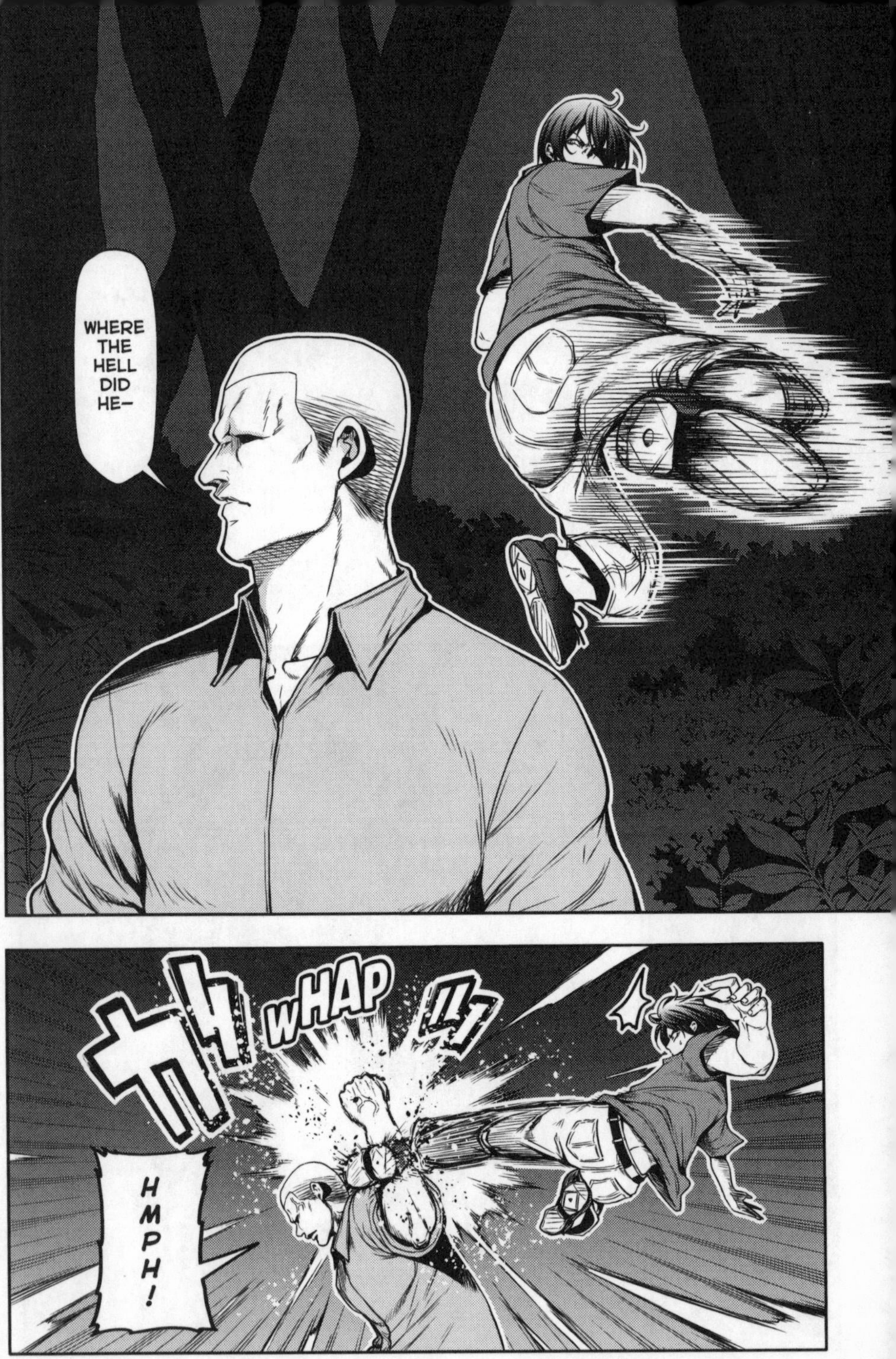
WHERE THE HELL DID HE–
WHAP
HMPH!

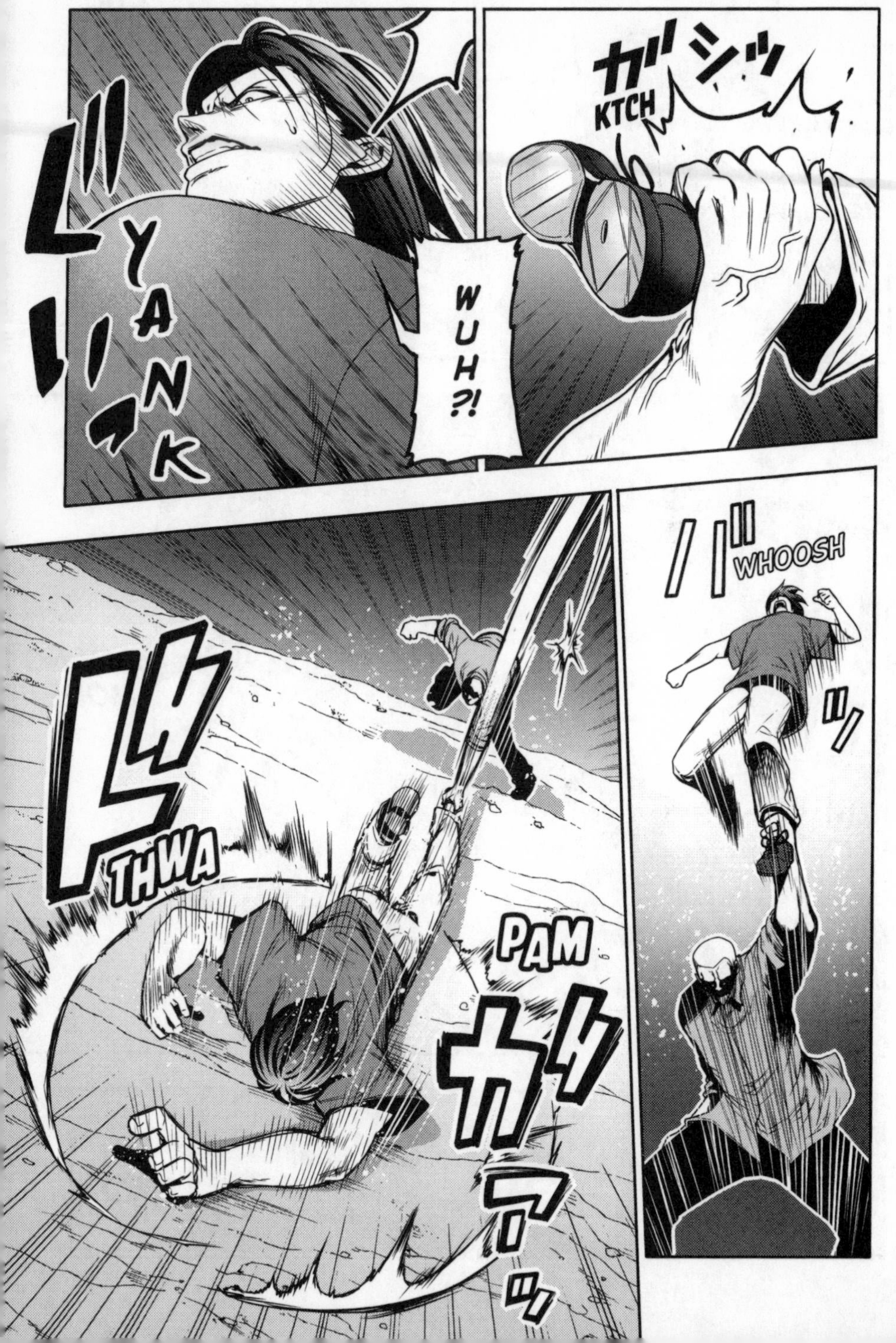
ガシッ
KTCH
YANK
WUH?!
WHOOSH
THWA
PAM

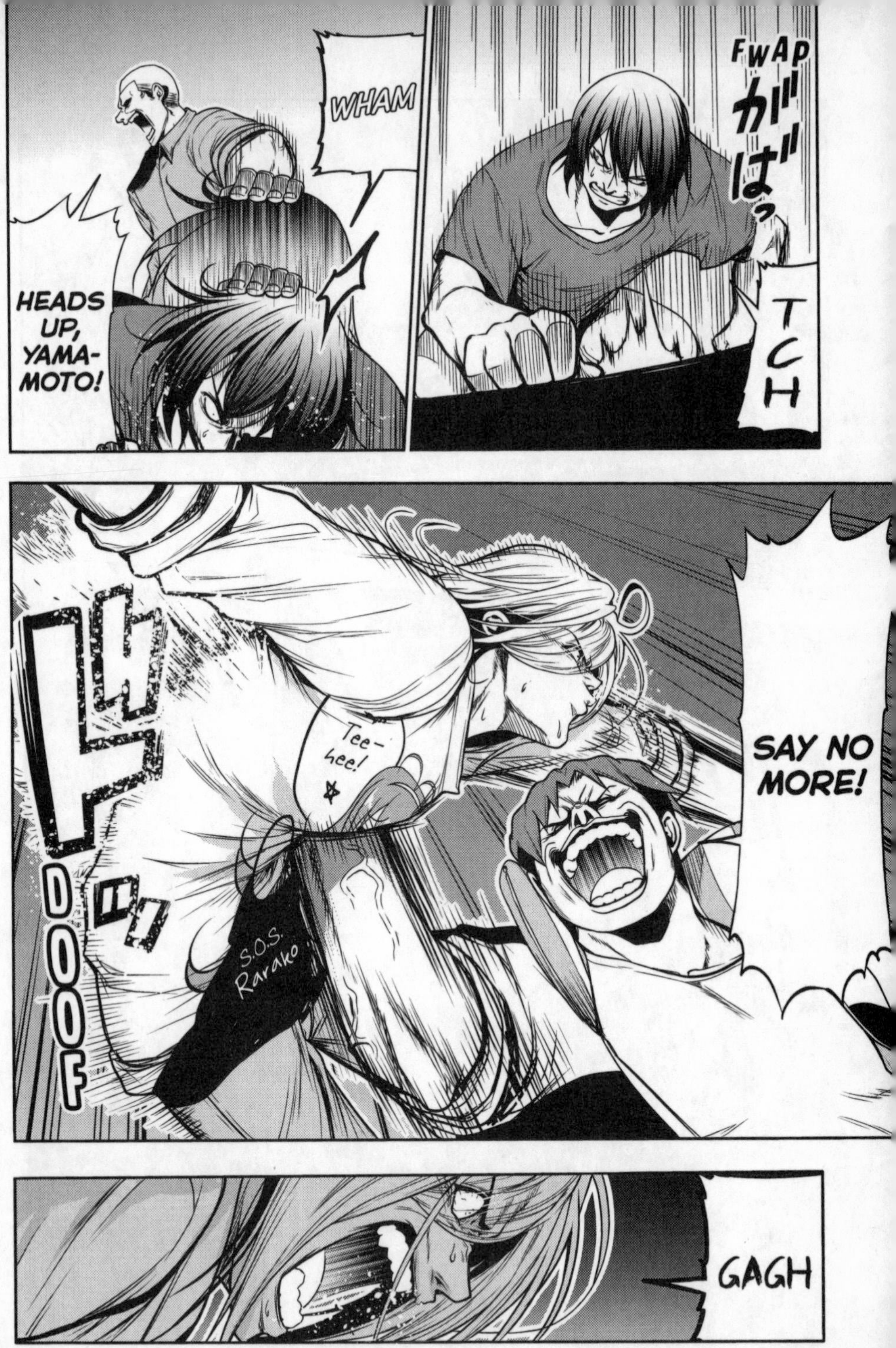
FWAP
がばっ
TCH
WHAM
HEADS UP, YAMA-MOTO!
SAY NO MORE!
Tee-hee!
S.O.S. Rarako
DOOF
GAGH

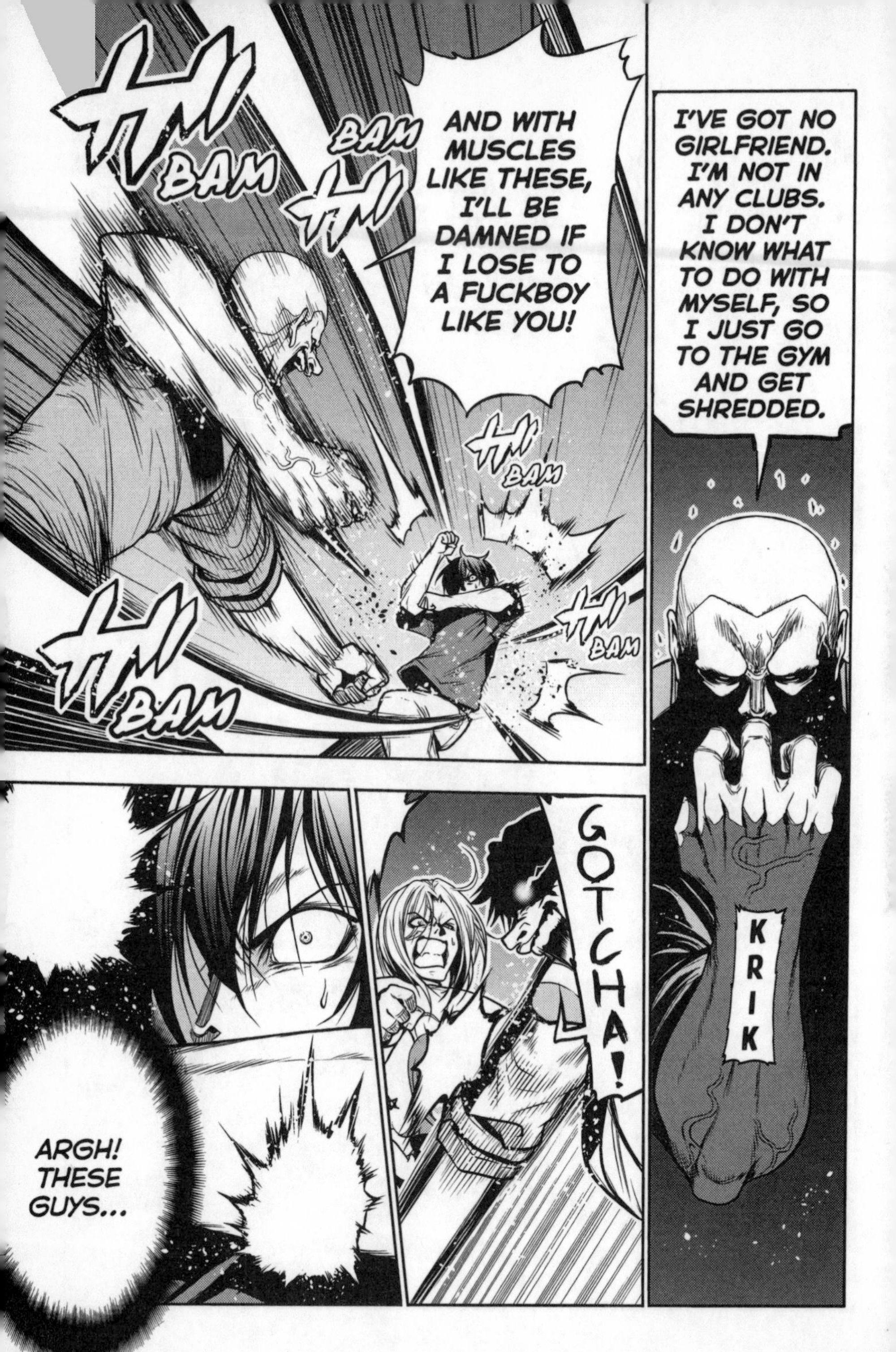
I'VE GOT NO GIRLFRIEND. I'M NOT IN ANY CLUBS. I DON'T KNOW WHAT TO DO WITH MYSELF, SO I JUST GO TO THE GYM AND GET SHREDDED.
KRIK
AND WITH MUSCLES LIKE THESE, I'LL BE DAMNED IF I LOSE TO A FUCKBOY LIKE YOU!
BAM
BAM
BAM
BAM
BAM
BAM
GOTCHA!
ARGH! THESE GUYS...

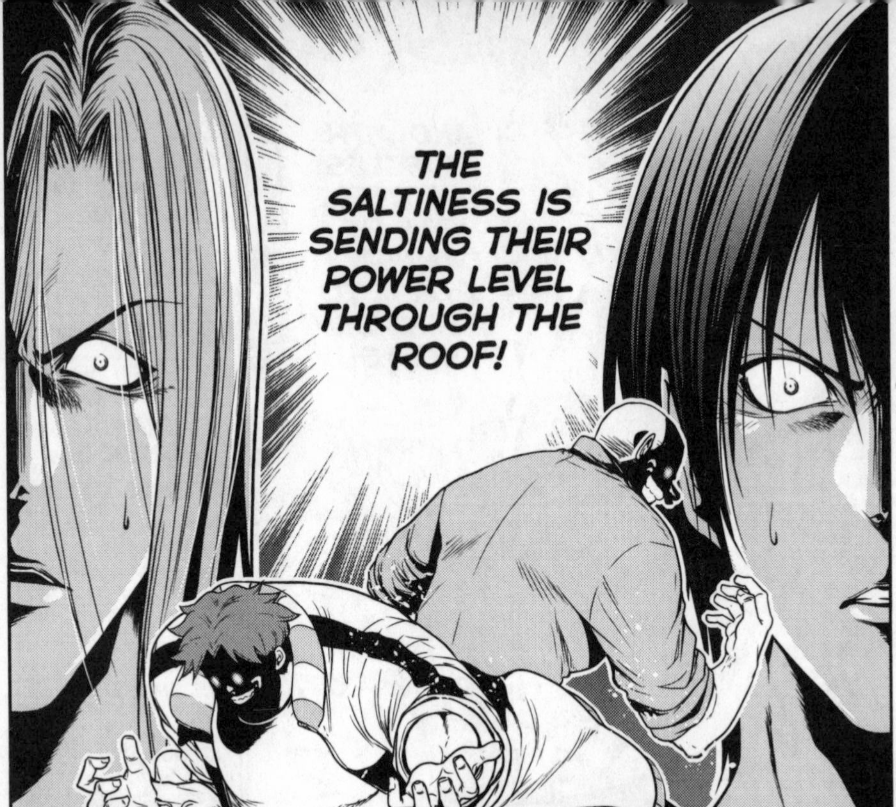
THE SALTINESS IS SENDING THEIR POWER LEVEL THROUGH THE ROOF!

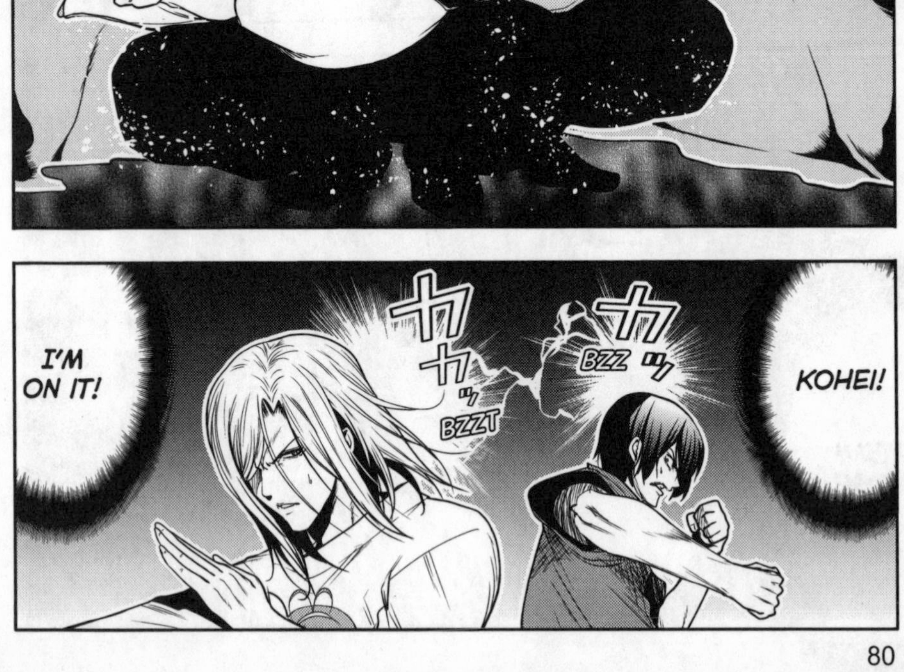
KOHEI!
BZZ
BZZT
I'M ON IT!

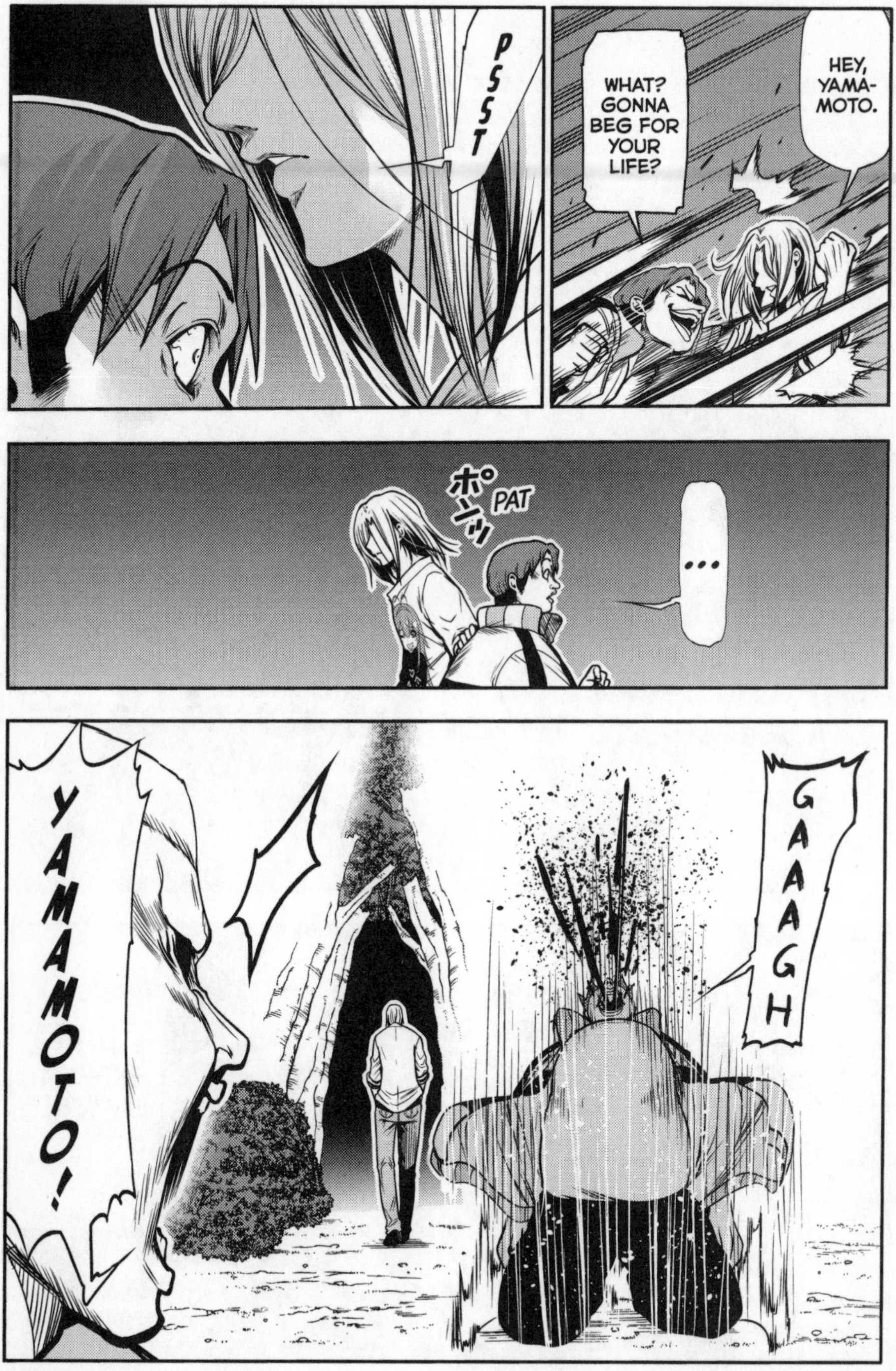
HEY, YAMA-
MOTO.
WHAT? GONNA BEG FOR YOUR LIFE?
PSSST
...
ポンッ PAT
GAAAGH
YAMAMOTO!

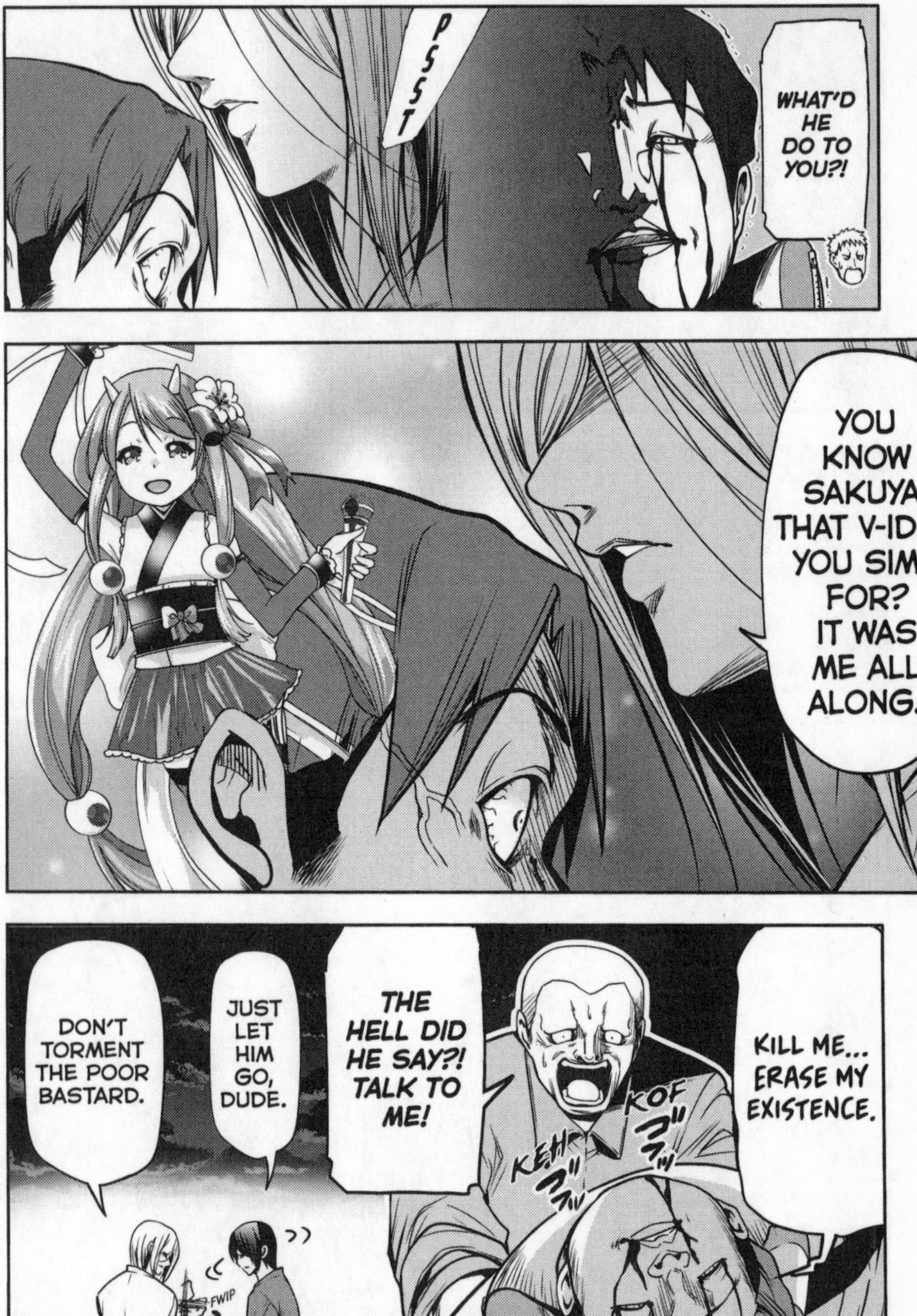
WHAT'D HE DO TO YOU?!
PSST
YOU KNOW SAKUYA, THAT V-IDOL YOU SIMP FOR? IT WAS ME ALL ALONG.
KILL ME... ERASE MY EXISTENCE.
KOF
KEH
THE HELL DID HE SAY?! TALK TO ME!
JUST LET HIM GO, DUDE.
DON'T TORMENT THE POOR BASTARD.
FWIP
FWIP

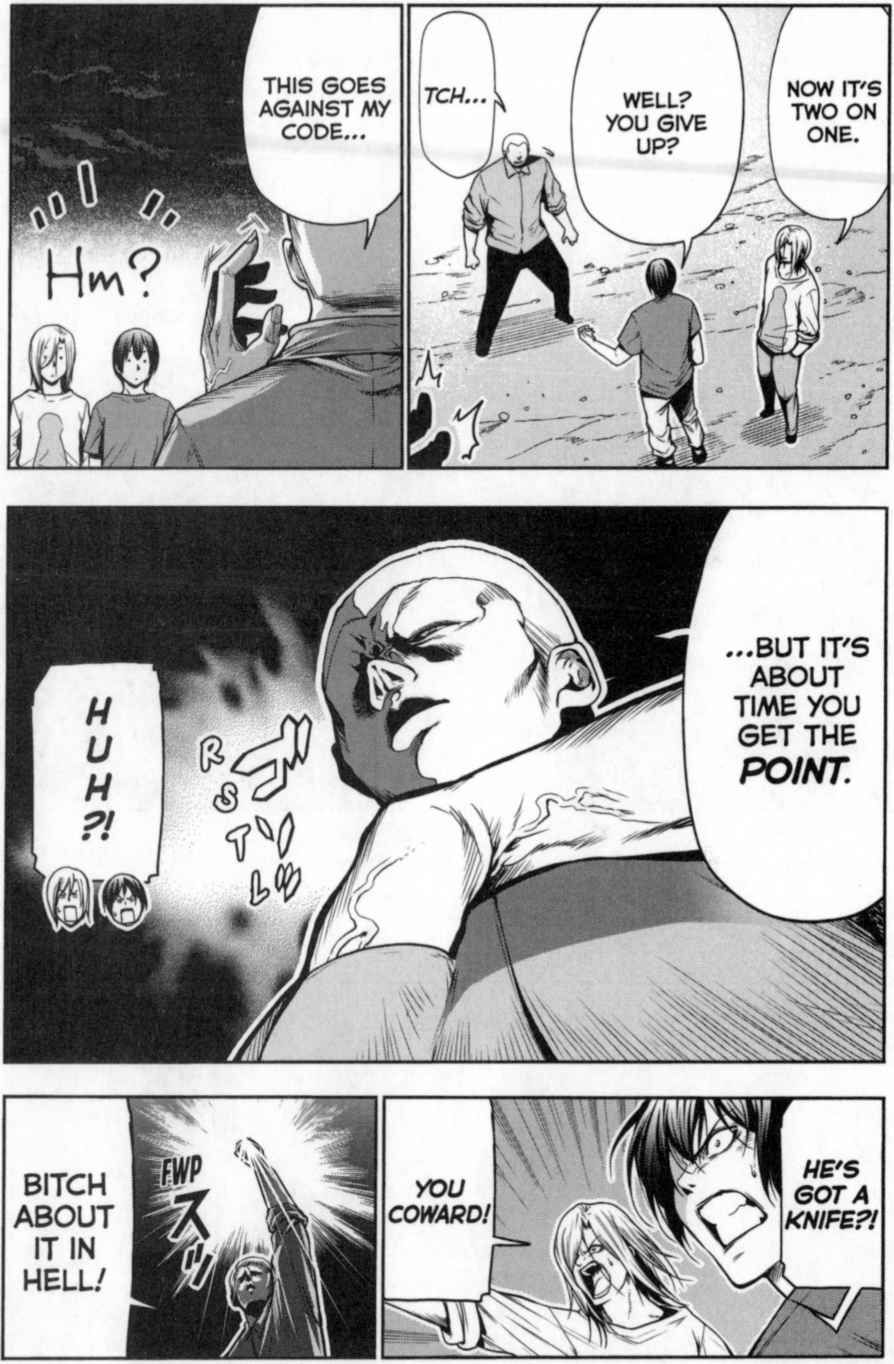
NOW IT'S TWO ON ONE.
WELL? YOU GIVE UP?
TCH...
THIS GOES AGAINST MY CODE...
Hm?
...BUT IT'S ABOUT TIME YOU GET THE POINT.
RSTL
HUH?!
HE'S GOT A KNIFE?!
YOU COWARD!
FWP
BITCH ABOUT IT IN HELL!

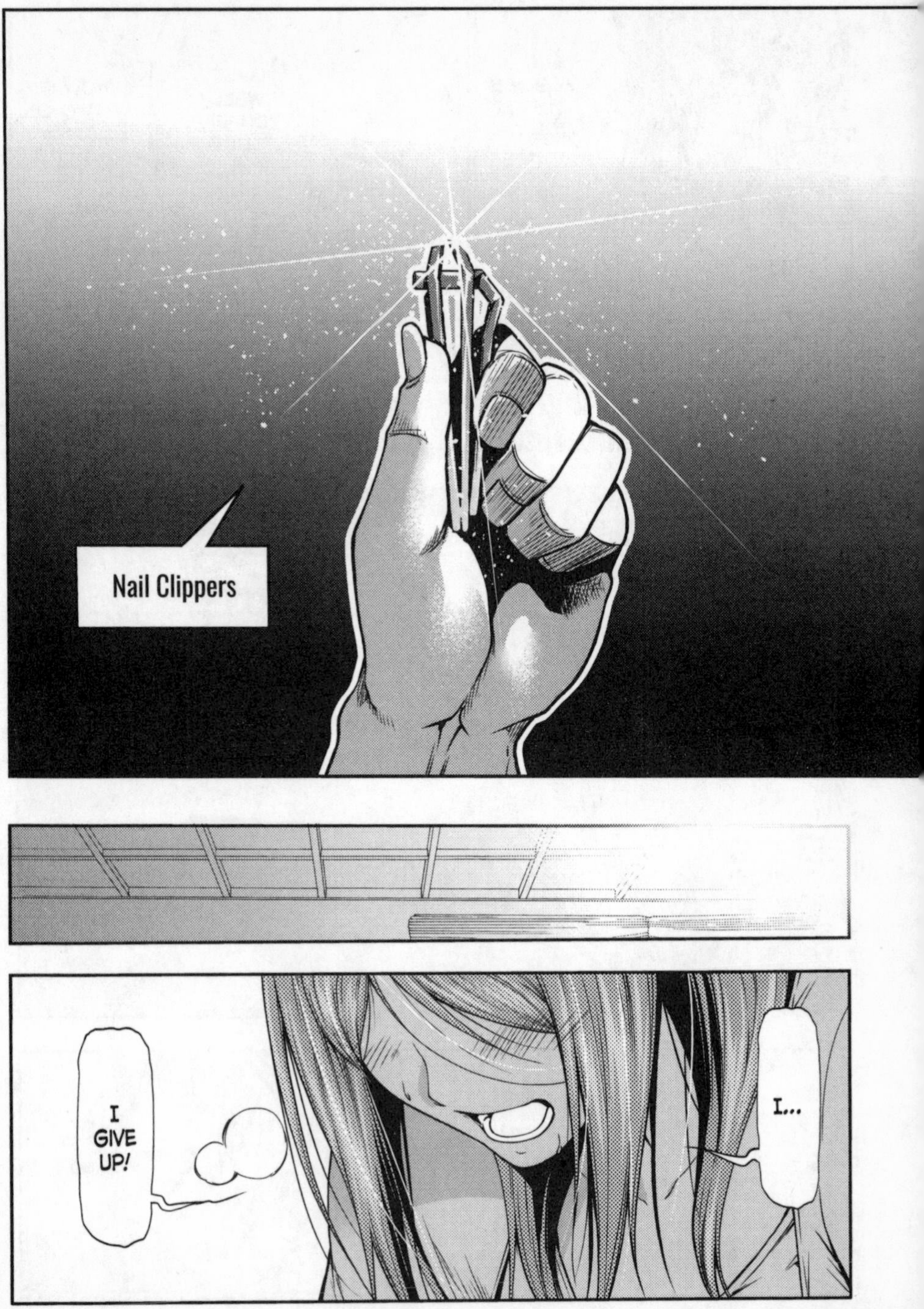
Nail Clippers
I...
I GIVE UP!

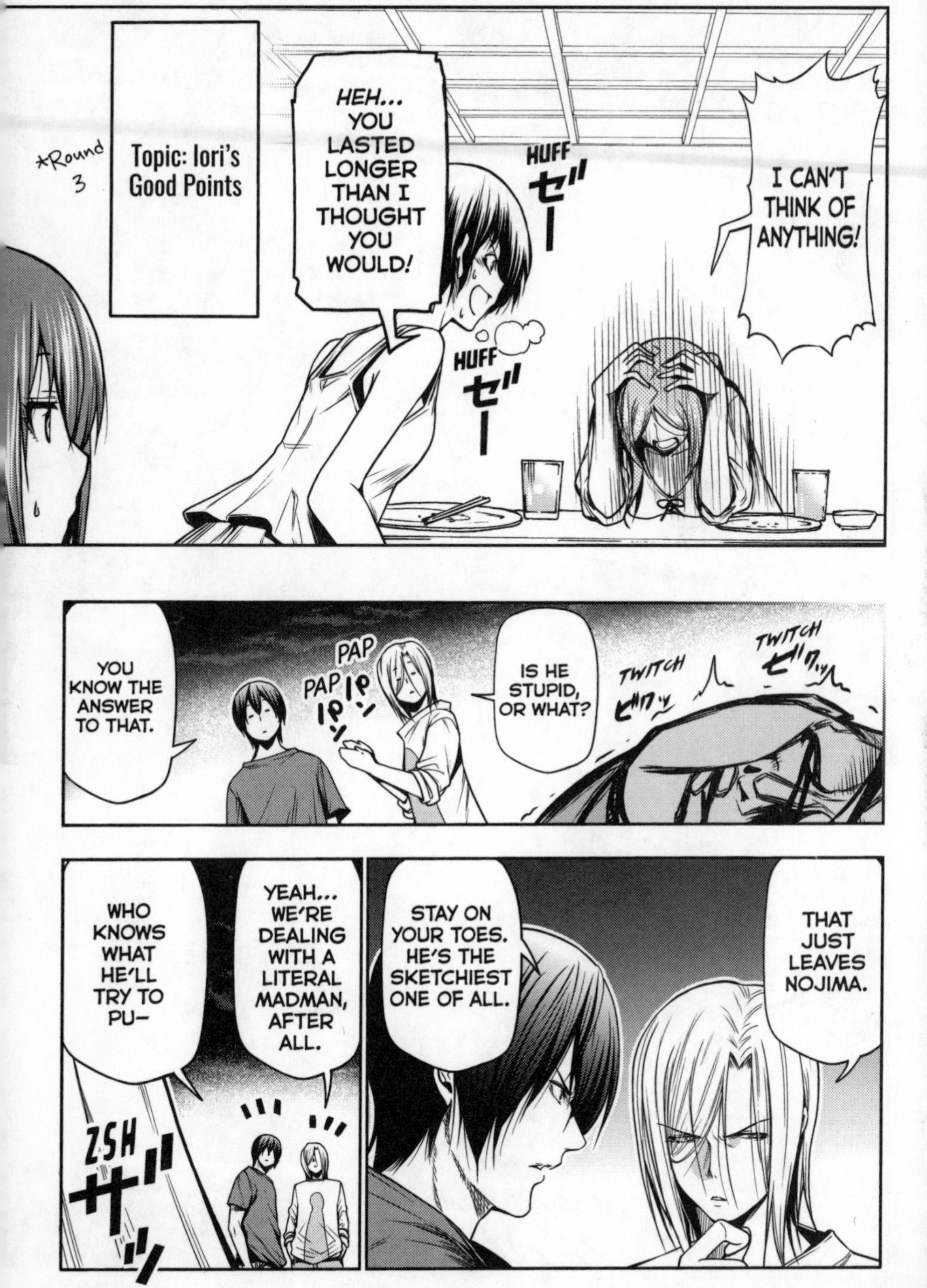
I CAN'T THINK OF ANYTHING!
HUFF
ゼー
HEH... YOU LASTED LONGER THAN I THOUGHT YOU WOULD!
HUFF
ゼー
Topic: Iori's Good Points
*Round 3
TWITCH
TWITCH
IS HE STUPID, OR WHAT?
PAP
PAP
YOU KNOW THE ANSWER TO THAT.
THAT JUST LEAVES NOJIMA.
STAY ON YOUR TOES. HE'S THE SKETCHIEST ONE OF ALL.
YEAH... WE'RE DEALING WITH A LITERAL MADMAN, AFTER ALL.
WHO KNOWS WHAT HE'LL TRY TO PU—
ZSH

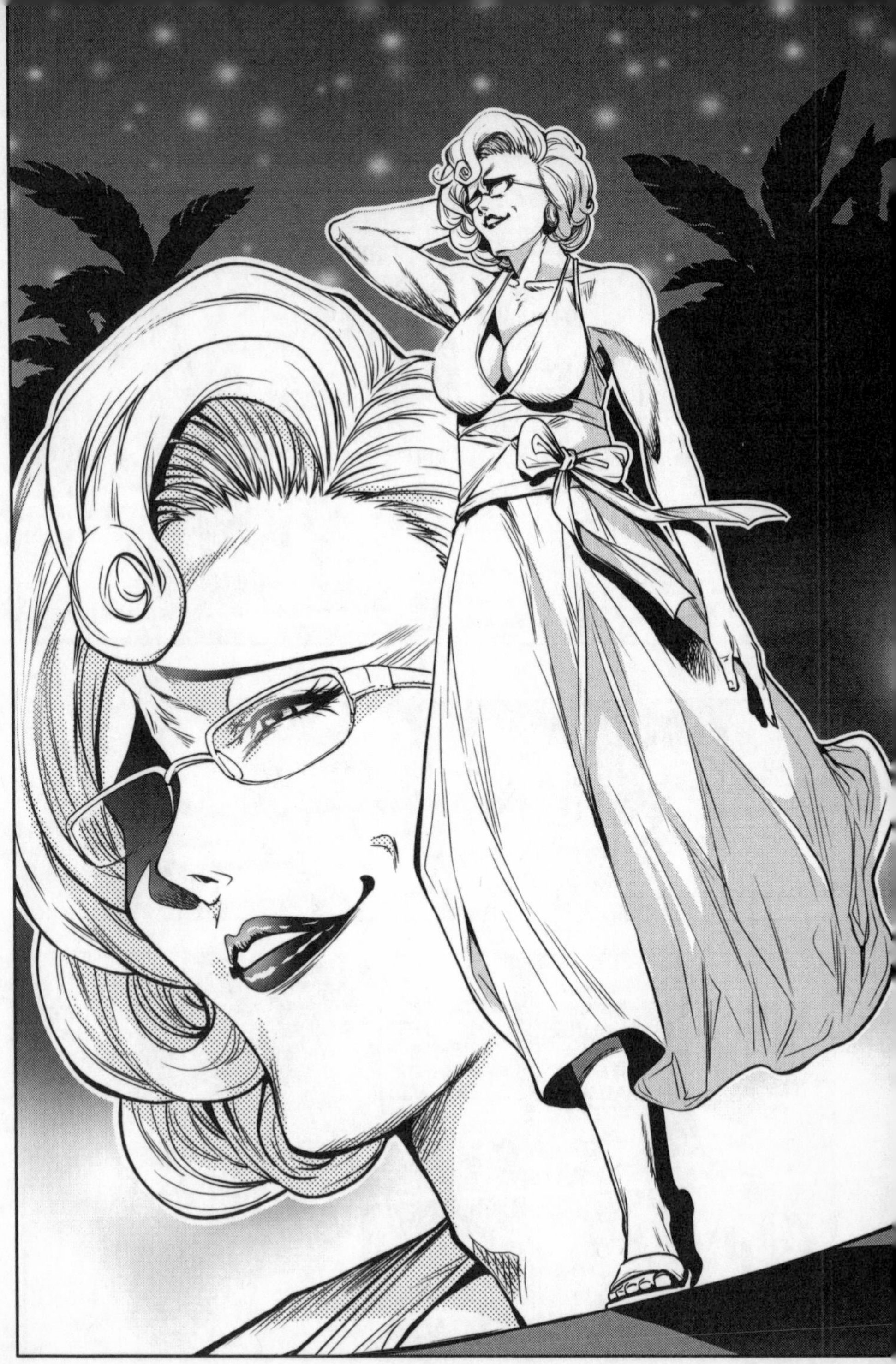

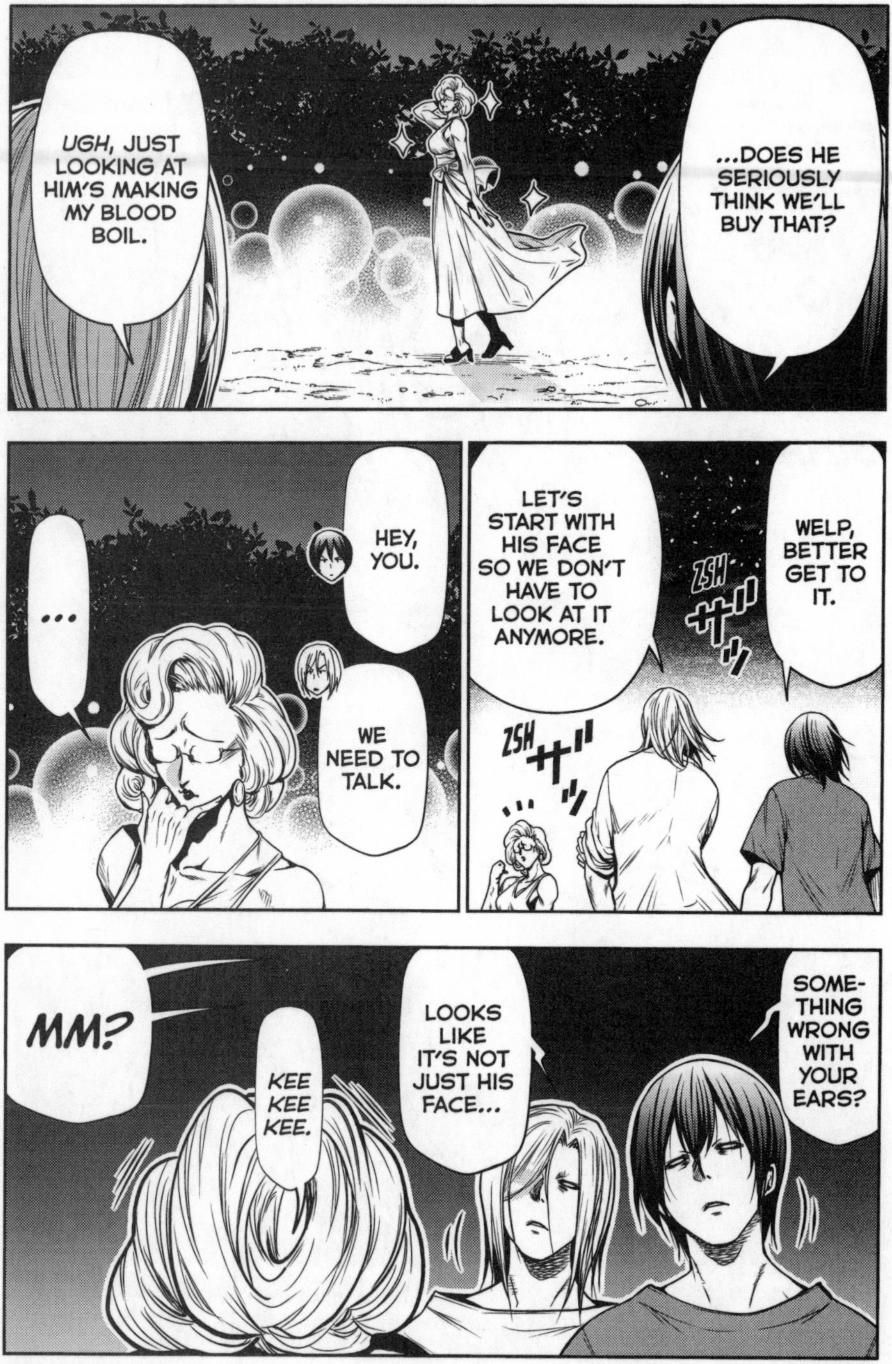

...DOES HE SERIOUSLY THINK WE'LL BUY THAT?
UGH, JUST LOOKING AT HIM'S MAKING MY BLOOD BOIL.
WELP, BETTER GET TO IT.
ZSH サッ
LET'S START WITH HIS FACE SO WE DON'T HAVE TO LOOK AT IT ANYMORE.
ZSH ザッ
...
HEY, YOU.
WE NEED TO TALK.
...
SOME-THING WRONG WITH YOUR EARS?
LOOKS LIKE IT'S NOT JUST HIS FACE...
KEE KEE KEE.
MM?

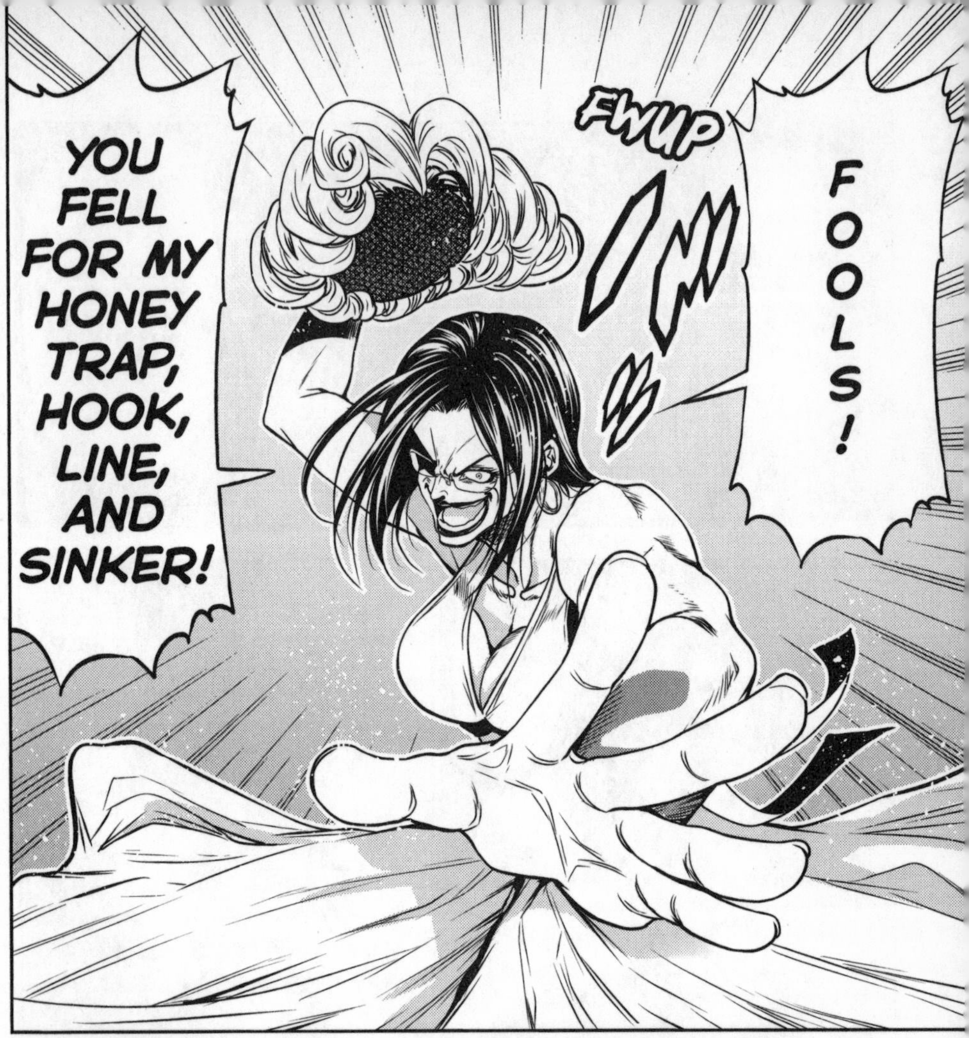
FOOLS!
FWUP
YOU FELL FOR MY HONEY TRAP, HOOK, LINE, AND SINKER!

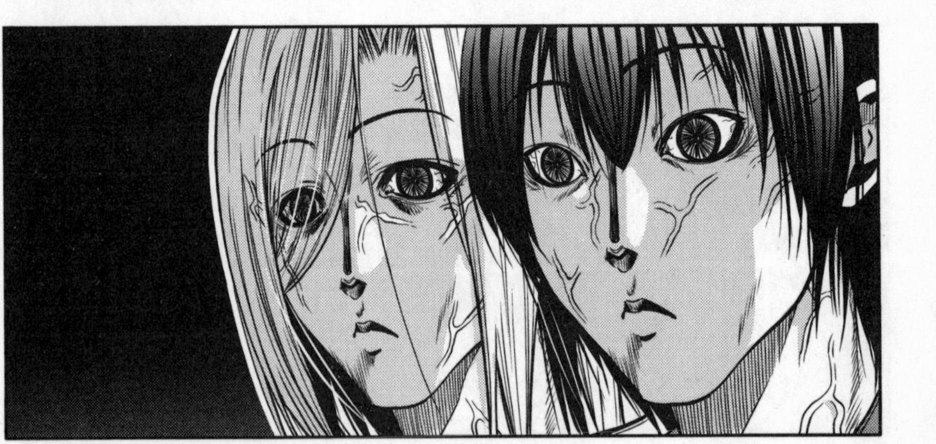

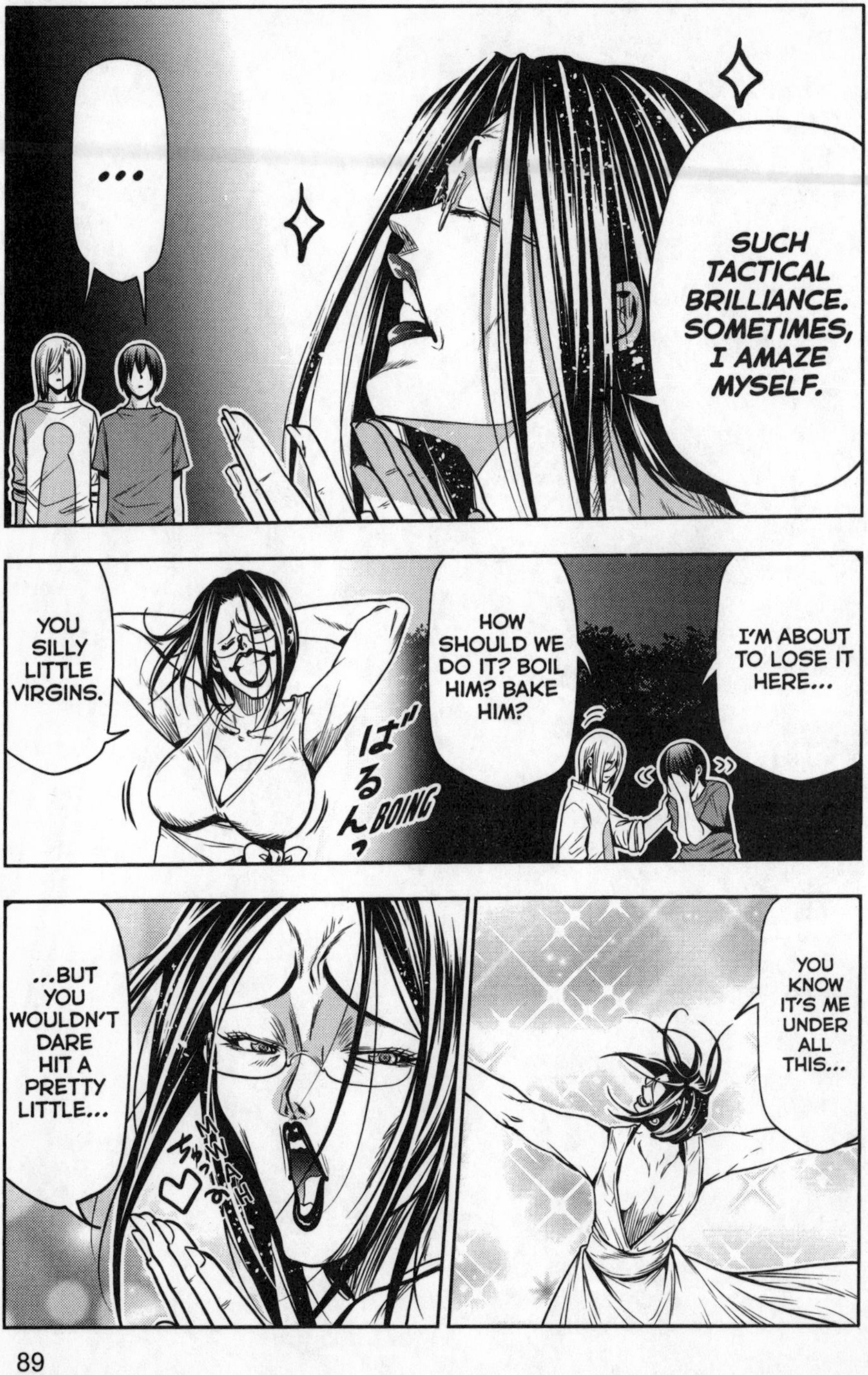
SUCH TACTICAL BRILLIANCE. SOMETIMES, I AMAZE MYSELF.
...
I'M ABOUT TO LOSE IT HERE...
HOW SHOULD WE DO IT? BOIL HIM? BAKE HIM?
ばるんっ
BOING
YOU SILLY LITTLE VIRGINS.
YOU KNOW IT'S ME UNDER ALL THIS...
...BUT YOU WOULDN'T DARE HIT A PRETTY LITTLE...
ちゅっ
MWAH

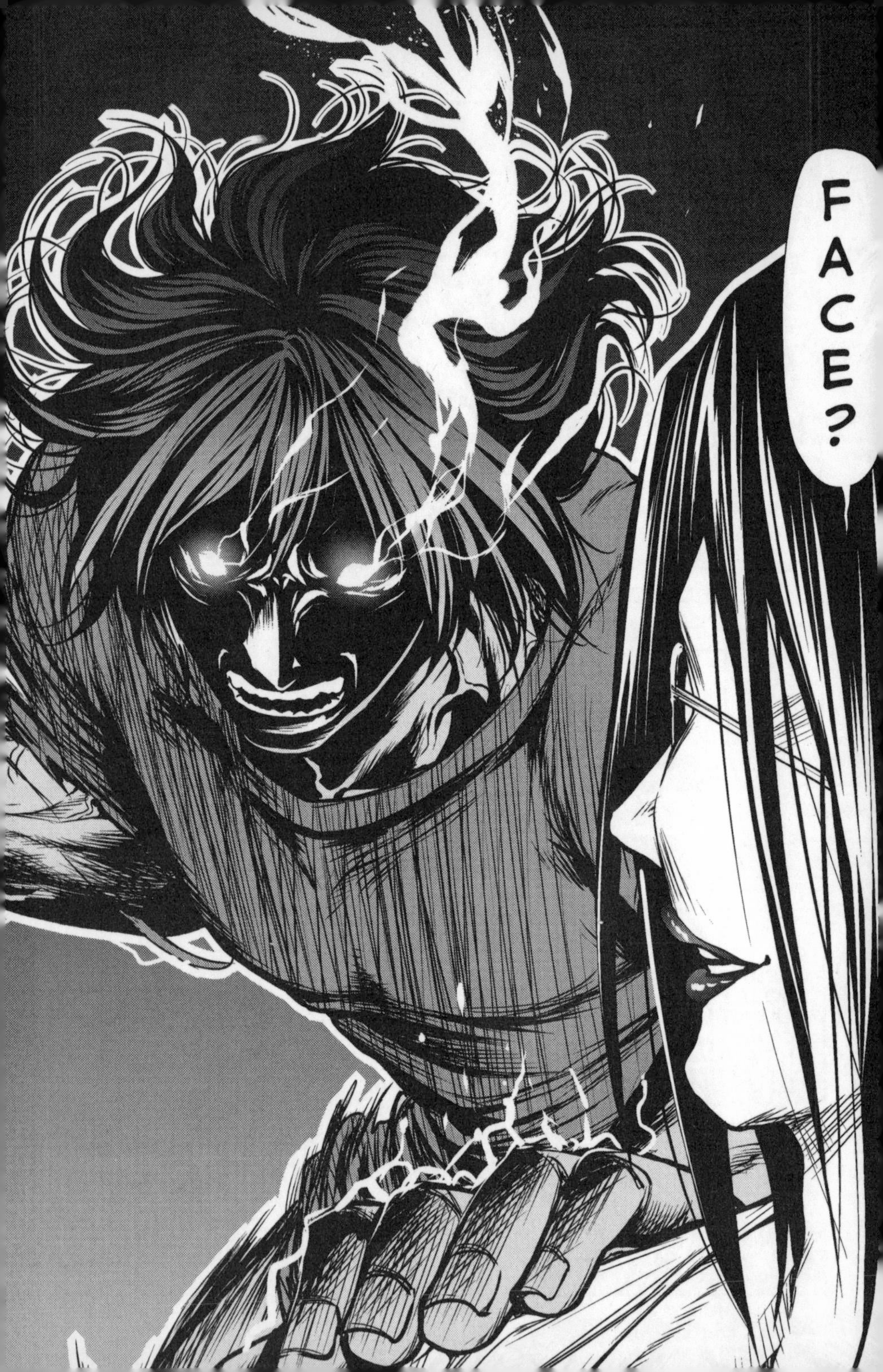
FACE?

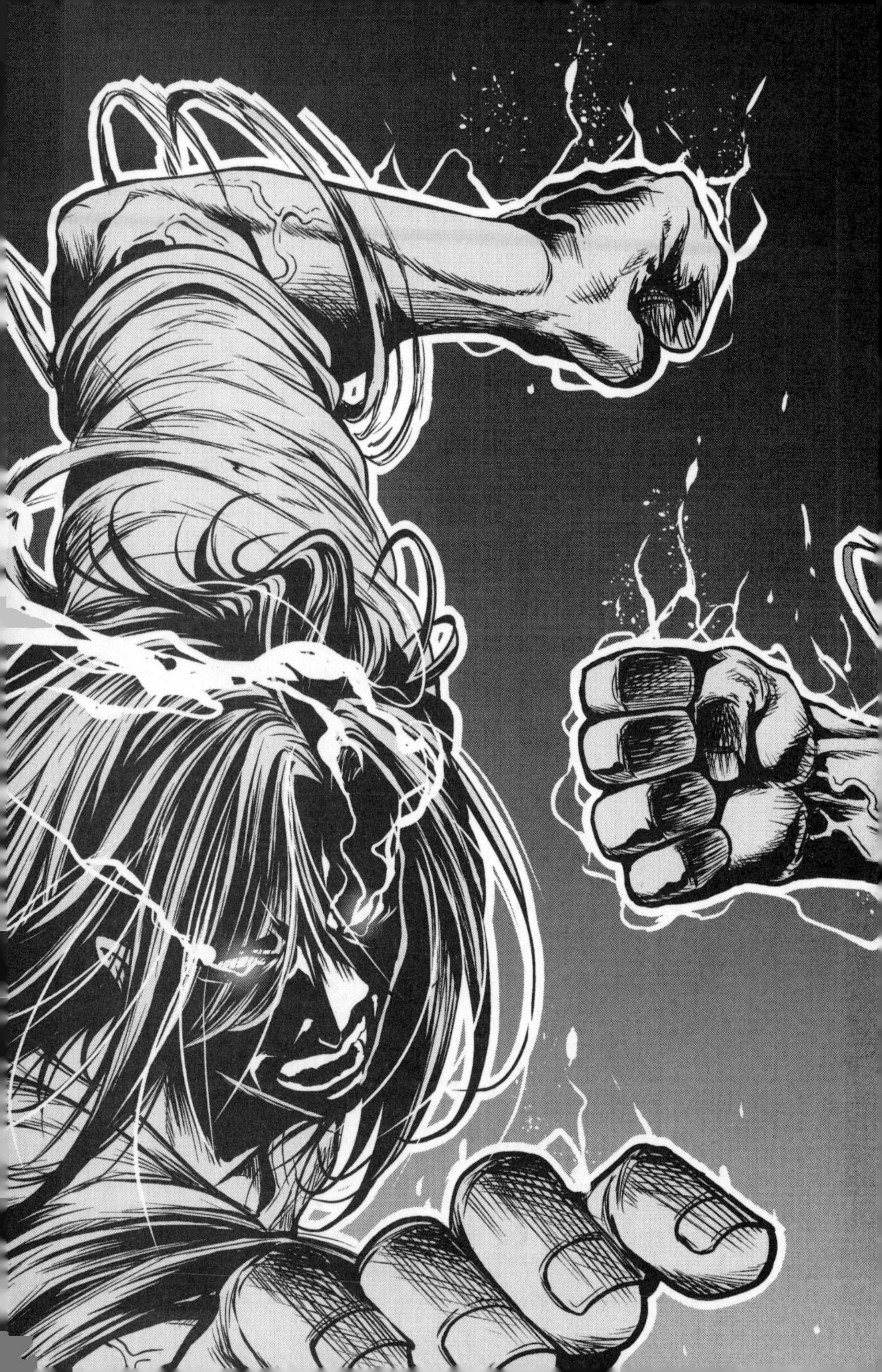

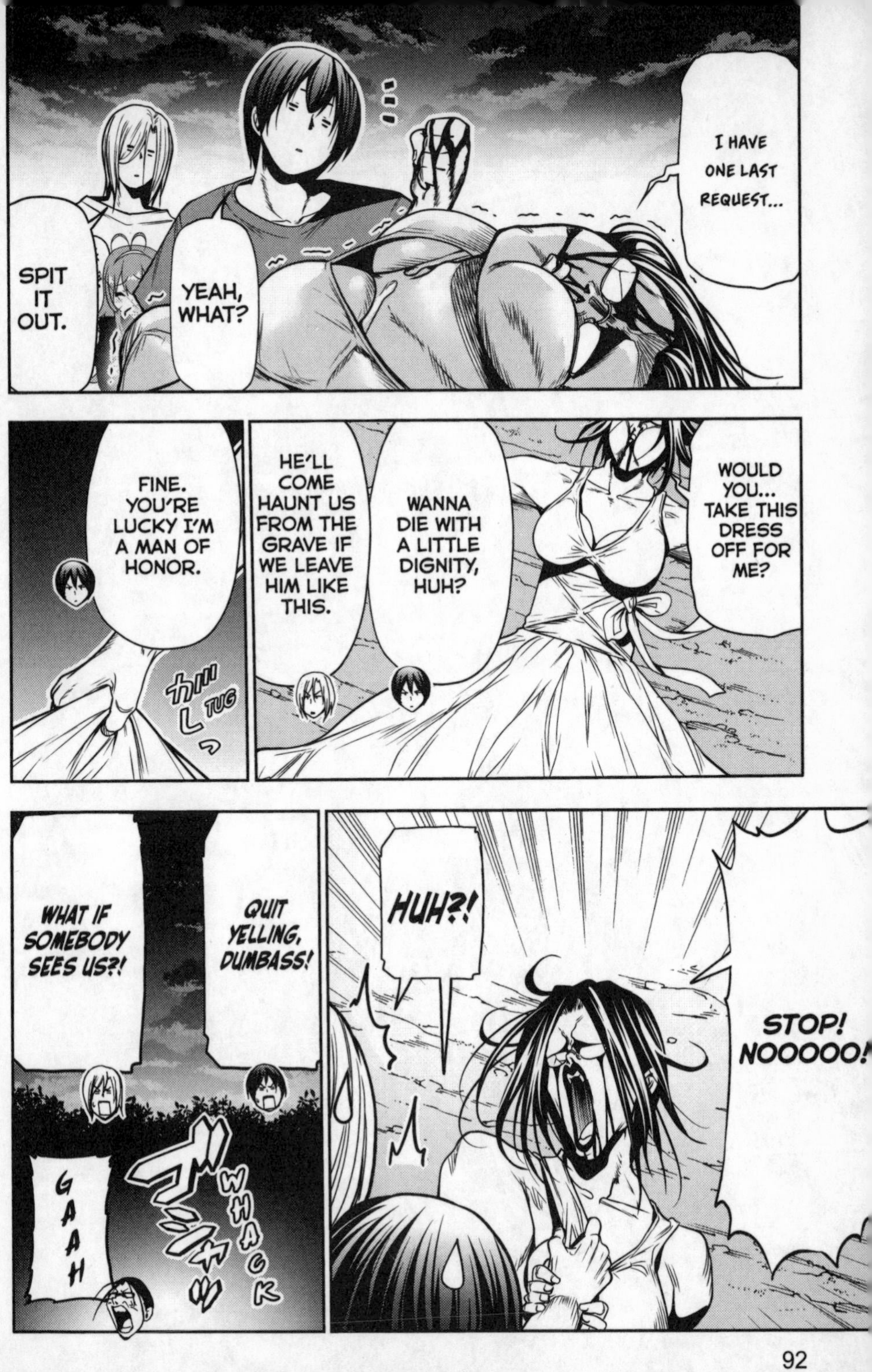
I HAVE ONE LAST REQUEST...
YEAH, WHAT?
SPIT IT OUT.
WOULD YOU... TAKE THIS DRESS OFF FOR ME?
WANNA DIE WITH A LITTLE DIGNITY, HUH?
HE'LL COME HAUNT US FROM THE GRAVE IF WE LEAVE HIM LIKE THIS.
FINE. YOU'RE LUCKY I'M A MAN OF HONOR.
TUG
STOP! NOOOOO!
HUH?!
QUIT YELLING, DUMBASS!
WHAT IF SOMEBODY SEES US?!
WHACK
GAAH

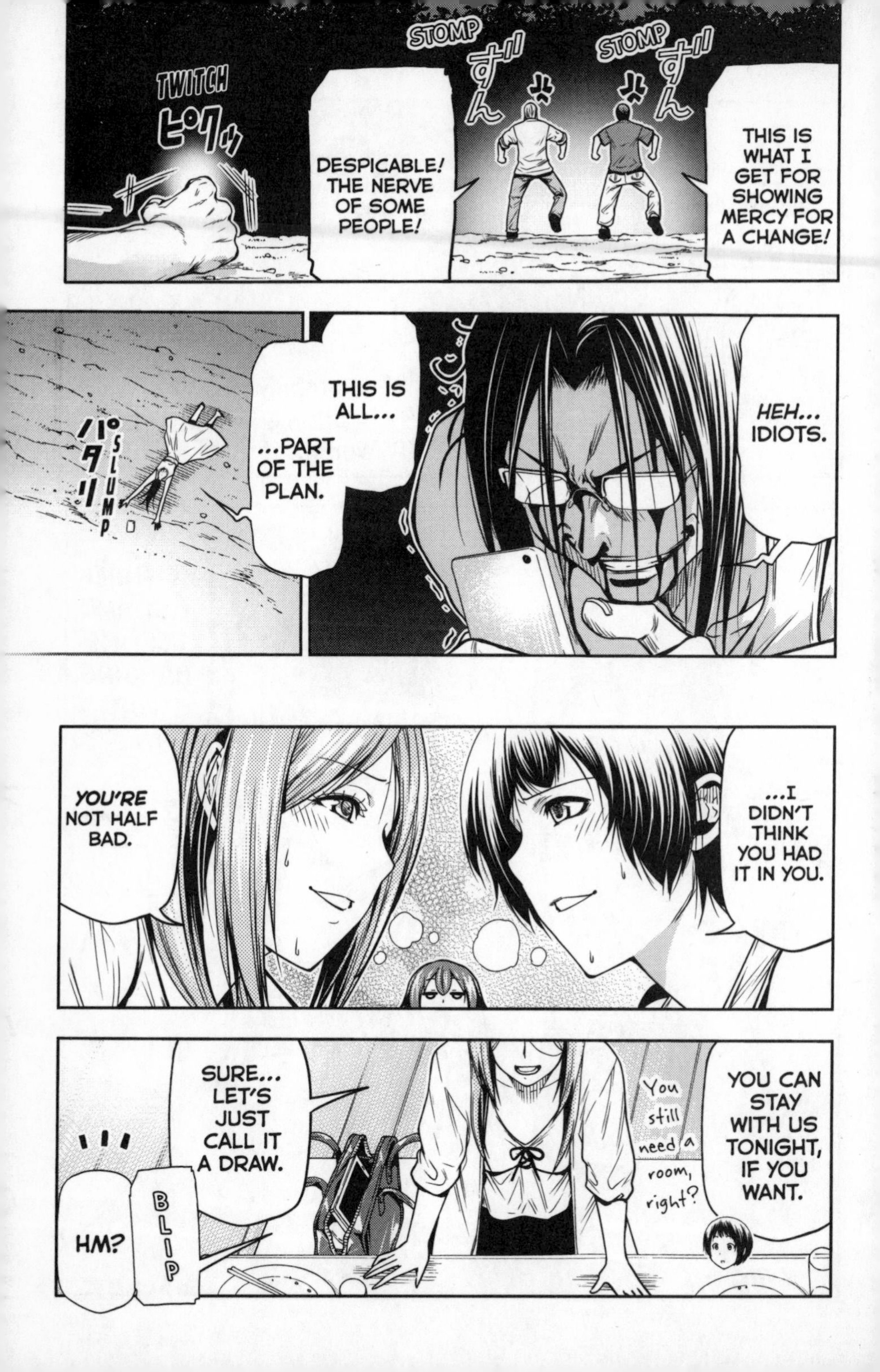
THIS IS WHAT I GET FOR SHOWING MERCY FOR A CHANGE!
STOMP
ずんッ
STOMP
ずんッ
DESPICABLE! THE NERVE OF SOME PEOPLE!
TWITCH
ピクッ
HEH... IDIOTS.
THIS IS ALL...
...PART OF THE PLAN.
SLUMP
パタリ
...I DIDN'T THINK YOU HAD IT IN YOU.
YOU'RE NOT HALF BAD.
YOU CAN STAY WITH US TONIGHT, IF YOU WANT.
You still need a room, right?
SURE... LET'S JUST CALL IT A DRAW.
BLIP
HM?
...

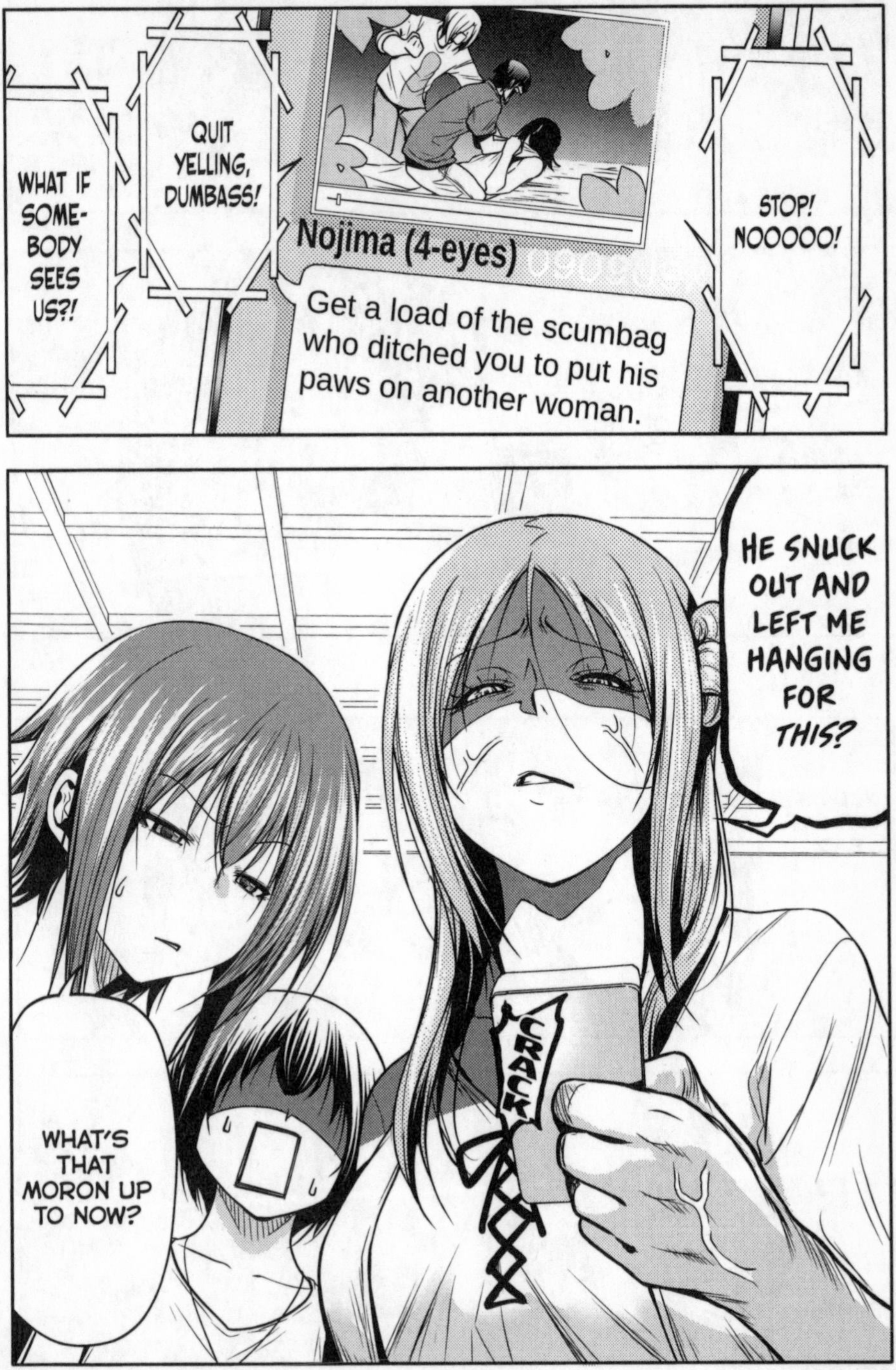
STOP! NOOOOO!
Nojima (4-eyes)
Get a load of the scumbag who ditched you to put his paws on another woman.
QUIT YELLING, DUMBASS!
WHAT IF SOME-BODY SEES US?!
HE SNUCK OUT AND LEFT ME HANGING FOR *THIS?*
CRACK
WHAT'S THAT MORON UP TO NOW?

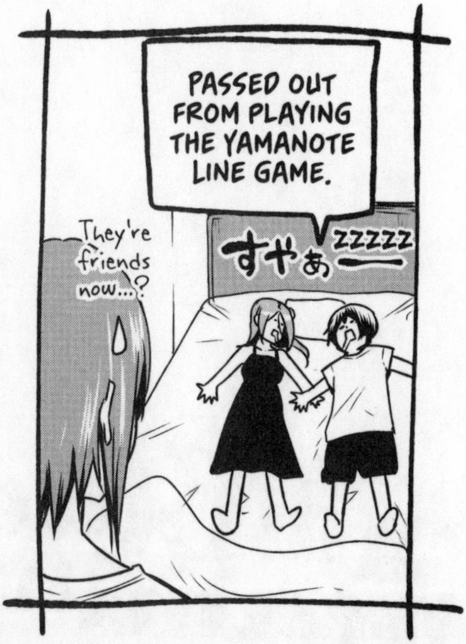
PASSED OUT FROM PLAYING THE YAMANOTE LINE GAME.
すやぁーー ZZZZZ
They're friends now...?

Grand Blue Dreaming

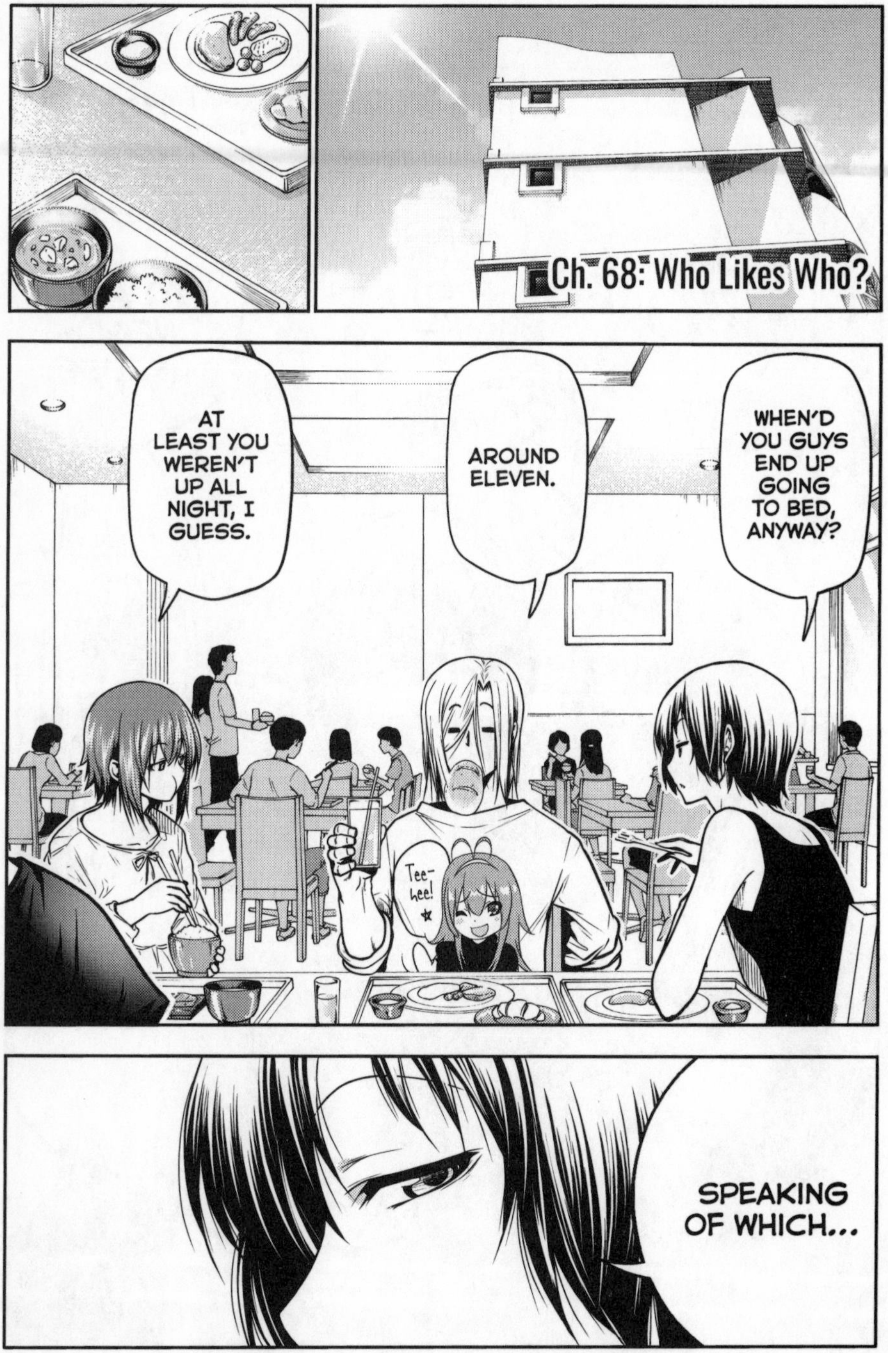
Ch. 68: Who Likes Who?
WHEN'D YOU GUYS END UP GOING TO BED, ANYWAY?
AROUND ELEVEN.
AT LEAST YOU WEREN'T UP ALL NIGHT, I GUESS.
Tee-hee! ☆
SPEAKING OF WHICH...

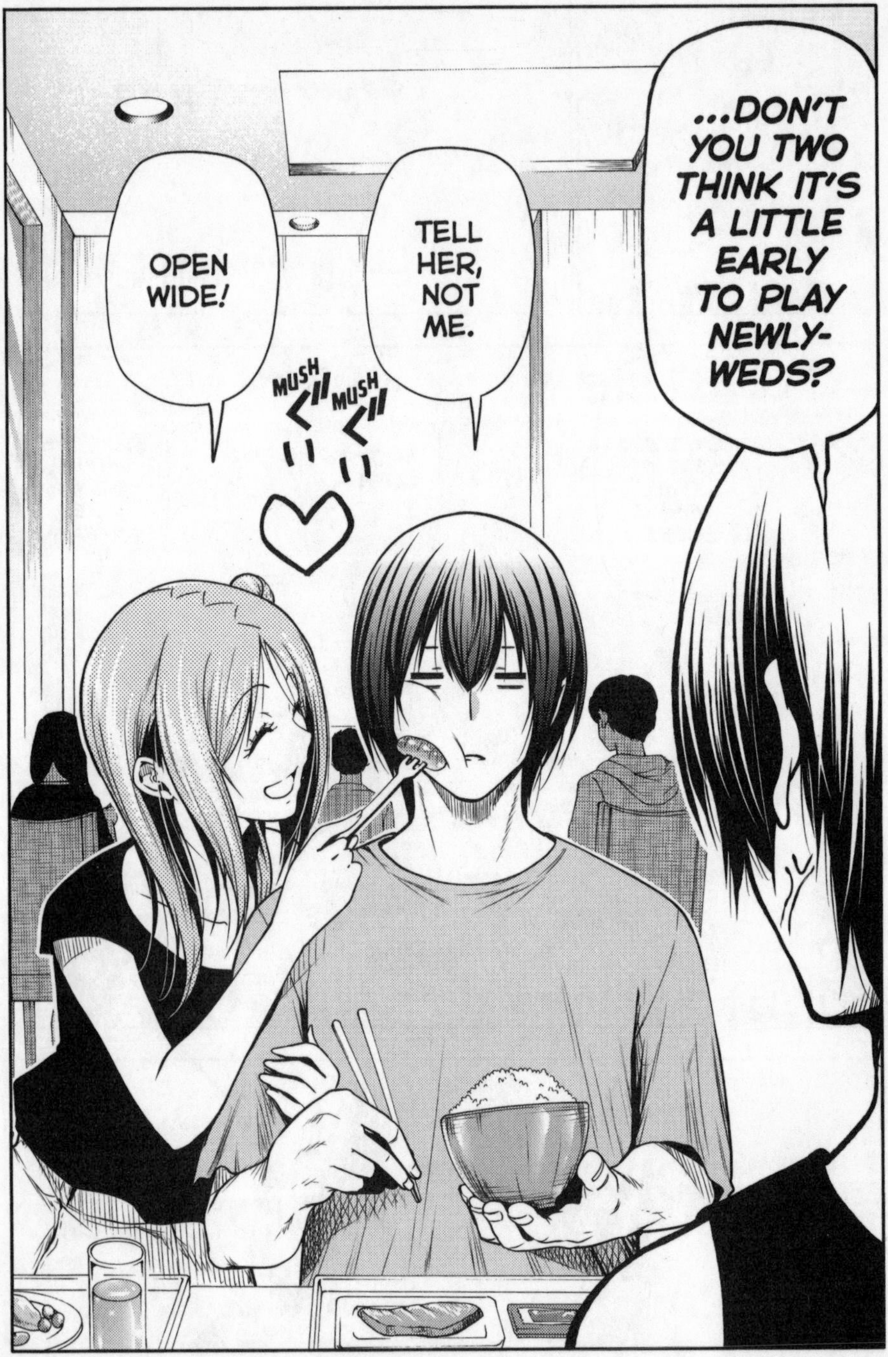
...DON'T YOU TWO THINK IT'S A LITTLE EARLY TO PLAY NEWLY-WEDS?
TELL HER, NOT ME.
MUSH MUSH
OPEN WIDE!

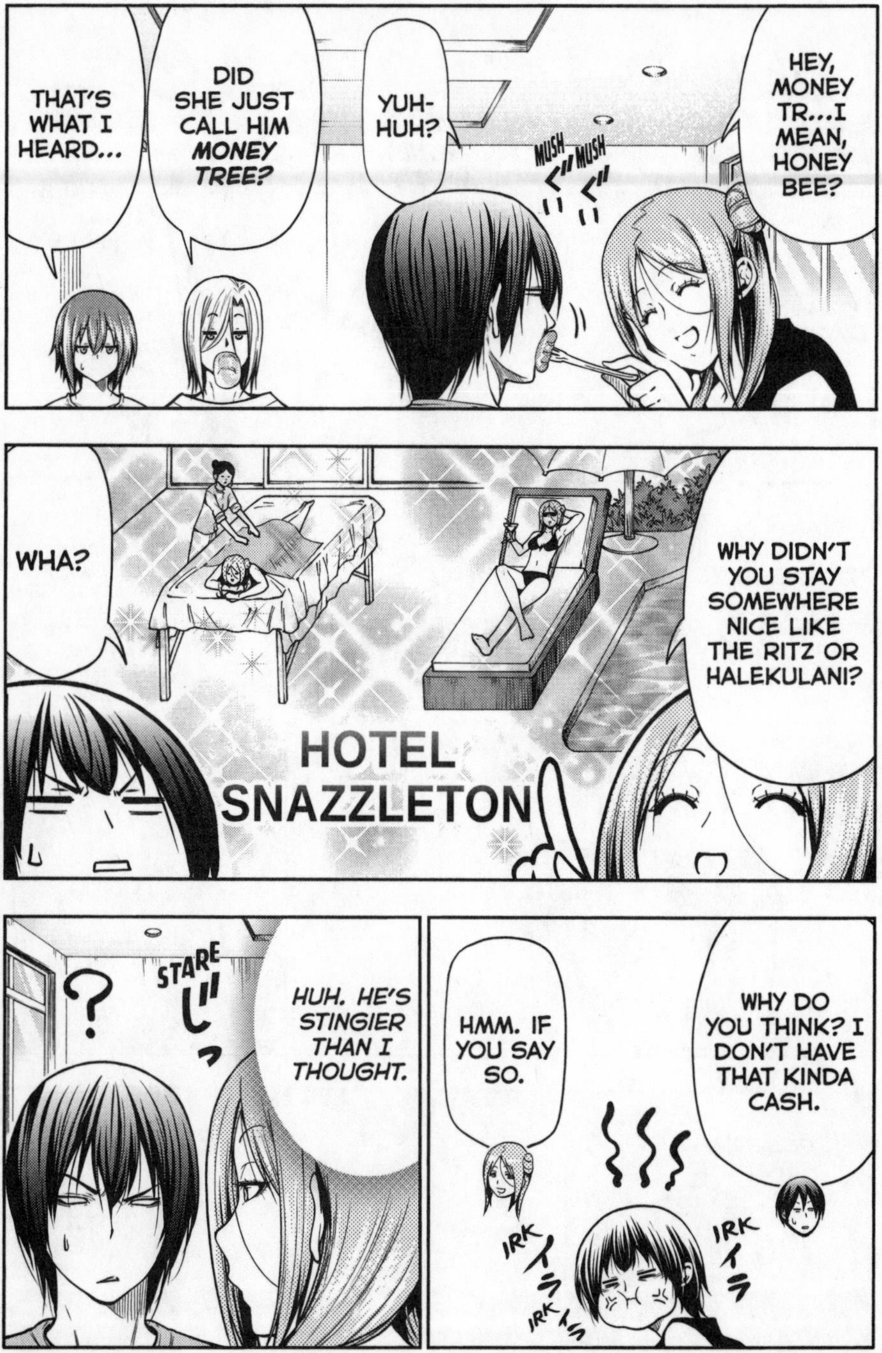
HEY, MONEY TR...I MEAN, HONEY BEE?
MUSH MUSH
YUH-HUH?
DID SHE JUST CALL HIM *MONEY TREE?*
THAT'S WHAT I HEARD...
WHY DIDN'T YOU STAY SOMEWHERE NICE LIKE THE RITZ OR HALEKULANI?
HOTEL SNAZZLETON
WHA?
WHY DO YOU THINK? I DON'T HAVE THAT KINDA CASH.
HMM. IF YOU SAY SO.
IRK
IRK
IRK
HUH. HE'S STINGIER THAN I THOUGHT.
STARE
?

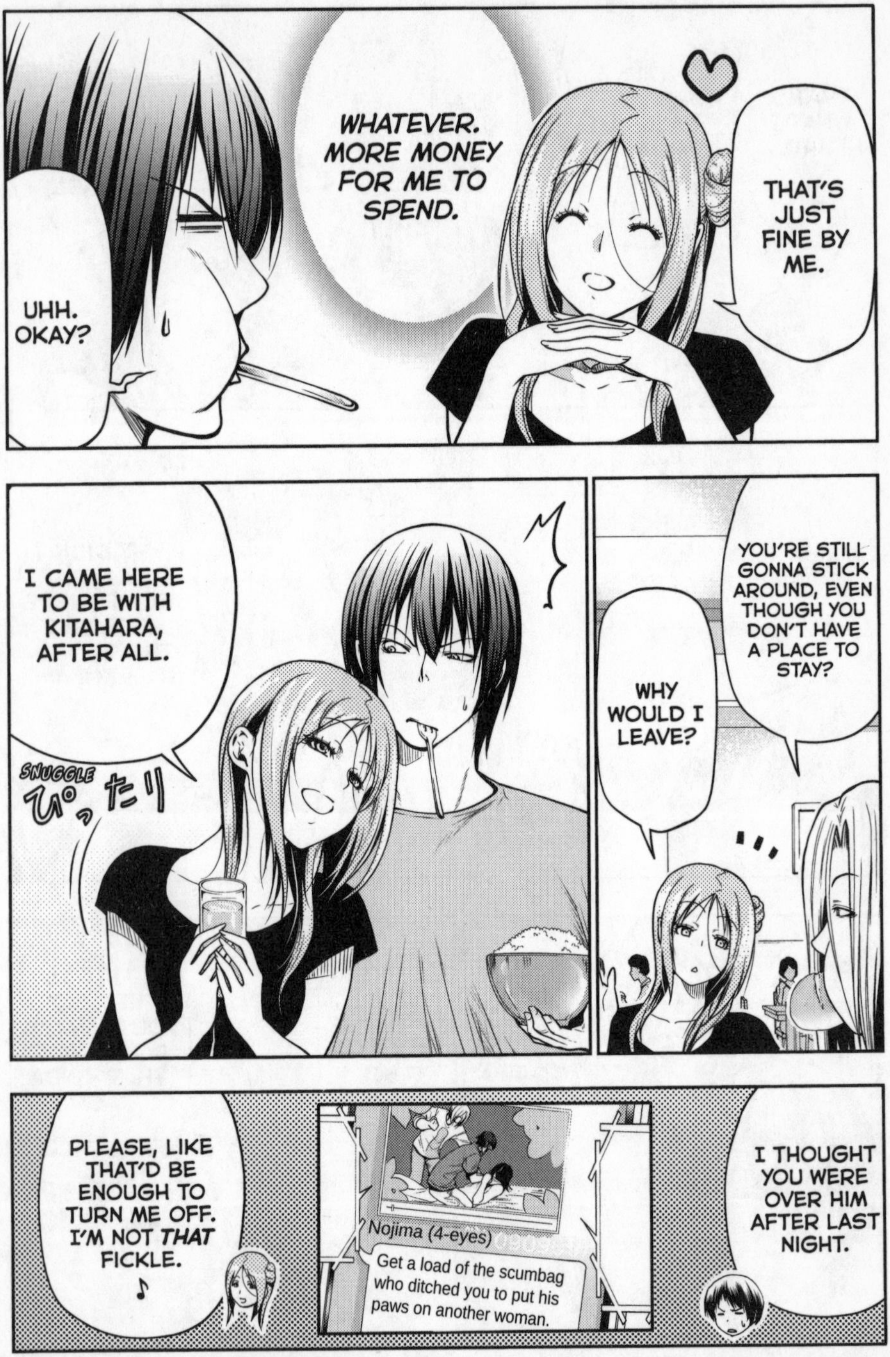
THAT'S JUST FINE BY ME.
WHATEVER. MORE MONEY FOR ME TO SPEND.
UHH. OKAY?
YOU'RE STILL GONNA STICK AROUND, EVEN THOUGH YOU DON'T HAVE A PLACE TO STAY?
WHY WOULD I LEAVE?
I CAME HERE TO BE WITH KITAHARA, AFTER ALL.
SNUGGLE
ぴったり
I THOUGHT YOU WERE OVER HIM AFTER LAST NIGHT.
Nojima (4-eyes)
Get a load of the scumbag who ditched you to put his paws on another woman.
PLEASE, LIKE THAT'D BE ENOUGH TO TURN ME OFF. I'M NOT *THAT* FICKLE. ♪

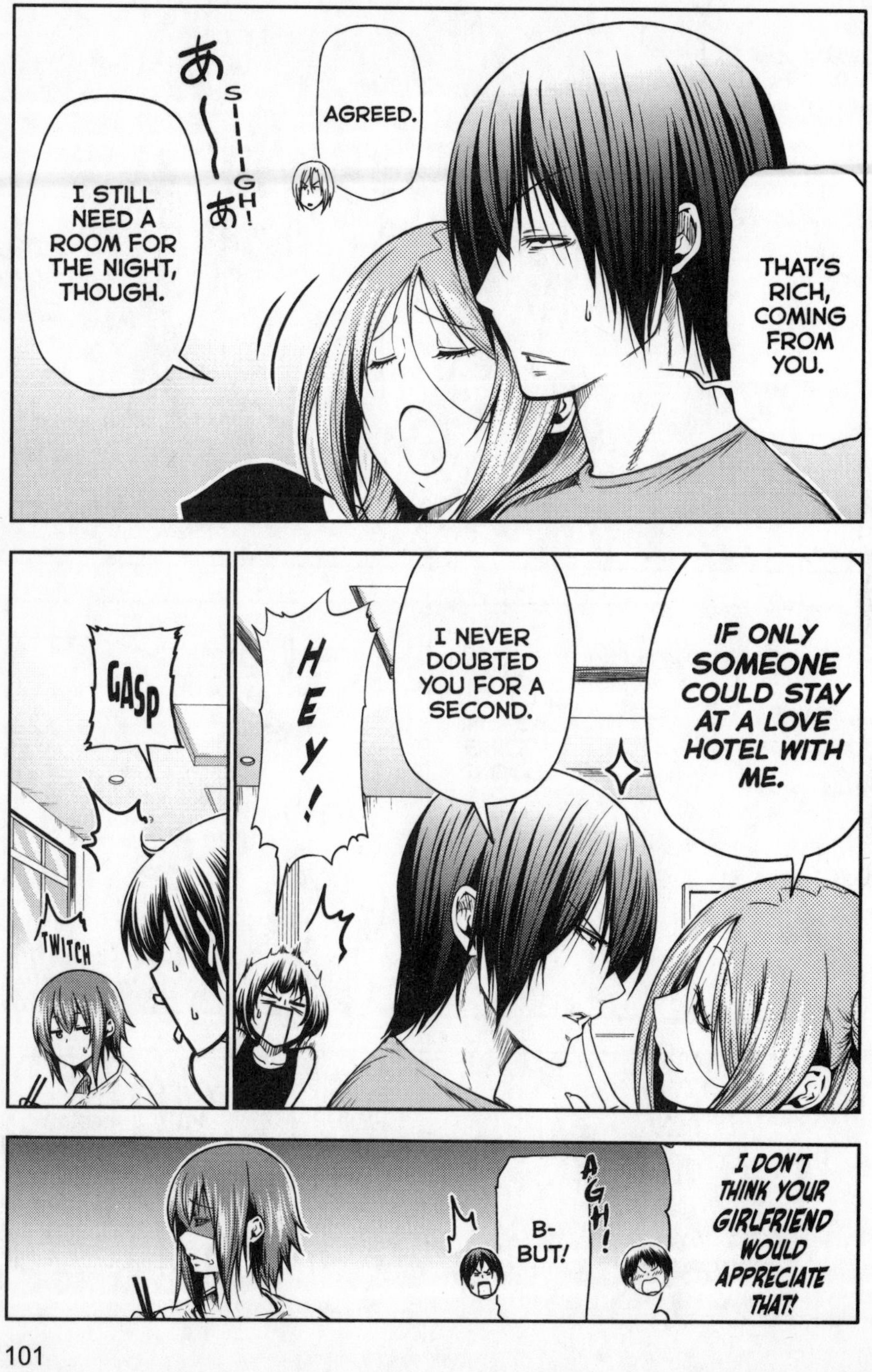
THAT'S RICH, COMING FROM YOU.
AGREED.
あ〜あ
SIIIGH!
I STILL NEED A ROOM FOR THE NIGHT, THOUGH.
IF ONLY SOMEONE COULD STAY AT A LOVE HOTEL WITH ME.
I NEVER DOUBTED YOU FOR A SECOND.
HEY!
GASP
TWITCH
I DON'T THINK YOUR GIRLFRIEND WOULD APPRECIATE THAT!
AGH!
B-BUT!

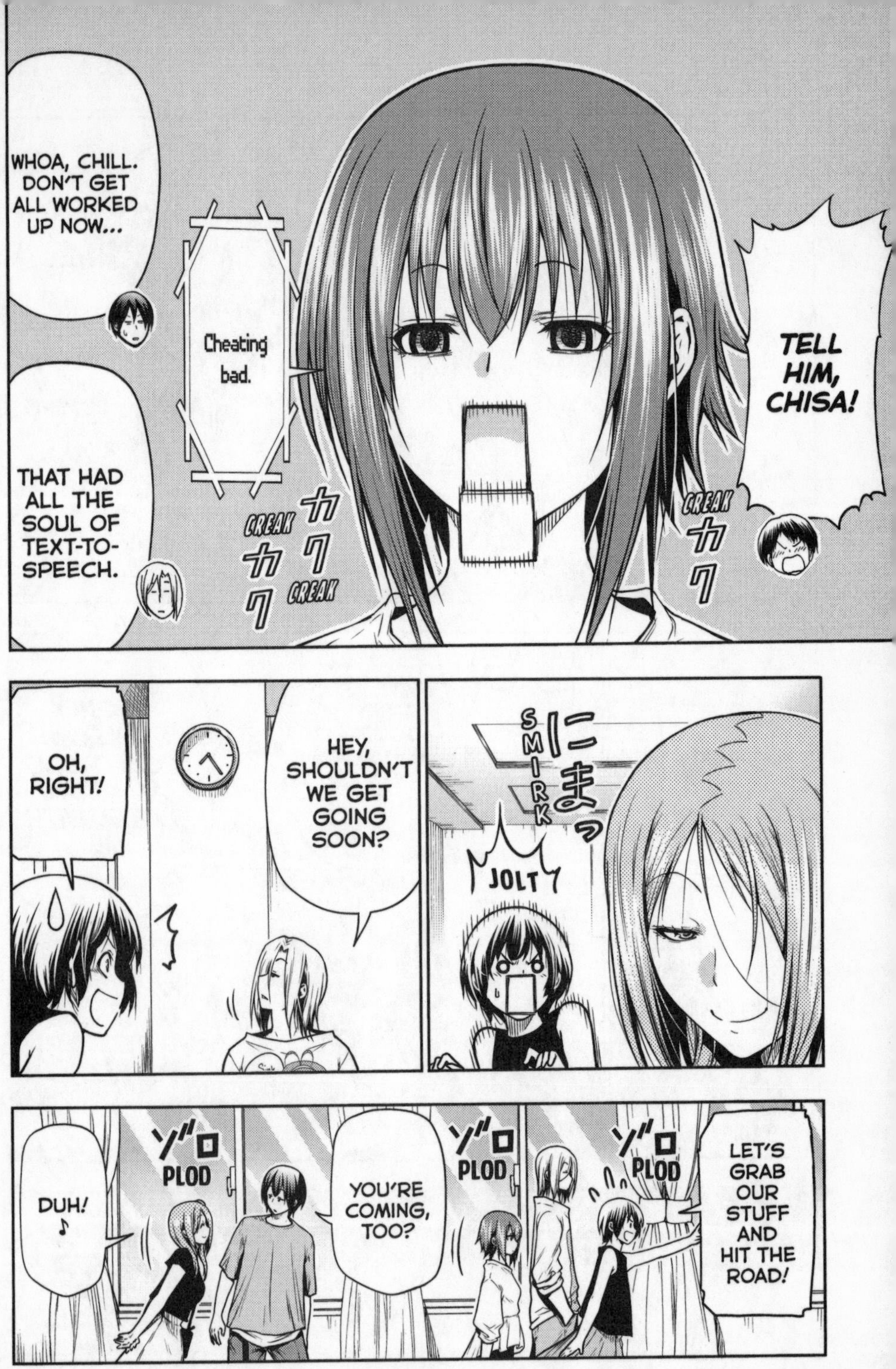

TELL HIM, CHISA!
CREAK
カク
Cheating bad.
CREAK
カク
CREAK
カク
WHOA, CHILL. DON'T GET ALL WORKED UP NOW...
THAT HAD ALL THE SOUL OF TEXT-TO-SPEECH.
にまっ
SMIRK
JOLT
HEY, SHOULDN'T WE GET GOING SOON?
OH, RIGHT!
LET'S GRAB OUR STUFF AND HIT THE ROAD!
ゾロ
PLOD
YOU'RE COMING, TOO?
ゾロ
PLOD
DUH! ♪
ゾロ
PLOD

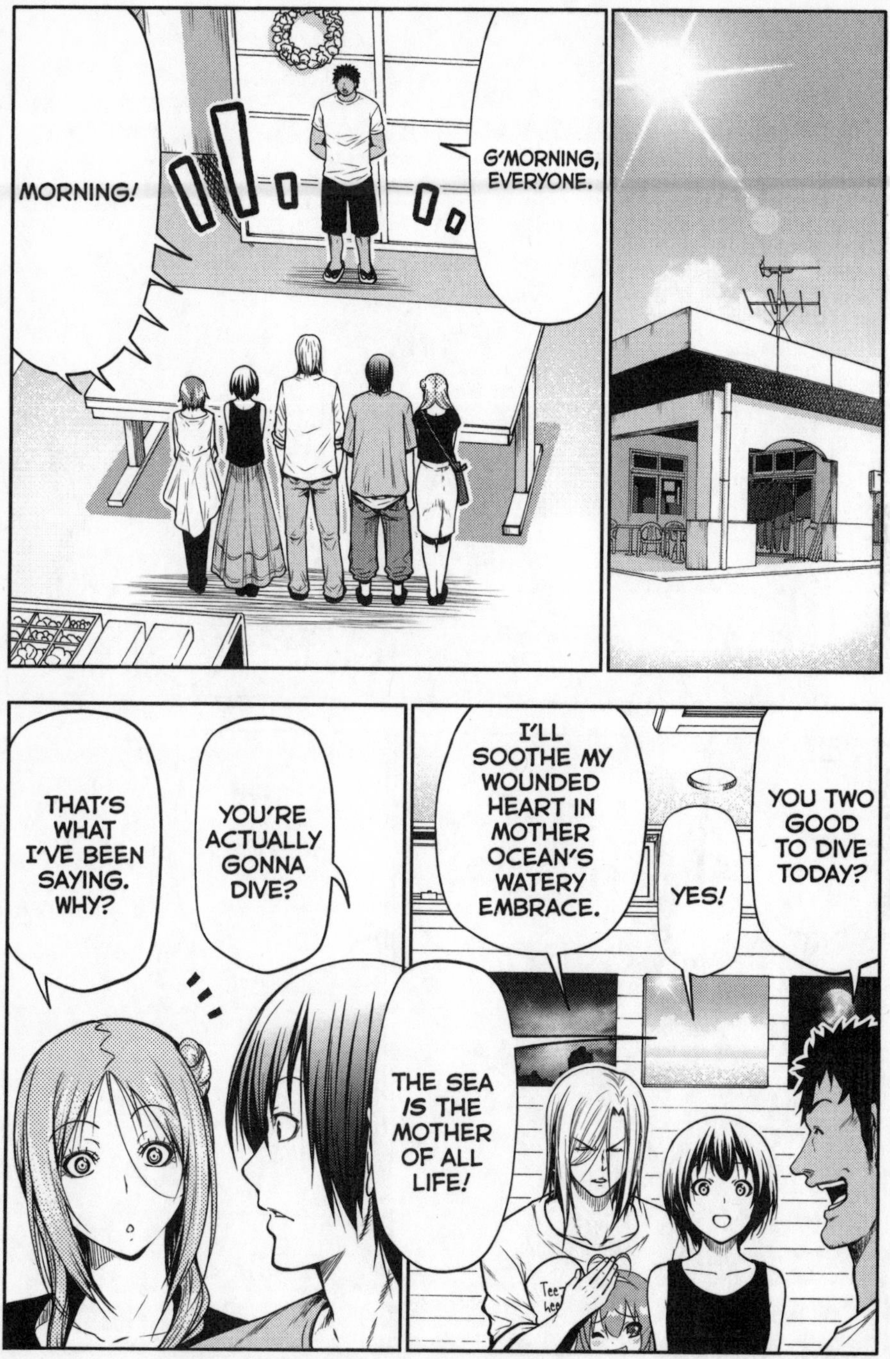
G'MORNING, EVERYONE.
MORNING!
YOU TWO GOOD TO DIVE TODAY?
YES!
I'LL SOOTHE MY WOUNDED HEART IN MOTHER OCEAN'S WATERY EMBRACE.
THE SEA IS THE MOTHER OF ALL LIFE!
Tee hee
YOU'RE ACTUALLY GONNA DIVE?
THAT'S WHAT I'VE BEEN SAYING. WHY?

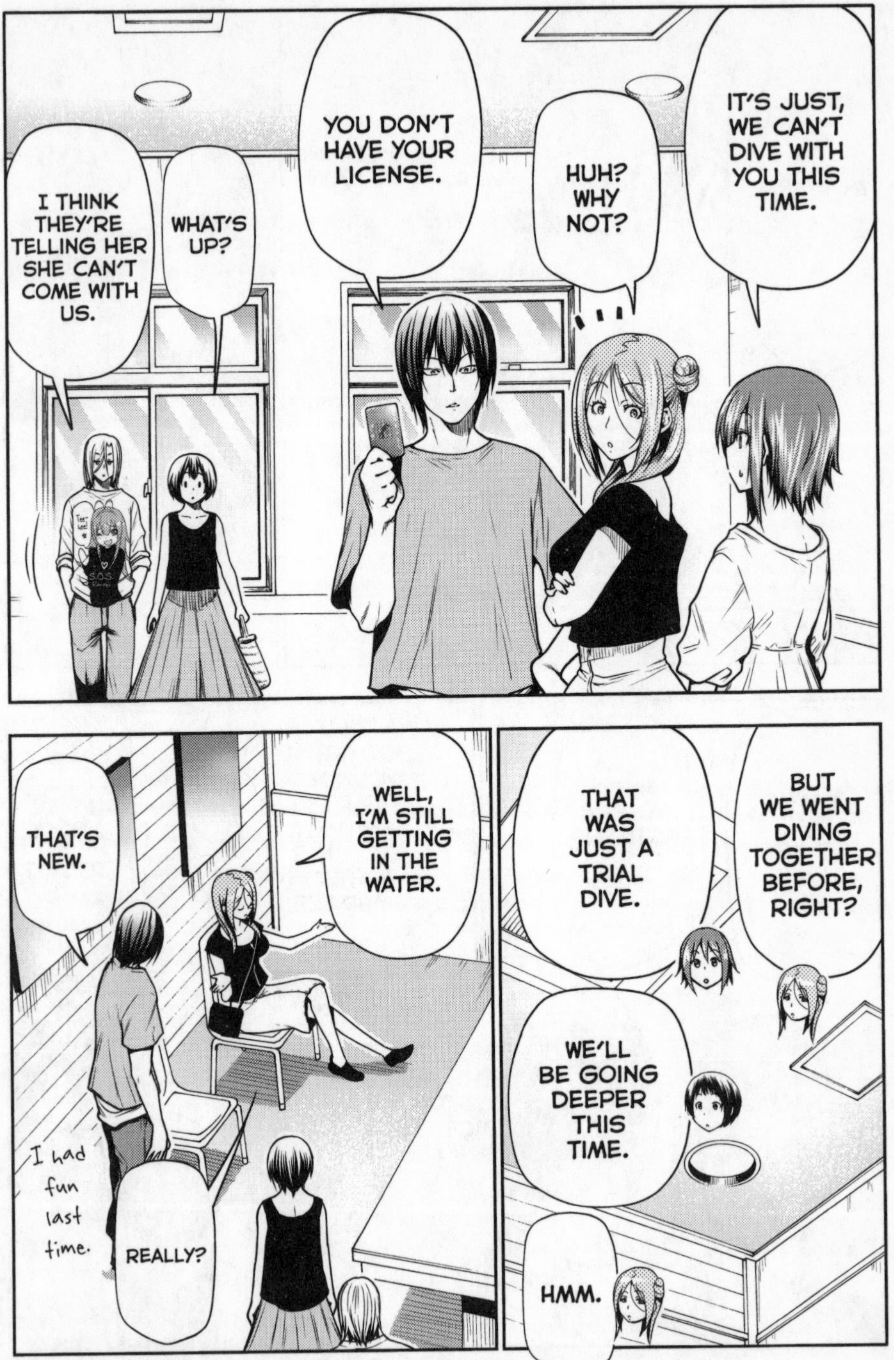
IT'S JUST, WE CAN'T DIVE WITH YOU THIS TIME.
HUH? WHY NOT?
YOU DON'T HAVE YOUR LICENSE.
WHAT'S UP?
I THINK THEY'RE TELLING HER SHE CAN'T COME WITH US.
BUT WE WENT DIVING TOGETHER BEFORE, RIGHT?
THAT WAS JUST A TRIAL DIVE.
WE'LL BE GOING DEEPER THIS TIME.
HMM.
WELL, I'M STILL GETTING IN THE WATER.
THAT'S NEW.
I had fun last time.
REALLY?

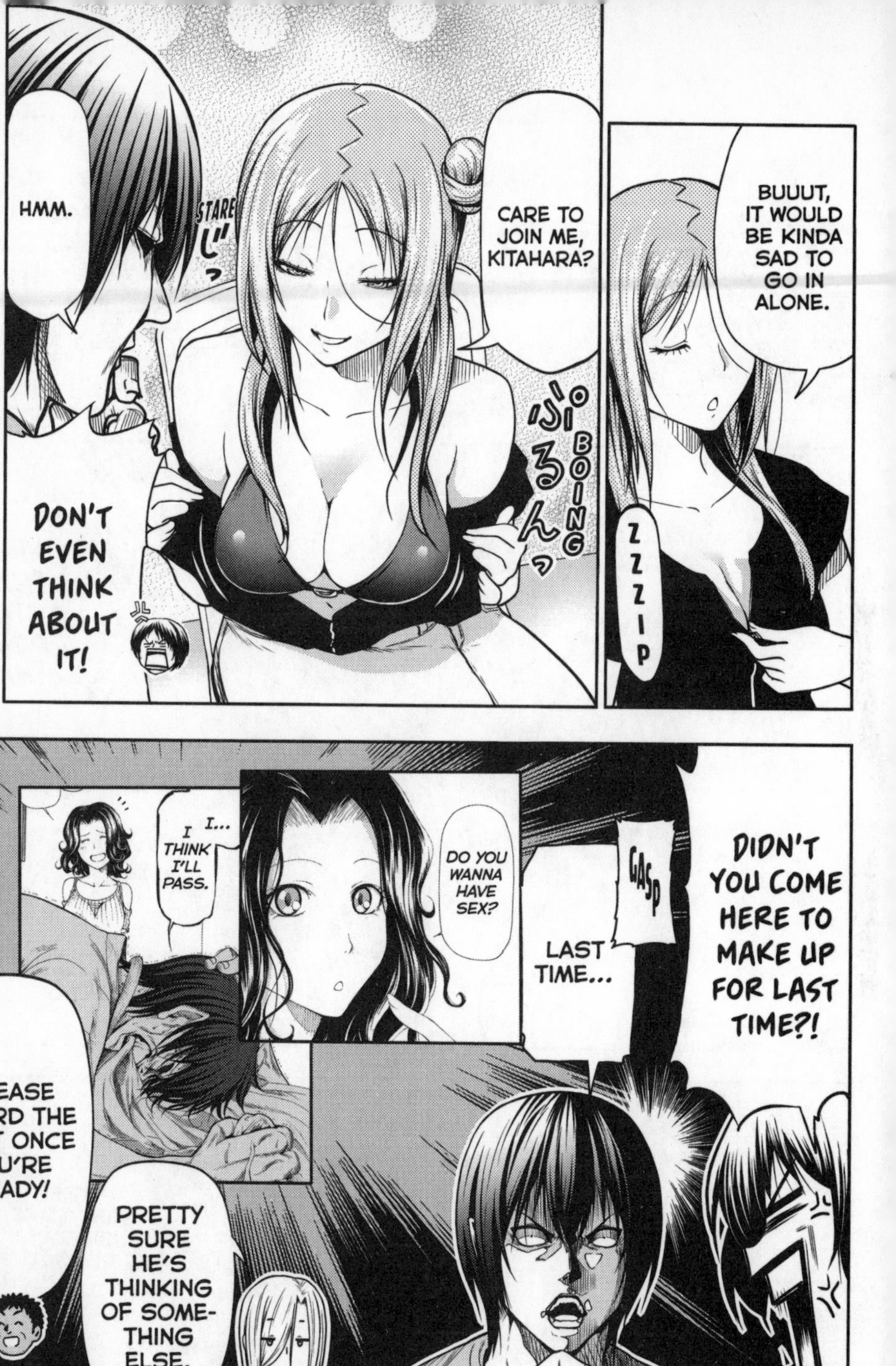
BUUUT, IT WOULD BE KINDA SAD TO GO IN ALONE.
ZZZIP
CARE TO JOIN ME, KITAHARA?
ぷるんっ
BOING
STARE
じっ
HMM.
DON'T EVEN THINK ABOUT IT!
DIDN'T YOU COME HERE TO MAKE UP FOR LAST TIME?!
GASP
LAST TIME...
DO YOU WANNA HAVE SEX?
I... I THINK I'LL PASS.
PLEASE BOARD THE BOAT ONCE YOU'RE READY!
PRETTY SURE HE'S THINKING OF SOME-THING ELSE.

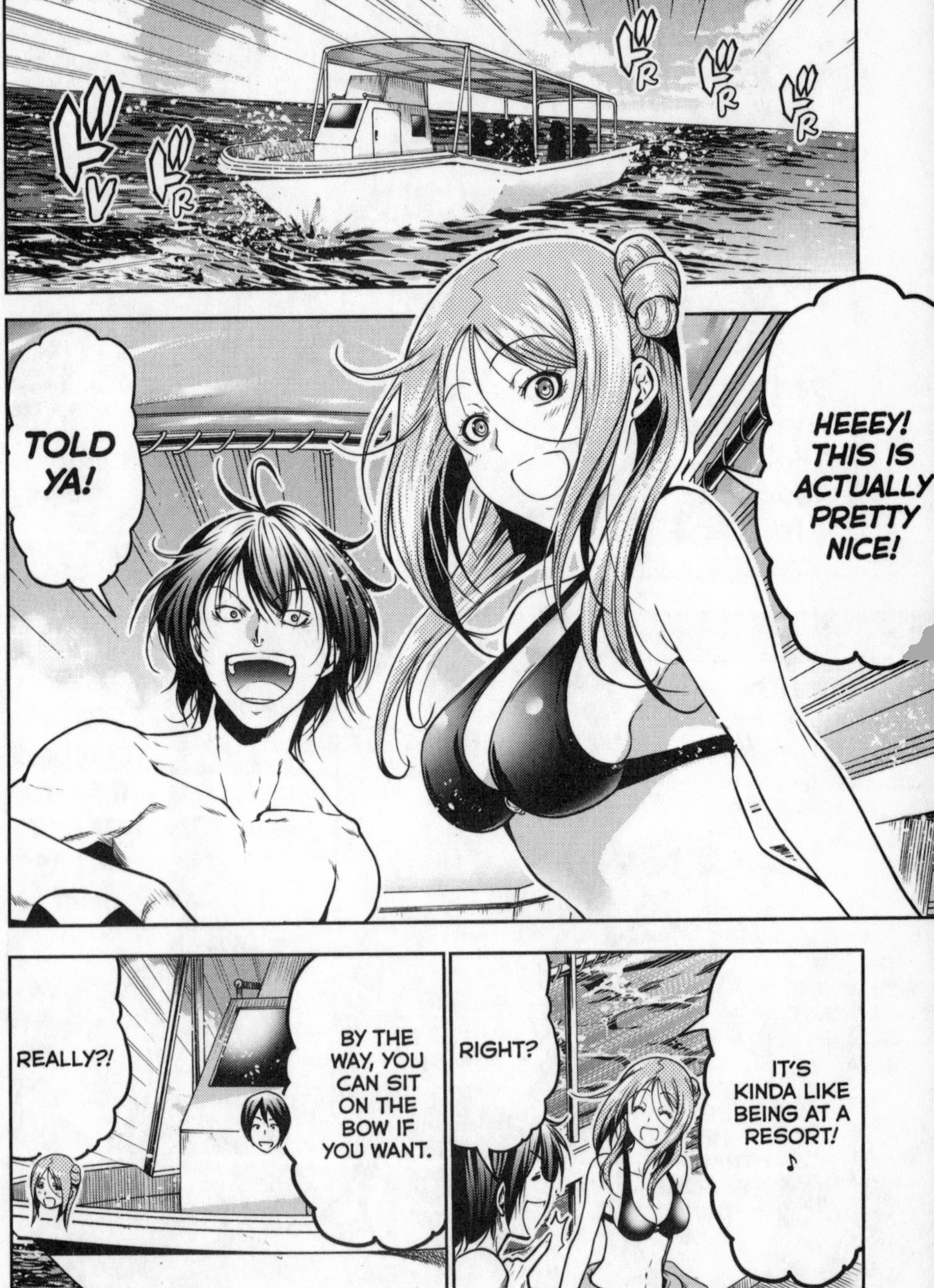
HEEEY! THIS IS ACTUALLY PRETTY NICE!
TOLD YA!
IT'S KINDA LIKE BEING AT A RESORT! ♪
RIGHT?
BY THE WAY, YOU CAN SIT ON THE BOW IF YOU WANT.
REALLY?!

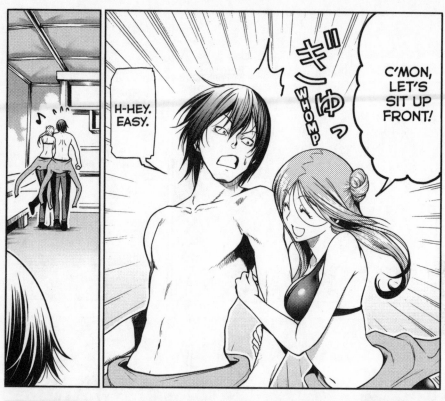

C'MON, LET'S SIT UP FRONT!
ぎゅっ
WHOMP
H-HEY. EASY.
COULD YOU LOOK ANY MORE ANNOYED?
じとー
STARE
WHAT DO YOU EXPECT?
I MEAN, SHE'S OBVIOUSLY JUST TRYING TO SEDUCE HIM.
ぷるーん
MOOSH
TRUE ENOUGH.

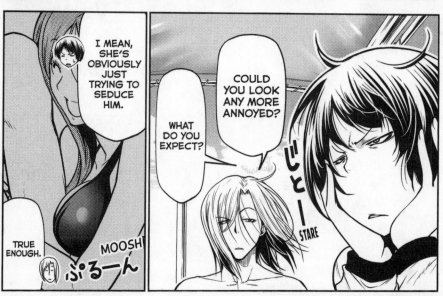

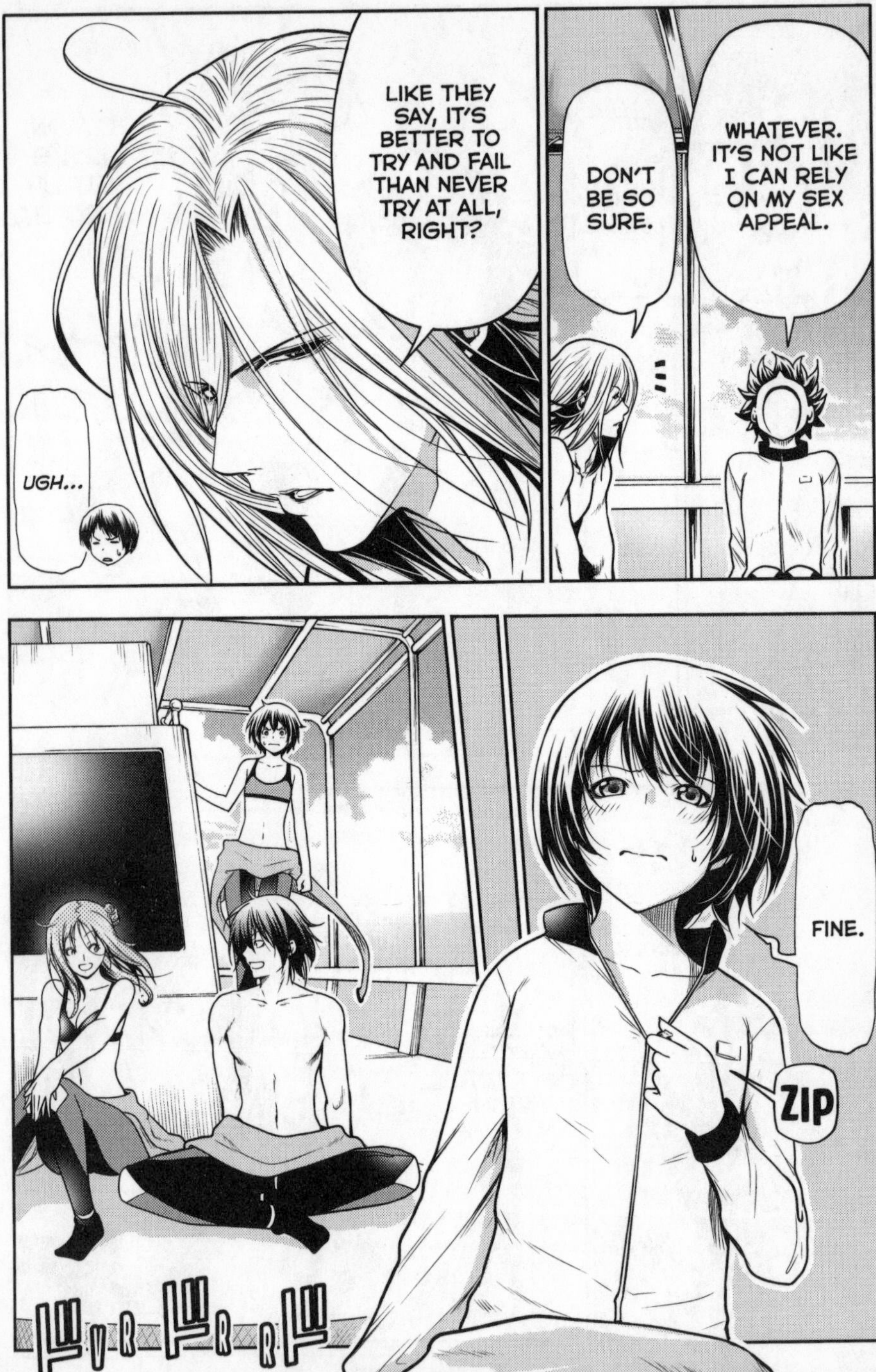
WHATEVER. IT'S NOT LIKE I CAN RELY ON MY SEX APPEAL.
DON'T BE SO SURE.
LIKE THEY SAY, IT'S BETTER TO TRY AND FAIL THAN NEVER TRY AT ALL, RIGHT?
UGH...
FINE.
ZIP

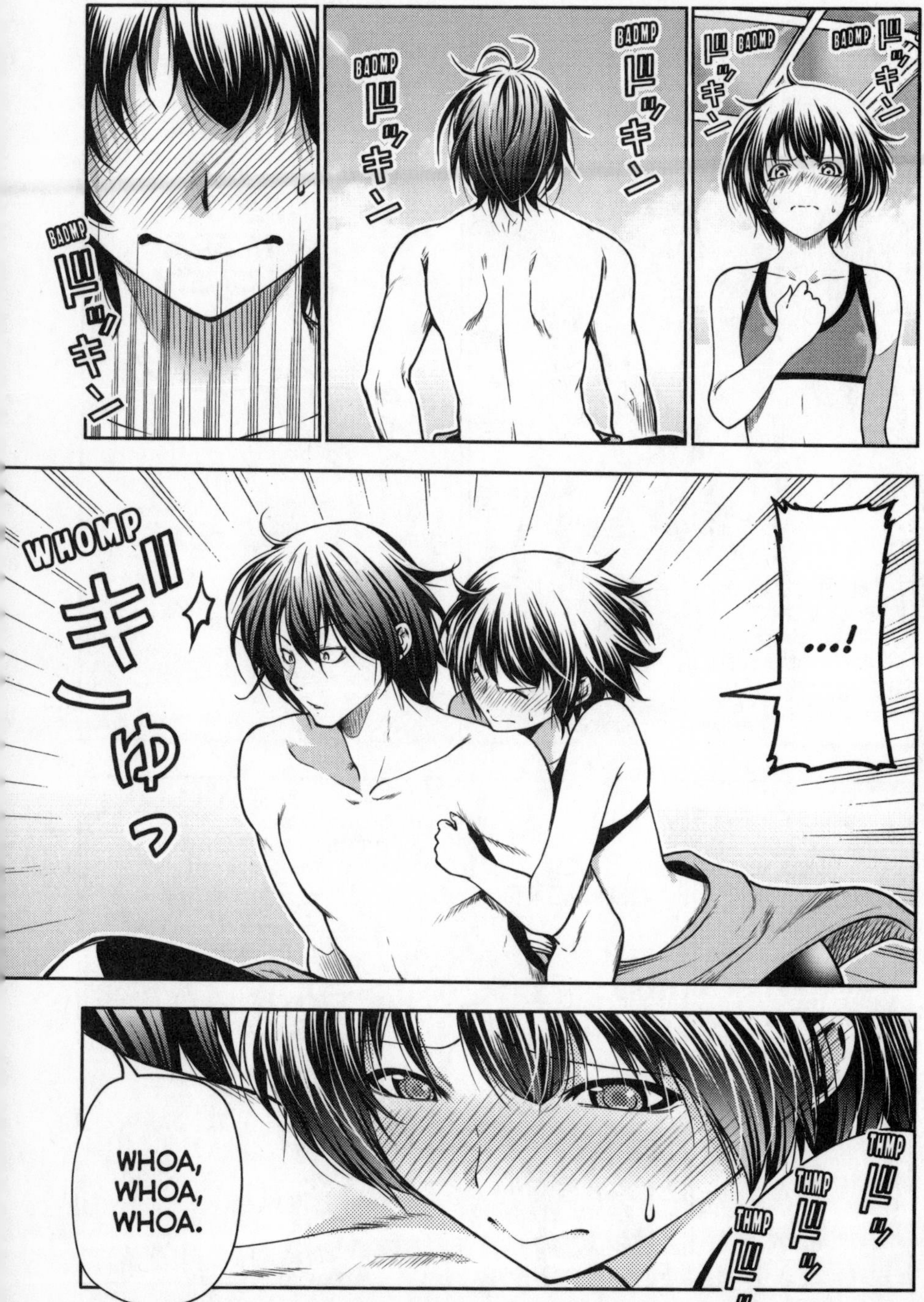
BADMP
ドッキン
BADMP
ドッキン
BADMP
ドッキン
BADMP
ドッキン
...!
WHOMP
WHOA, WHOA, WHOA.
THMP
ドッ
THMP
ドッ
THMP
ドッ

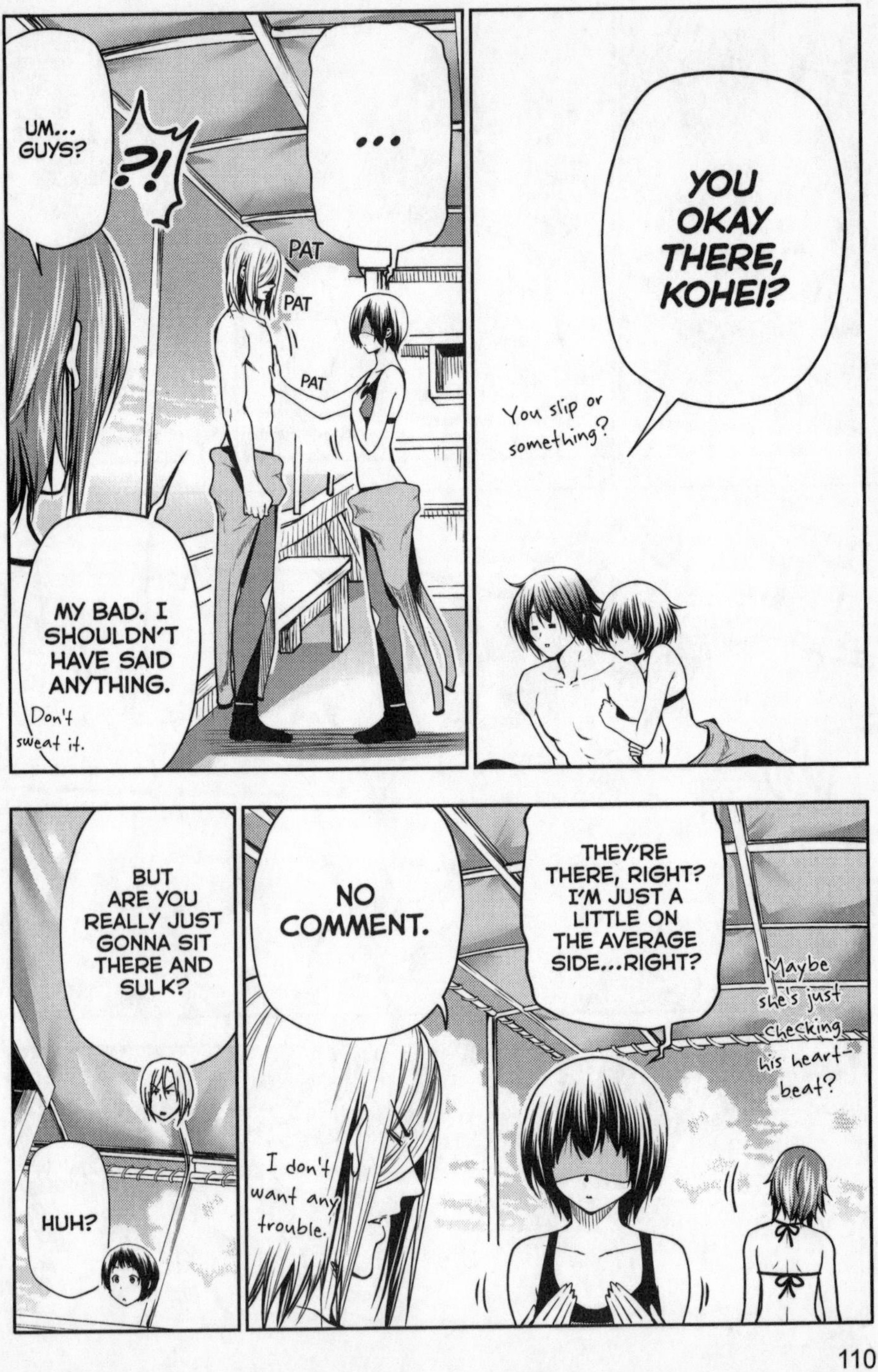
YOU OKAY THERE, KOHEI?
You slip or something?
...
UM... GUYS?
?!
PAT
PAT
PAT
MY BAD. I SHOULDN'T HAVE SAID ANYTHING.
Don't sweat it.
THEY'RE THERE, RIGHT? I'M JUST A LITTLE ON THE AVERAGE SIDE...RIGHT?
Maybe she's just checking his heart-beat?
NO COMMENT.
I don't want any trouble.
BUT ARE YOU REALLY JUST GONNA SIT THERE AND SULK?
HUH?

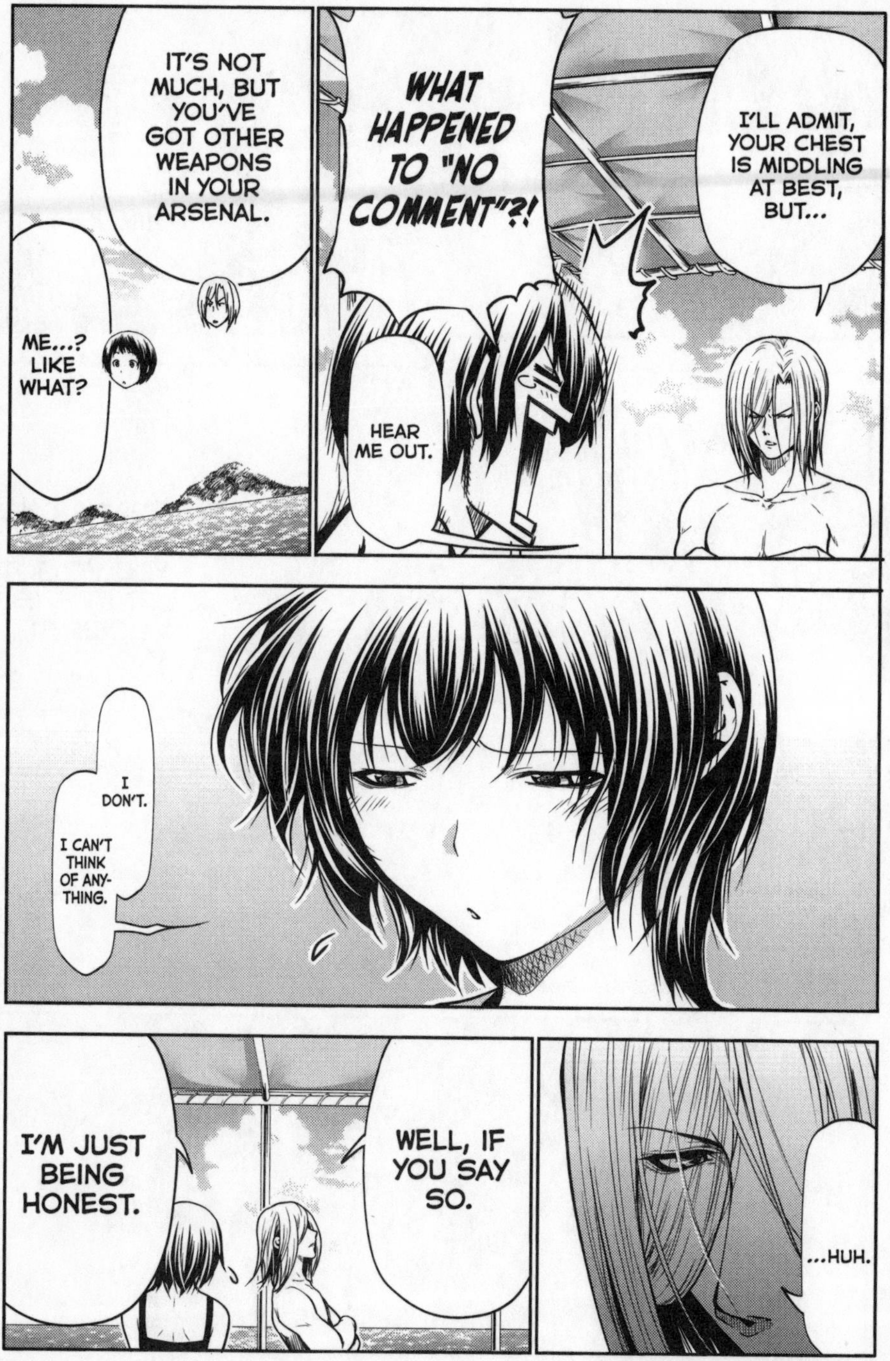
I'LL ADMIT, YOUR CHEST IS MIDDLING AT BEST, BUT...
WHAT HAPPENED TO "NO COMMENT"?!
HEAR ME OUT.
IT'S NOT MUCH, BUT YOU'VE GOT OTHER WEAPONS IN YOUR ARSENAL.
ME...? LIKE WHAT?
I DON'T.
I CAN'T THINK OF ANY-THING.
...HUH.
WELL, IF YOU SAY SO.
I'M JUST BEING HONEST.

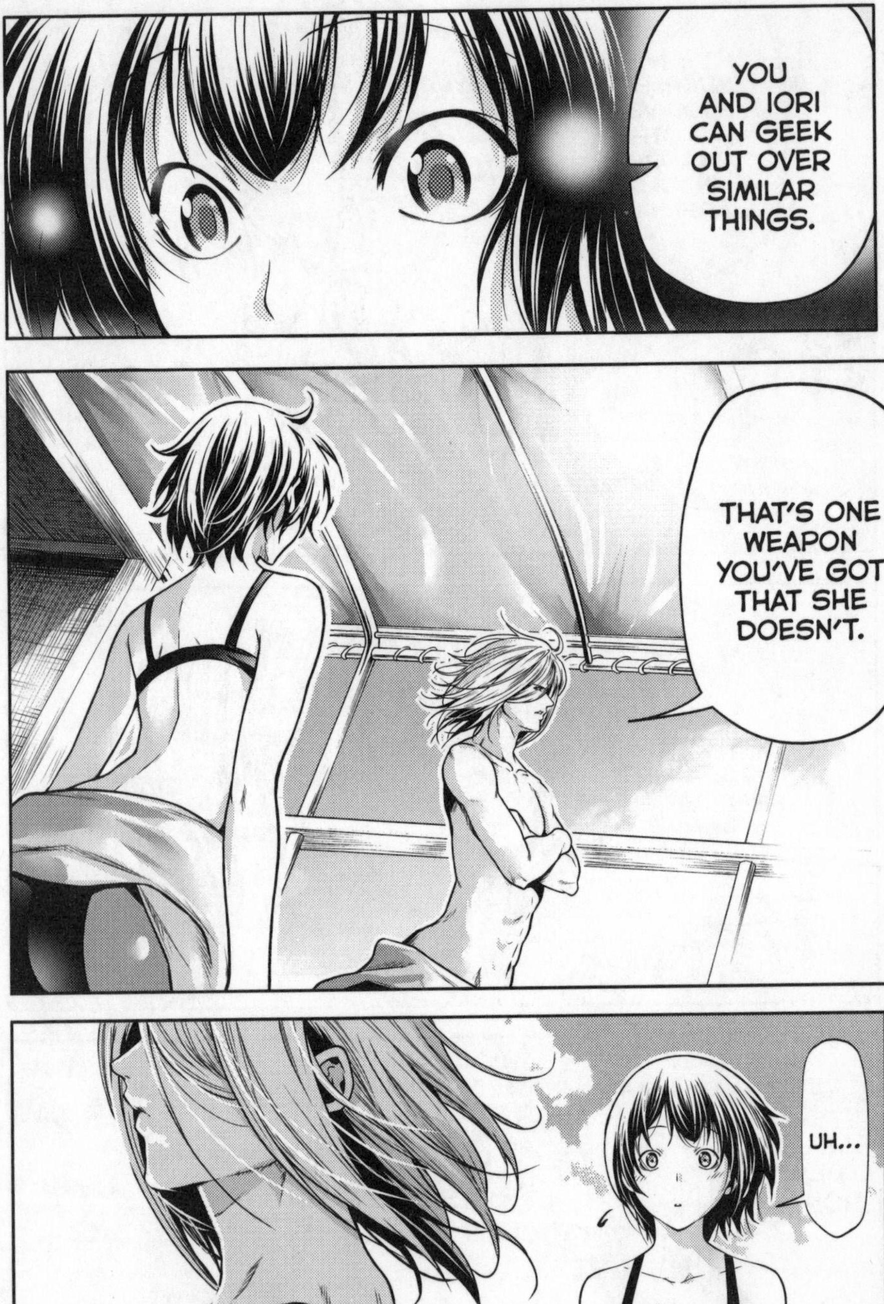
YOU AND IORI CAN GEEK OUT OVER SIMILAR THINGS.
THAT'S ONE WEAPON YOU'VE GOT THAT SHE DOESN'T.
UH...

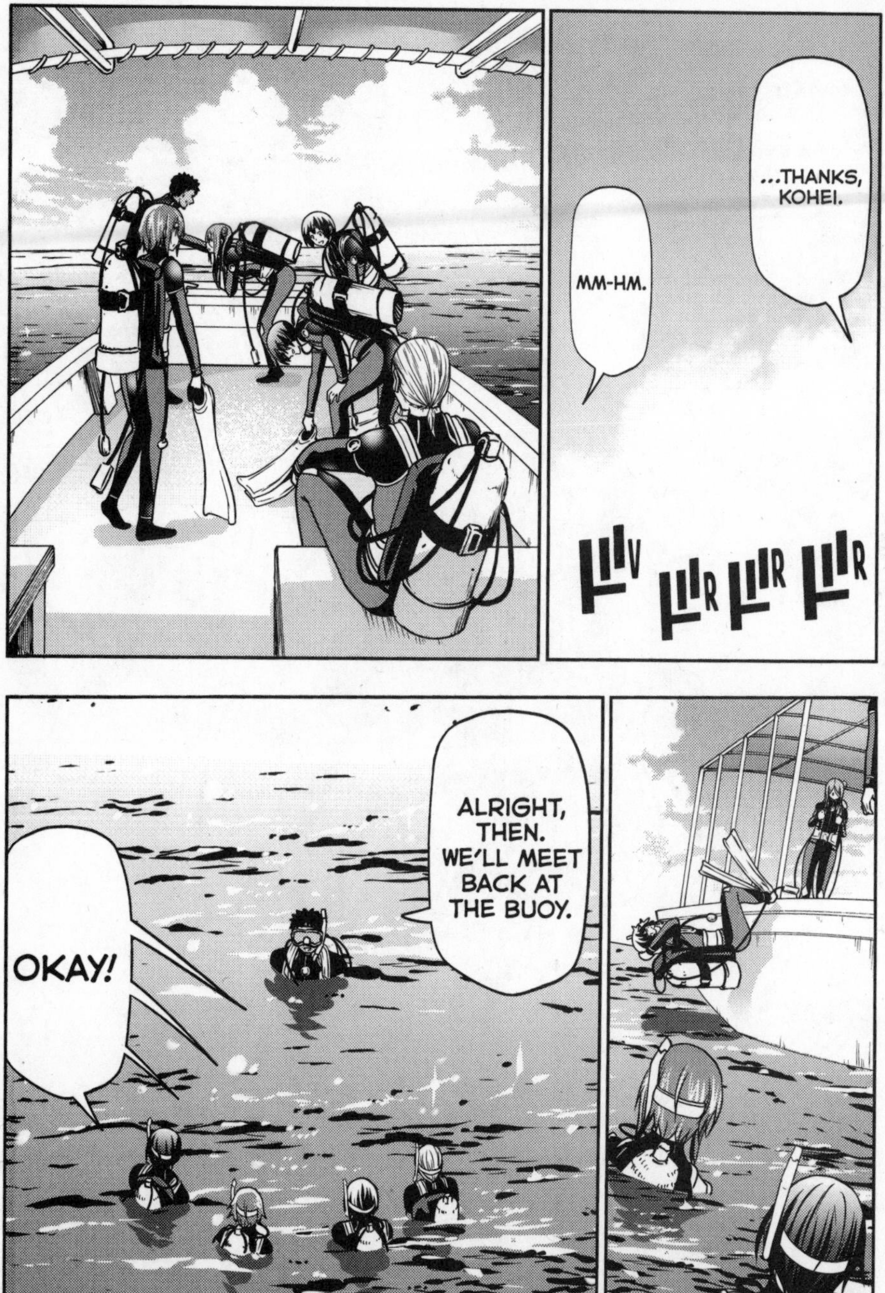
...THANKS, KOHEI.
MM-HM.
ALRIGHT, THEN. WE'LL MEET BACK AT THE BUOY.
OKAY!

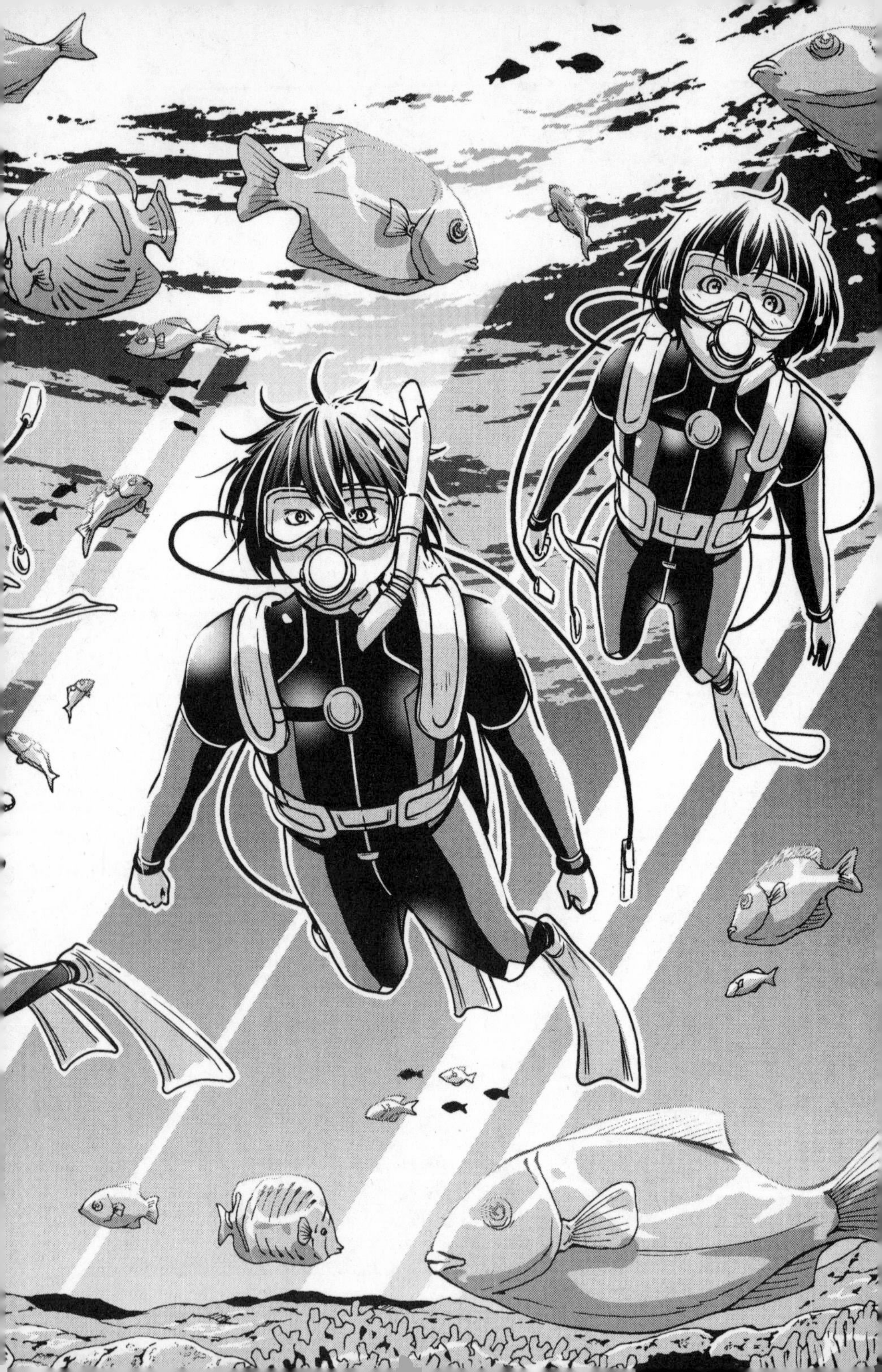

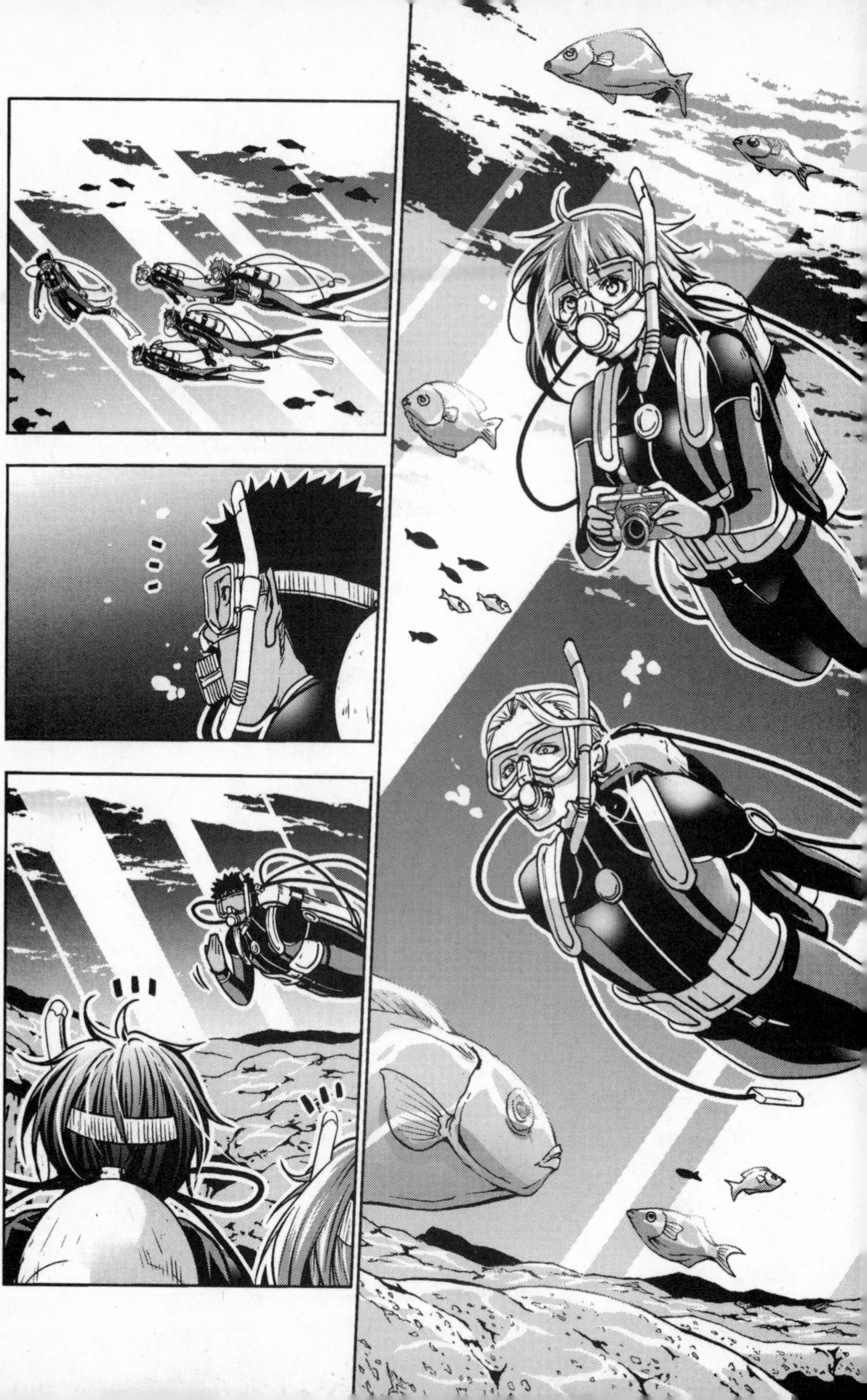
...
...
...

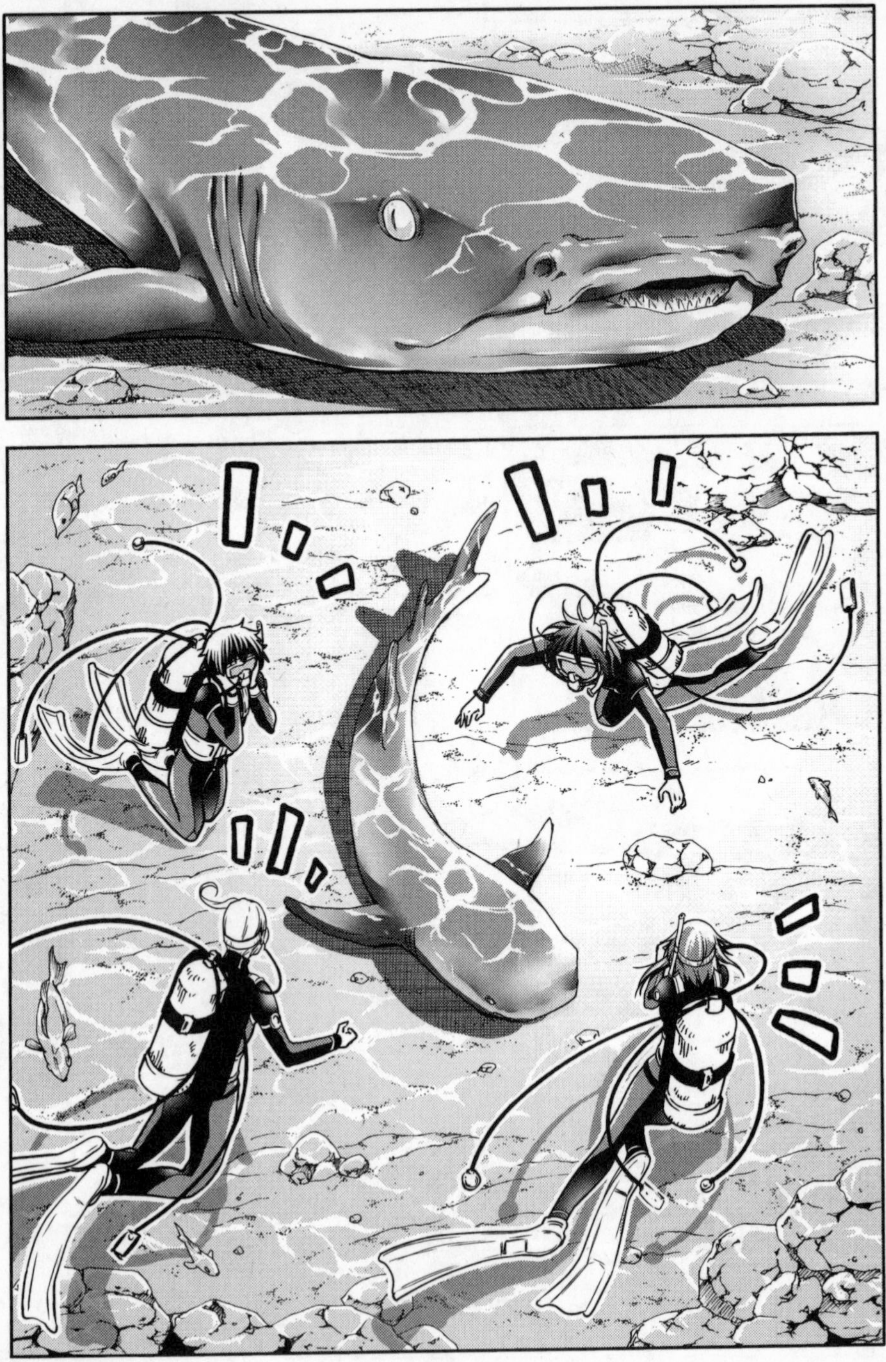

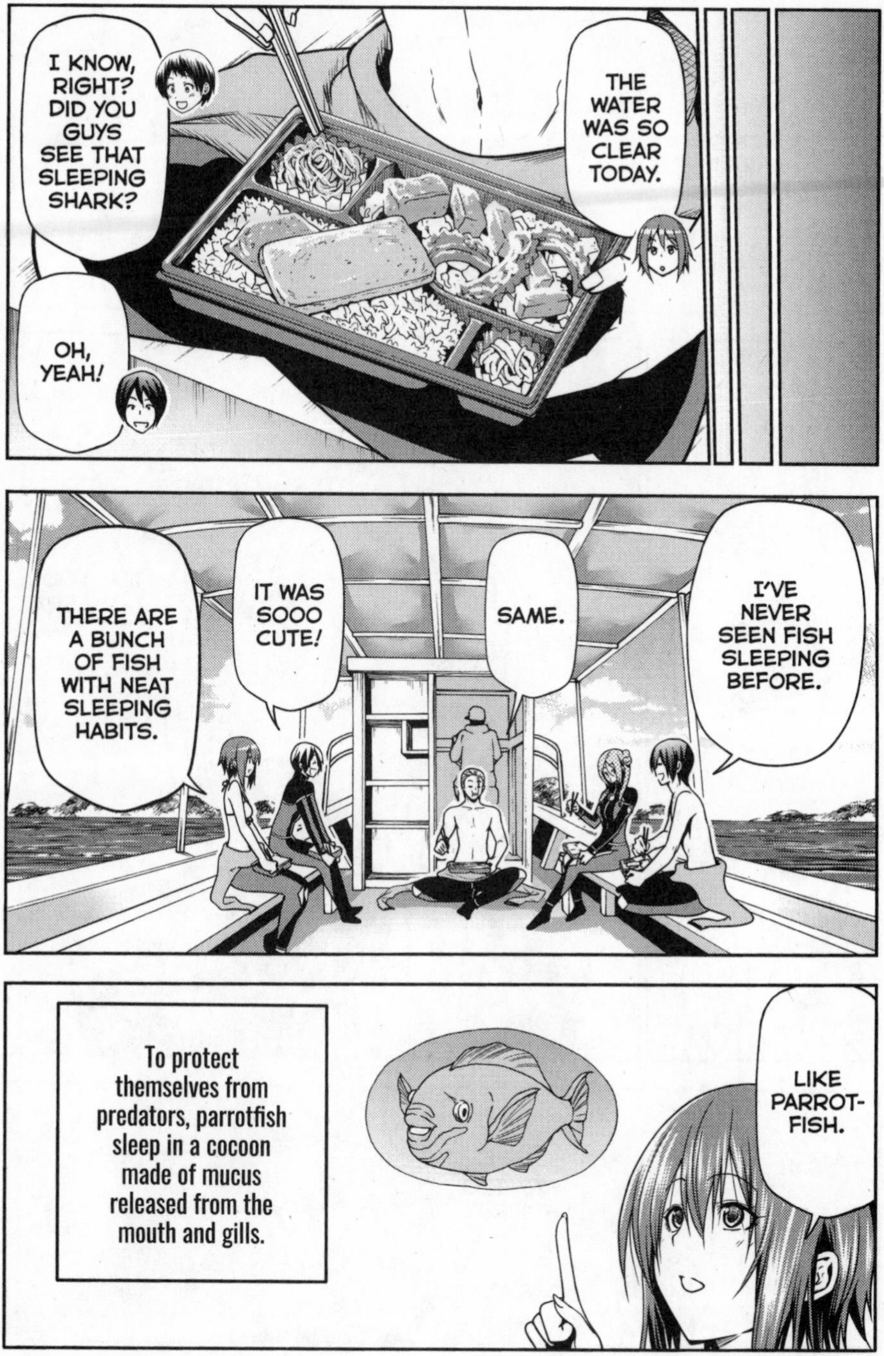
THE WATER WAS SO CLEAR TODAY.
I KNOW, RIGHT? DID YOU GUYS SEE THAT SLEEPING SHARK?
OH, YEAH!
I'VE NEVER SEEN FISH SLEEPING BEFORE.
SAME.
IT WAS SOOO CUTE!
THERE ARE A BUNCH OF FISH WITH NEAT SLEEPING HABITS.
LIKE PARROT-FISH.
To protect themselves from predators, parrotfish sleep in a cocoon made of mucus released from the mouth and gills.

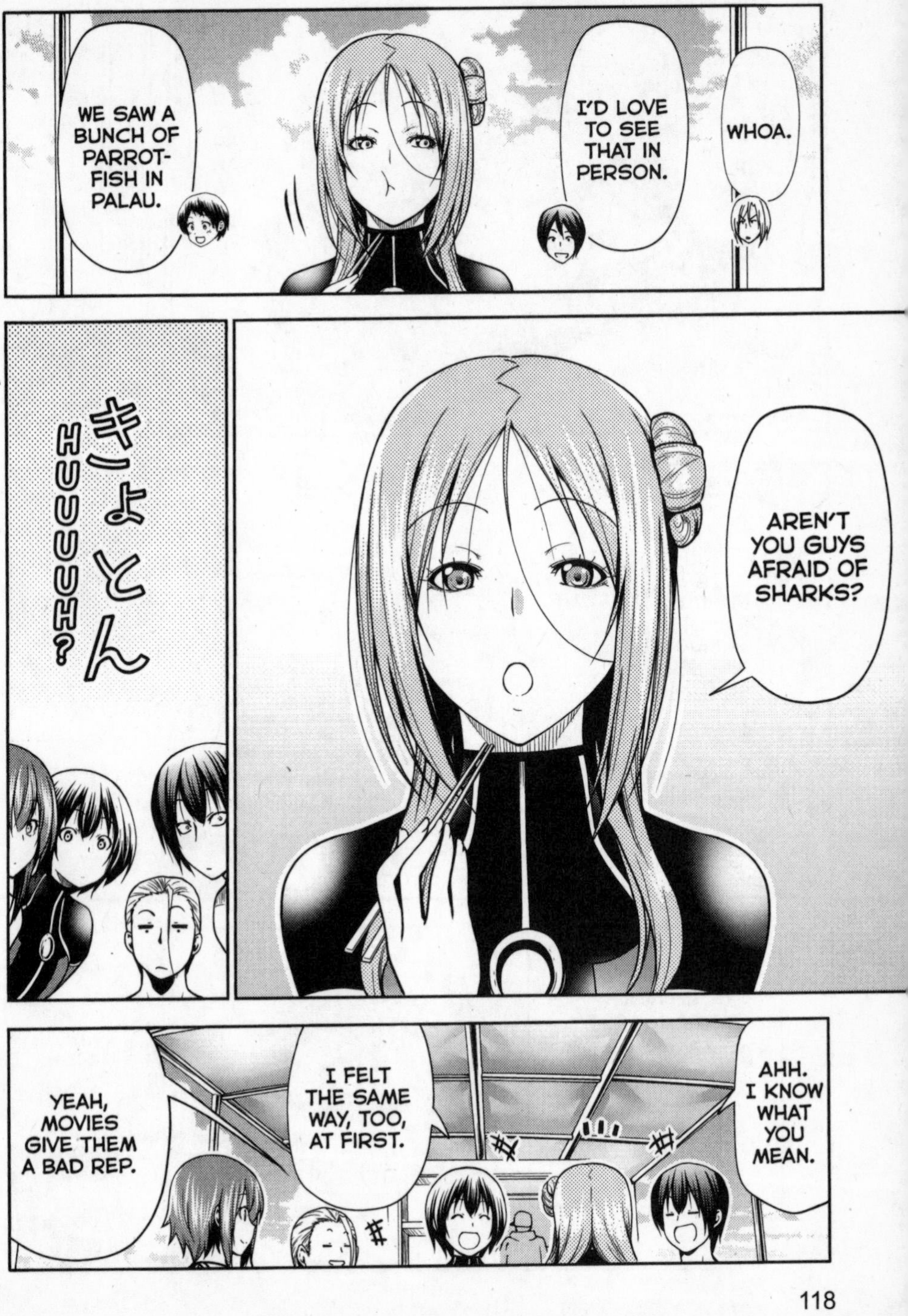
WHOA.
I'D LOVE TO SEE THAT IN PERSON.
WE SAW A BUNCH OF PARROT-FISH IN PALAU.
AREN'T YOU GUYS AFRAID OF SHARKS?
きょとん
HUUUUUH?
AHH. I KNOW WHAT YOU MEAN.
I FELT THE SAME WAY, TOO, AT FIRST.
YEAH, MOVIES GIVE THEM A BAD REP.

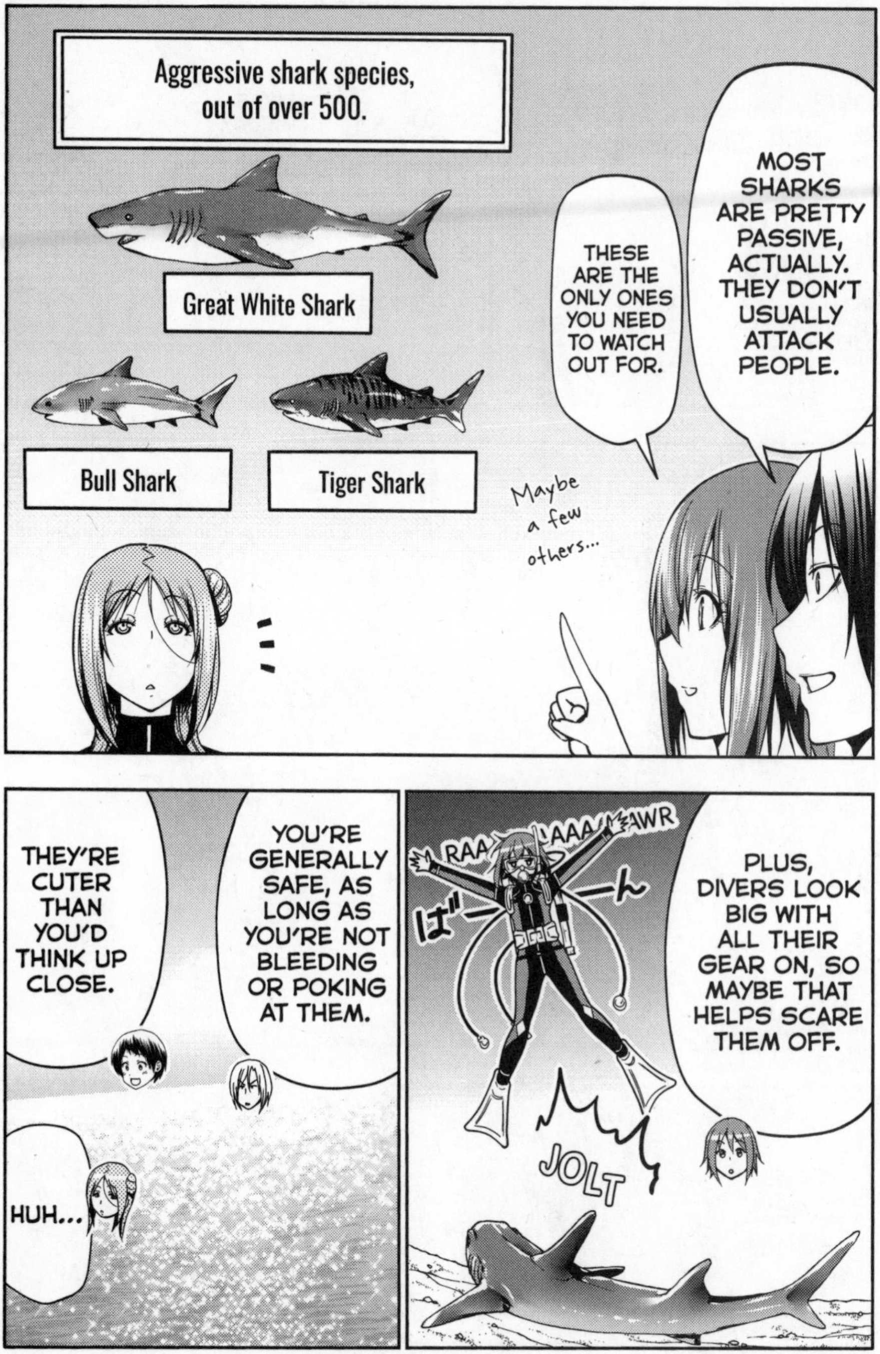
MOST SHARKS ARE PRETTY PASSIVE, ACTUALLY. THEY DON'T USUALLY ATTACK PEOPLE.
THESE ARE THE ONLY ONES YOU NEED TO WATCH OUT FOR.
Aggressive shark species, out of over 500.
Great White Shark
Tiger Shark
Bull Shark
Maybe a few others...
PLUS, DIVERS LOOK BIG WITH ALL THEIR GEAR ON, SO MAYBE THAT HELPS SCARE THEM OFF.
ば―ん
JOLT
YOU'RE GENERALLY SAFE, AS LONG AS YOU'RE NOT BLEEDING OR POKING AT THEM.
THEY'RE CUTER THAN YOU'D THINK UP CLOSE.
HUH...

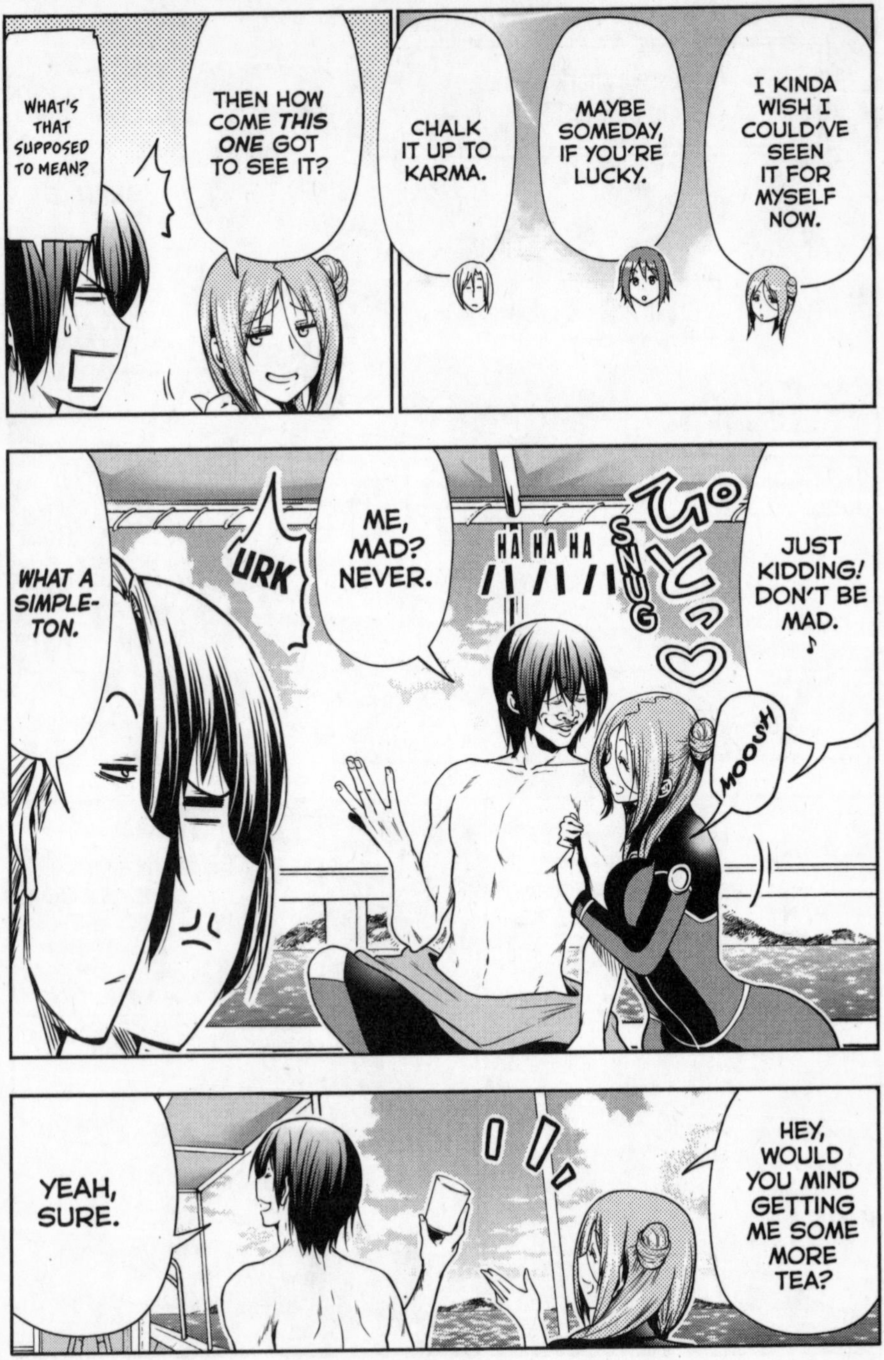
I KINDA WISH I COULD'VE SEEN IT FOR MYSELF NOW.
MAYBE SOMEDAY, IF YOU'RE LUCKY.
CHALK IT UP TO KARMA.
THEN HOW COME *THIS ONE* GOT TO SEE IT?
WHAT'S THAT SUPPOSED TO MEAN?
JUST KIDDING! DON'T BE MAD. ♪
MOOSH
ぴとっ♡
SNUG
HA HA HA
ハハハ
ME, MAD? NEVER.
URK
WHAT A SIMPLETON.
HEY, WOULD YOU MIND GETTING ME SOME MORE TEA?
YEAH, SURE.

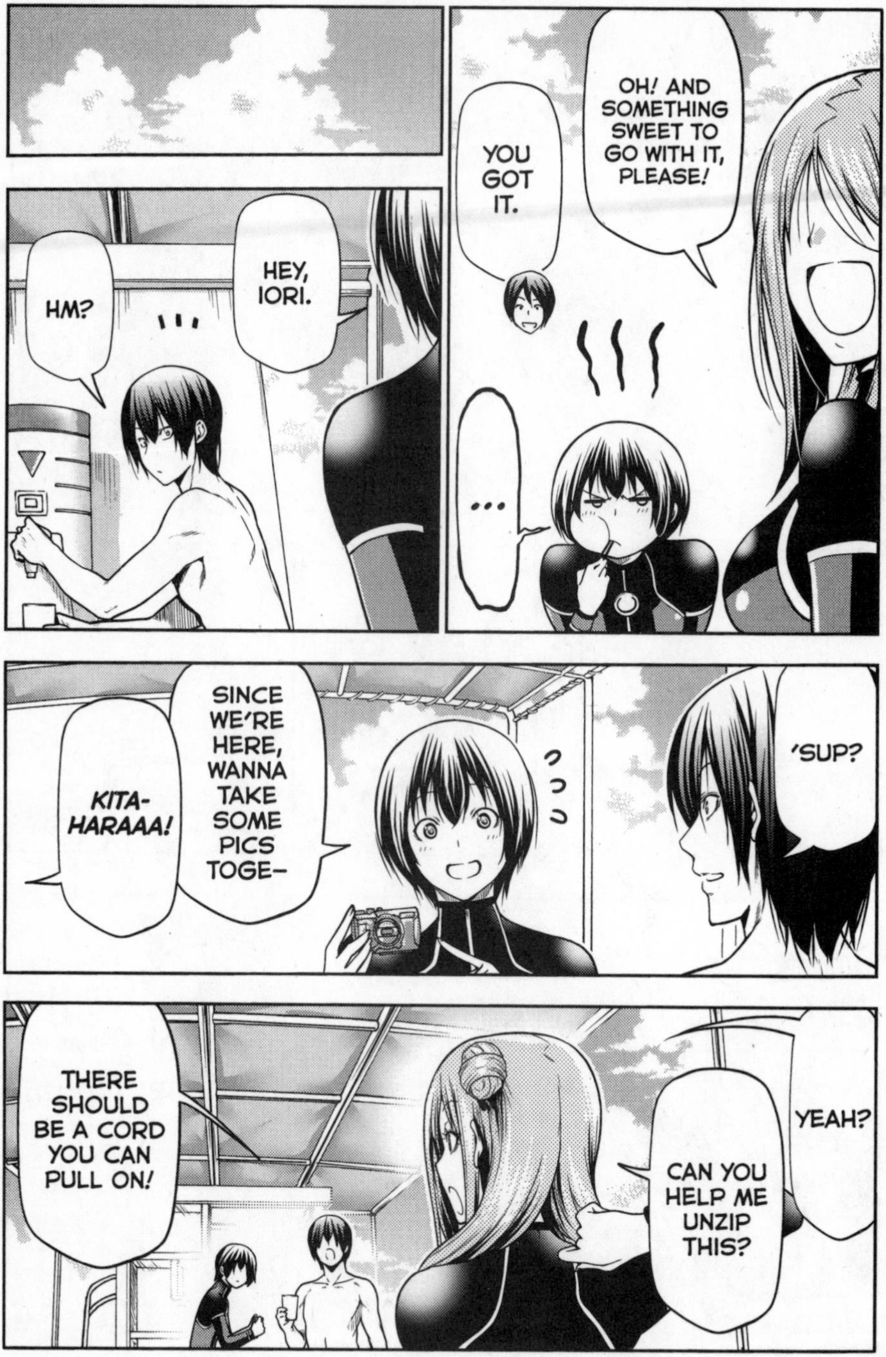
OH! AND SOMETHING SWEET TO GO WITH IT, PLEASE!
YOU GOT IT.
...
HEY, IORI.
HM?
'SUP?
SINCE WE'RE HERE, WANNA TAKE SOME PICS TOGE–
KITA-HARAAA!
YEAH?
CAN YOU HELP ME UNZIP THIS?
THERE SHOULD BE A CORD YOU CAN PULL ON!

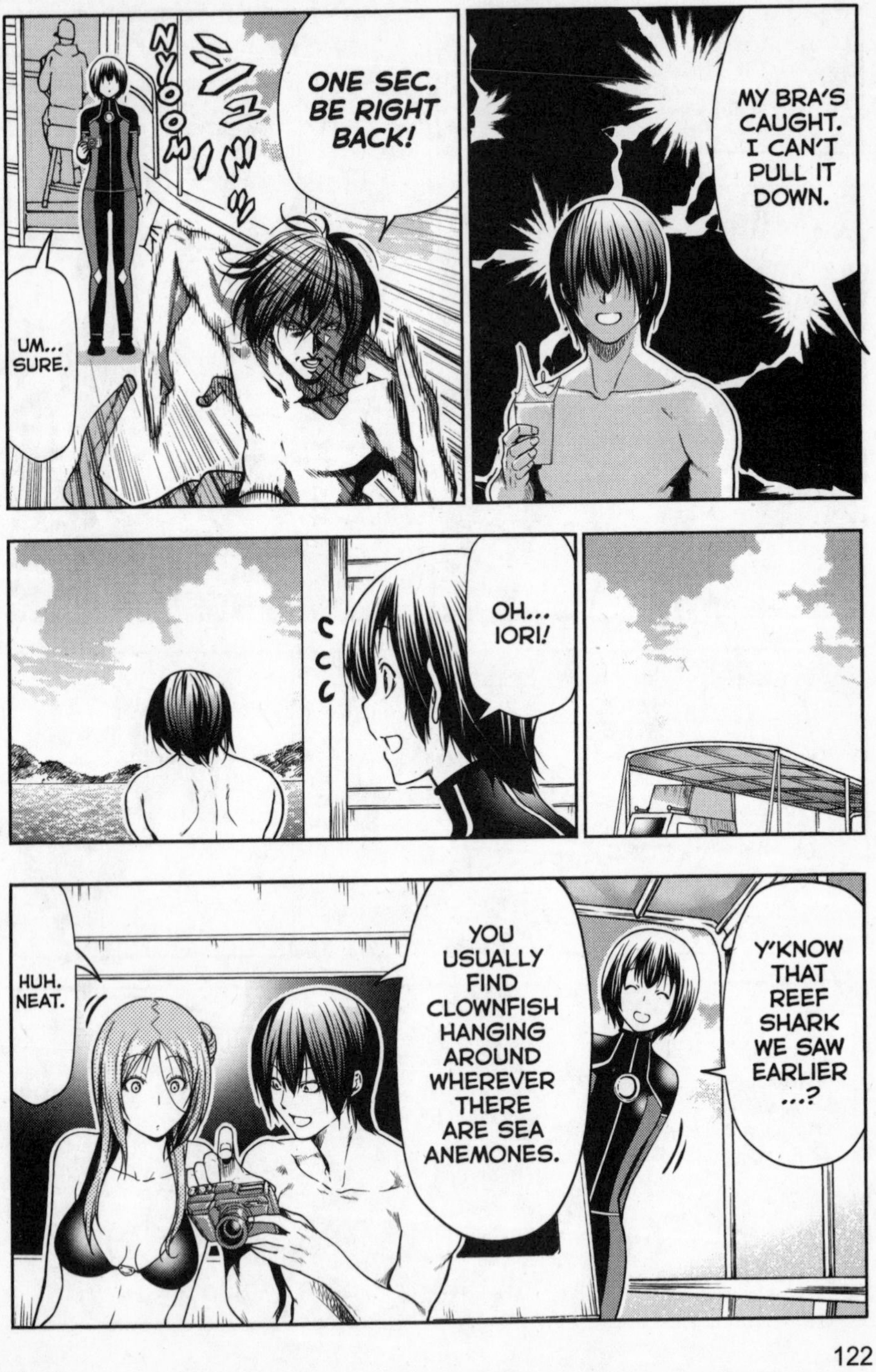
MY BRA'S CAUGHT. I CAN'T PULL IT DOWN.
ONE SEC. BE RIGHT BACK!
NYOOM
UM... SURE.
OH... IORI!
Y'KNOW THAT REEF SHARK WE SAW EARLIER ...?
YOU USUALLY FIND CLOWNFISH HANGING AROUND WHEREVER THERE ARE SEA ANEMONES.
HUH. NEAT.

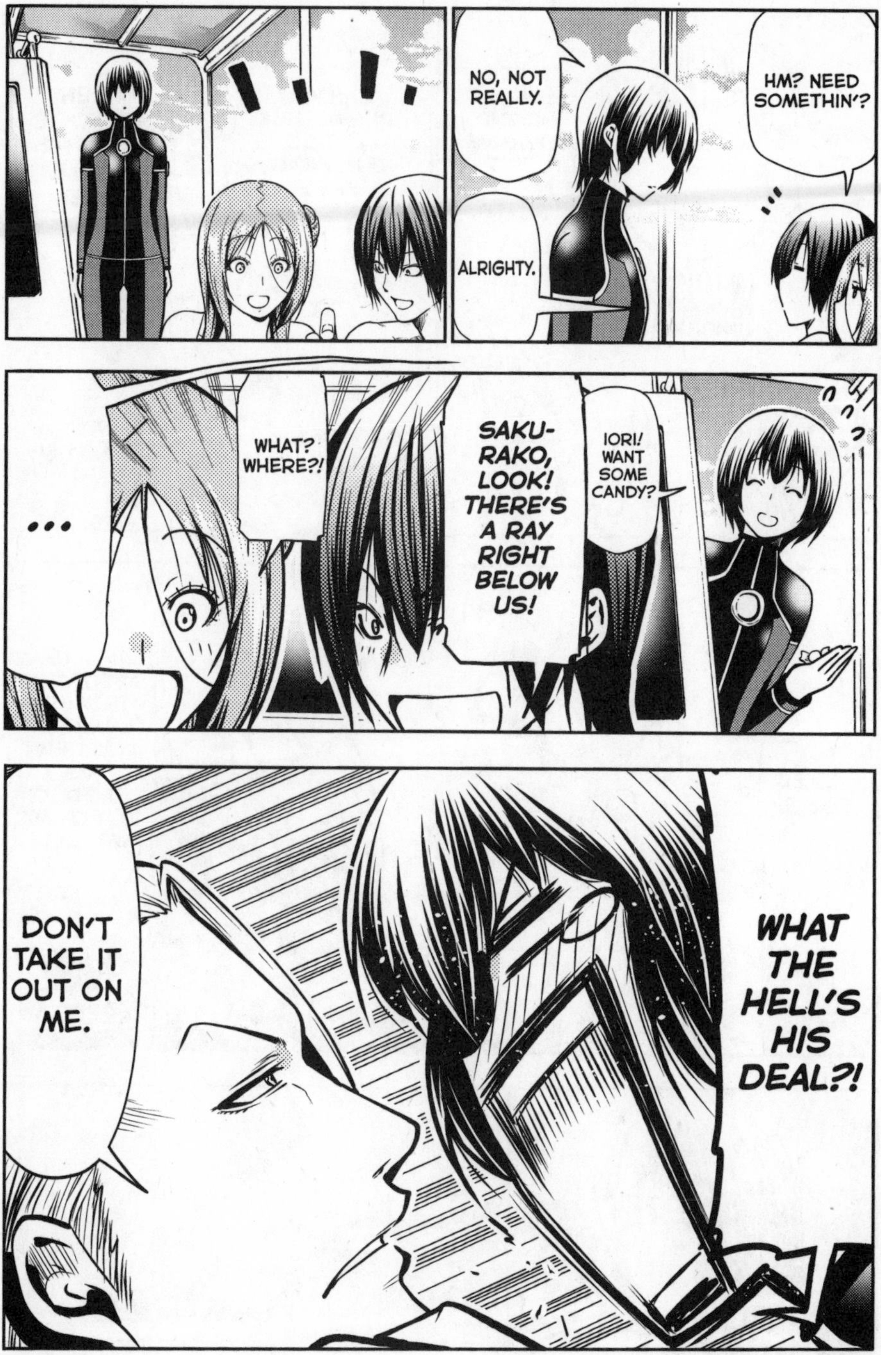
HM? NEED SOMETHIN'?
NO, NOT REALLY.
ALRIGHTY.
IORI! WANT SOME CANDY?
SAKU-RAKO, LOOK! THERE'S A RAY RIGHT BELOW US!
WHAT? WHERE?!
...
WHAT THE HELL'S HIS DEAL?!
DON'T TAKE IT OUT ON ME.

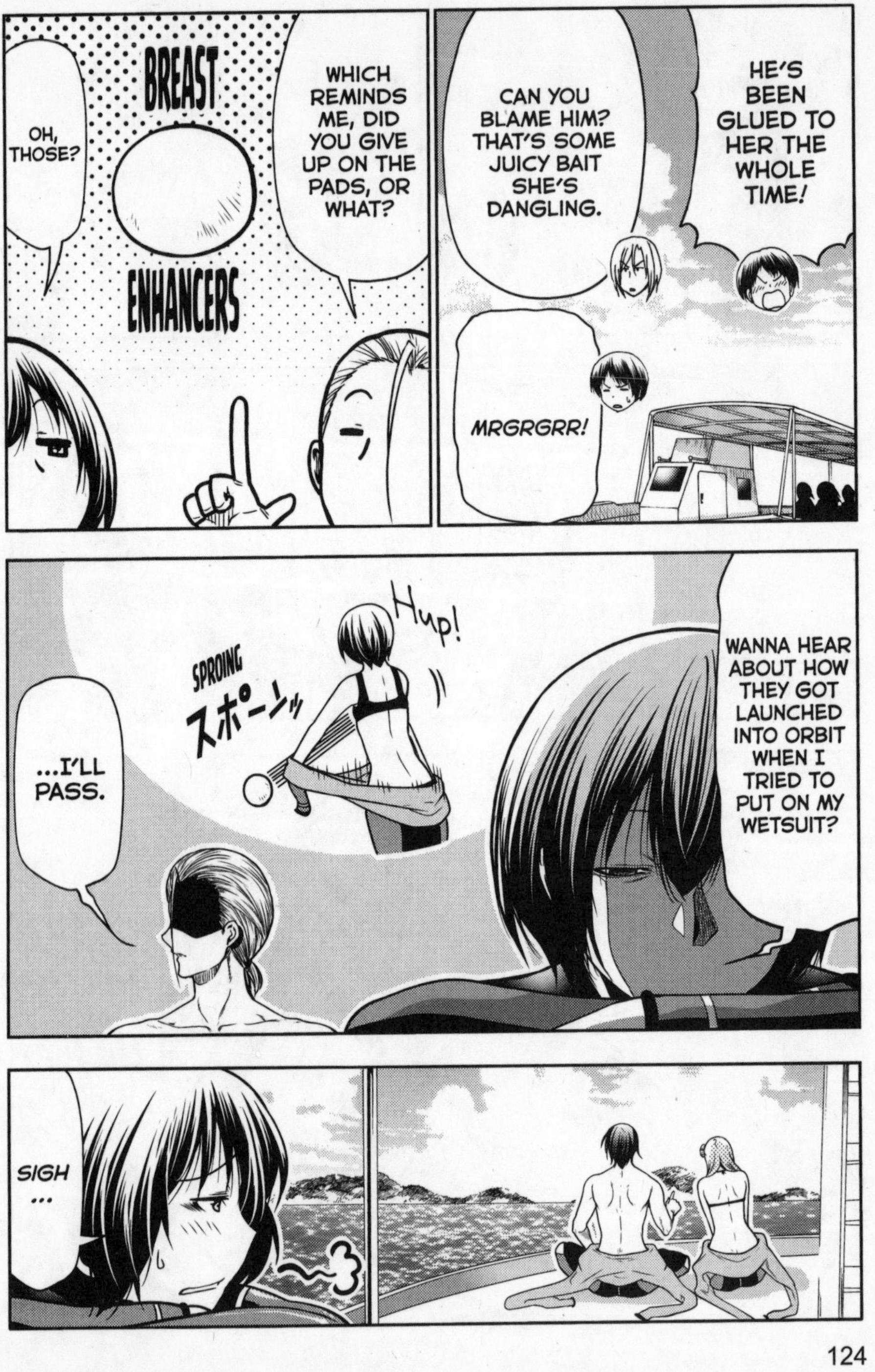
HE'S BEEN GLUED TO HER THE WHOLE TIME!
CAN YOU BLAME HIM? THAT'S SOME JUICY BAIT SHE'S DANGLING.
MRGRGRR!
WHICH REMINDS ME, DID YOU GIVE UP ON THE PADS, OR WHAT?
BREAST
ENHANCERS
OH, THOSE?
WANNA HEAR ABOUT HOW THEY GOT LAUNCHED INTO ORBIT WHEN I TRIED TO PUT ON MY WETSUIT?
Hup!
SPROING
スポーンッ
...I'LL PASS.
SIGH ...

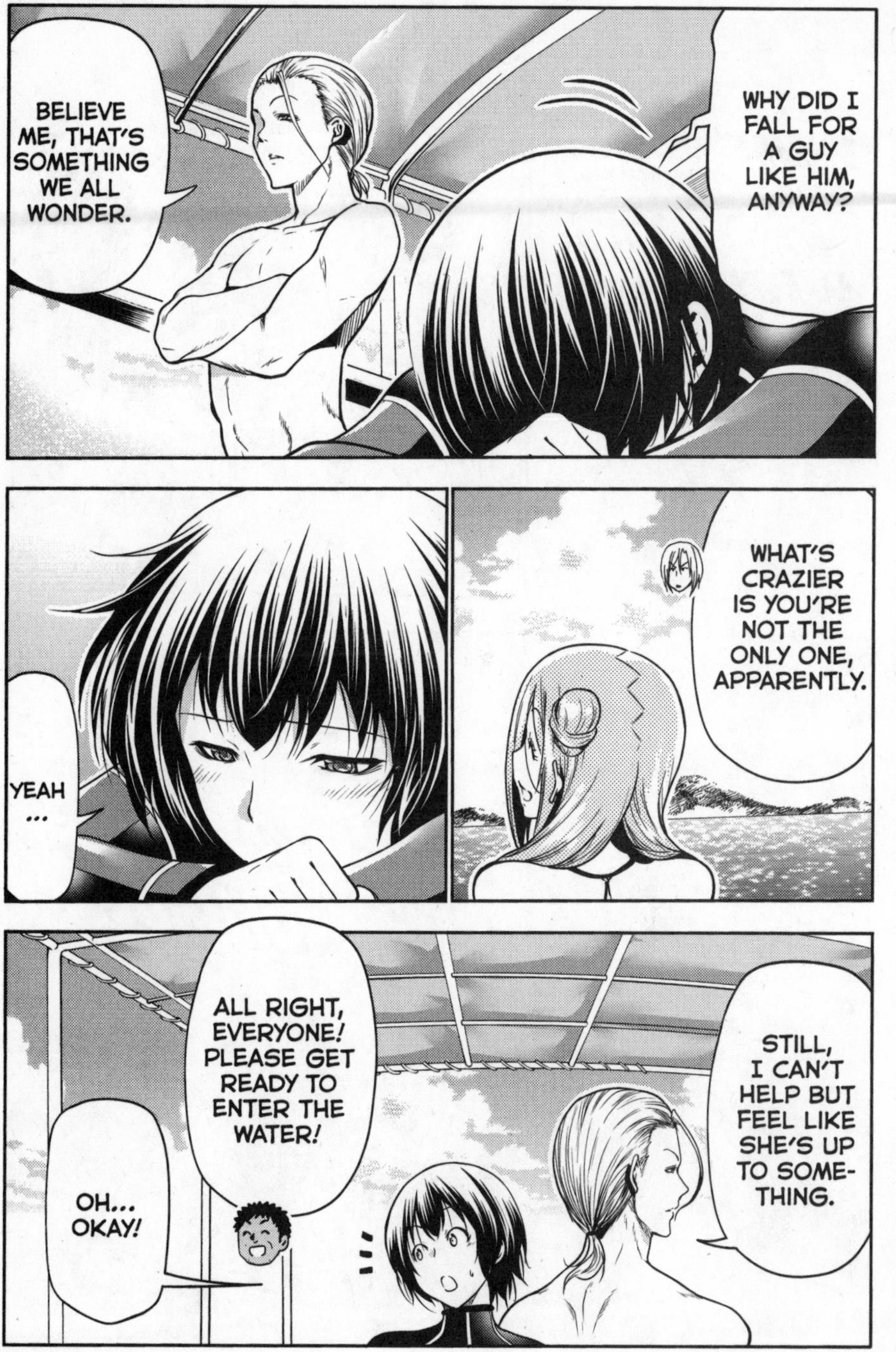
WHY DID I FALL FOR A GUY LIKE HIM, ANYWAY?
BELIEVE ME, THAT'S SOMETHING WE ALL WONDER.
WHAT'S CRAZIER IS YOU'RE NOT THE ONLY ONE, APPARENTLY.
YEAH ...
STILL, I CAN'T HELP BUT FEEL LIKE SHE'S UP TO SOME-THING.
ALL RIGHT, EVERYONE! PLEASE GET READY TO ENTER THE WATER!
OH... OKAY!

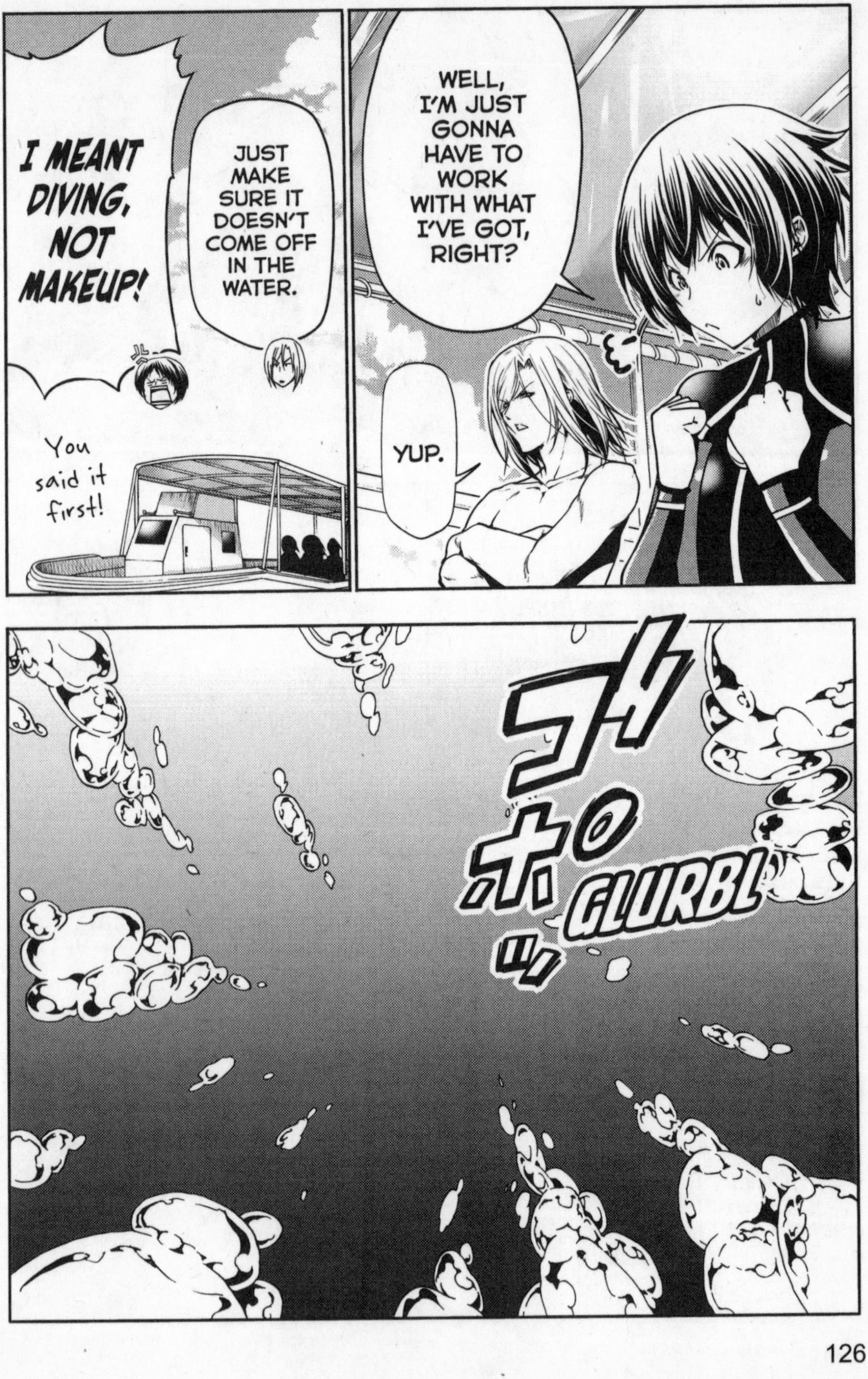
WELL, I'M JUST GONNA HAVE TO WORK WITH WHAT I'VE GOT, RIGHT?
YUP.
JUST MAKE SURE IT DOESN'T COME OFF IN THE WATER.
I MEANT DIVING, NOT MAKEUP!
You said it first!
ゴポッ
GLURBL

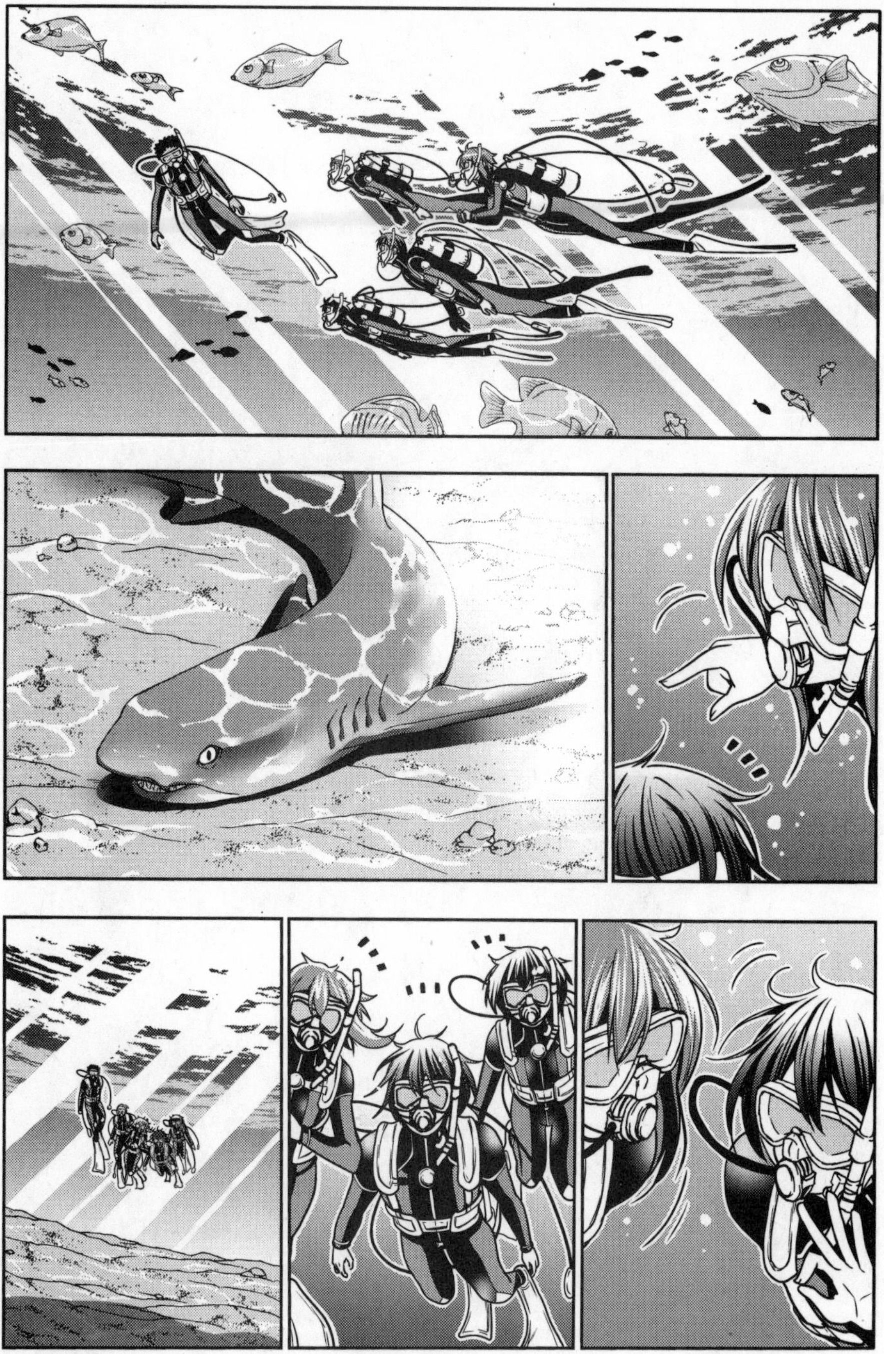
...
...
...
...

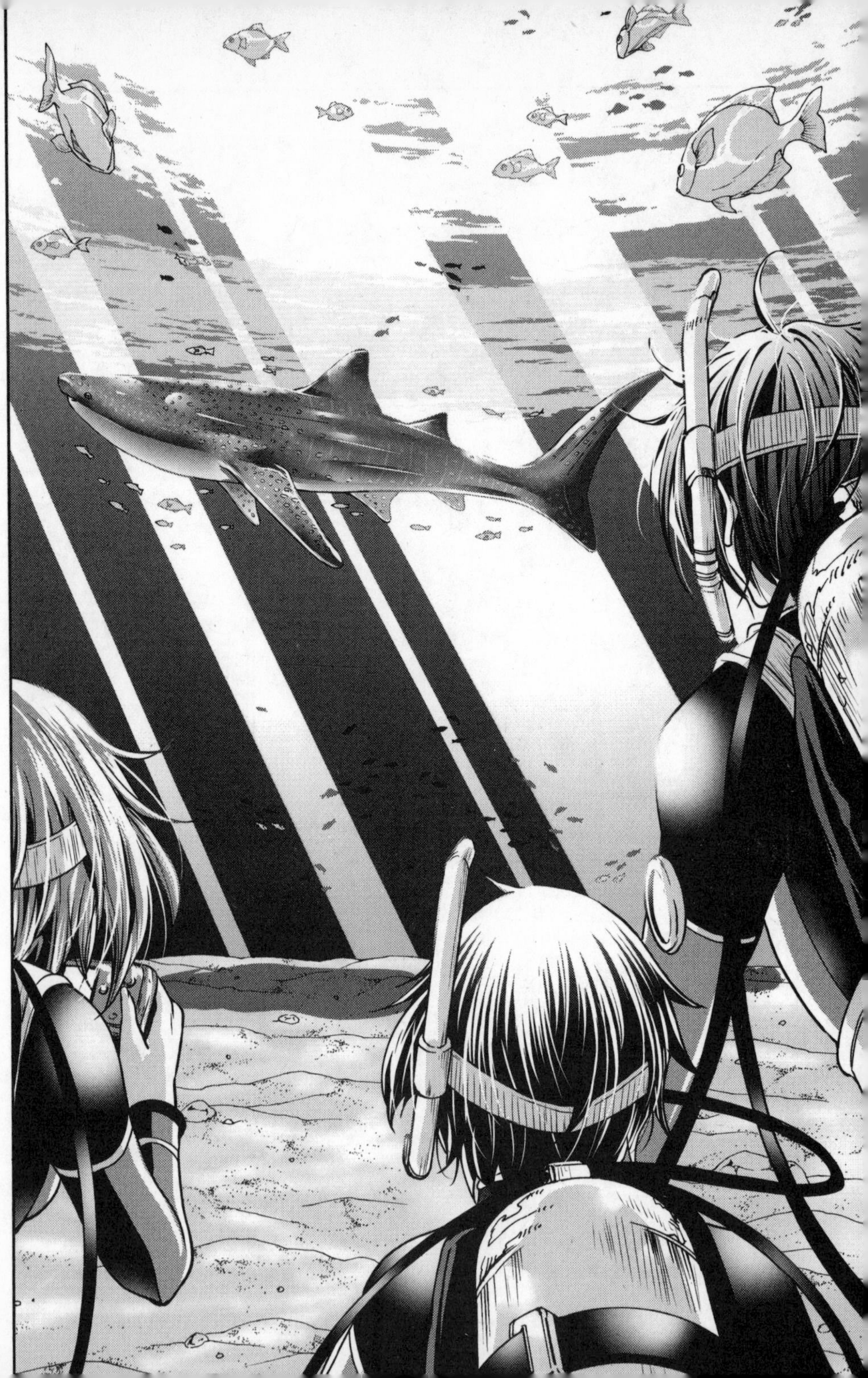

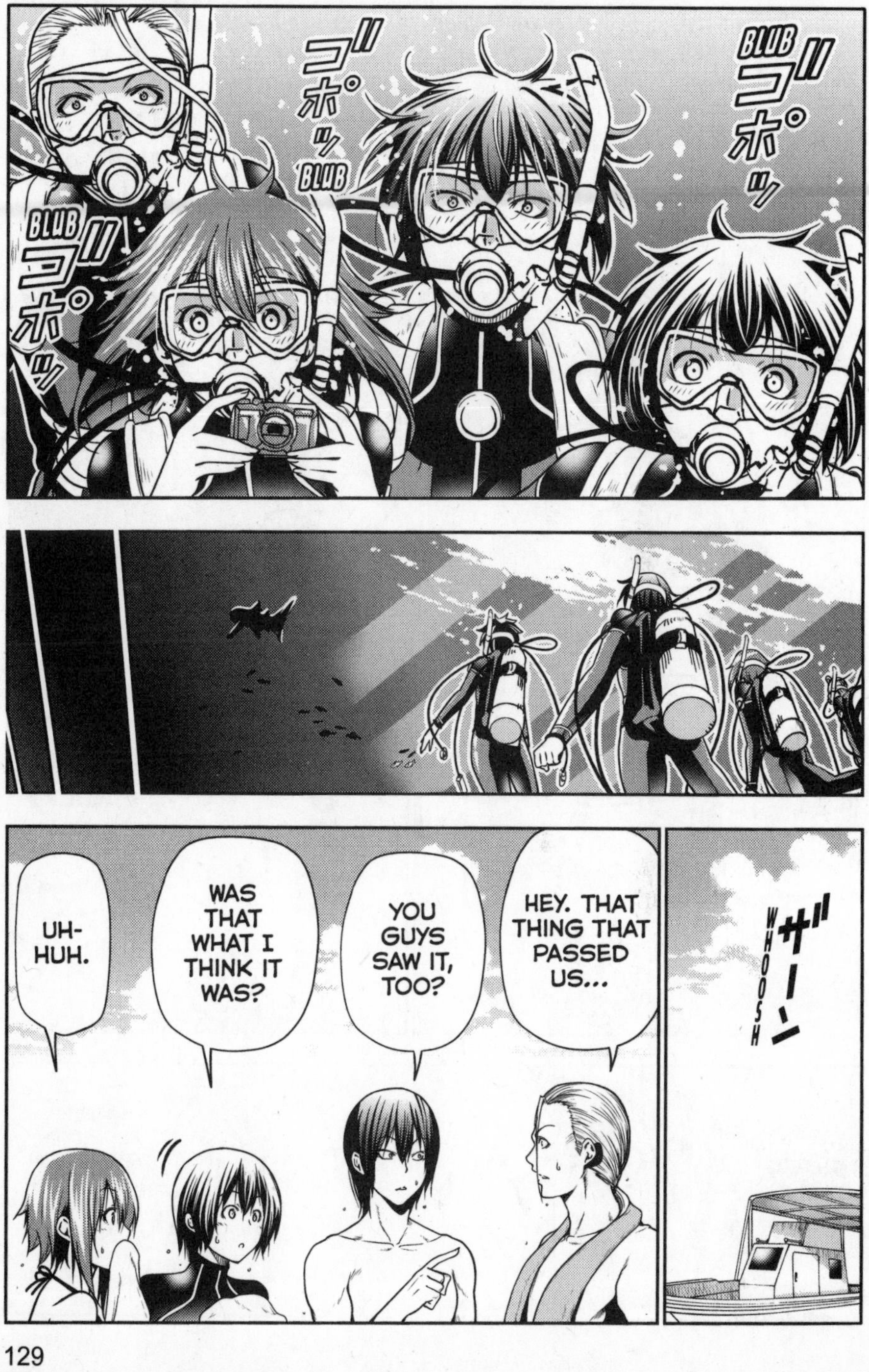
BLUB
ゴポッ
ゴポッ
BLUB
BLUB
ゴポッ
ザーン
WHOOSH
HEY. THAT THING THAT PASSED US...
YOU GUYS SAW IT, TOO?
WAS THAT WHAT I THINK IT WAS?
UH-HUH.

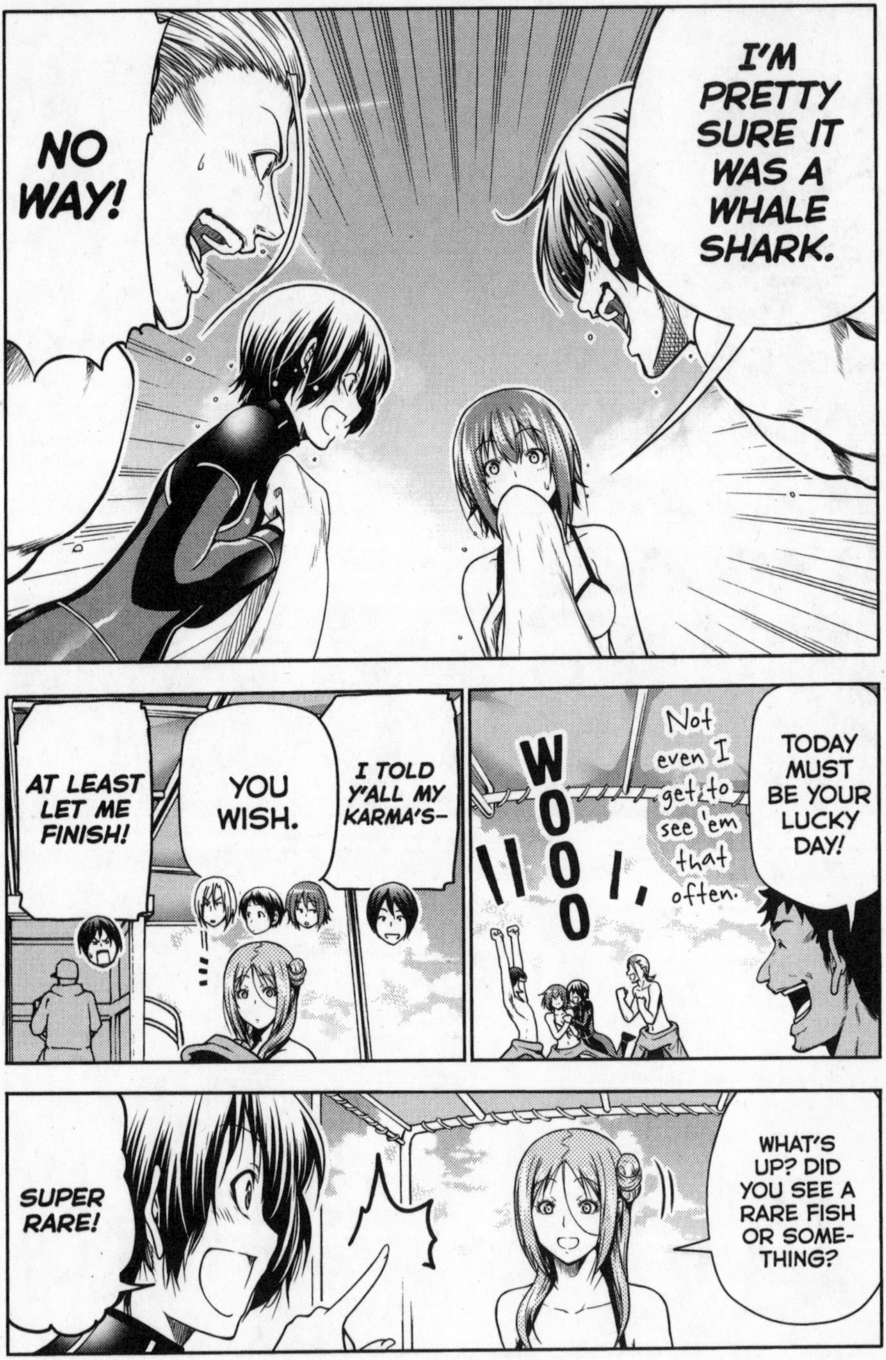
I'M PRETTY SURE IT WAS A WHALE SHARK.
NO WAY!
TODAY MUST BE YOUR LUCKY DAY!
Not even I get to see 'em that often.
WOOO!!
I TOLD Y'ALL MY KARMA'S–
YOU WISH.
AT LEAST LET ME FINISH!
WHAT'S UP? DID YOU SEE A RARE FISH OR SOME-THING?
SUPER RARE!

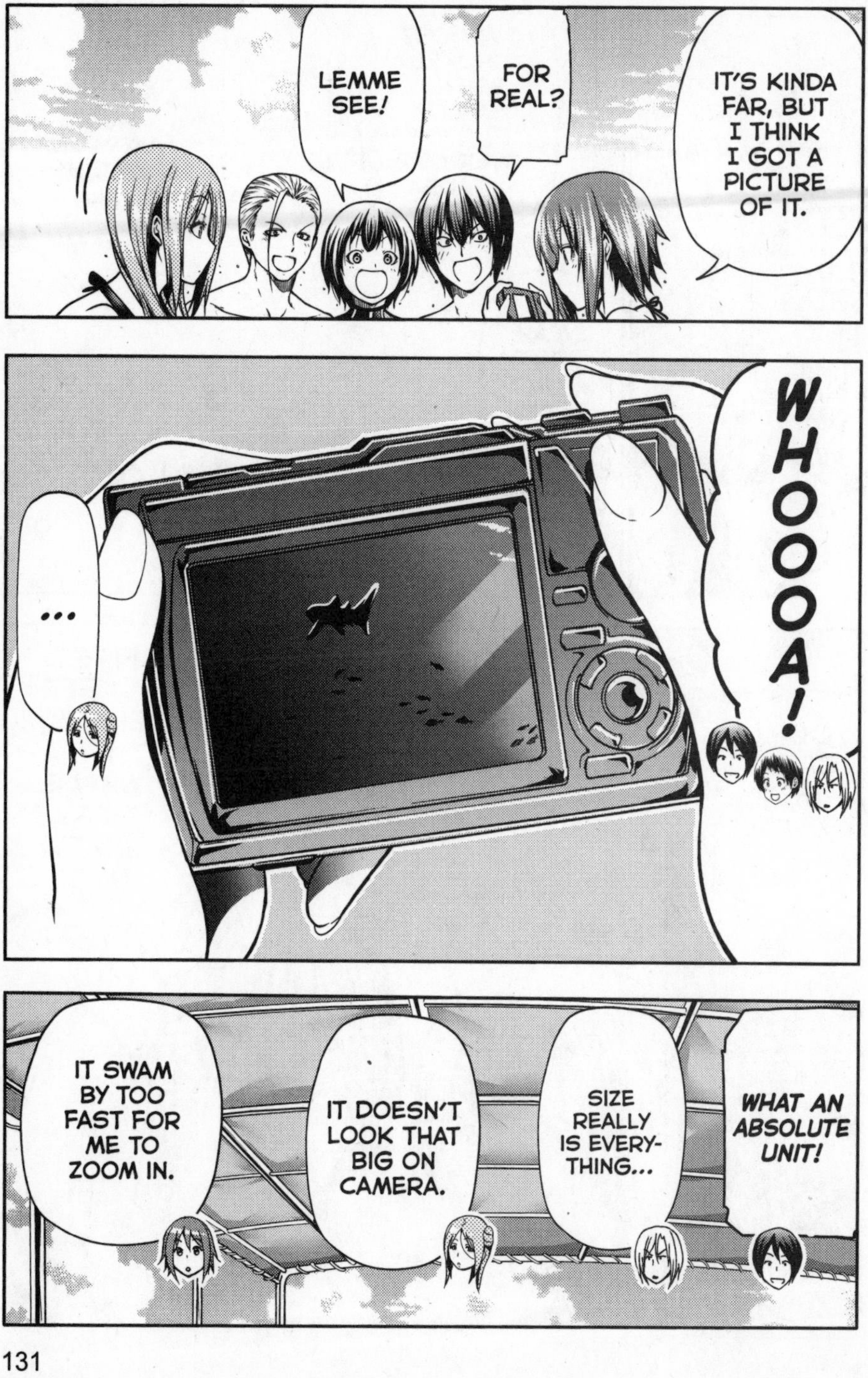
IT'S KINDA FAR, BUT I THINK I GOT A PICTURE OF IT.
FOR REAL?
LEMME SEE!
WHOOOA!
...
WHAT AN ABSOLUTE UNIT!
SIZE REALLY IS EVERY-THING...
IT DOESN'T LOOK THAT BIG ON CAMERA.
IT SWAM BY TOO FAST FOR ME TO ZOOM IN.

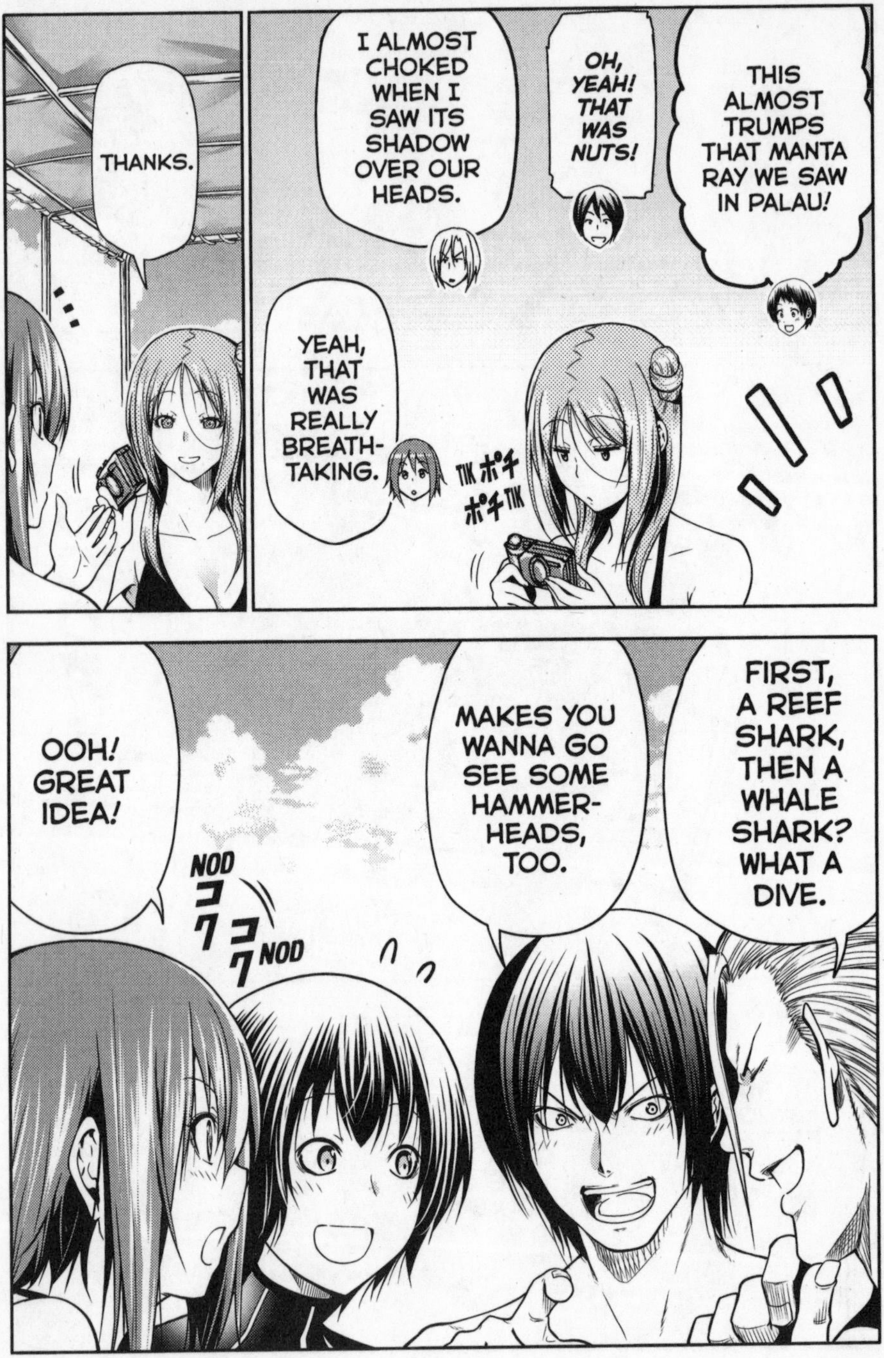
THIS ALMOST TRUMPS THAT MANTA RAY WE SAW IN PALAU!
OH, YEAH! THAT WAS NUTS!
I ALMOST CHOKED WHEN I SAW ITS SHADOW OVER OUR HEADS.
!!
TIK ポチ
ポチ TIK
YEAH, THAT WAS REALLY BREATH-TAKING.
THANKS.
...
FIRST, A REEF SHARK, THEN A WHALE SHARK? WHAT A DIVE.
MAKES YOU WANNA GO SEE SOME HAMMER-HEADS, TOO.
NOD コク
コク NOD
OOH! GREAT IDEA!

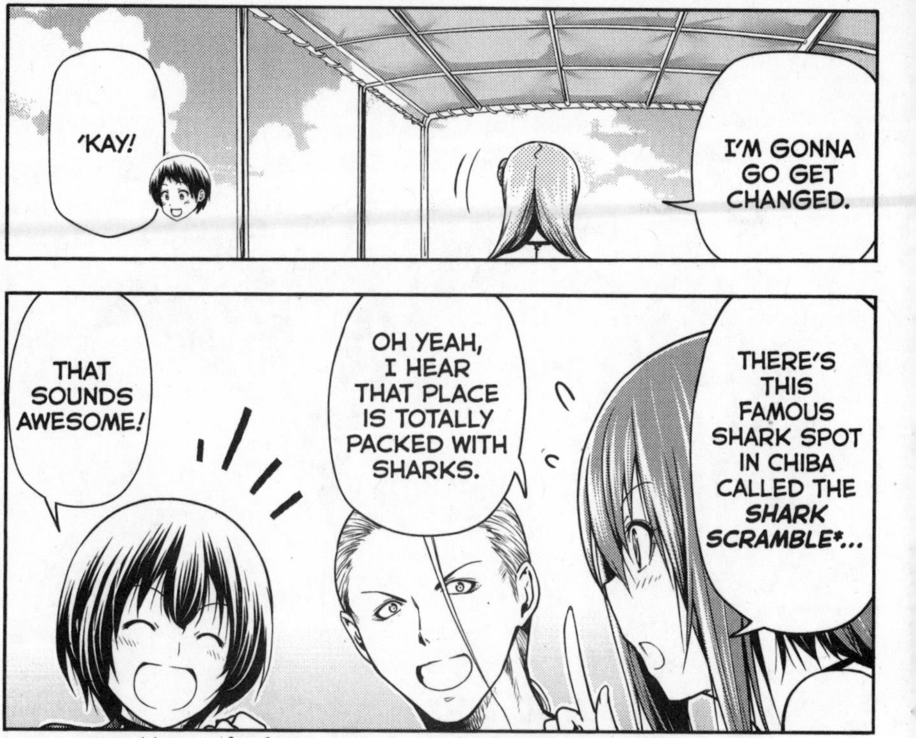
I'M GONNA GO GET CHANGED.
'KAY!
THERE'S THIS FAMOUS SHARK SPOT IN CHIBA CALLED THE *SHARK SCRAMBLE**...
OH YEAH, I HEAR THAT PLACE IS TOTALLY PACKED WITH SHARKS.
THAT SOUNDS AWESOME!

*A type of pedestrian crossing, such as the notoriously busy crossing in Shibuya.

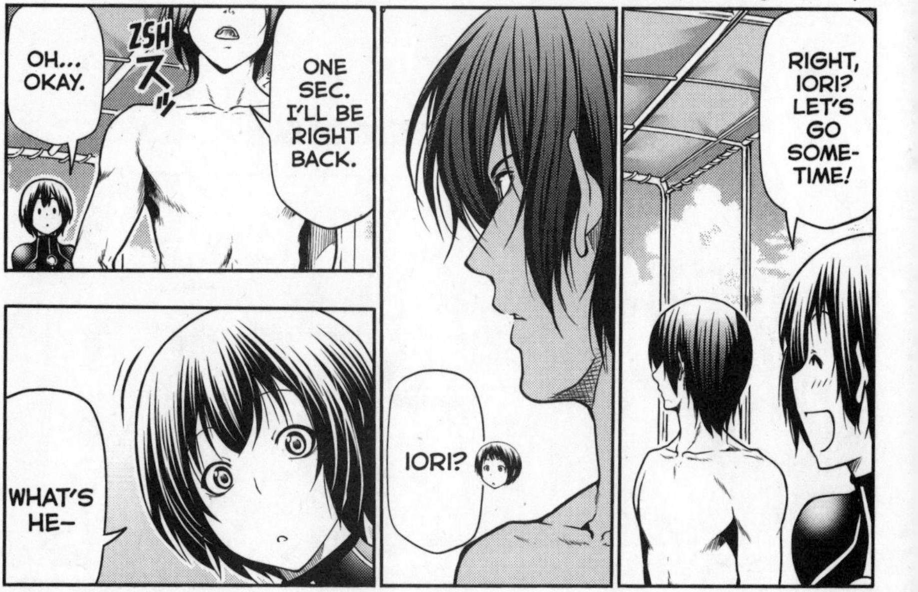
RIGHT, IORI? LET'S GO SOME-TIME!
IORI?
ONE SEC. I'LL BE RIGHT BACK.
ZSH
OH... OKAY.
WHAT'S HE–

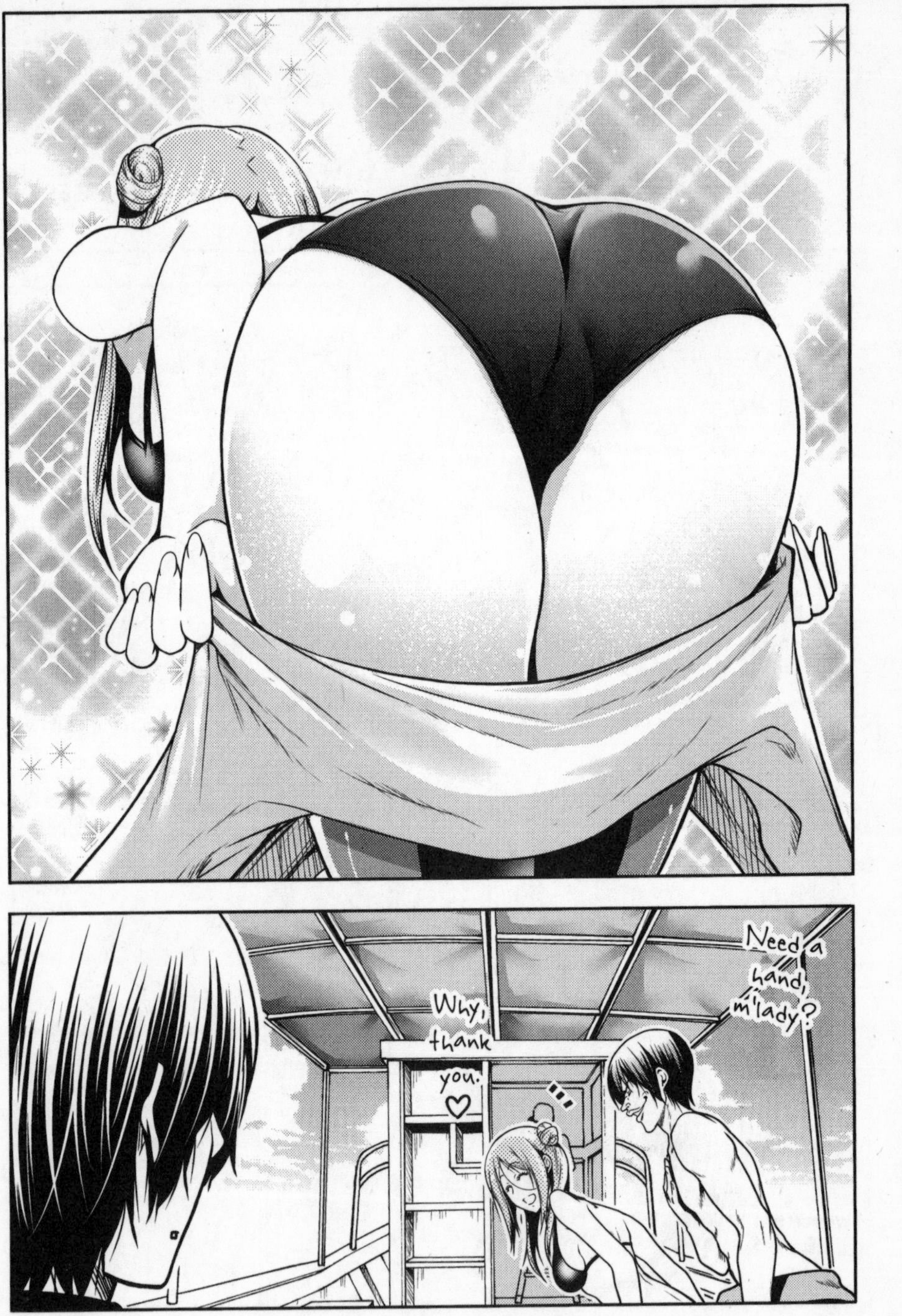
Need a hand, m'lady?
Why, thank you. ♡

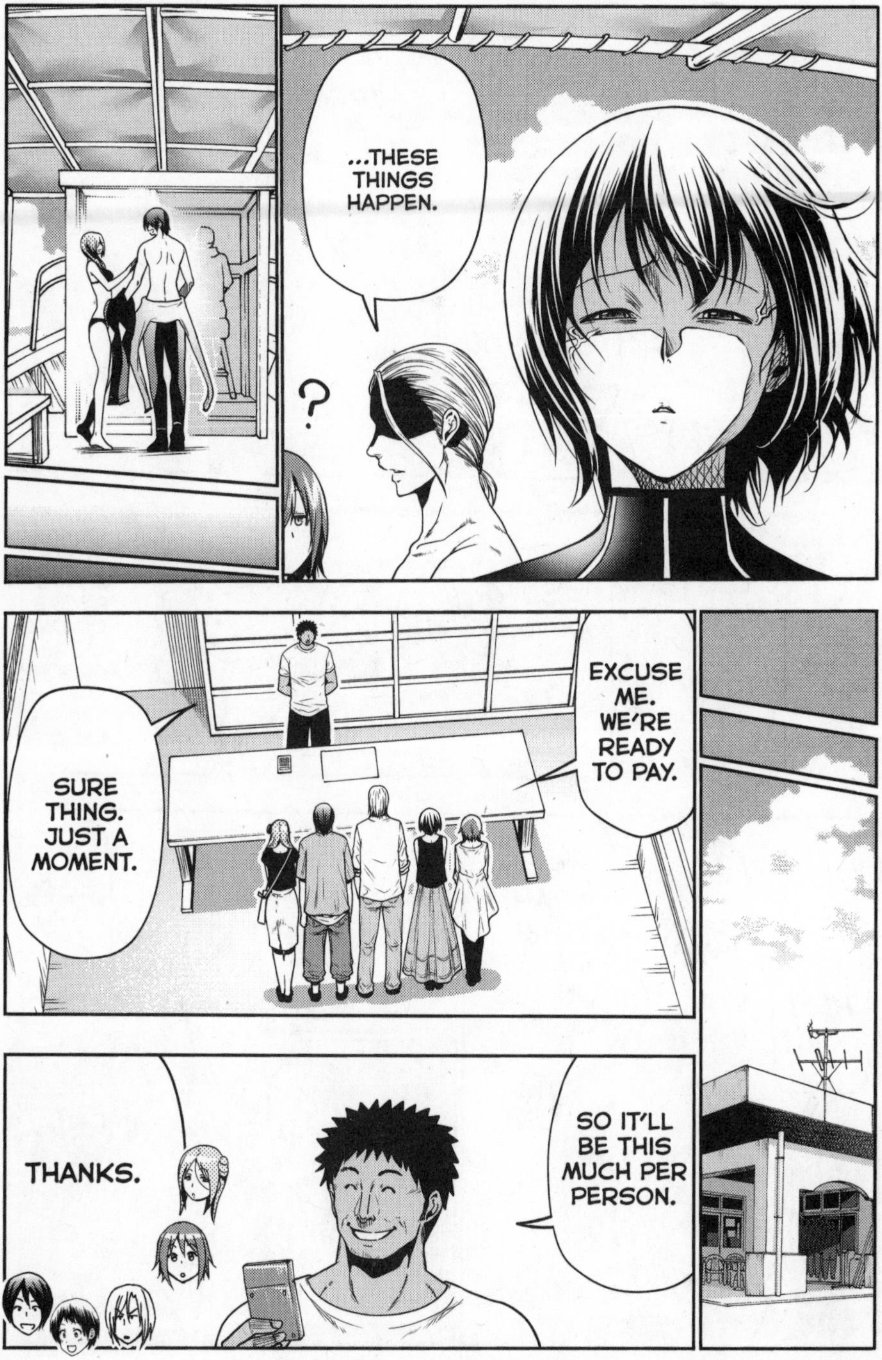
...THESE THINGS HAPPEN.
?
EXCUSE ME. WE'RE READY TO PAY.
SURE THING. JUST A MOMENT.
SO IT'LL BE THIS MUCH PER PERSON.
THANKS.

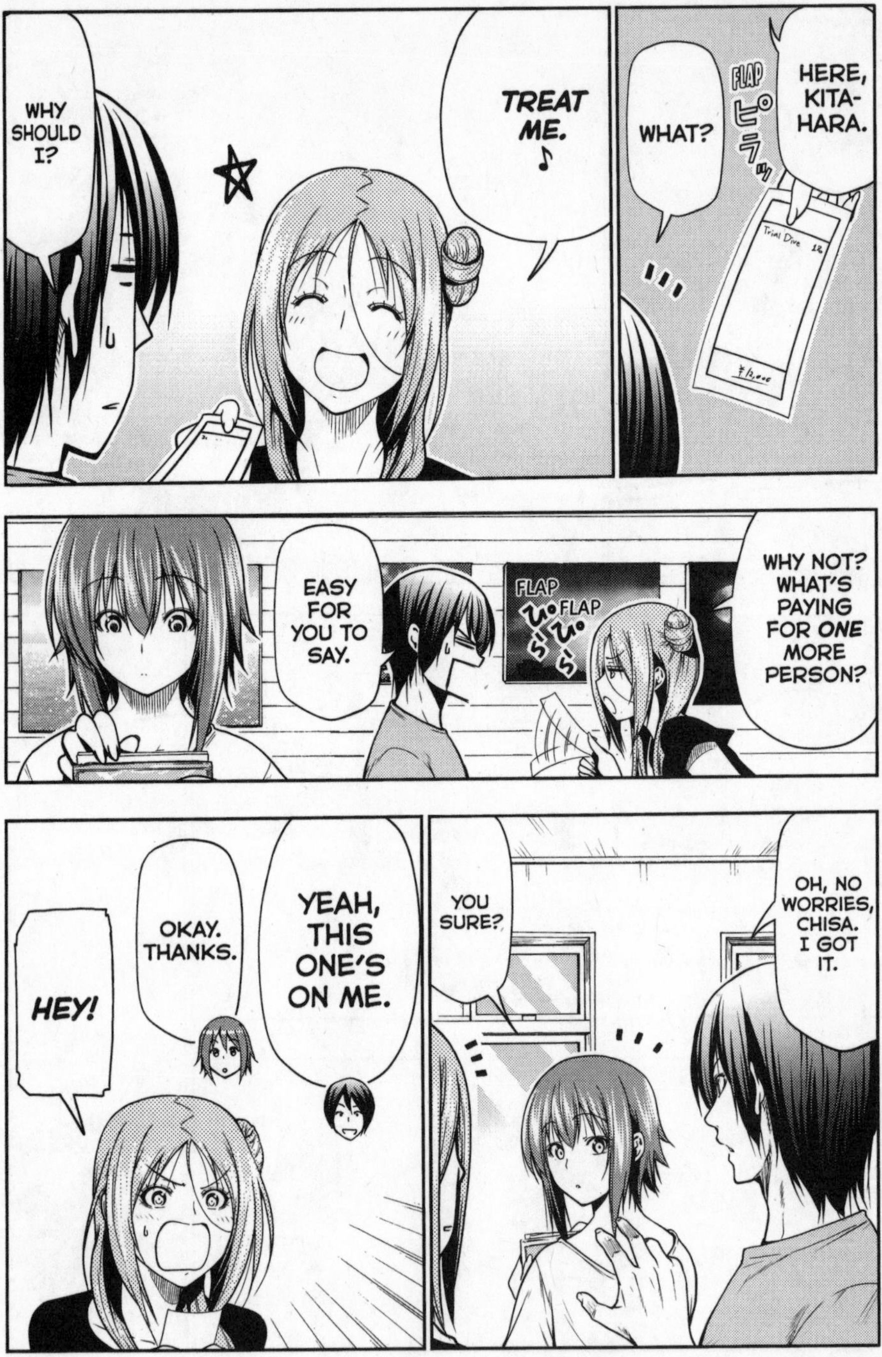

HERE, KITA-HARA.
FLAP ピラッ
WHAT?
TREAT ME. ♪
WHY SHOULD I?
WHY NOT? WHAT'S PAYING FOR ONE MORE PERSON?
FLAP ひら FLAP ひら
EASY FOR YOU TO SAY.
OH, NO WORRIES, CHISA. I GOT IT.
YOU SURE?
YEAH, THIS ONE'S ON ME.
OKAY. THANKS.
HEY!

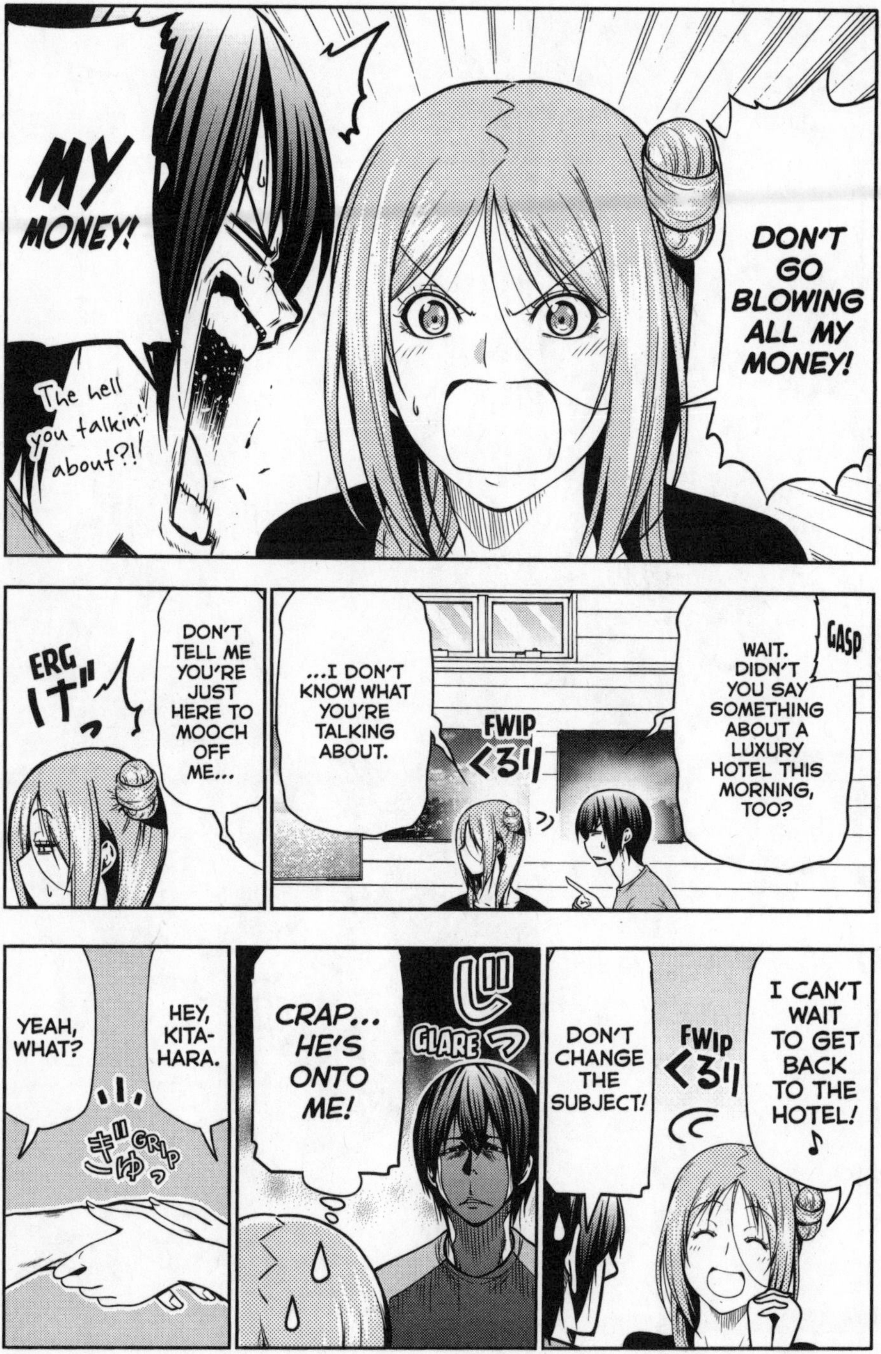

DON'T GO BLOWING ALL MY MONEY!
MY MONEY!
The hell you talkin' about?!
GASP
WAIT. DIDN'T YOU SAY SOMETHING ABOUT A LUXURY HOTEL THIS MORNING, TOO?
FWIP くるり
...I DON'T KNOW WHAT YOU'RE TALKING ABOUT.
DON'T TELL ME YOU'RE JUST HERE TO MOOCH OFF ME...
ERG げっ
I CAN'T WAIT TO GET BACK TO THE HOTEL! ♪
FWIP くるり
DON'T CHANGE THE SUBJECT!
じーっ
GLARE
CRAP... HE'S ONTO ME!
HEY, KITA-HARA.
YEAH, WHAT?
ぎゅっ GRIP

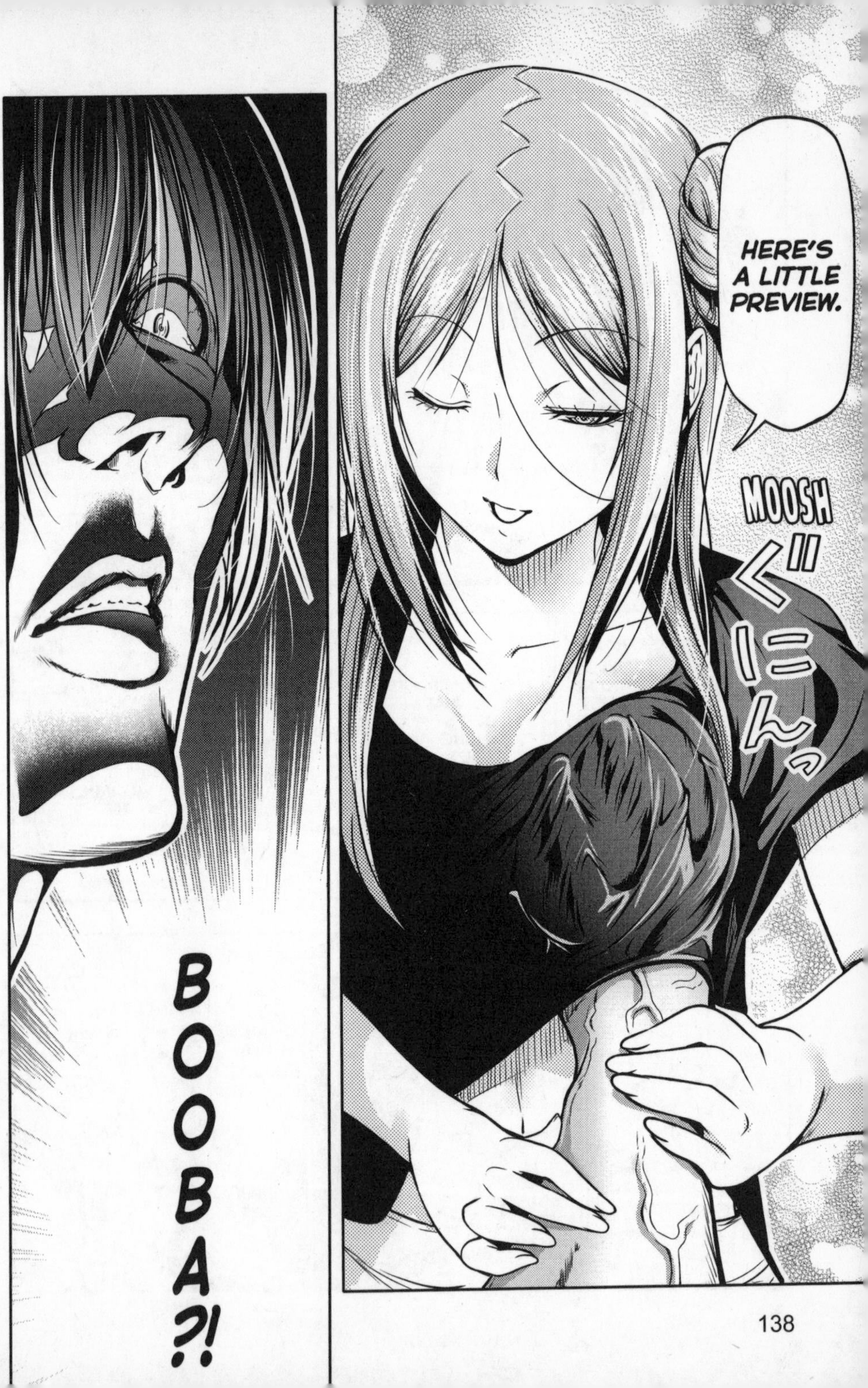
HERE'S A LITTLE PREVIEW.
MOOSH
ぐにんっ
BOOBA?!

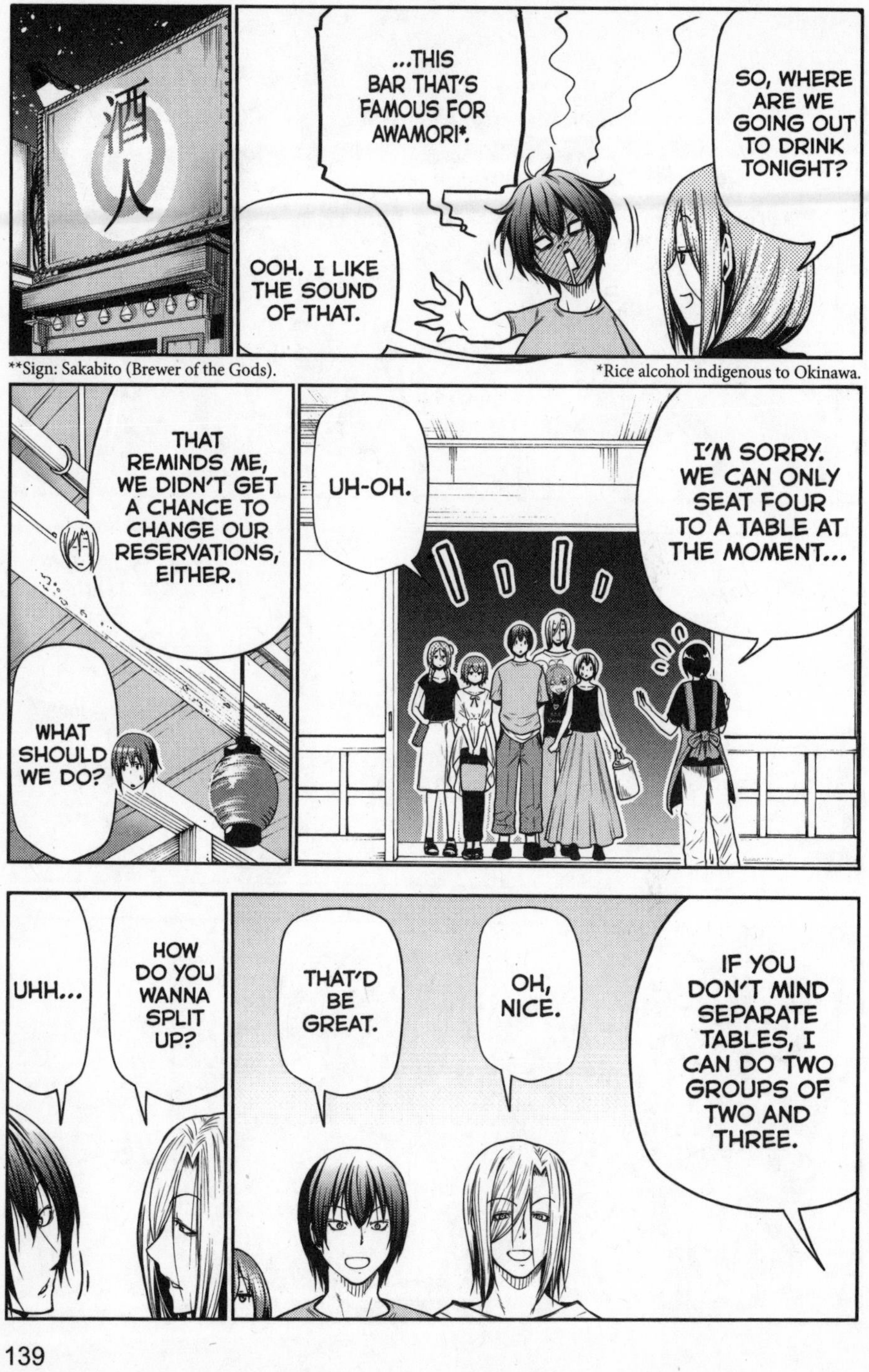
SO, WHERE ARE WE GOING OUT TO DRINK TONIGHT?
...THIS BAR THAT'S FAMOUS FOR AWAMORI*.
OOH. I LIKE THE SOUND OF THAT.
酒人
I'M SORRY. WE CAN ONLY SEAT FOUR TO A TABLE AT THE MOMENT...
UH-OH.
THAT REMINDS ME, WE DIDN'T GET A CHANCE TO CHANGE OUR RESERVATIONS, EITHER.
WHAT SHOULD WE DO?
IF YOU DON'T MIND SEPARATE TABLES, I CAN DO TWO GROUPS OF TWO AND THREE.
OH, NICE.
THAT'D BE GREAT.
HOW DO YOU WANNA SPLIT UP?
UHH...
*Rice alcohol indigenous to Okinawa.

**Sign: Sakabito (Brewer of the Gods).

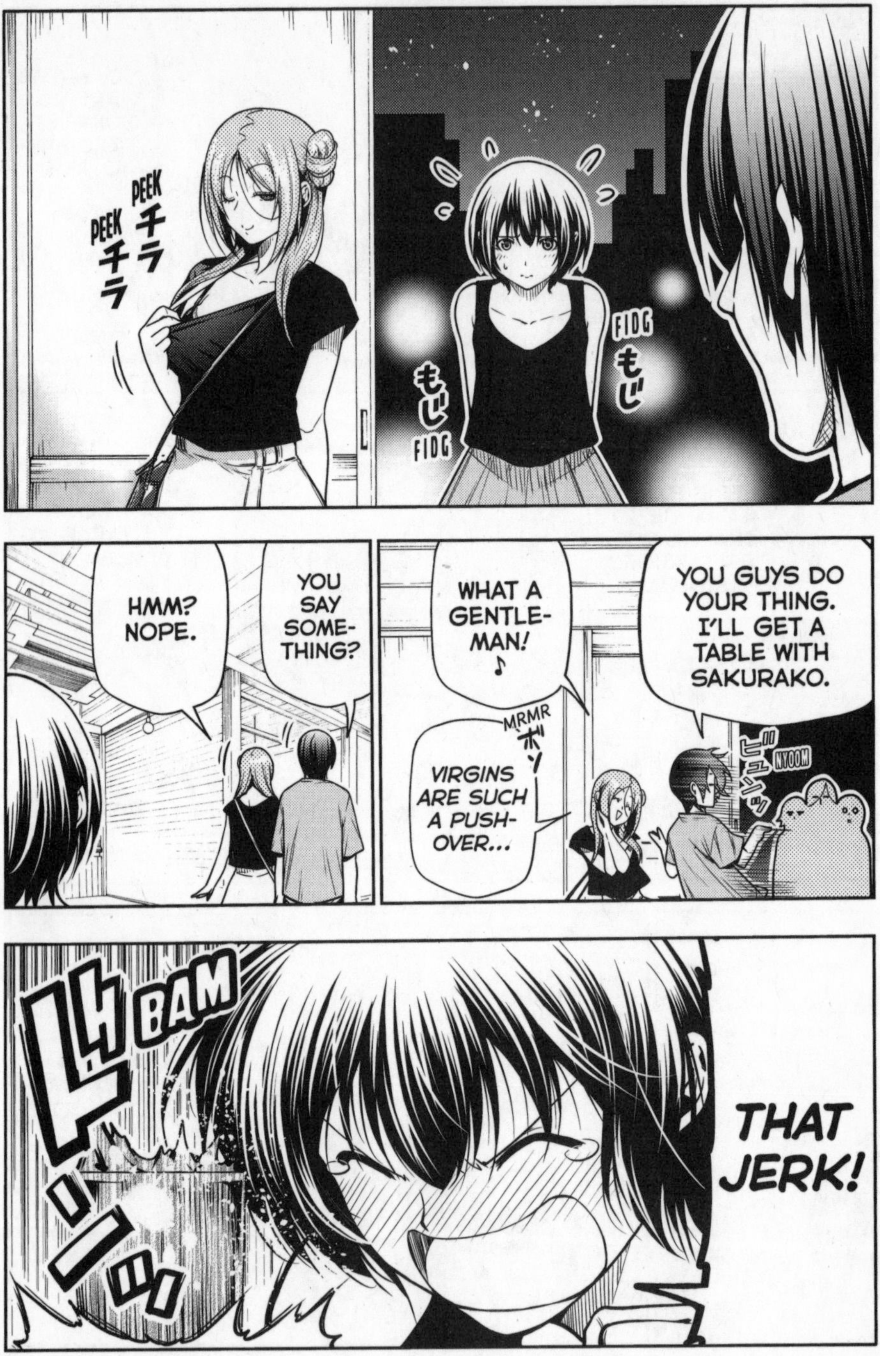
FIDG もじ
もじ FIDG
PEEK チラ
PEEK チラ
YOU GUYS DO YOUR THING. I'LL GET A TABLE WITH SAKURAKO.
ビュンッ NYOOM
WHAT A GENTLEMAN! ♪
MRMR ボソ
VIRGINS ARE SUCH A PUSHOVER...
YOU SAY SOMETHING?
HMM? NOPE.
ドンッ!! BAM
THAT JERK!

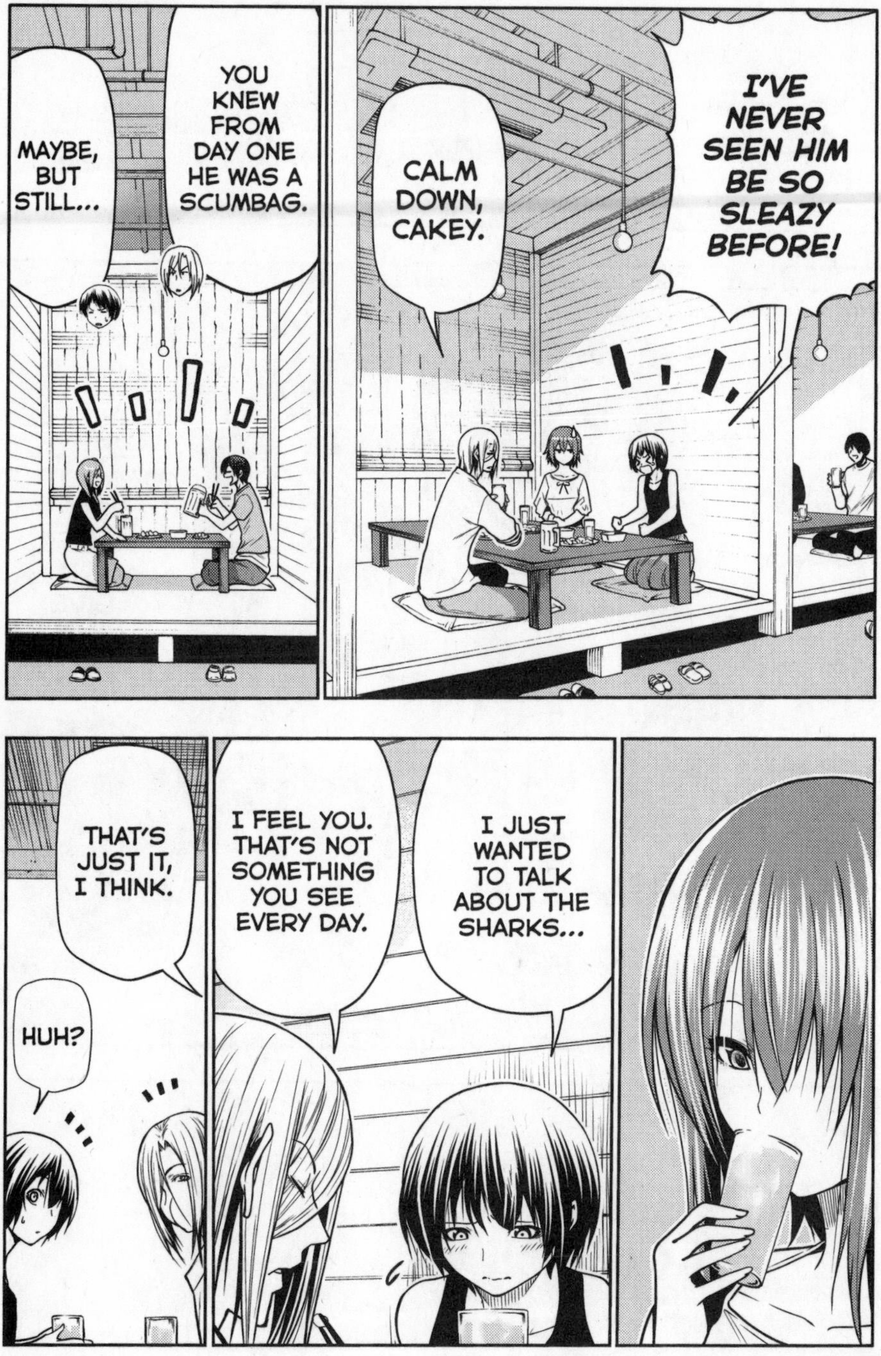
I'VE NEVER SEEN HIM BE SO SLEAZY BEFORE!
CALM DOWN, CAKEY.
YOU KNEW FROM DAY ONE HE WAS A SCUMBAG.
MAYBE, BUT STILL...
I JUST WANTED TO TALK ABOUT THE SHARKS...
I FEEL YOU. THAT'S NOT SOMETHING YOU SEE EVERY DAY.
THAT'S JUST IT, I THINK.
HUH?

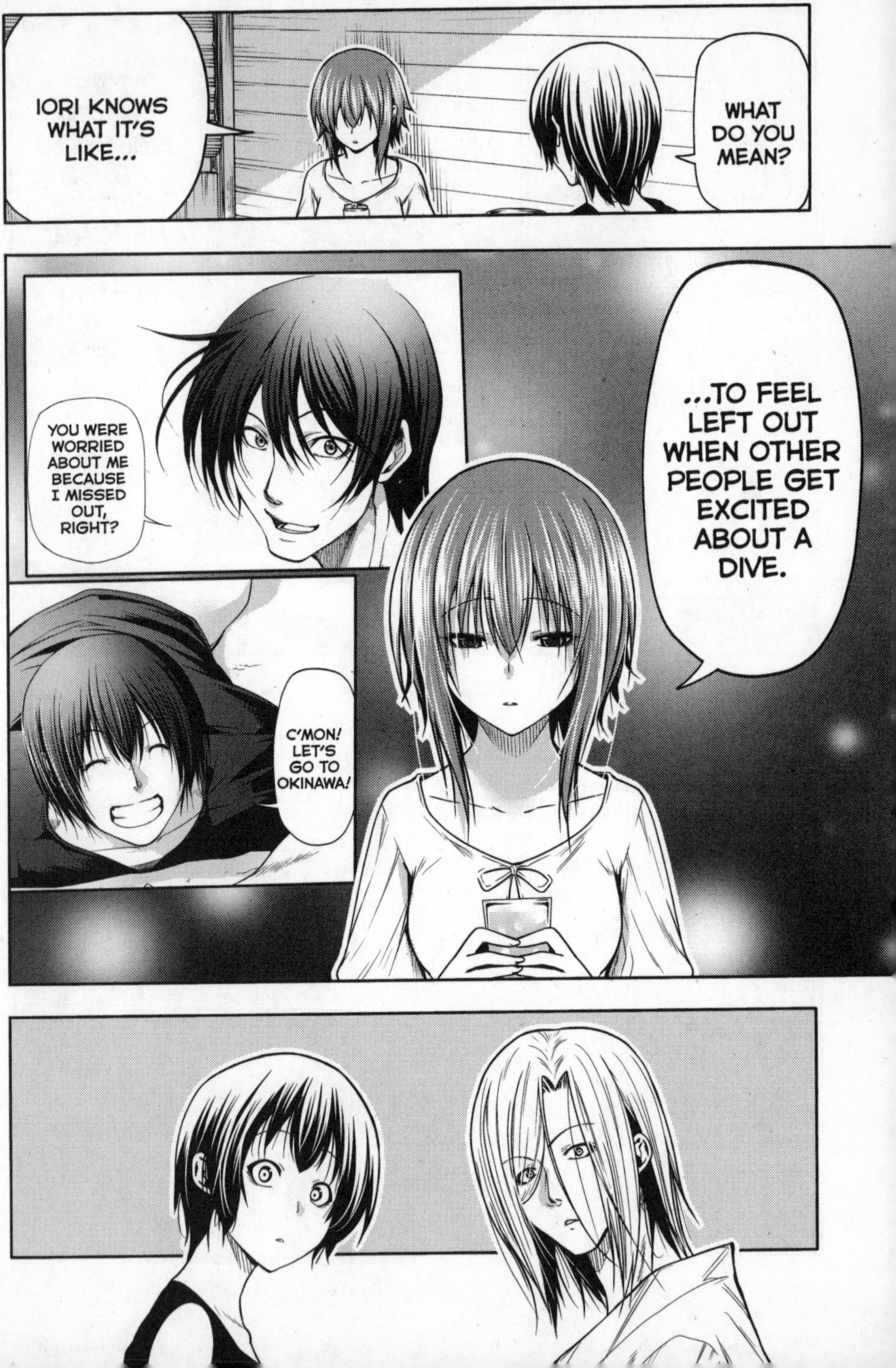
WHAT DO YOU MEAN?
IORI KNOWS WHAT IT'S LIKE...
...TO FEEL LEFT OUT WHEN OTHER PEOPLE GET EXCITED ABOUT A DIVE.
YOU WERE WORRIED ABOUT ME BECAUSE I MISSED OUT, RIGHT?
C'MON! LET'S GO TO OKINAWA!

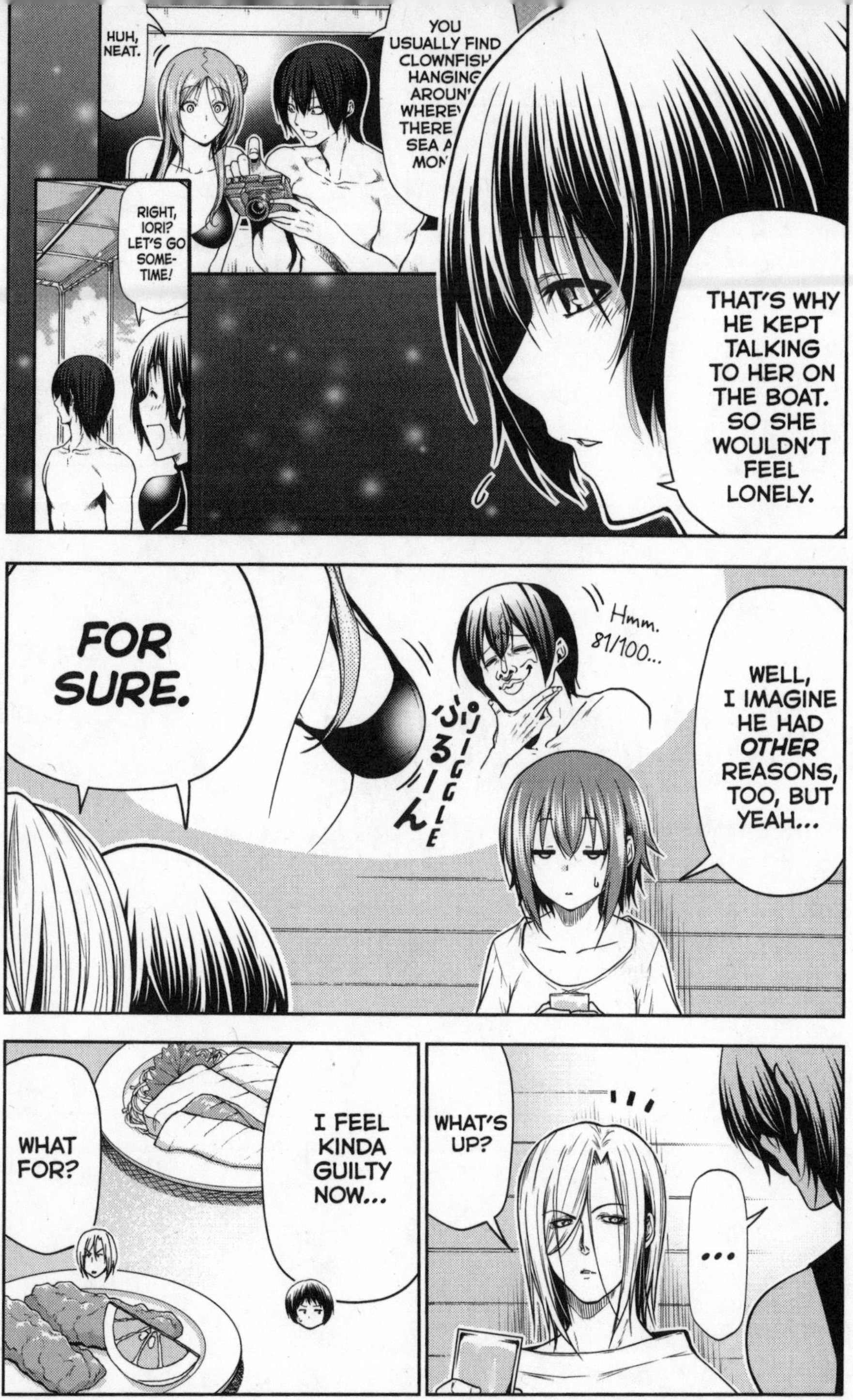
THAT'S WHY HE KEPT TALKING TO HER ON THE BOAT. SO SHE WOULDN'T FEEL LONELY.
YOU USUALLY FIND CLOWNFISH HANGING AROUN WHEREV THERE SEA A MON
HUH, NEAT.
RIGHT, IORI? LET'S GO SOME-TIME!
WELL, I IMAGINE HE HAD *OTHER* REASONS, TOO, BUT YEAH...
Hmm. 81/100...
ぷるーん
JIGGLE
FOR SURE.
WHAT'S UP?
...
I FEEL KINDA GUILTY NOW...
WHAT FOR?

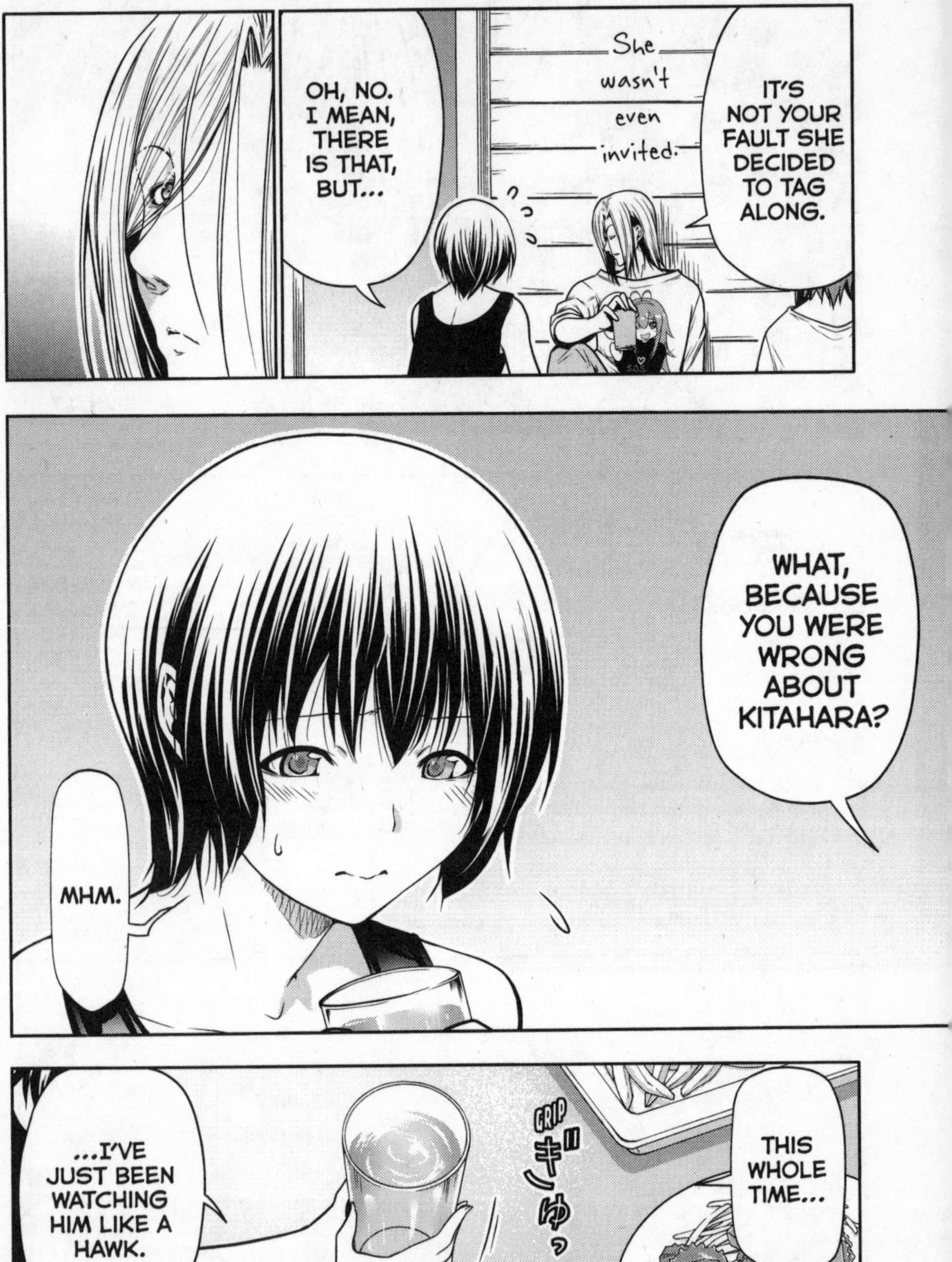
IT'S NOT YOUR FAULT SHE DECIDED TO TAG ALONG.
She wasn't even invited.
OH, NO. I MEAN, THERE IS THAT, BUT...
WHAT, BECAUSE YOU WERE WRONG ABOUT KITAHARA?
MHM.
THIS WHOLE TIME...
GRIP
...I'VE JUST BEEN WATCHING HIM LIKE A HAWK.

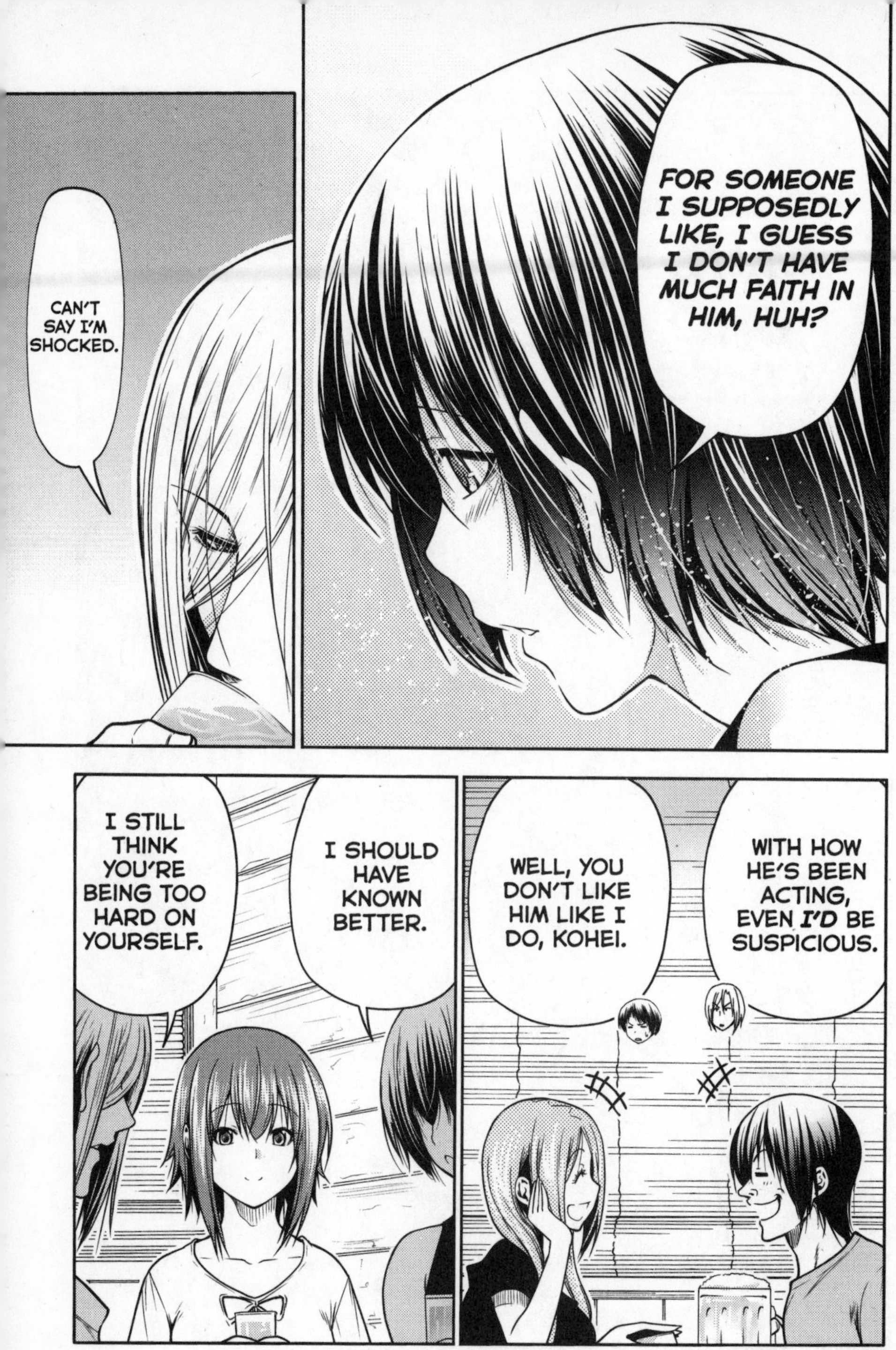
FOR SOMEONE I SUPPOSEDLY LIKE, I GUESS I DON'T HAVE MUCH FAITH IN HIM, HUH?
CAN'T SAY I'M SHOCKED.
WITH HOW HE'S BEEN ACTING, EVEN *I'D* BE SUSPICIOUS.
WELL, YOU DON'T LIKE HIM LIKE I DO, KOHEI.
I SHOULD HAVE KNOWN BETTER.
I STILL THINK YOU'RE BEING TOO HARD ON YOURSELF.

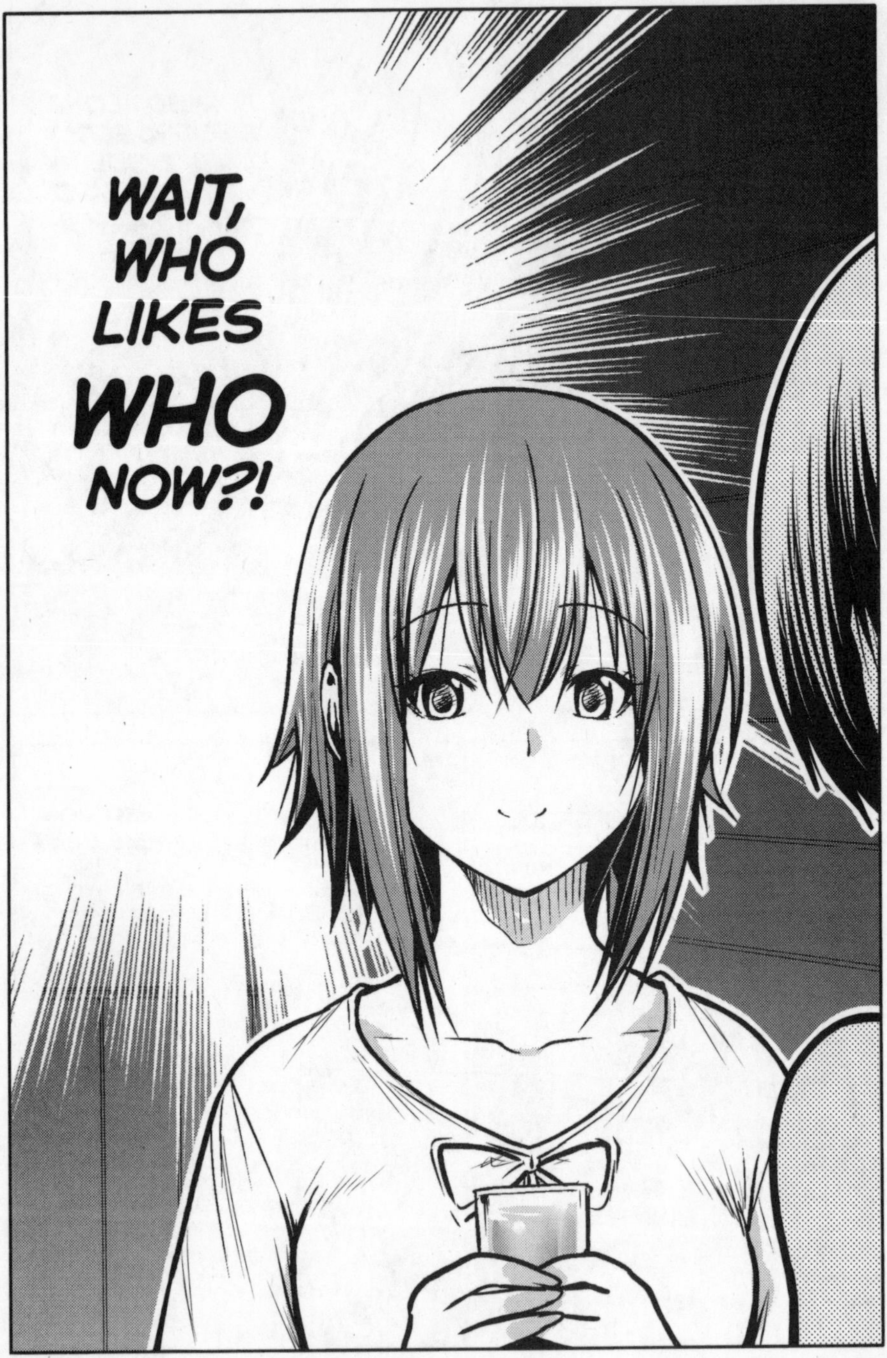
WAIT, WHO LIKES WHO NOW?!

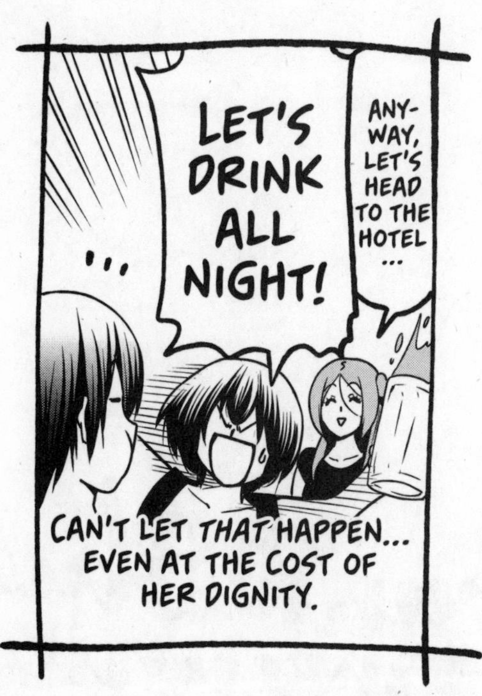
ANY-WAY, LET'S HEAD TO THE HOTEL ...
LET'S DRINK ALL NIGHT!
...
CAN'T LET THAT HAPPEN... EVEN AT THE COST OF HER DIGNITY.

Grand Blue
Dreaming

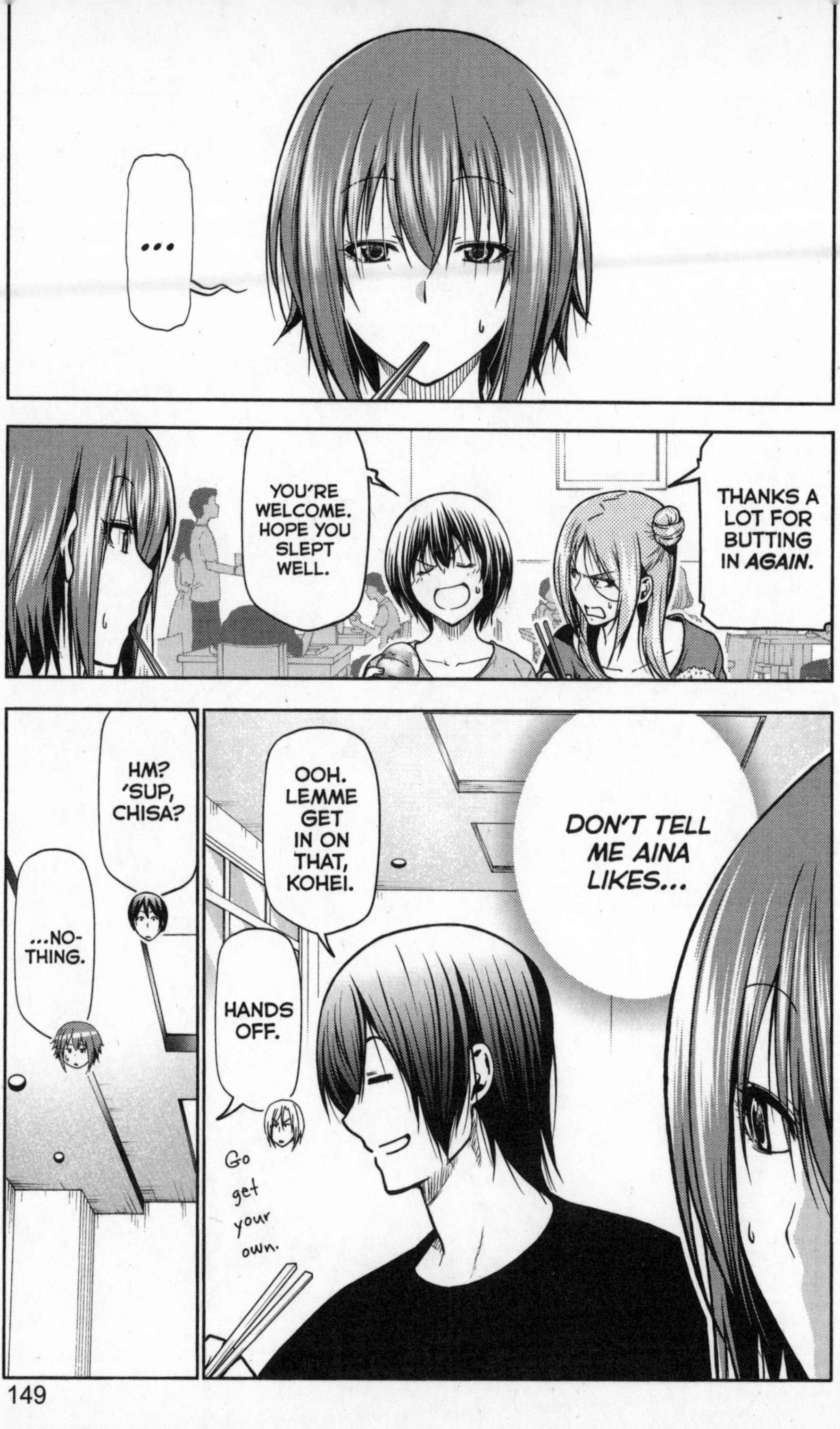
...
THANKS A LOT FOR BUTTING IN AGAIN.
YOU'RE WELCOME. HOPE YOU SLEPT WELL.
DON'T TELL ME AINA LIKES...
OOH. LEMME GET IN ON THAT, KOHEI.
HANDS OFF.
Go get your own.
HM? 'SUP, CHISA?
...NO-THING.

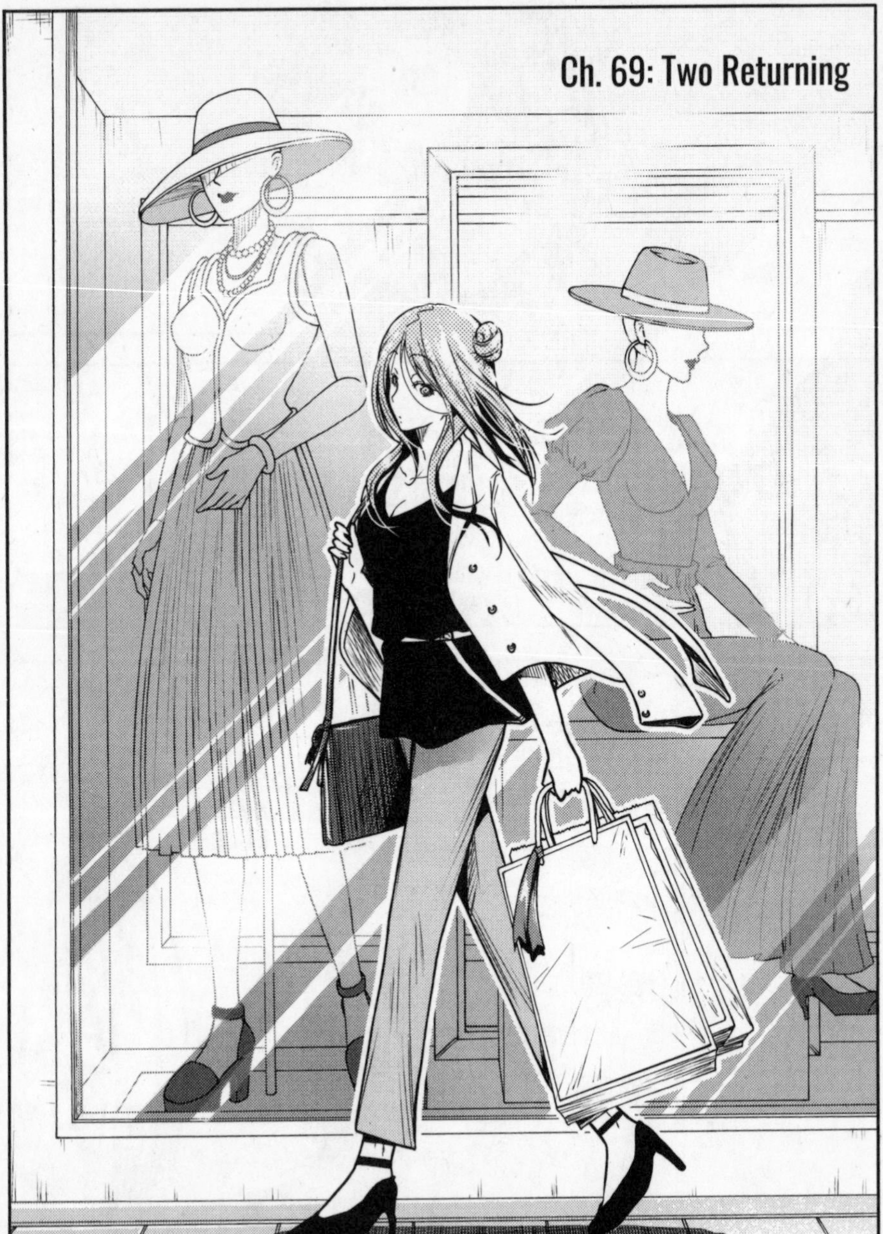
Ch. 69: Two Returning

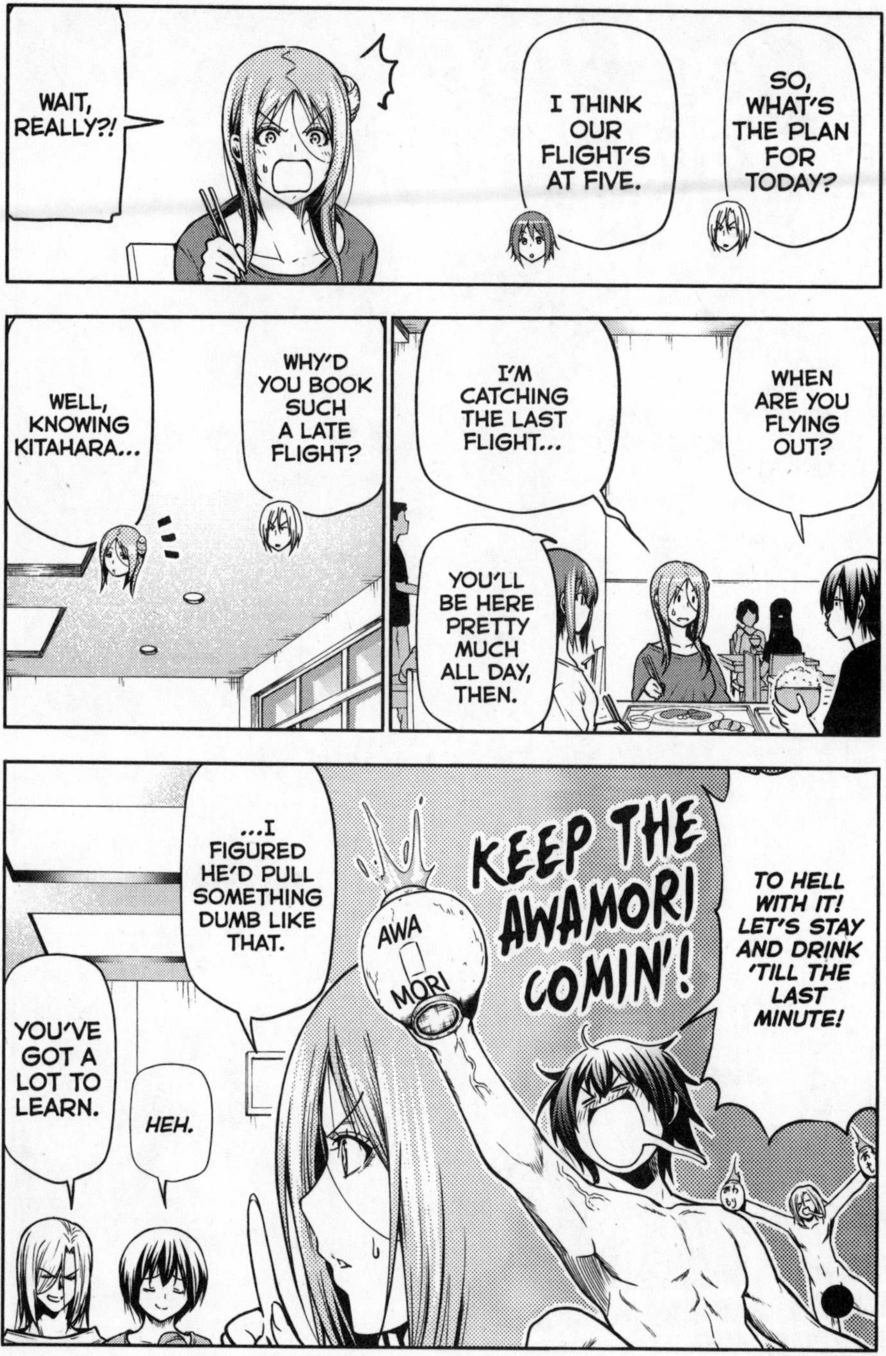
SO, WHAT'S THE PLAN FOR TODAY?
I THINK OUR FLIGHT'S AT FIVE.
WAIT, REALLY?!
WHEN ARE YOU FLYING OUT?
I'M CATCHING THE LAST FLIGHT...
YOU'LL BE HERE PRETTY MUCH ALL DAY, THEN.
WHY'D YOU BOOK SUCH A LATE FLIGHT?
WELL, KNOWING KITAHARA...
TO HELL WITH IT! LET'S STAY AND DRINK 'TILL THE LAST MINUTE!
KEEP THE AWAMORI COMIN'!
AWA MORI
...I FIGURED HE'D PULL SOMETHING DUMB LIKE THAT.
HEH.
YOU'VE GOT A LOT TO LEARN.

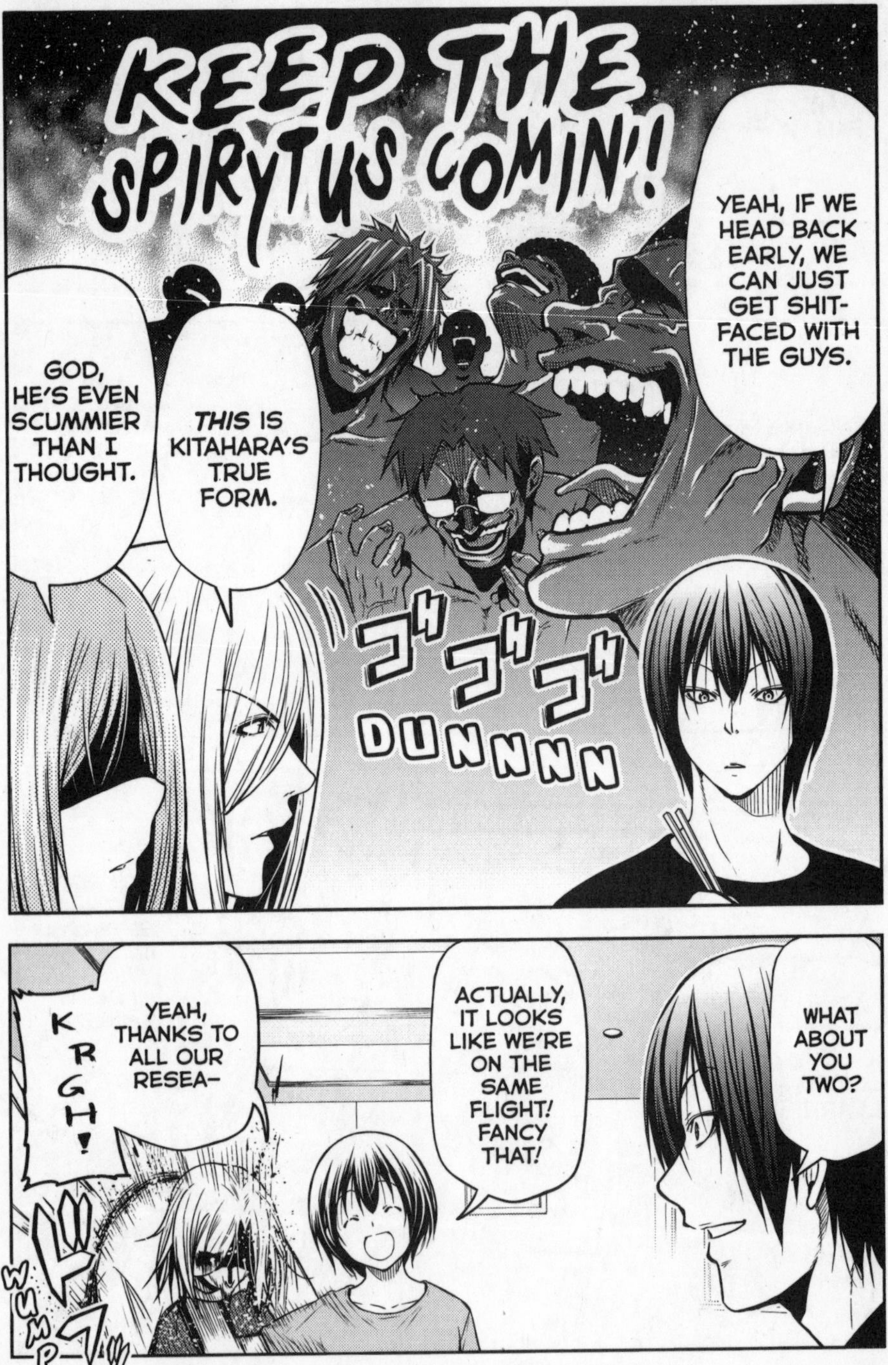
YEAH, IF WE HEAD BACK EARLY, WE CAN JUST GET SHIT-FACED WITH THE GUYS.
KEEP THE SPIRYTUS COMIN'!
THIS IS KITAHARA'S TRUE FORM.
GOD, HE'S EVEN SCUMMIER THAN I THOUGHT.
DUNNNNN
WHAT ABOUT YOU TWO?
ACTUALLY, IT LOOKS LIKE WE'RE ON THE SAME FLIGHT! FANCY THAT!
YEAH, THANKS TO ALL OUR RESEA–
KRGH!
WUMP

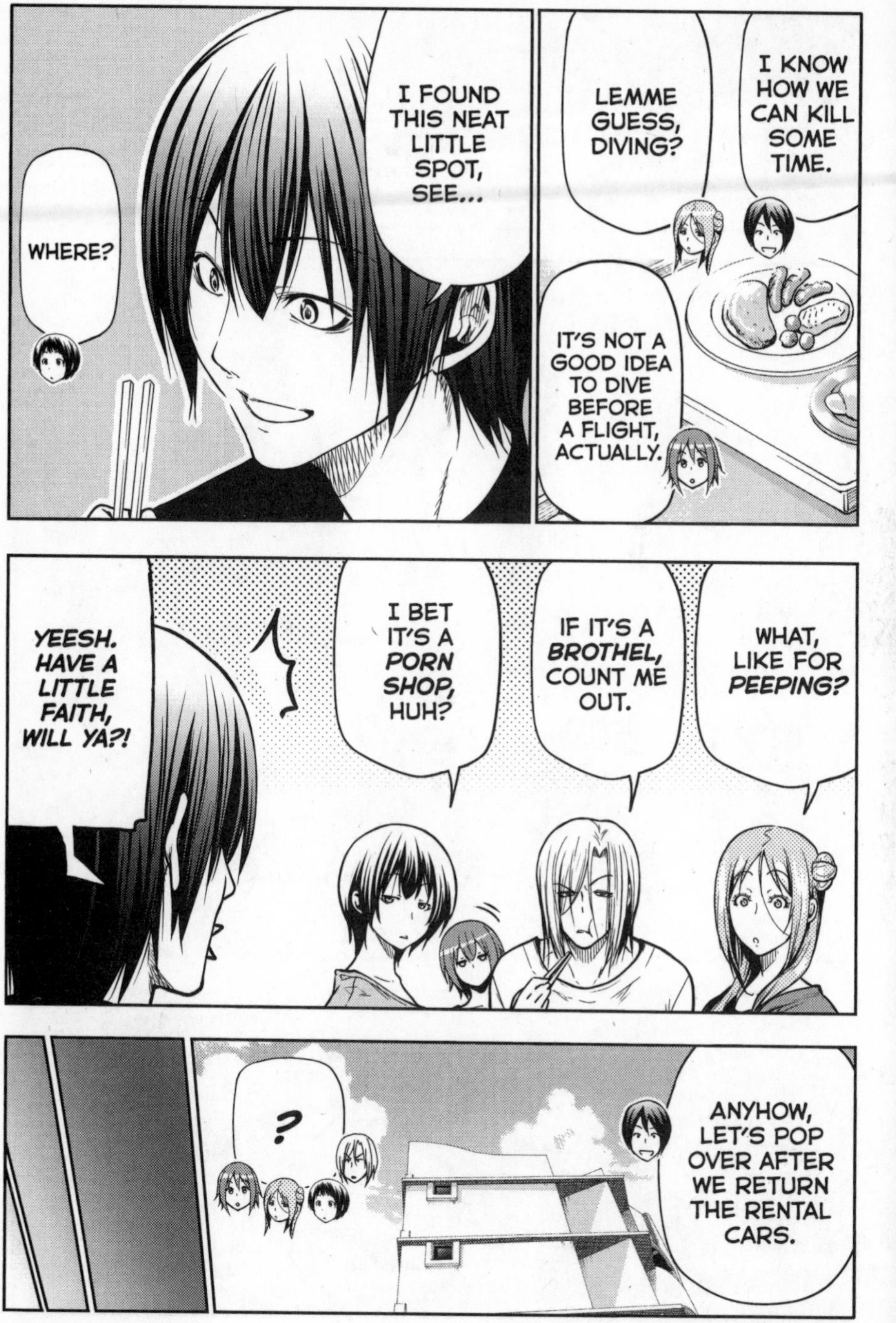
I KNOW HOW WE CAN KILL SOME TIME.
LEMME GUESS, DIVING?
IT'S NOT A GOOD IDEA TO DIVE BEFORE A FLIGHT, ACTUALLY.
I FOUND THIS NEAT LITTLE SPOT, SEE...
WHERE?
WHAT, LIKE FOR *PEEPING?*
IF IT'S A *BROTHEL,* COUNT ME OUT.
I BET IT'S A *PORN SHOP,* HUH?
YEESH. HAVE A LITTLE FAITH, WILL YA?!
ANYHOW, LET'S POP OVER AFTER WE RETURN THE RENTAL CARS.
?

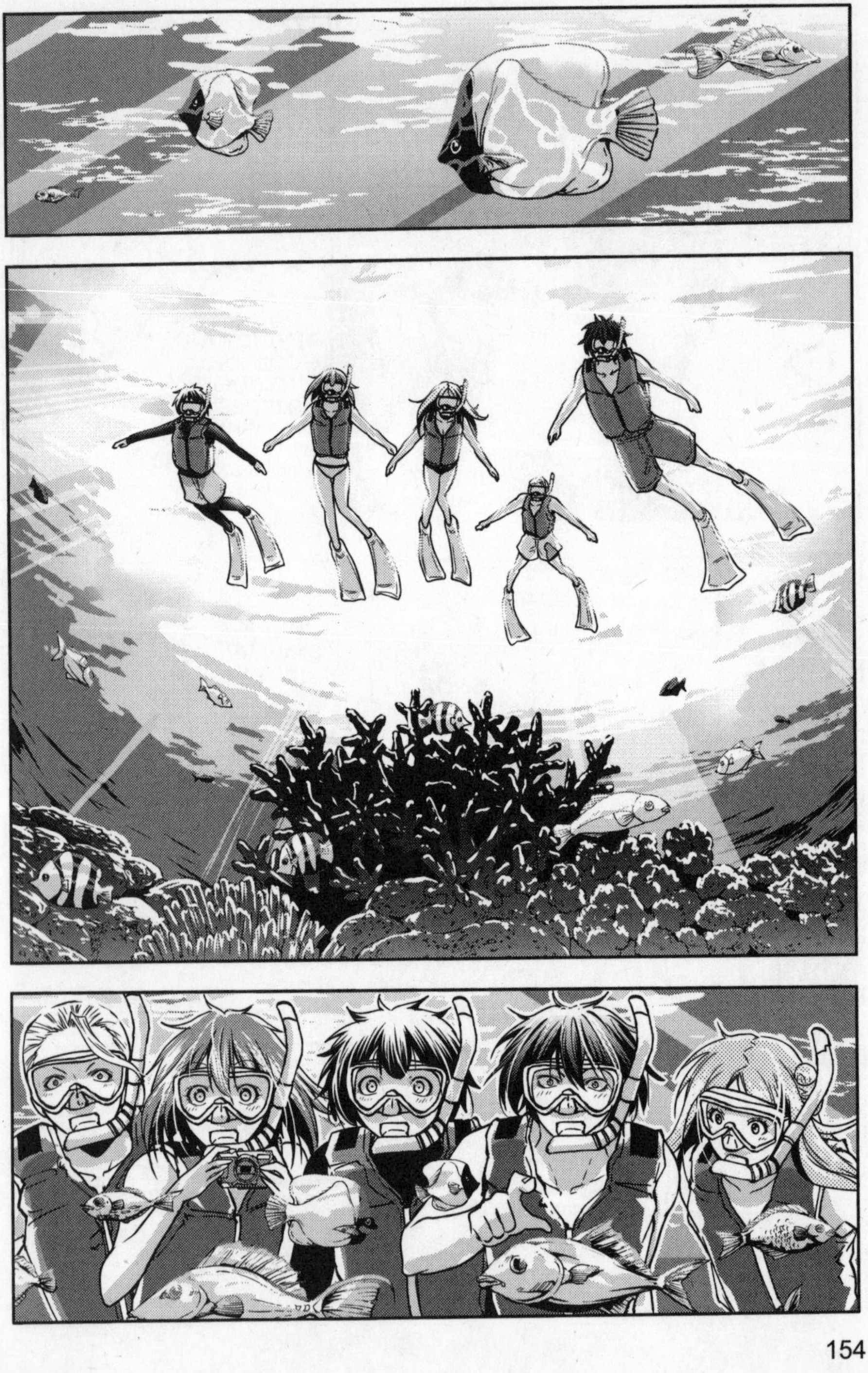

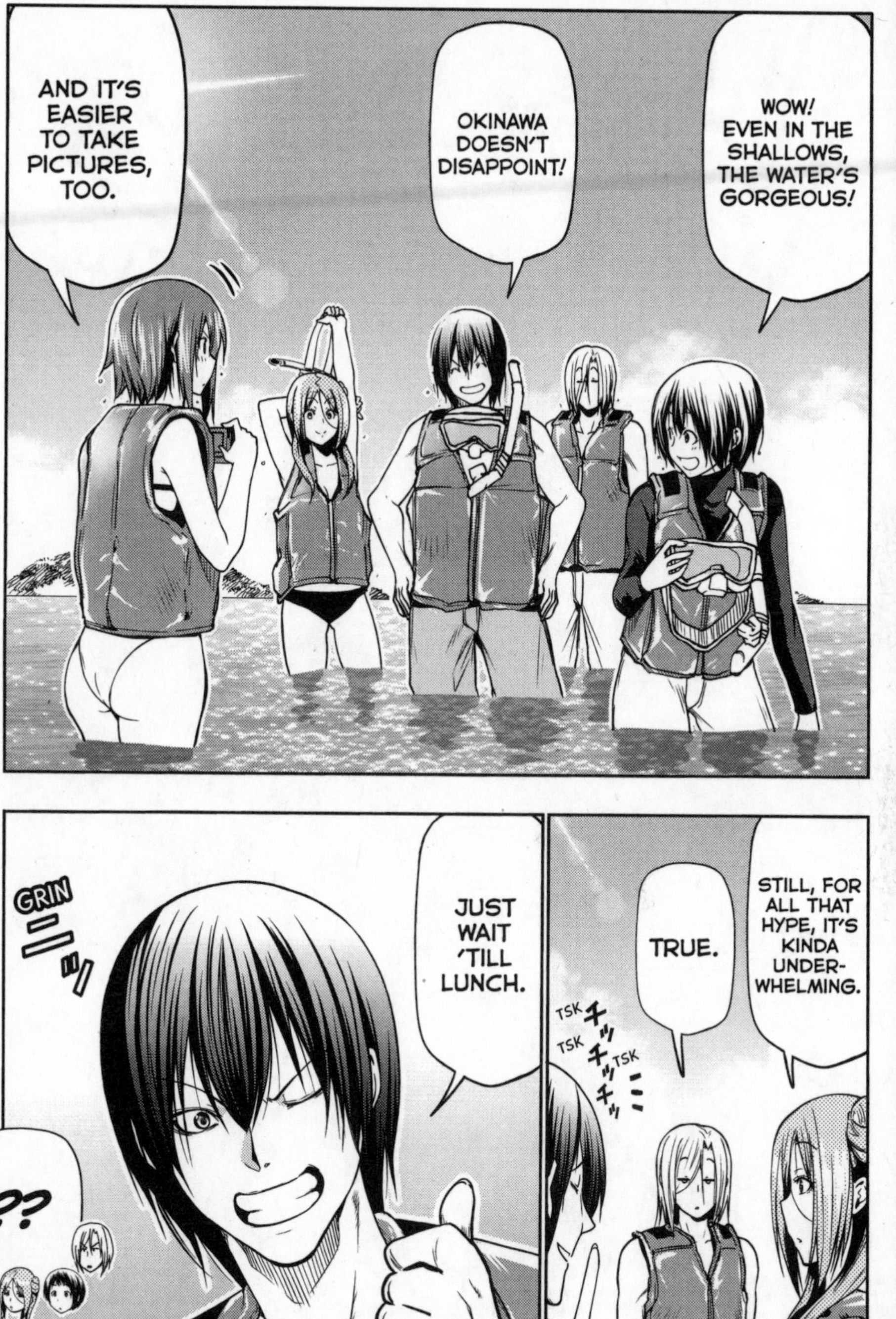
WOW! EVEN IN THE SHALLOWS, THE WATER'S GORGEOUS!
OKINAWA DOESN'T DISAPPOINT!
AND IT'S EASIER TO TAKE PICTURES, TOO.
STILL, FOR ALL THAT HYPE, IT'S KINDA UNDER-WHELMING.
TRUE.
TSK TSK TSK
JUST WAIT 'TILL LUNCH.
GRIN
??

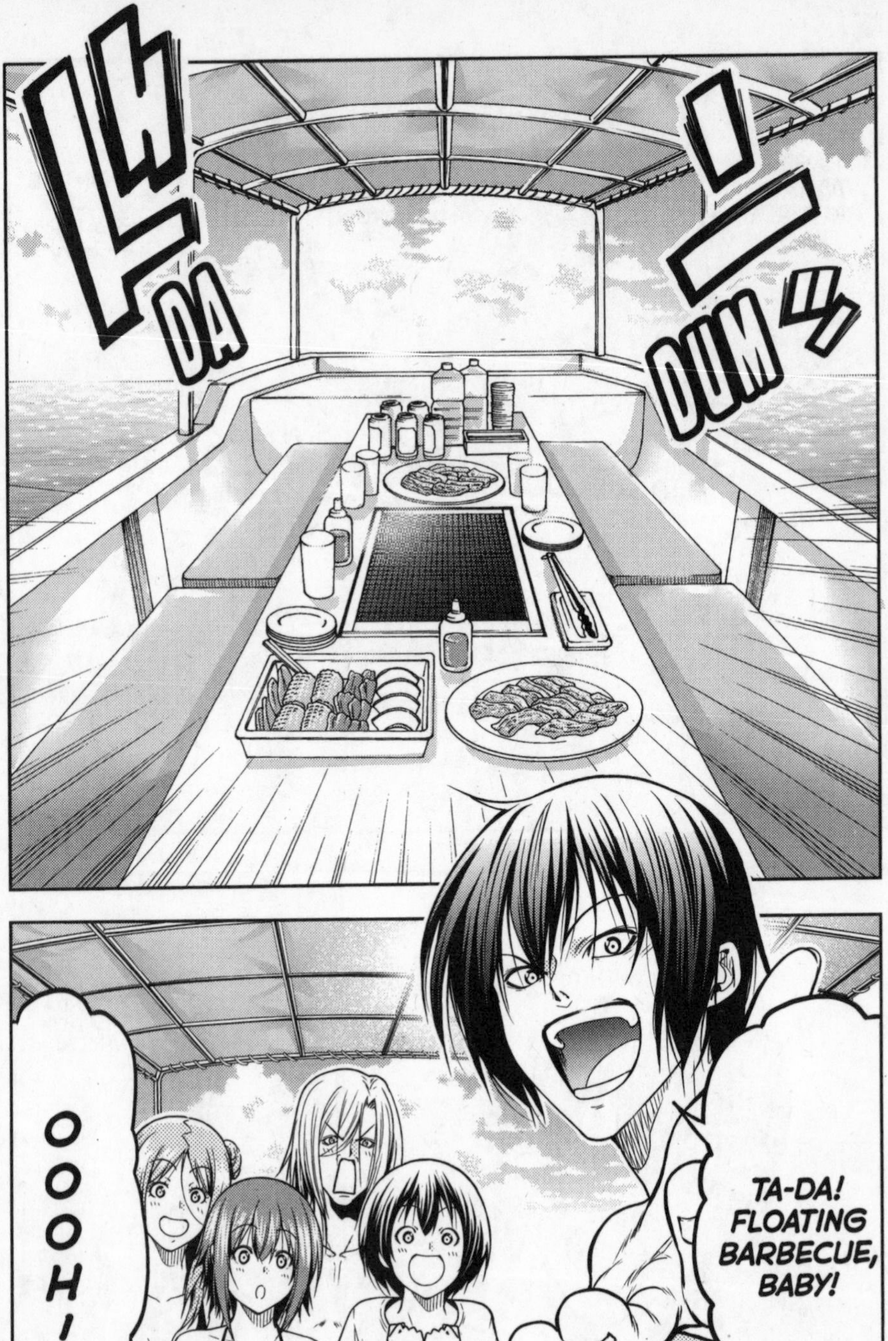
DA
DUM
TA-DA! FLOATING BARBECUE, BABY!
OOOOH!

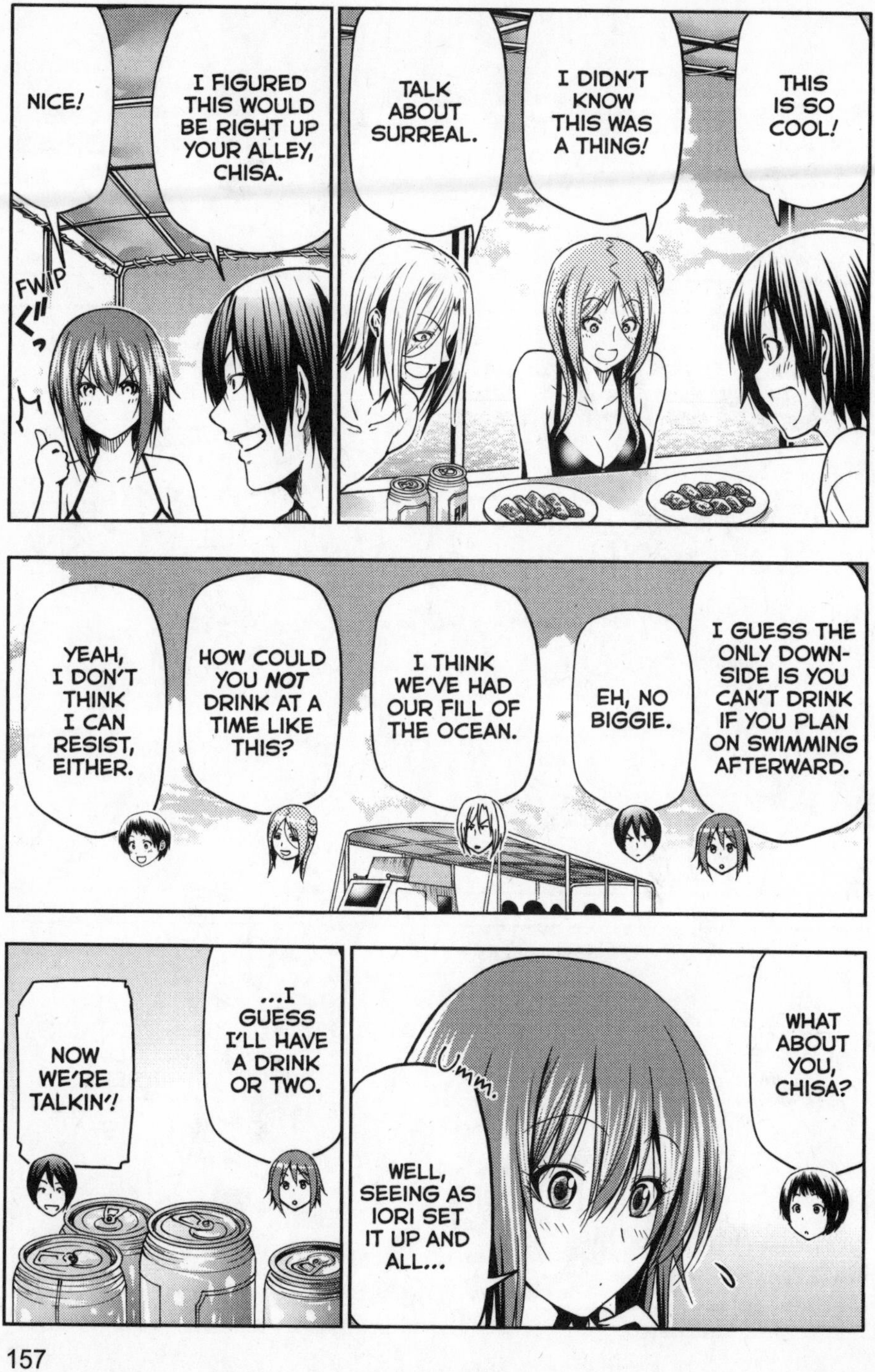
THIS IS SO COOL!
I DIDN'T KNOW THIS WAS A THING!
TALK ABOUT SURREAL.
I FIGURED THIS WOULD BE RIGHT UP YOUR ALLEY, CHISA.
NICE!
FWIP
I GUESS THE ONLY DOWN-SIDE IS YOU CAN'T DRINK IF YOU PLAN ON SWIMMING AFTERWARD.
EH, NO BIGGIE.
I THINK WE'VE HAD OUR FILL OF THE OCEAN.
HOW COULD YOU *NOT* DRINK AT A TIME LIKE THIS?
YEAH, I DON'T THINK I CAN RESIST, EITHER.
WHAT ABOUT YOU, CHISA?
Umm.
WELL, SEEING AS IORI SET IT UP AND ALL...
...I GUESS I'LL HAVE A DRINK OR TWO.
NOW WE'RE TALKIN'!

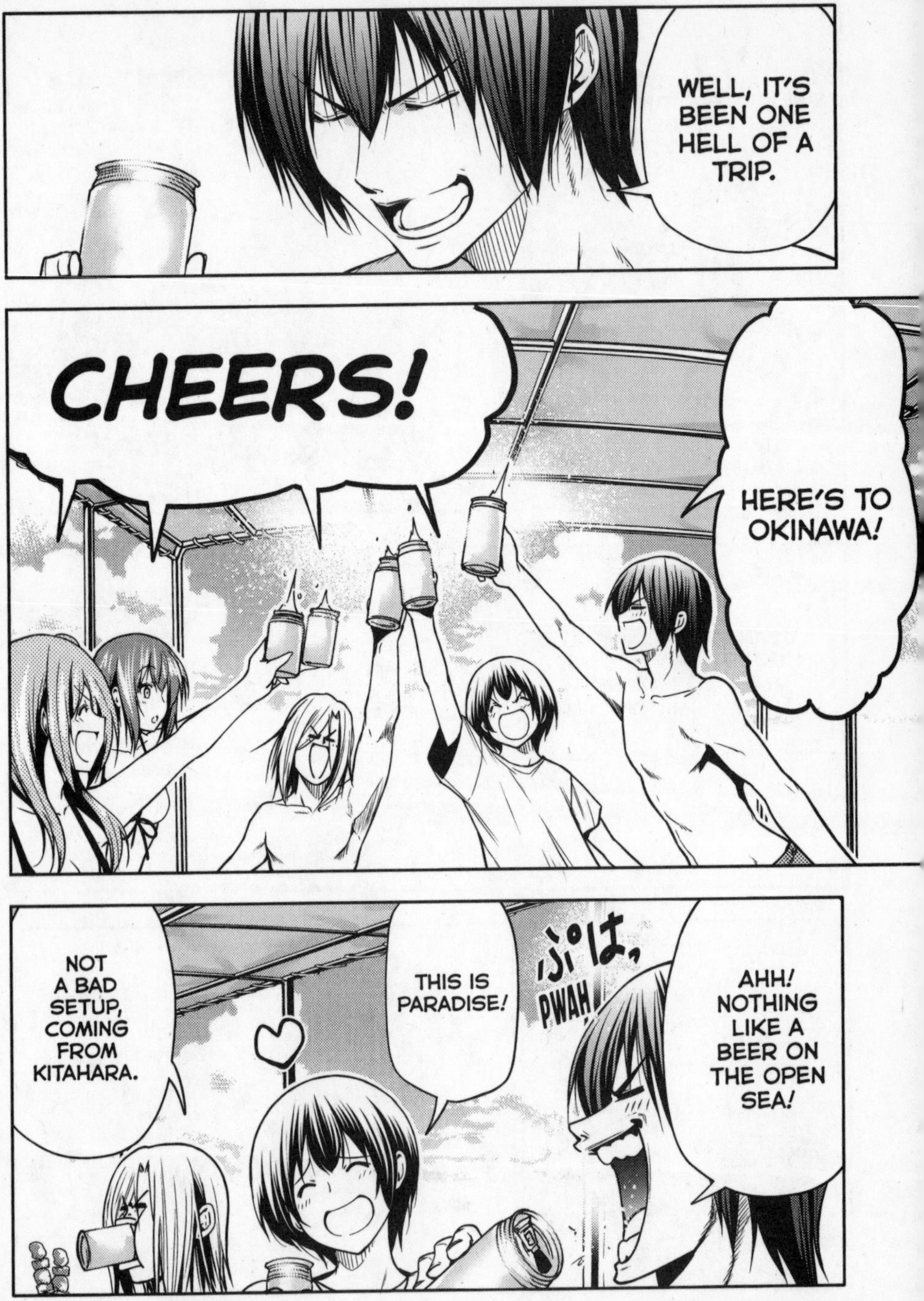
WELL, IT'S BEEN ONE HELL OF A TRIP.
HERE'S TO OKINAWA!
CHEERS!
AHH! NOTHING LIKE A BEER ON THE OPEN SEA!
ぷは、
PWAH
THIS IS PARADISE!
NOT A BAD SETUP, COMING FROM KITAHARA.

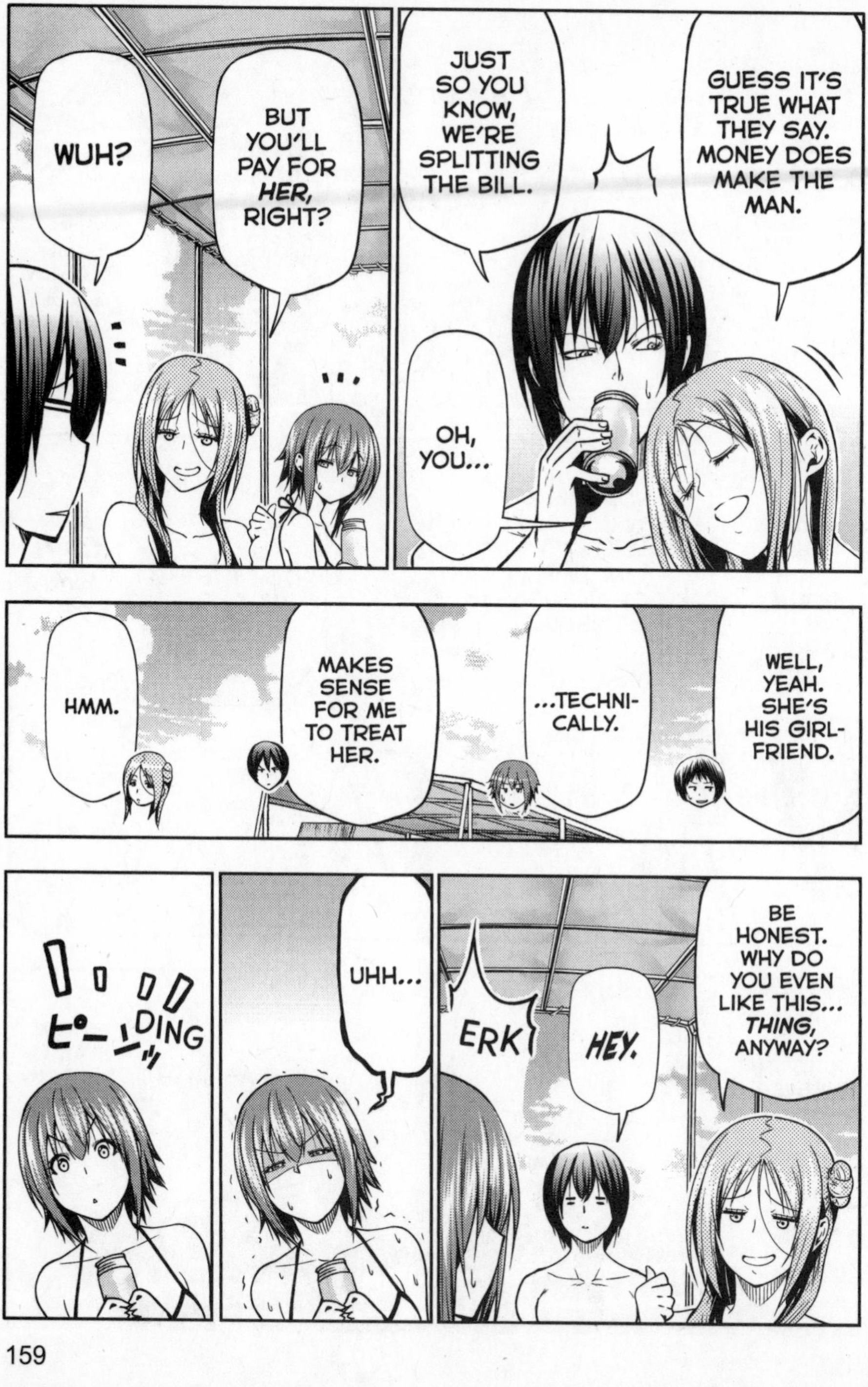

GUESS IT'S TRUE WHAT THEY SAY. MONEY DOES MAKE THE MAN.
JUST SO YOU KNOW, WE'RE SPLITTING THE BILL.
OH, YOU...
BUT YOU'LL PAY FOR *HER*, RIGHT?
WUH?
WELL, YEAH. SHE'S HIS GIRL-FRIEND.
...TECHNI-CALLY.
MAKES SENSE FOR ME TO TREAT HER.
HMM.
BE HONEST. WHY DO YOU EVEN LIKE THIS... *THING*, ANYWAY?
HEY.
ERK
UHH...
ピーンッ
DING

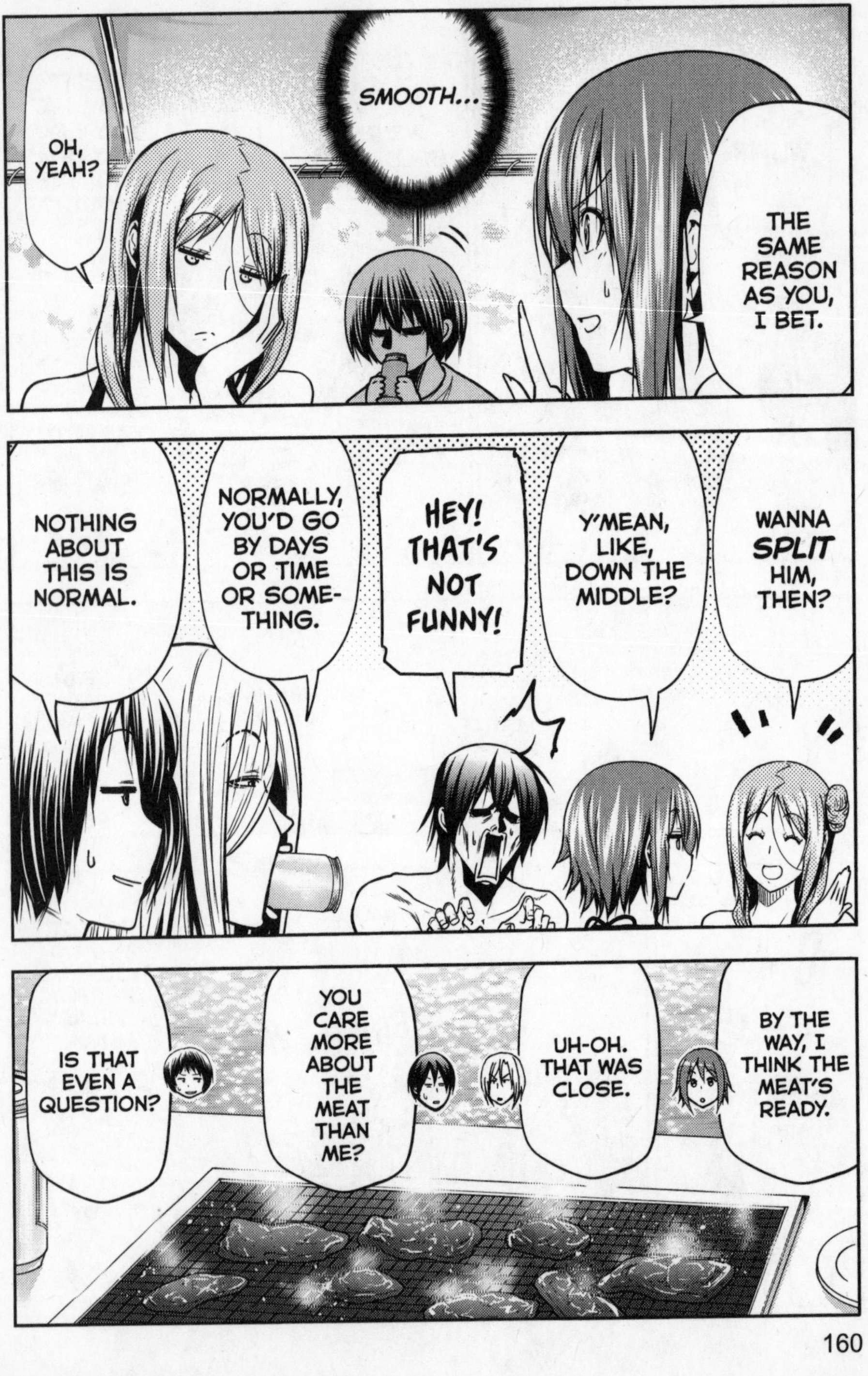
THE SAME REASON AS YOU, I BET.
SMOOTH...
OH, YEAH?
WANNA SPLIT HIM, THEN?
Y'MEAN, LIKE, DOWN THE MIDDLE?
HEY! THAT'S NOT FUNNY!
NORMALLY, YOU'D GO BY DAYS OR TIME OR SOME-THING.
NOTHING ABOUT THIS IS NORMAL.
BY THE WAY, I THINK THE MEAT'S READY.
UH-OH. THAT WAS CLOSE.
YOU CARE MORE ABOUT THE MEAT THAN ME?
IS THAT EVEN A QUESTION?

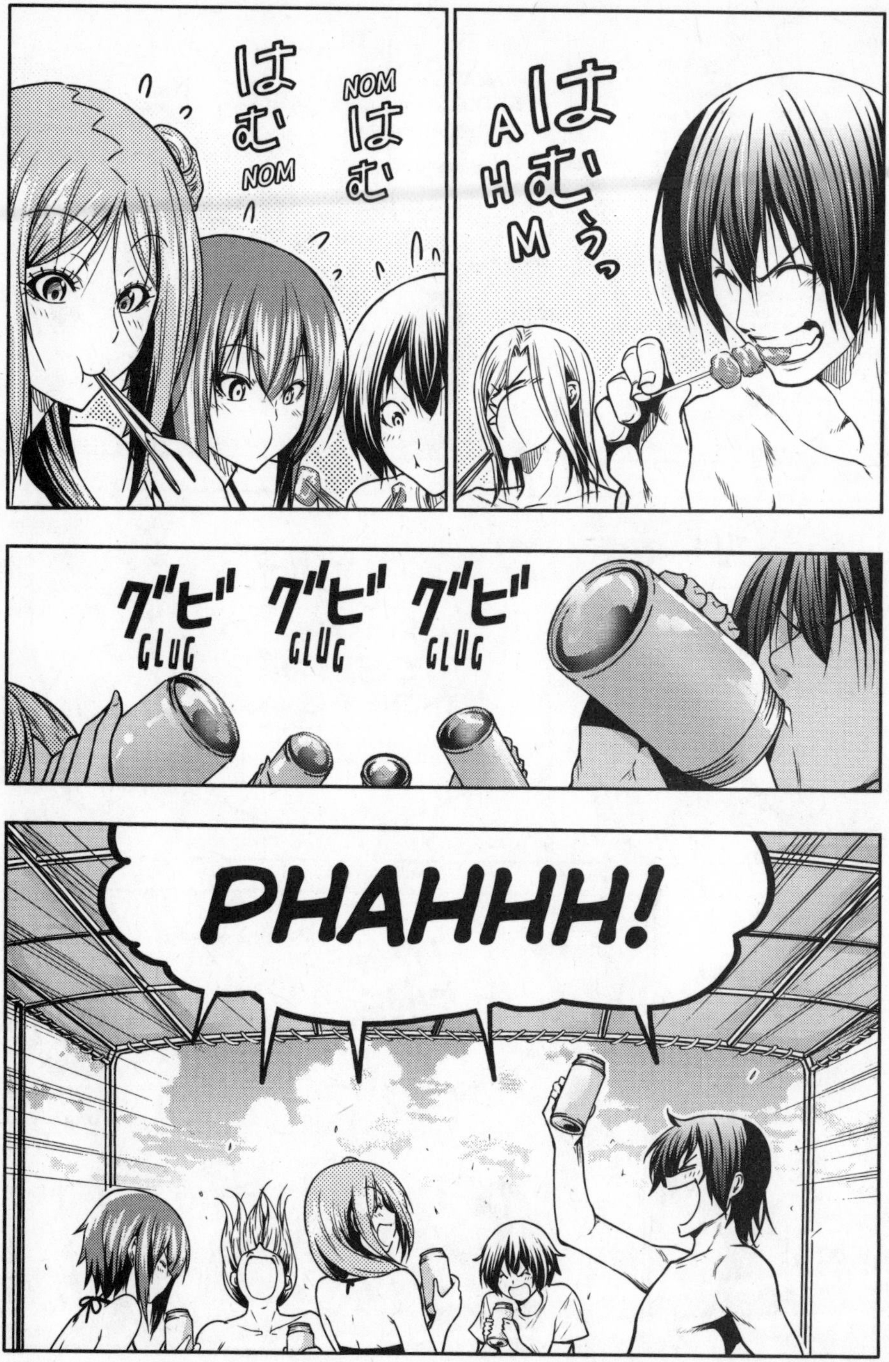

はむぅっ
AHM
NOM
はむ
はむ
NOM
グビ
GLUG
グビ
GLUG
グビ
GLUG
PHAHHH!

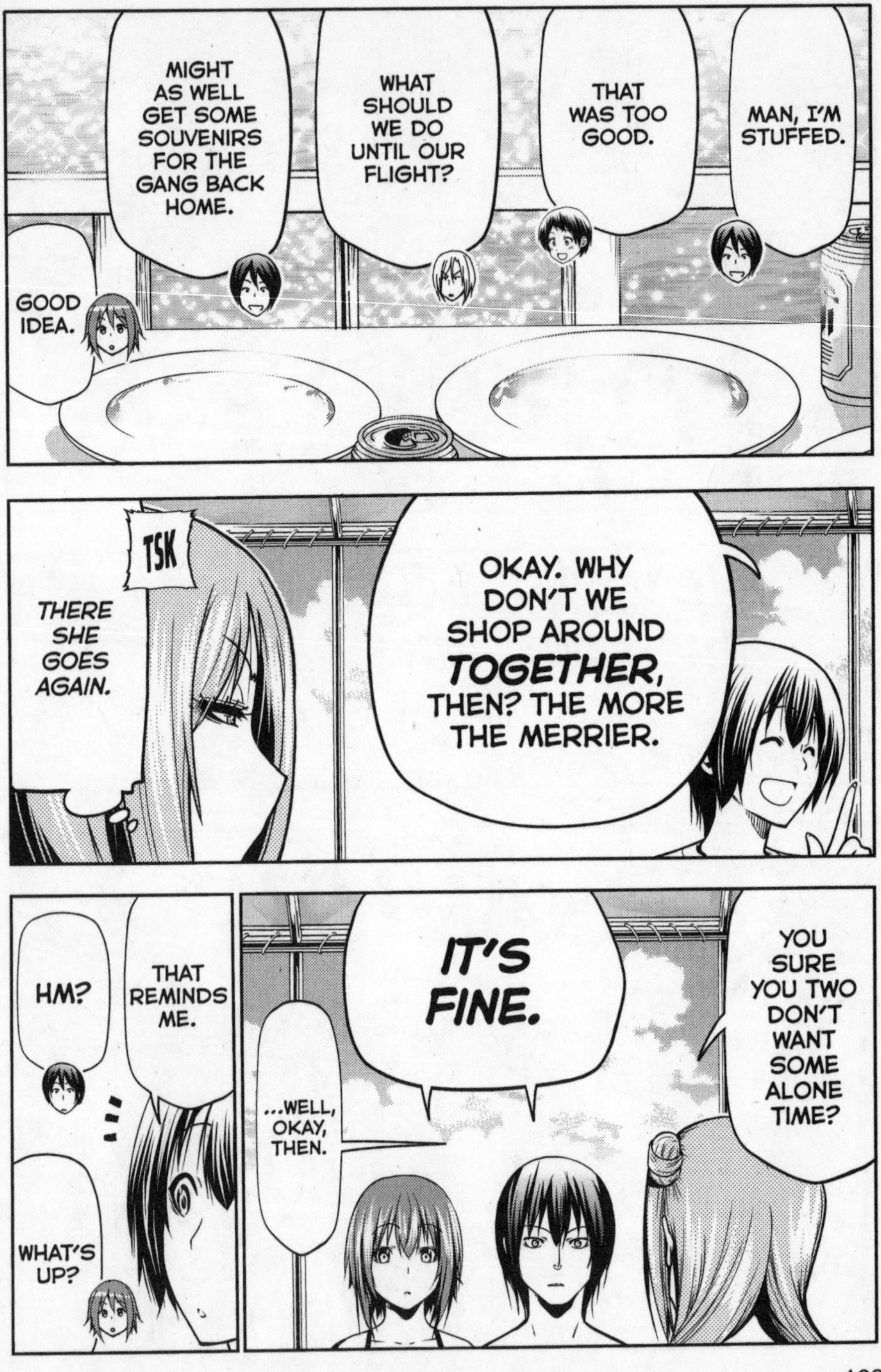
MAN, I'M STUFFED.
THAT WAS TOO GOOD.
WHAT SHOULD WE DO UNTIL OUR FLIGHT?
MIGHT AS WELL GET SOME SOUVENIRS FOR THE GANG BACK HOME.
GOOD IDEA.
OKAY. WHY DON'T WE SHOP AROUND TOGETHER, THEN? THE MORE THE MERRIER.
TSK
THERE SHE GOES AGAIN.
YOU SURE YOU TWO DON'T WANT SOME ALONE TIME?
IT'S FINE.
...WELL, OKAY, THEN.
THAT REMINDS ME.
HM?
WHAT'S UP?

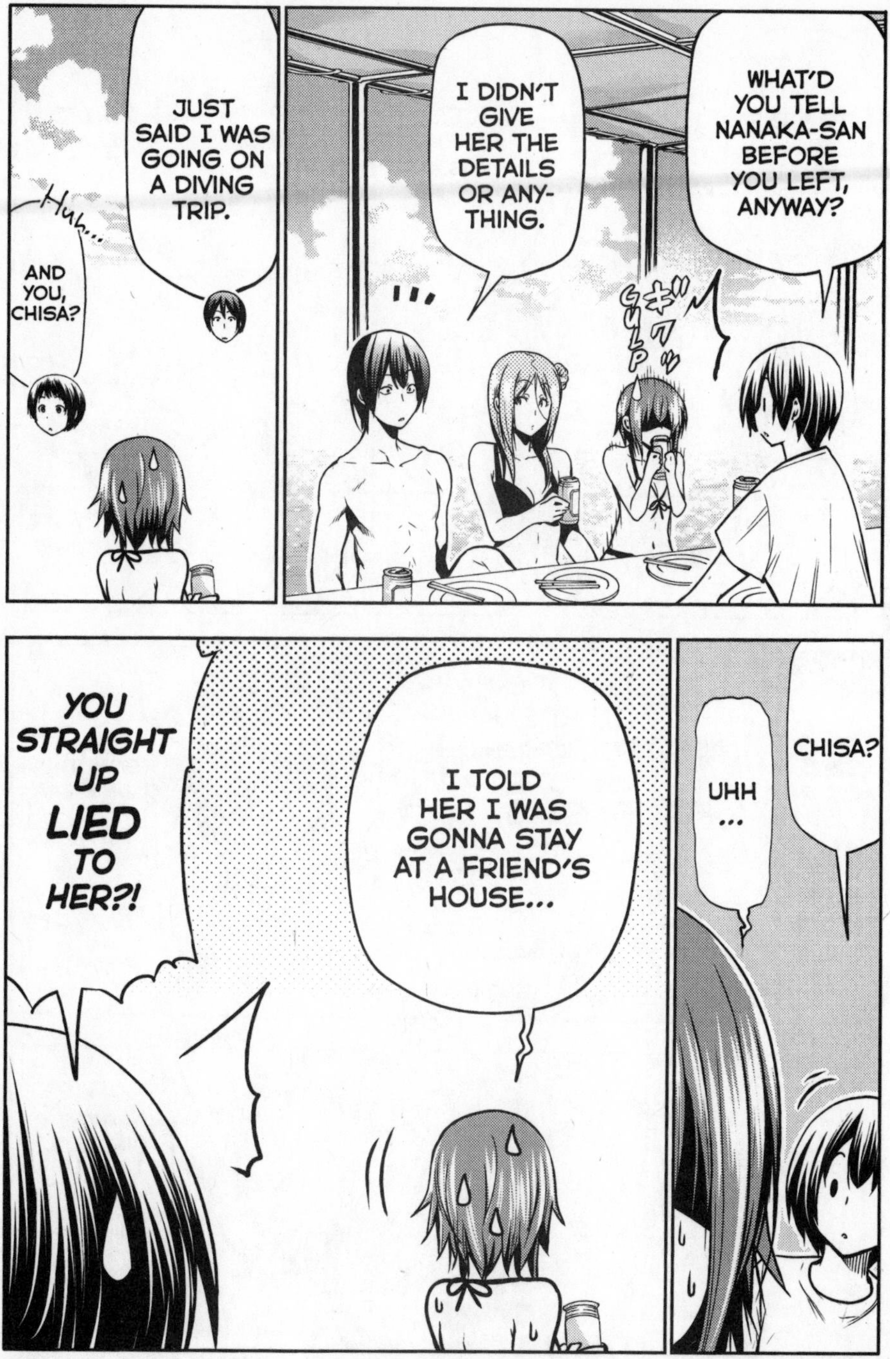
WHAT'D YOU TELL NANAKA-SAN BEFORE YOU LEFT, ANYWAY?
I DIDN'T GIVE HER THE DETAILS OR ANY-THING.
GULP
JUST SAID I WAS GOING ON A DIVING TRIP.
Huh...
AND YOU, CHISA?
CHISA?
UHH ...
I TOLD HER I WAS GONNA STAY AT A FRIEND'S HOUSE...
YOU STRAIGHT UP LIED TO HER?!

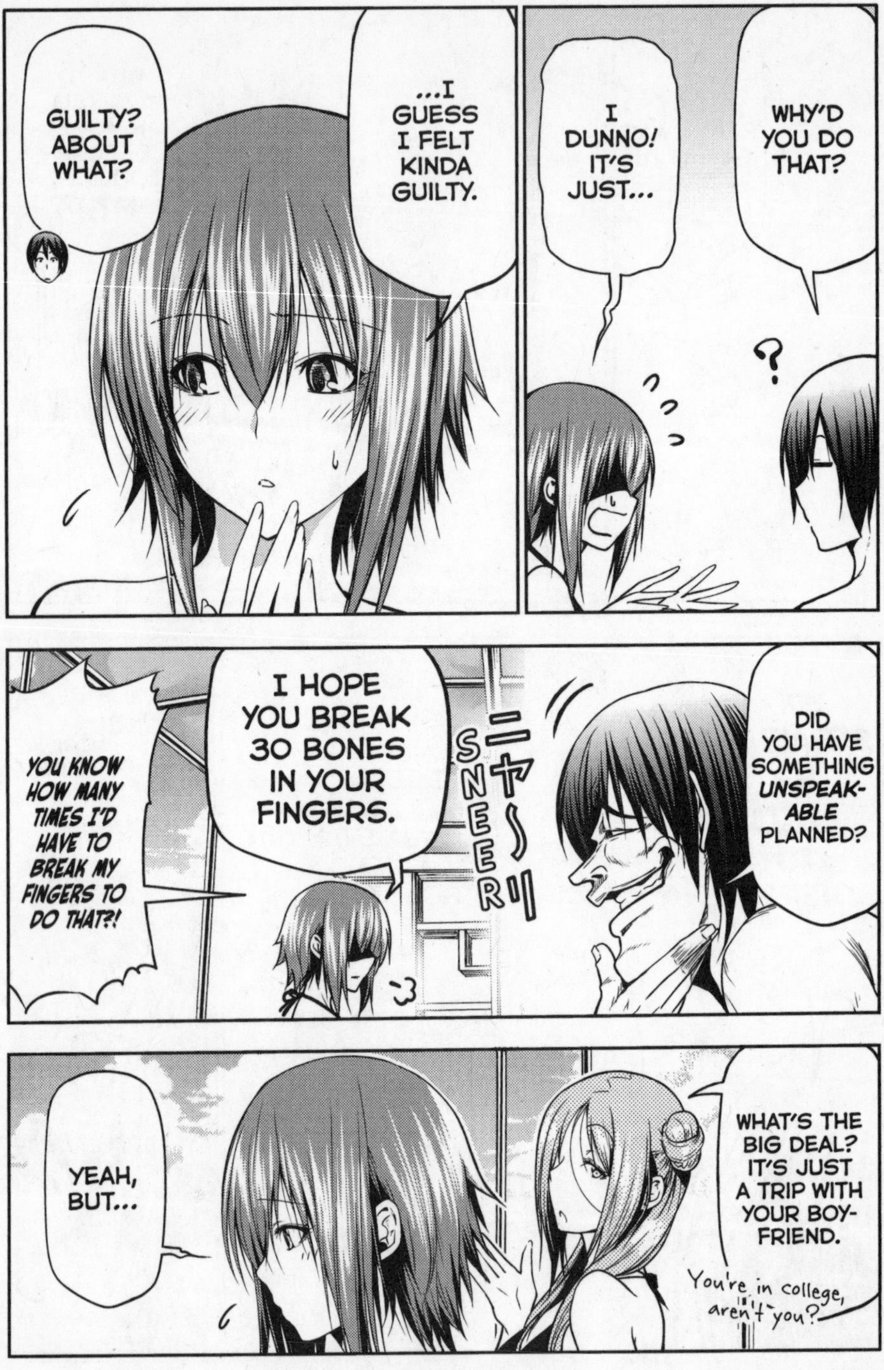
WHY'D YOU DO THAT?
I DUNNO! IT'S JUST...
...I GUESS I FELT KINDA GUILTY.
GUILTY? ABOUT WHAT?
DID YOU HAVE SOMETHING *UNSPEAKABLE* PLANNED?
SNEER
I HOPE YOU BREAK 30 BONES IN YOUR FINGERS.
YOU KNOW HOW MANY TIMES I'D HAVE TO BREAK MY FINGERS TO DO THAT?!
WHAT'S THE BIG DEAL? IT'S JUST A TRIP WITH YOUR BOY-FRIEND.
You're in college, aren't you?
YEAH, BUT...

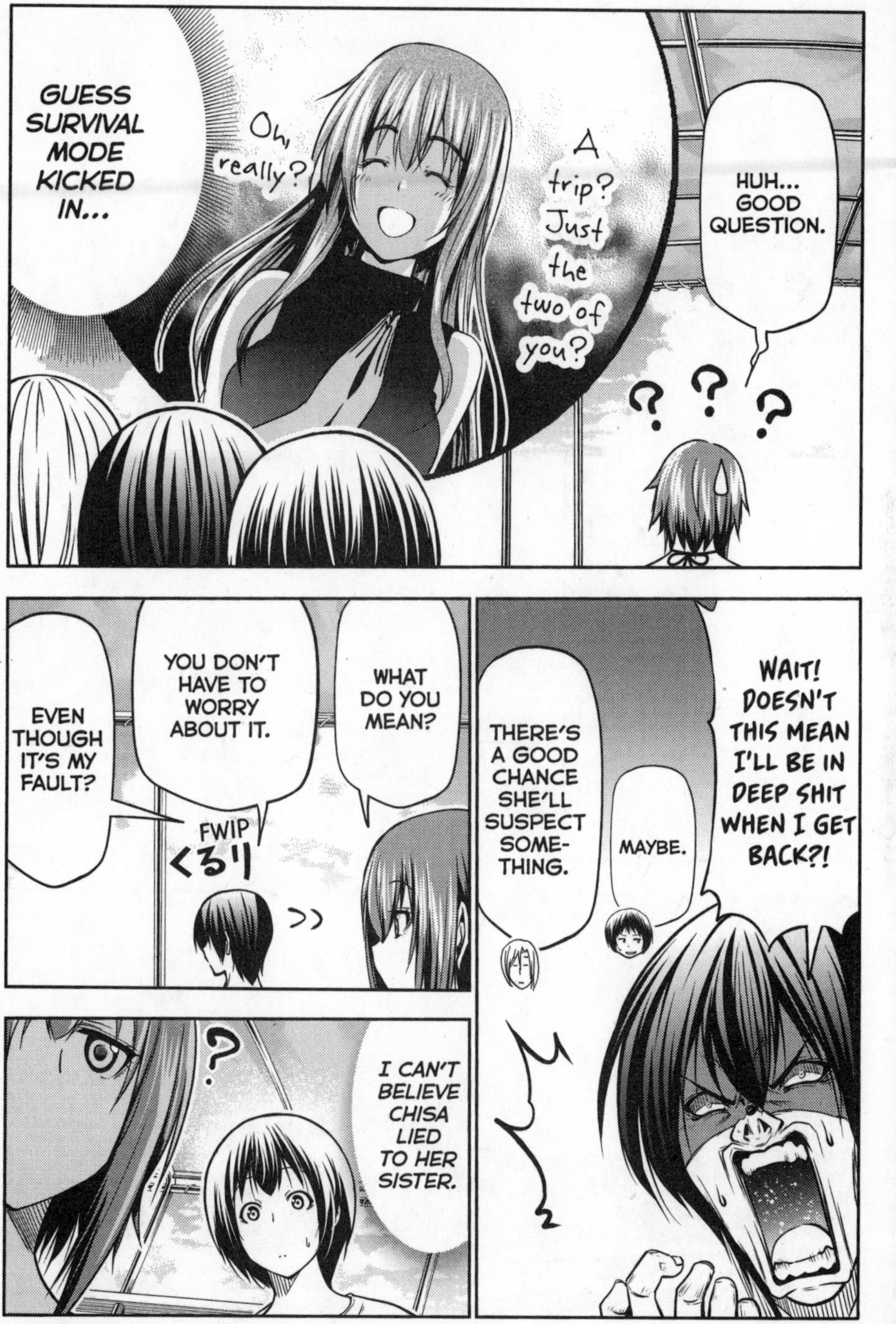
HUH... GOOD QUESTION.
A trip? Just the two of you?
Oh, really?
GUESS SURVIVAL MODE KICKED IN...
WAIT! DOESN'T THIS MEAN I'LL BE IN DEEP SHIT WHEN I GET BACK?!
MAYBE.
THERE'S A GOOD CHANCE SHE'LL SUSPECT SOMETHING.
WHAT DO YOU MEAN?
YOU DON'T HAVE TO WORRY ABOUT IT.
EVEN THOUGH IT'S MY FAULT?
FWIP
くるり
I CAN'T BELIEVE CHISA LIED TO HER SISTER.

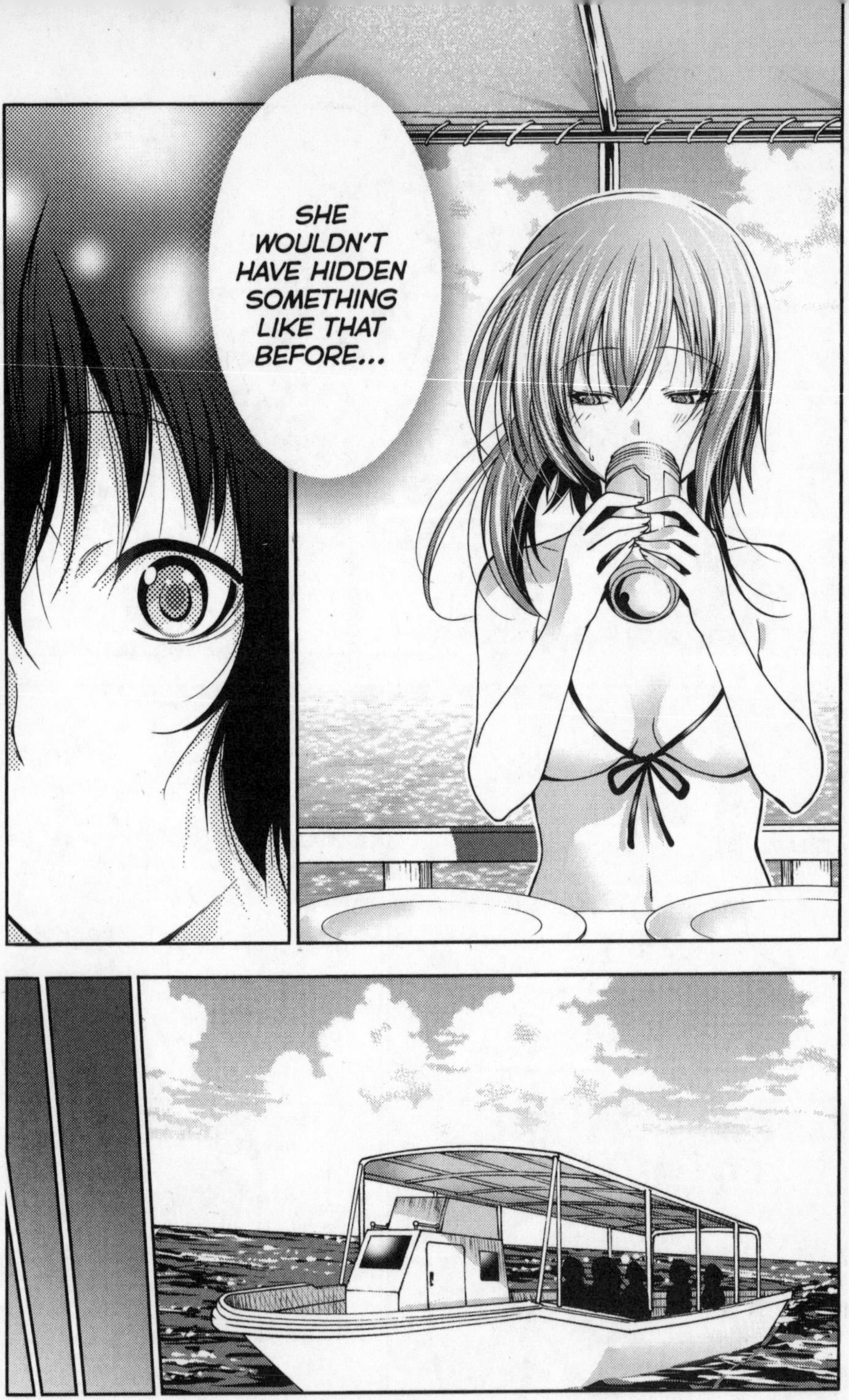
SHE WOULDN'T HAVE HIDDEN SOMETHING LIKE THAT BEFORE...

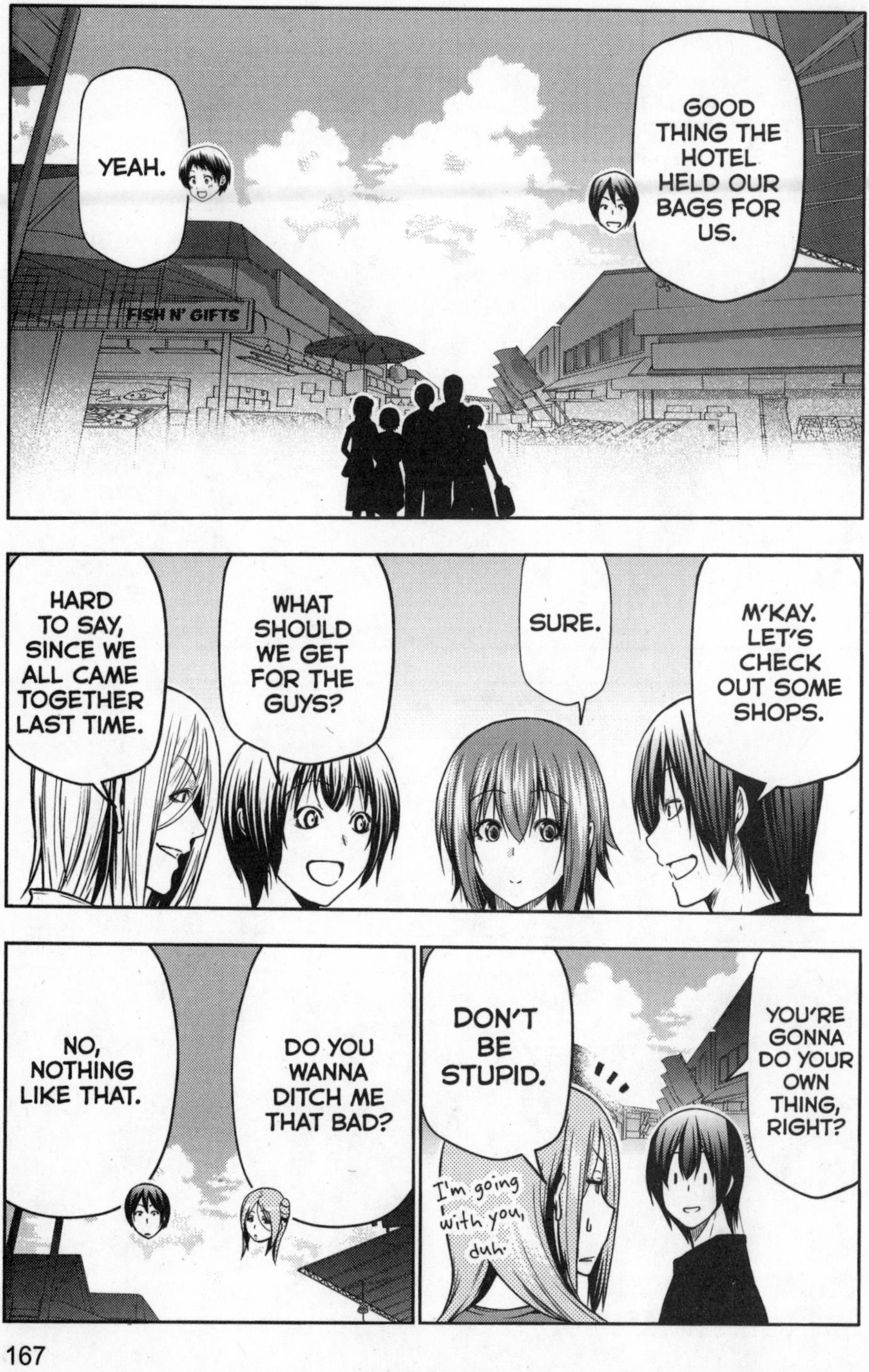
GOOD THING THE HOTEL HELD OUR BAGS FOR US.
YEAH.
FISH N' GIFTS
M'KAY. LET'S CHECK OUT SOME SHOPS.
SURE.
WHAT SHOULD WE GET FOR THE GUYS?
HARD TO SAY, SINCE WE ALL CAME TOGETHER LAST TIME.
YOU'RE GONNA DO YOUR OWN THING, RIGHT?
...
DON'T BE STUPID.
I'm going with you, duh.
DO YOU WANNA DITCH ME THAT BAD?
NO, NOTHING LIKE THAT.

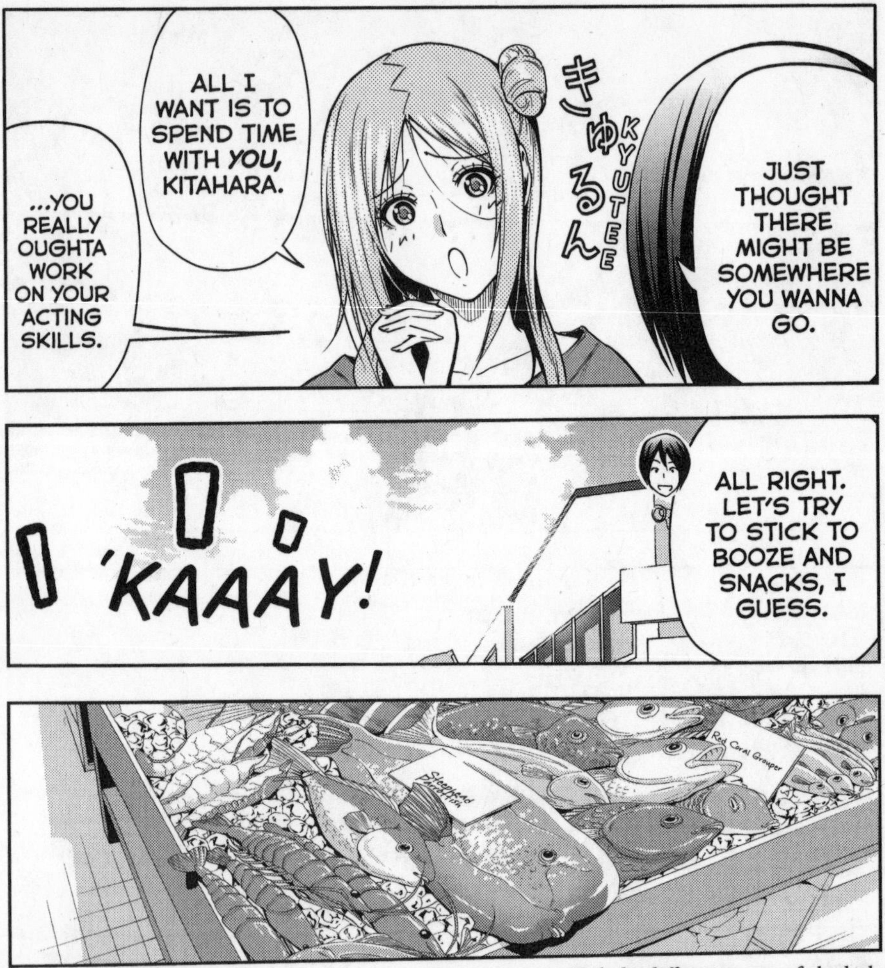
JUST THOUGHT THERE MIGHT BE SOMEWHERE YOU WANNA GO.
きゅるん
KYUTEE
ALL I WANT IS TO SPEND TIME WITH *YOU,* KITAHARA.
...YOU REALLY OUGHTA WORK ON YOUR ACTING SKILLS.
ALL RIGHT. LET'S TRY TO STICK TO BOOZE AND SNACKS, I GUESS.
'KAAAY!
Red Coral Grouper

*Labels: different types of alcohol.

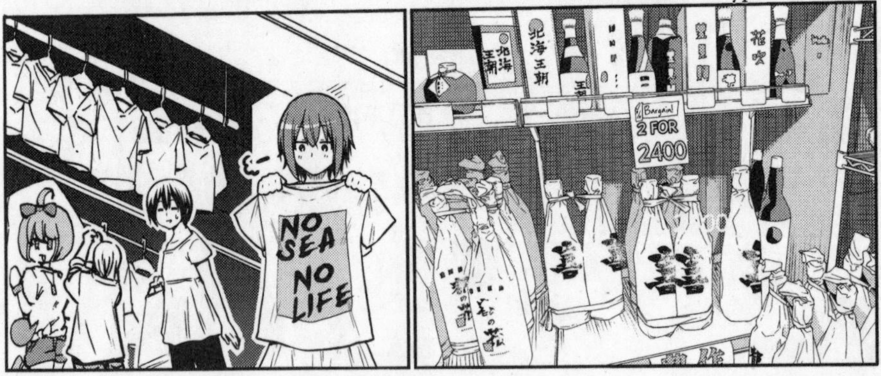
北海王朝
Bargain!
2 FOR
2400
NO SEA NO LIFE

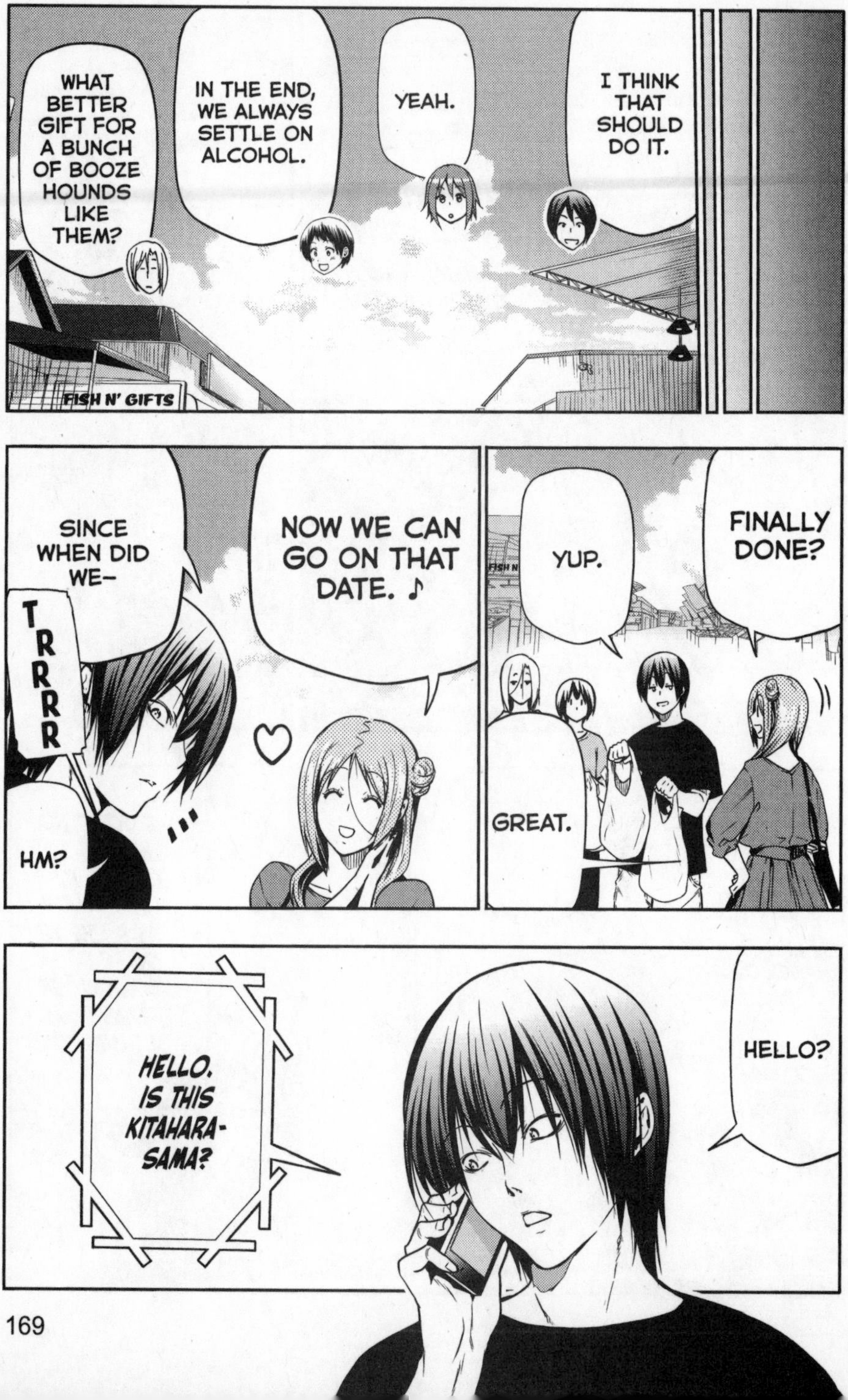
I THINK THAT SHOULD DO IT.
YEAH.
IN THE END, WE ALWAYS SETTLE ON ALCOHOL.
WHAT BETTER GIFT FOR A BUNCH OF BOOZE HOUNDS LIKE THEM?
FISH N' GIFTS
FINALLY DONE?
YUP.
GREAT.
NOW WE CAN GO ON THAT DATE. ♪
SINCE WHEN DID WE–
TRRRR
HM?
HELLO?
HELLO. IS THIS KITAHARA-SAMA?

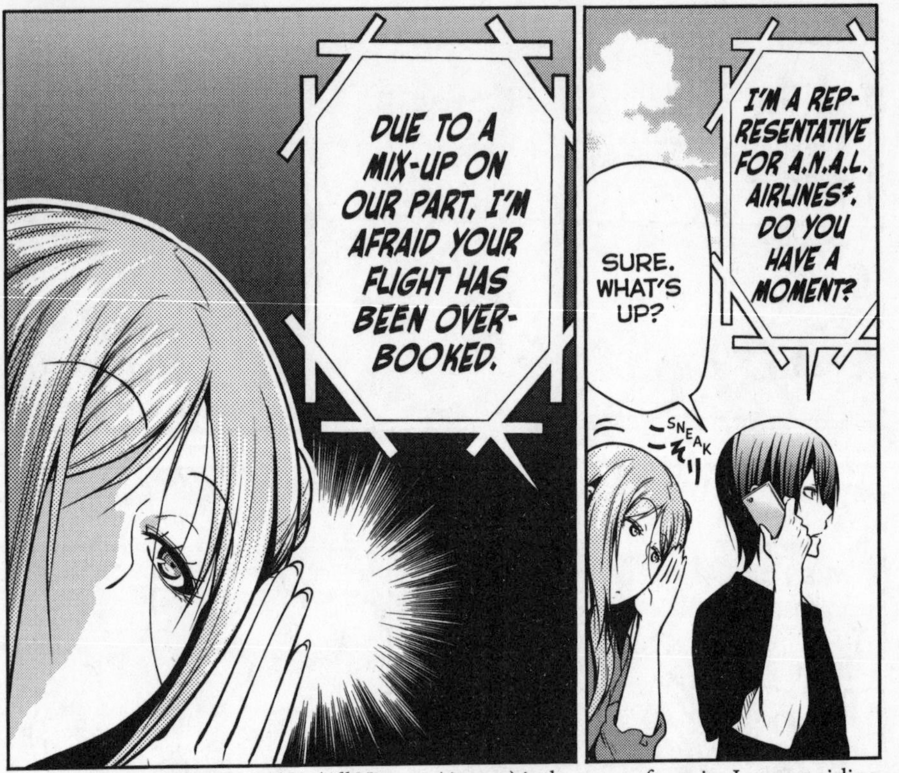
I'M A REP-RESENTATIVE FOR A.N.A.L. AIRLINES*. DO YOU HAVE A MOMENT?
SURE. WHAT'S UP?
SNEAK
DUE TO A MIX-UP ON OUR PART, I'M AFRAID YOUR FLIGHT HAS BEEN OVER-BOOKED.

*ANA (All Nippon Airways) is the name of a major Japanese airline.

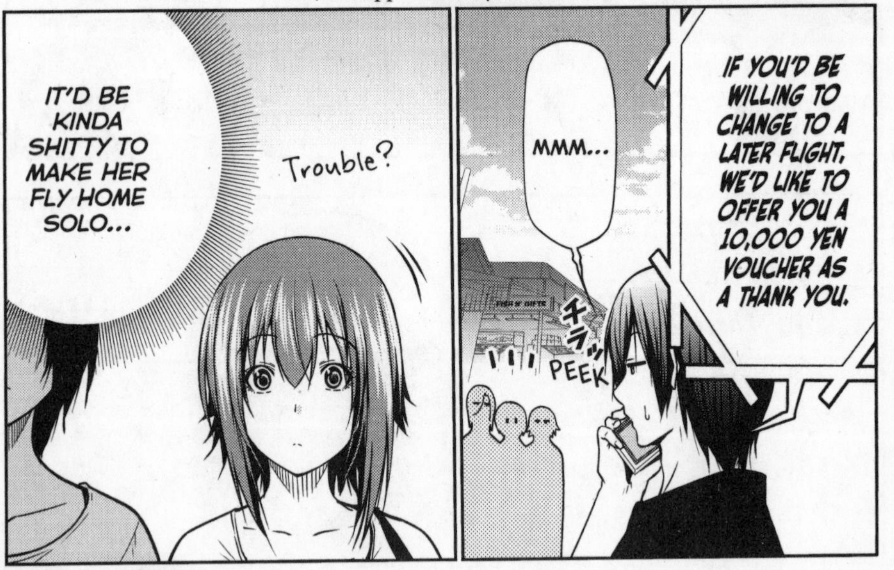
IF YOU'D BE WILLING TO CHANGE TO A LATER FLIGHT, WE'D LIKE TO OFFER YOU A 10,000 YEN VOUCHER AS A THANK YOU.
MMM...
チラッ
PEEK
Trouble?
IT'D BE KINDA SHITTY TO MAKE HER FLY HOME SOLO...

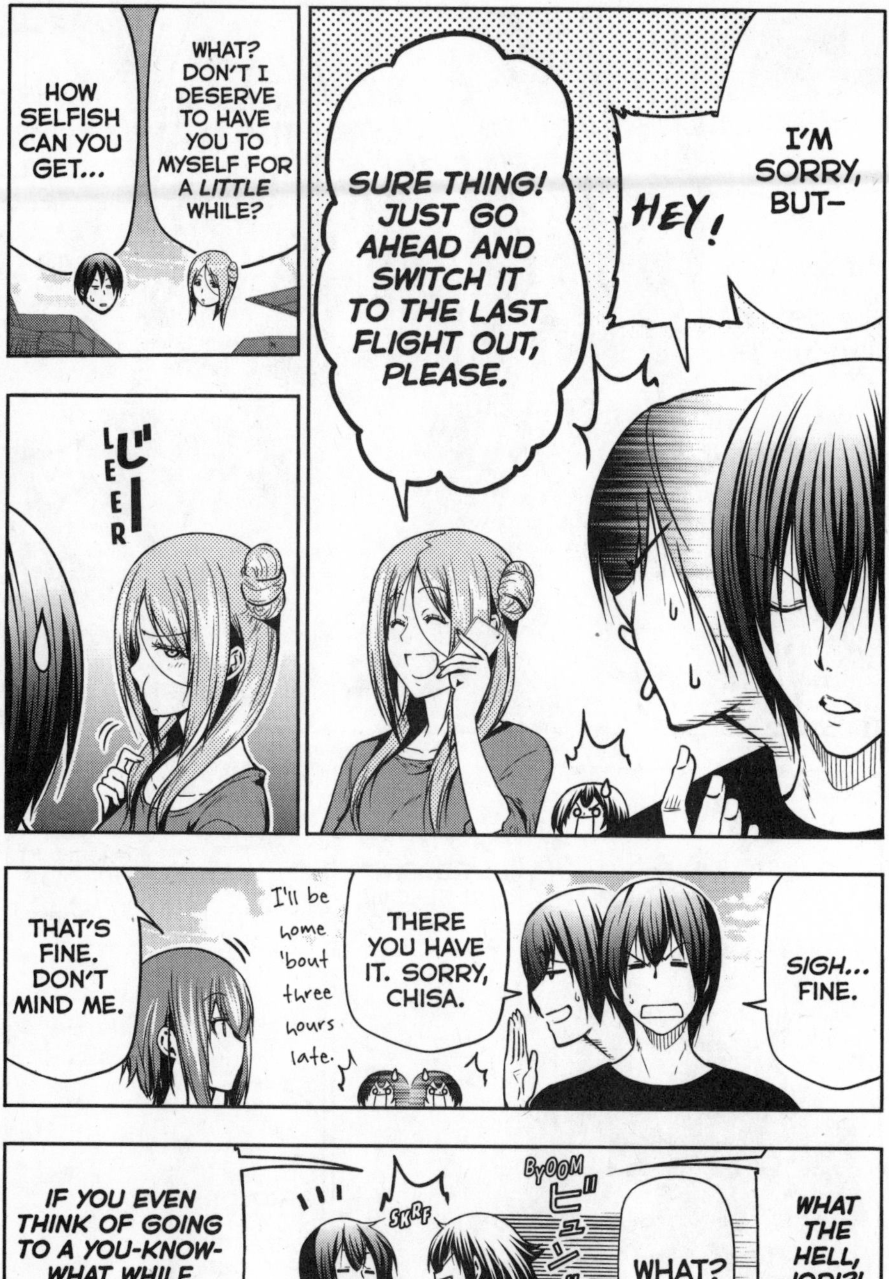
I'M SORRY, BUT-
HEY!
SURE THING! JUST GO AHEAD AND SWITCH IT TO THE LAST FLIGHT OUT, PLEASE.
WHAT? DON'T I DESERVE TO HAVE YOU TO MYSELF FOR A LITTLE WHILE?
HOW SELFISH CAN YOU GET...
じー
LEER
SIGH... FINE.
THERE YOU HAVE IT. SORRY, CHISA.
I'll be home 'bout three hours late.
THAT'S FINE. DON'T MIND ME.
WHAT THE HELL, IORI?!
BYOOM
WHAT?
SKRF
IF YOU EVEN THINK OF GOING TO A YOU-KNOW-WHAT WHILE CHISA'S GONE...

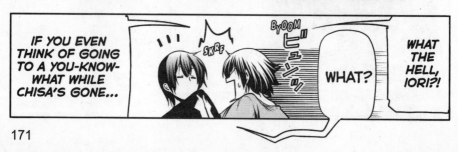

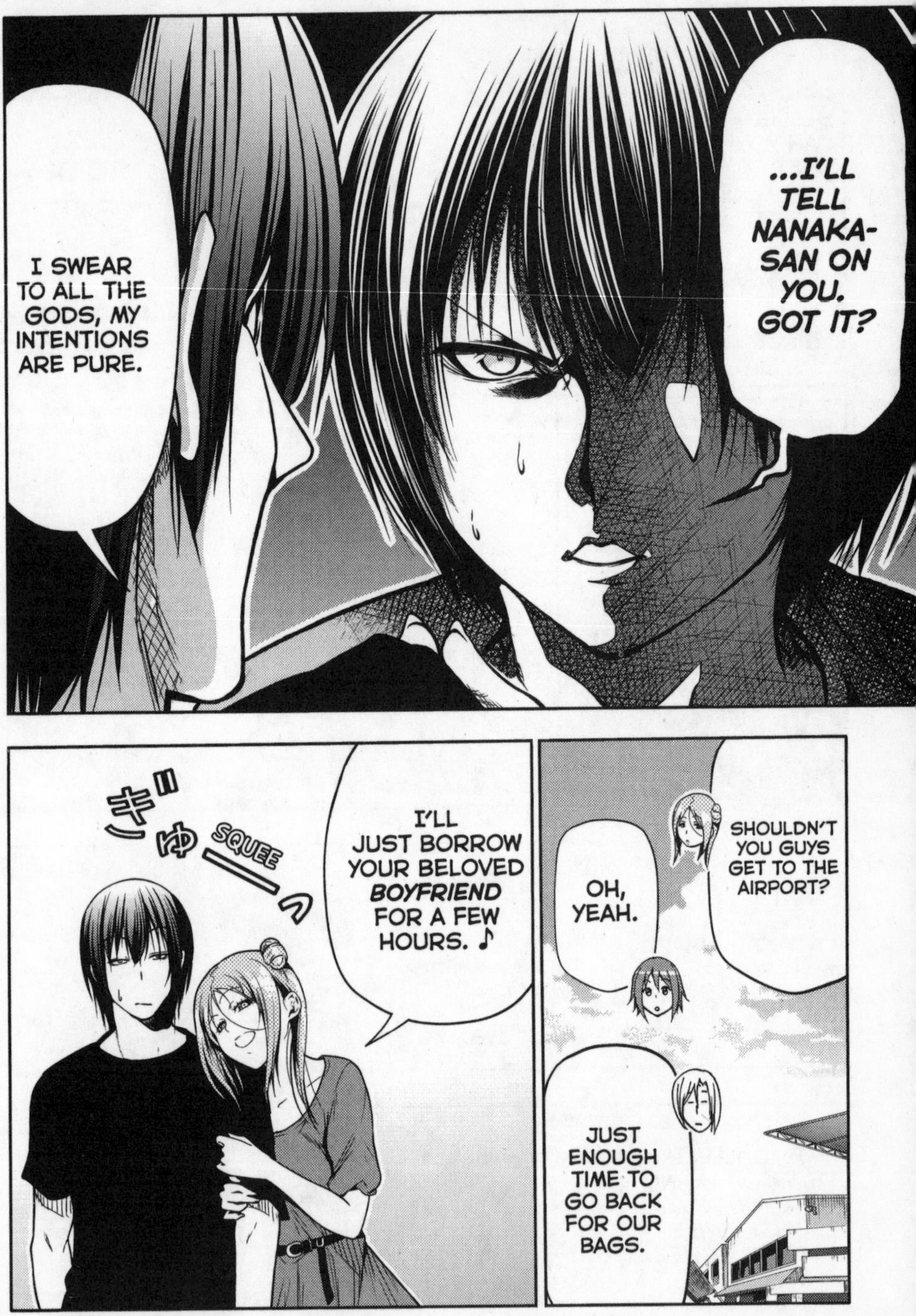
...I'LL TELL NANAKA-SAN ON YOU. GOT IT?
I SWEAR TO ALL THE GODS, MY INTENTIONS ARE PURE.
SHOULDN'T YOU GUYS GET TO THE AIRPORT?
OH, YEAH.
JUST ENOUGH TIME TO GO BACK FOR OUR BAGS.
I'LL JUST BORROW YOUR BELOVED *BOYFRIEND* FOR A FEW HOURS. ♪
ぎゅーっ
SQUEE

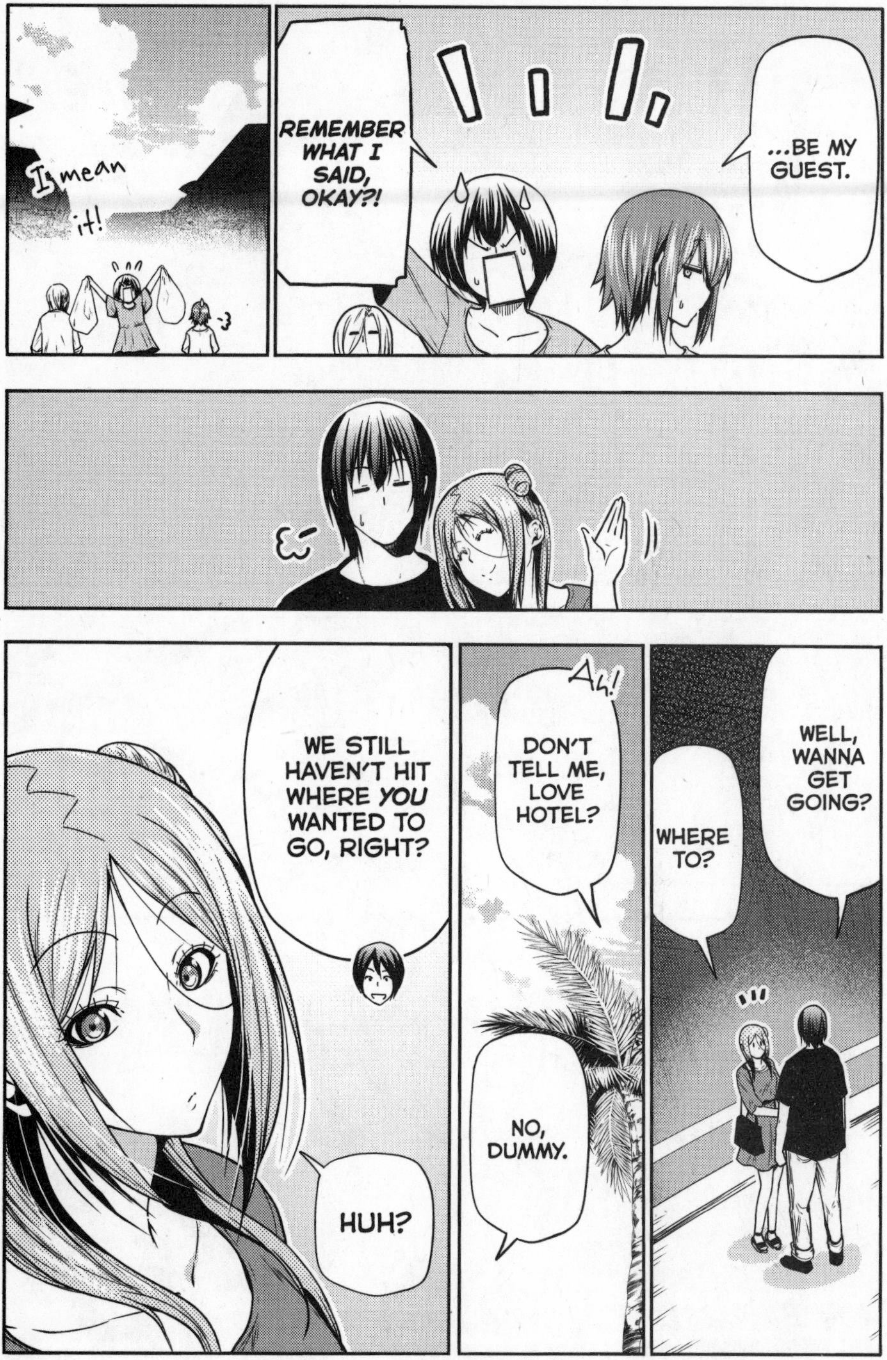
...BE MY GUEST.
REMEMBER WHAT I SAID, OKAY?!
I mean it!
WELL, WANNA GET GOING?
WHERE TO?
Ah!
DON'T TELL ME, LOVE HOTEL?
NO, DUMMY.
WE STILL HAVEN'T HIT WHERE *YOU* WANTED TO GO, RIGHT?
HUH?

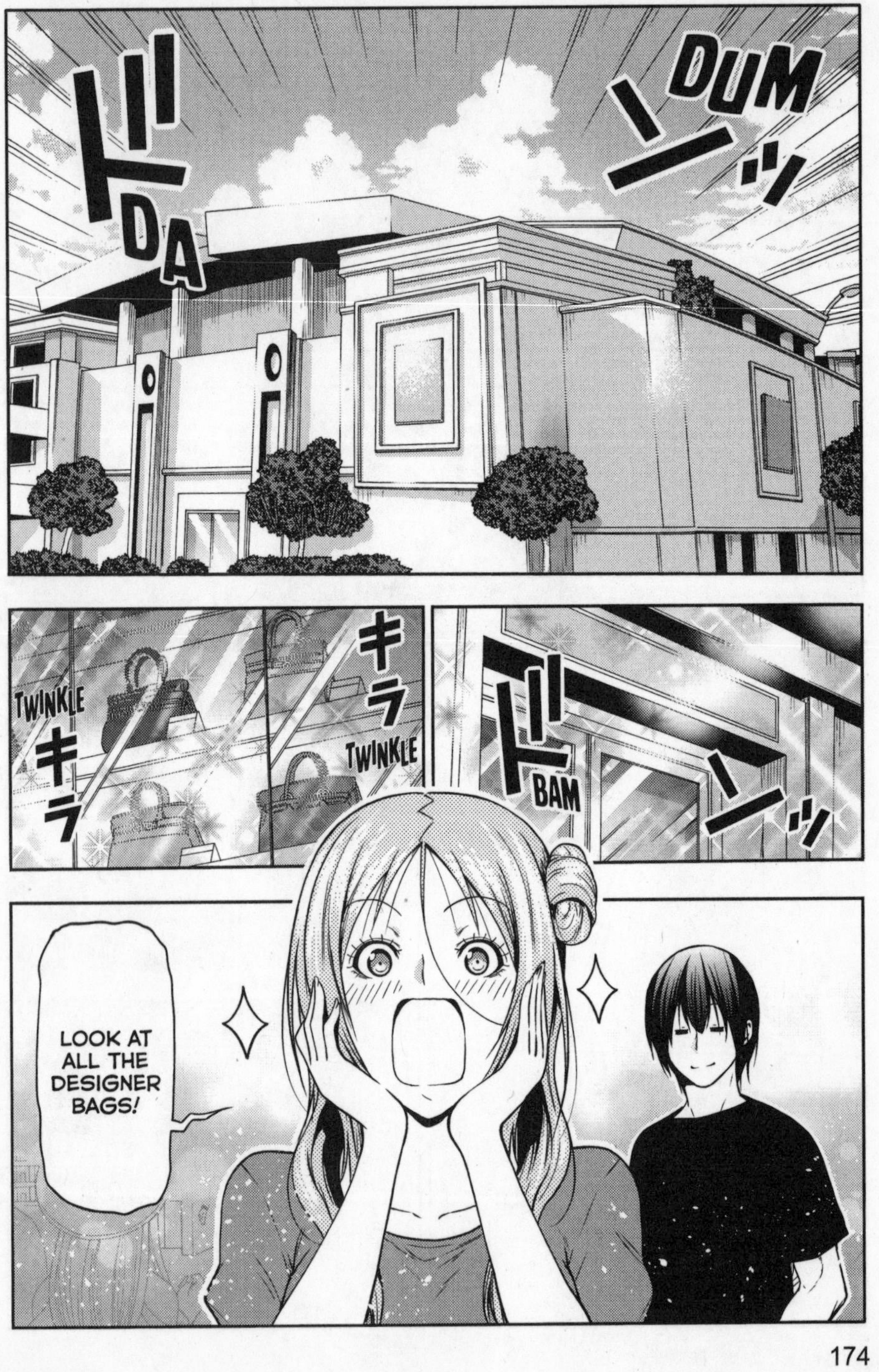
ーンッ
DUM
ド
DA
ドーンッ
BAM
キラ
TWINKLE
キラ
TWINKLE
LOOK AT ALL THE DESIGNER BAGS!

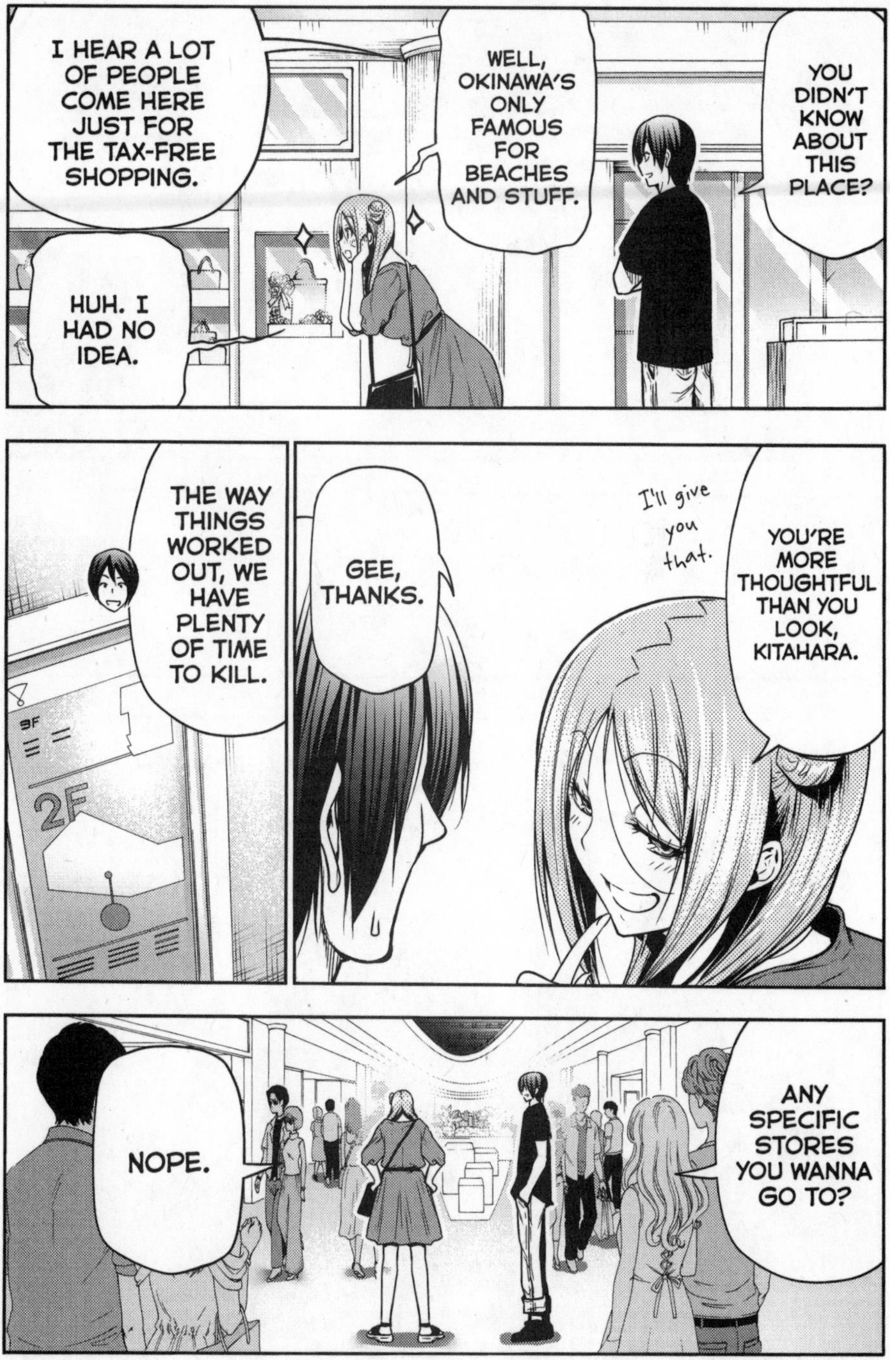
YOU DIDN'T KNOW ABOUT THIS PLACE?
WELL, OKINAWA'S ONLY FAMOUS FOR BEACHES AND STUFF.
I HEAR A LOT OF PEOPLE COME HERE JUST FOR THE TAX-FREE SHOPPING.
HUH. I HAD NO IDEA.
YOU'RE MORE THOUGHTFUL THAN YOU LOOK, KITAHARA.
I'll give you that.
GEE, THANKS.
THE WAY THINGS WORKED OUT, WE HAVE PLENTY OF TIME TO KILL.
2F
ANY SPECIFIC STORES YOU WANNA GO TO?
NOPE.

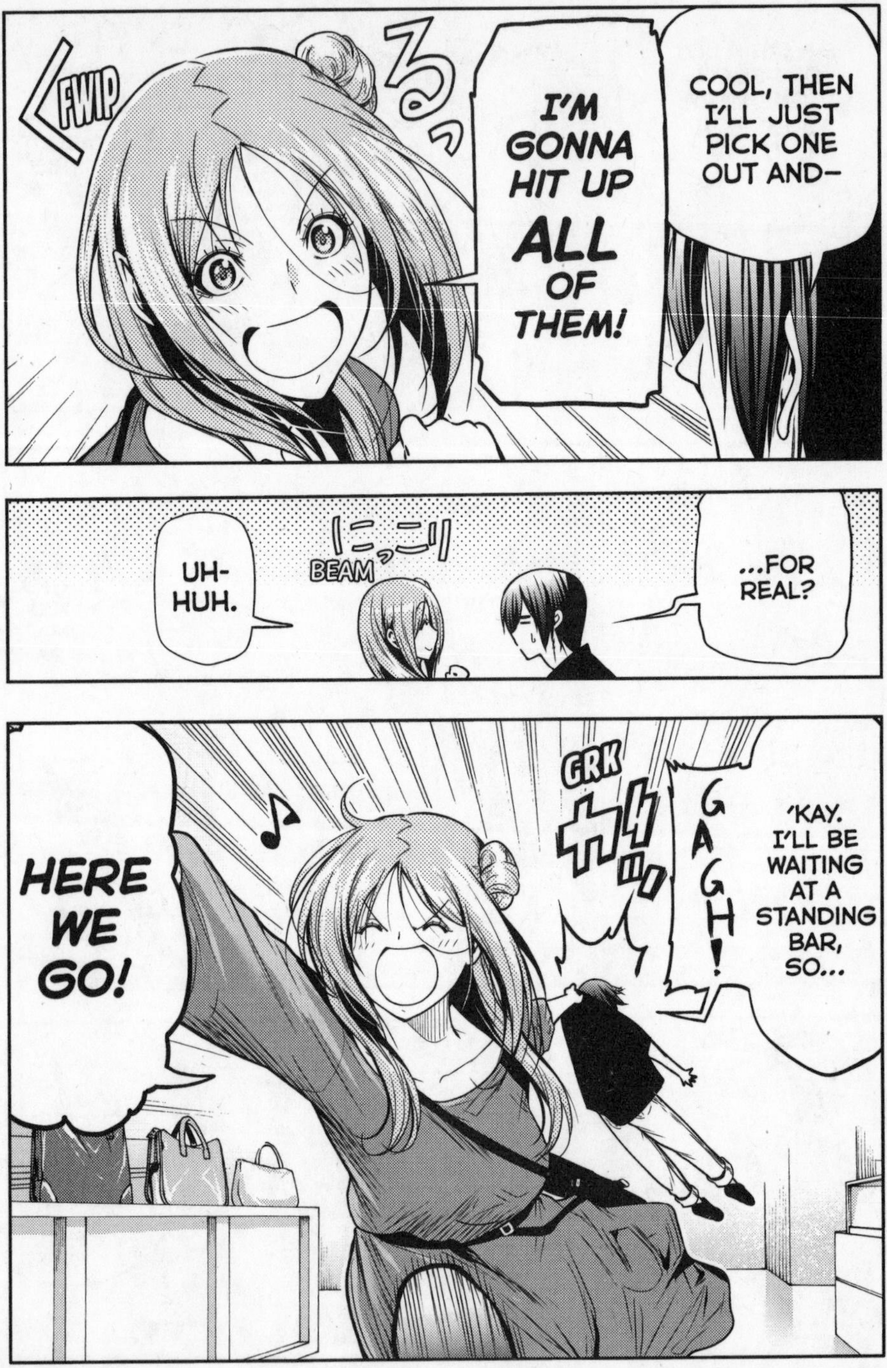
COOL, THEN I'LL JUST PICK ONE OUT AND–
I'M GONNA HIT UP ALL OF THEM!
FWIP
...FOR REAL?
BEAM
UH-HUH.
'KAY. I'LL BE WAITING AT A STANDING BAR, SO...
GAGH!
GRK
HERE WE GO!

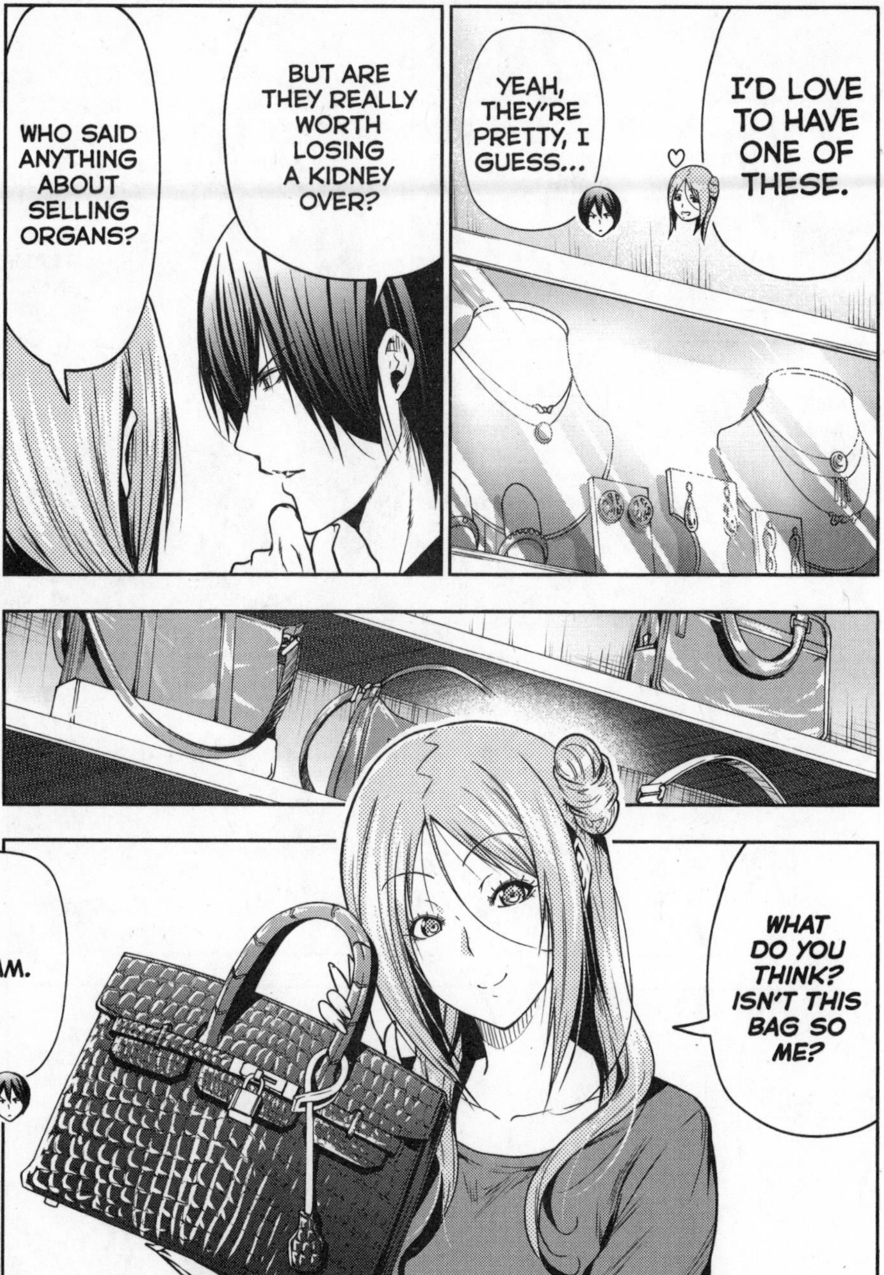
I'D LOVE TO HAVE ONE OF THESE.
YEAH, THEY'RE PRETTY, I GUESS...
BUT ARE THEY REALLY WORTH LOSING A KIDNEY OVER?
WHO SAID ANYTHING ABOUT SELLING ORGANS?
WHAT DO YOU THINK? ISN'T THIS BAG SO ME?
HMM.

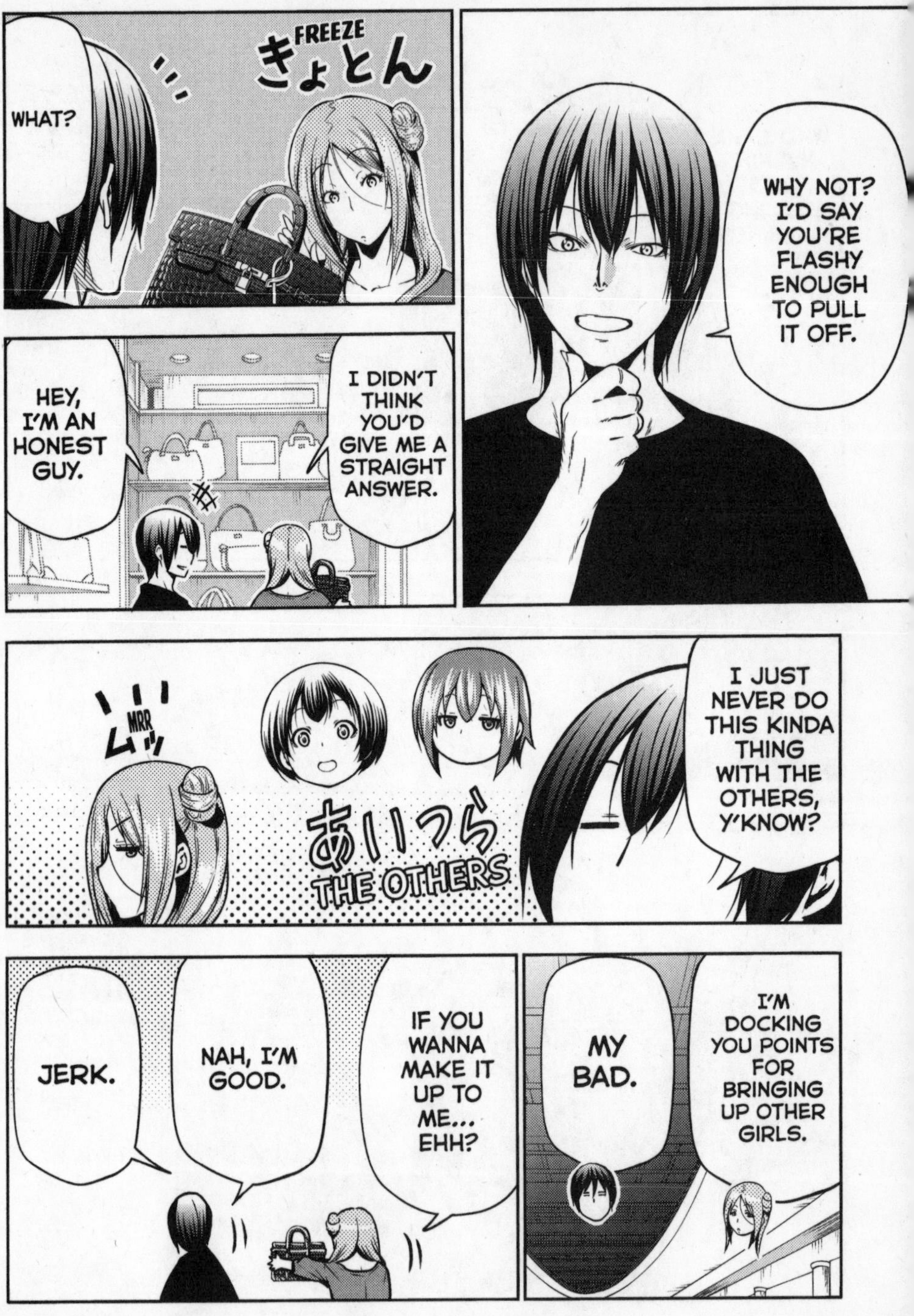
WHY NOT? I'D SAY YOU'RE FLASHY ENOUGH TO PULL IT OFF.
FREEZE
きょとん
WHAT?
I DIDN'T THINK YOU'D GIVE ME A STRAIGHT ANSWER.
HEY, I'M AN HONEST GUY.
I JUST NEVER DO THIS KINDA THING WITH THE OTHERS, Y'KNOW?
あいつら
THE OTHERS
MRR
ムッ
I'M DOCKING YOU POINTS FOR BRINGING UP OTHER GIRLS.
MY BAD.
IF YOU WANNA MAKE IT UP TO ME... EHH?
NAH, I'M GOOD.
JERK.

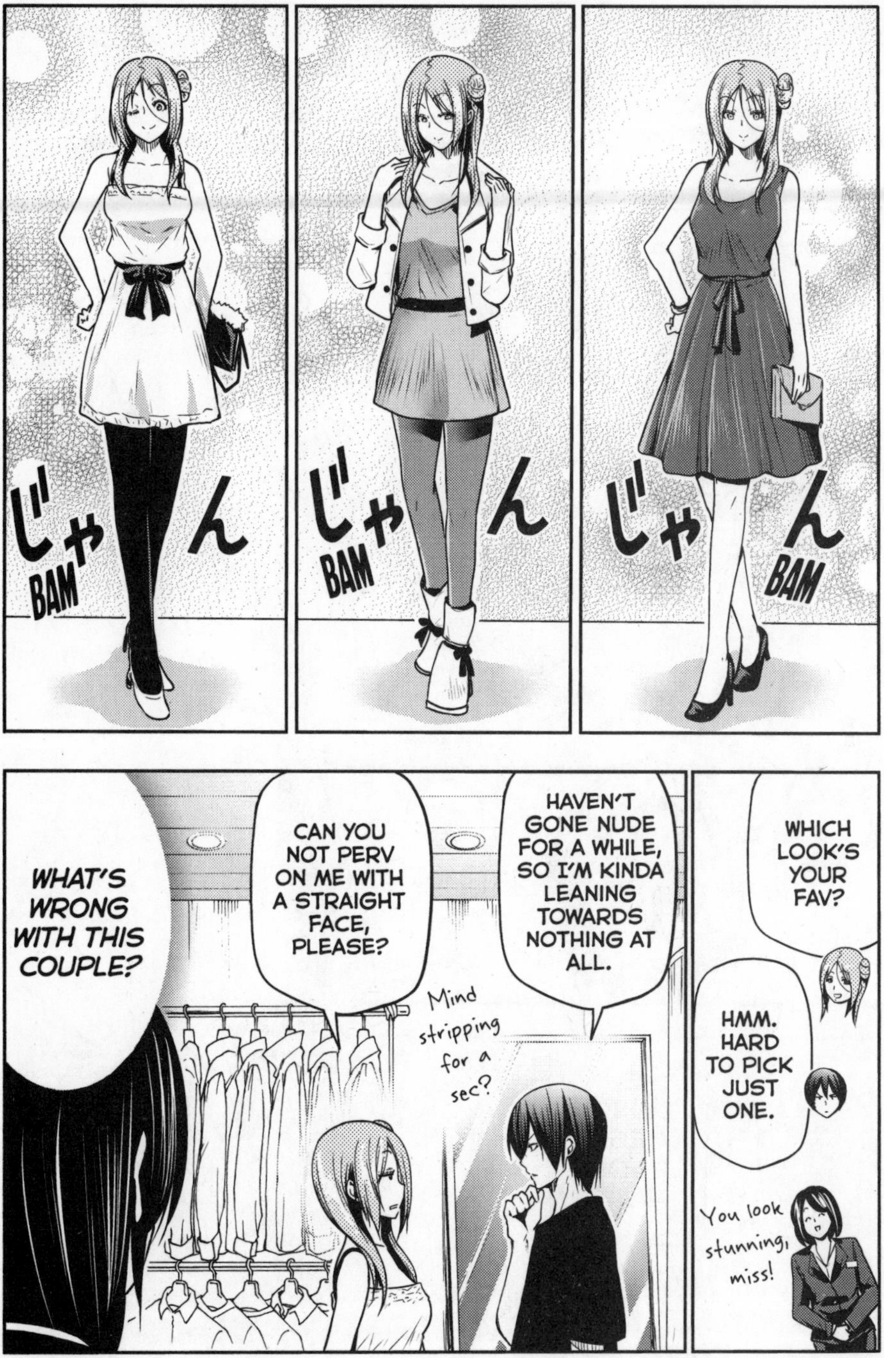
じゃん
BAM
じゃん
BAM
じゃん
BAM
WHICH LOOK'S YOUR FAV?
HMM. HARD TO PICK JUST ONE.
You look stunning, miss!
HAVEN'T GONE NUDE FOR A WHILE, SO I'M KINDA LEANING TOWARDS NOTHING AT ALL.
Mind stripping for a sec?
CAN YOU NOT PERV ON ME WITH A STRAIGHT FACE, PLEASE?
WHAT'S WRONG WITH THIS COUPLE?

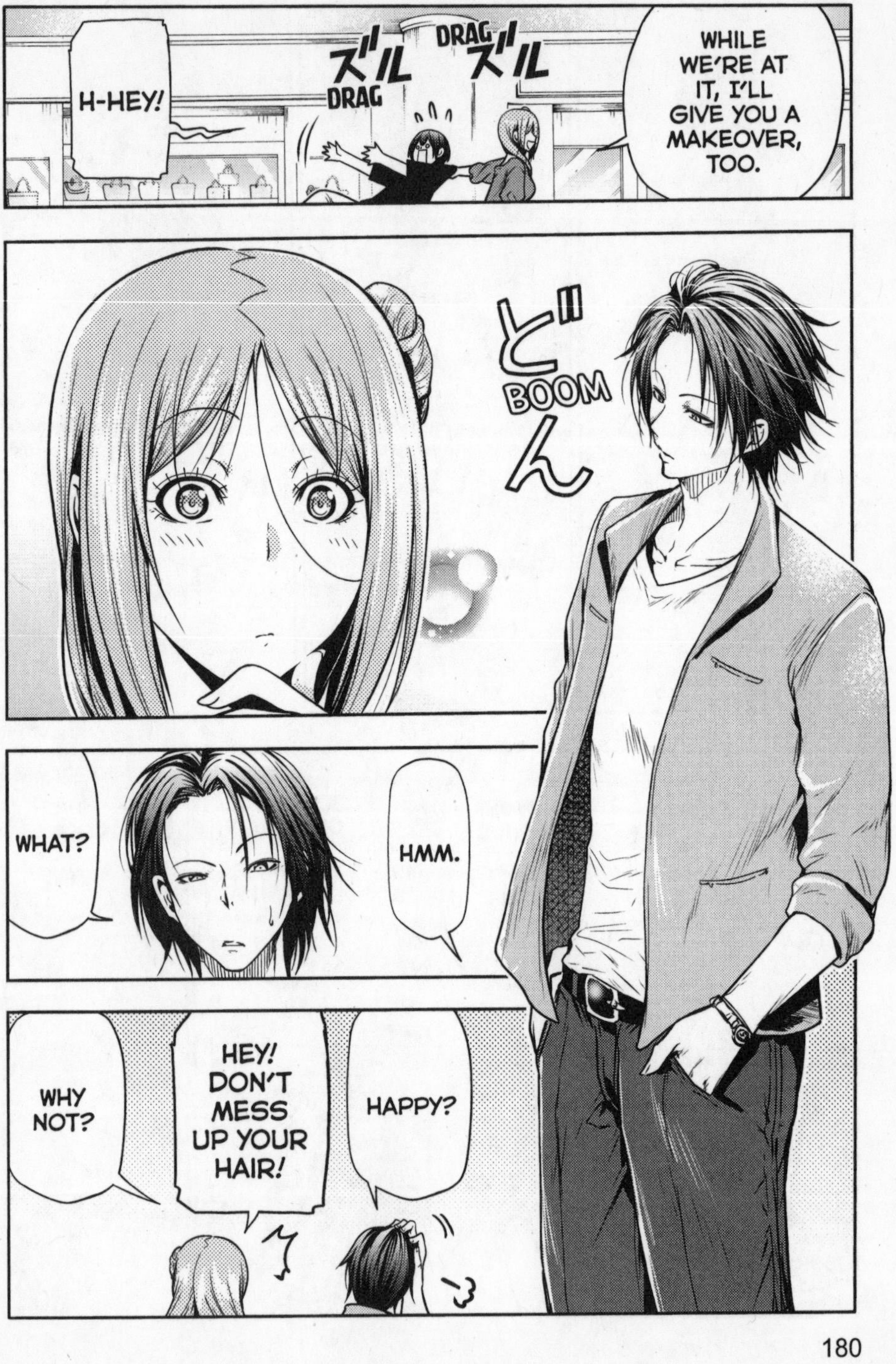
WHILE WE'RE AT IT, I'LL GIVE YOU A MAKEOVER, TOO.
ズル DRAG
ズル DRAG
H-HEY!
どん BOOM
HMM.
WHAT?
HAPPY?
HEY! DON'T MESS UP YOUR HAIR!
WHY NOT?

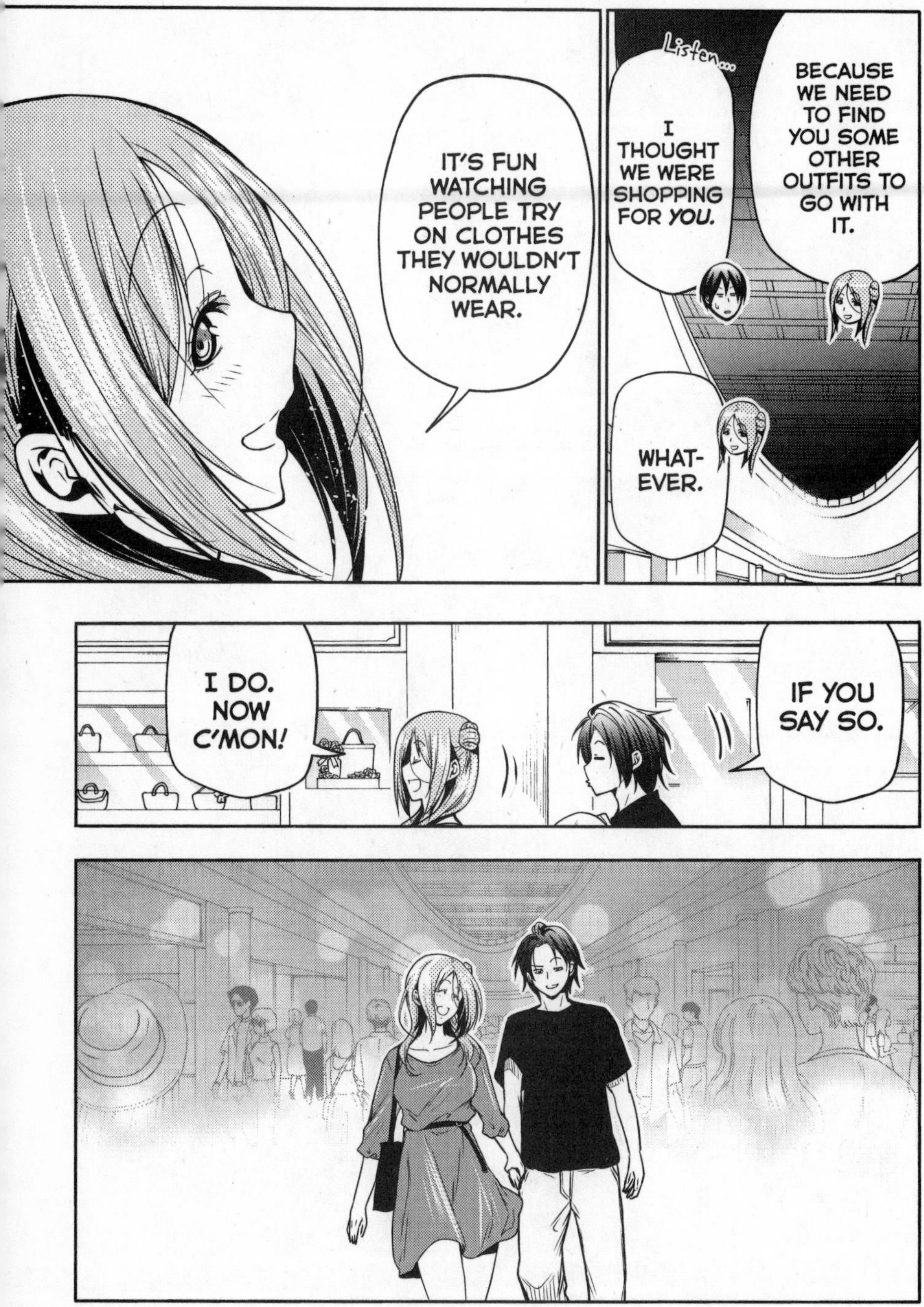
Listen...
I THOUGHT WE WERE SHOPPING FOR *YOU.*
BECAUSE WE NEED TO FIND YOU SOME OTHER OUTFITS TO GO WITH IT.
WHAT-EVER.
IT'S FUN WATCHING PEOPLE TRY ON CLOTHES THEY WOULDN'T NORMALLY WEAR.
IF YOU SAY SO.
I DO. NOW C'MON!

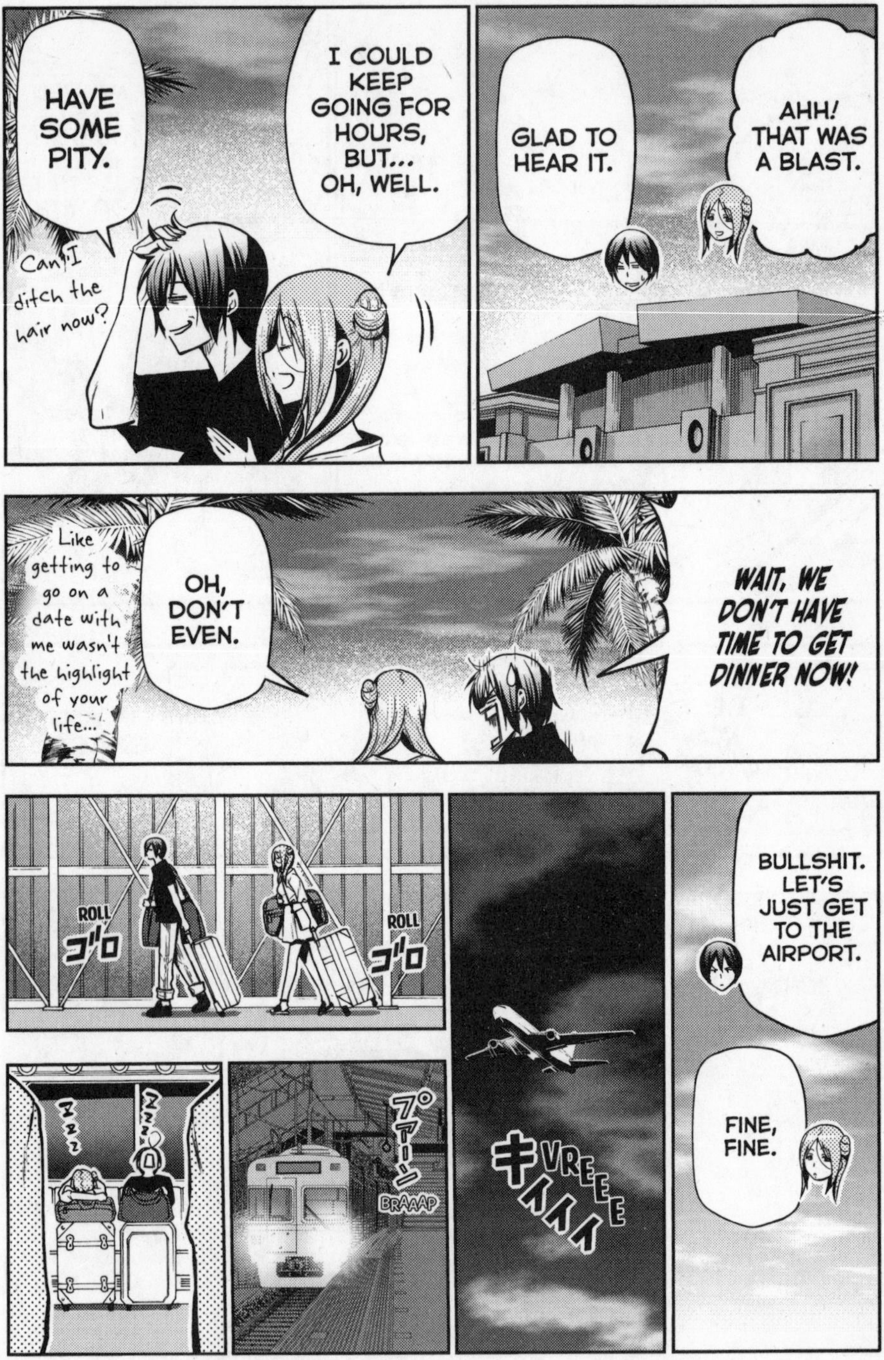
AHH! THAT WAS A BLAST.
GLAD TO HEAR IT.
I COULD KEEP GOING FOR HOURS, BUT... OH, WELL.
HAVE SOME PITY.
Can I ditch the hair now?
WAIT, WE DON'T HAVE TIME TO GET DINNER NOW!
OH, DON'T EVEN.
Like getting to go on a date with me wasn't the highlight of your life...
BULLSHIT. LET'S JUST GET TO THE AIRPORT.
FINE, FINE.
キイイイ
VREEEE
ゴロ
ROLL
ゴロ
ROLL
プアーン
BRAAAP

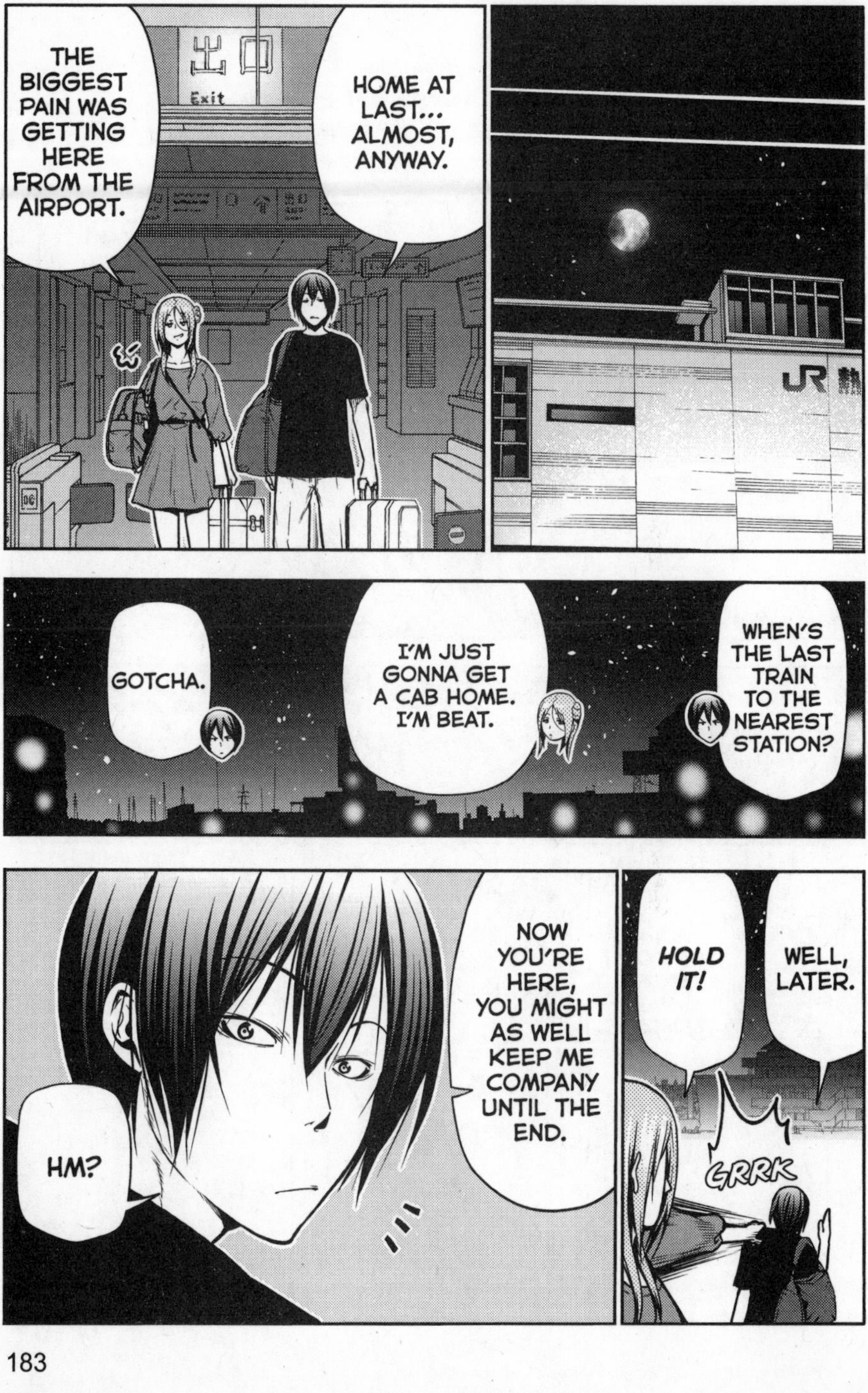
JR
出口
Exit
HOME AT LAST... ALMOST, ANYWAY.
THE BIGGEST PAIN WAS GETTING HERE FROM THE AIRPORT.
WHEN'S THE LAST TRAIN TO THE NEAREST STATION?
I'M JUST GONNA GET A CAB HOME. I'M BEAT.
GOTCHA.
WELL, LATER.
HOLD IT!
GRRK
NOW YOU'RE HERE, YOU MIGHT AS WELL KEEP ME COMPANY UNTIL THE END.
HM?

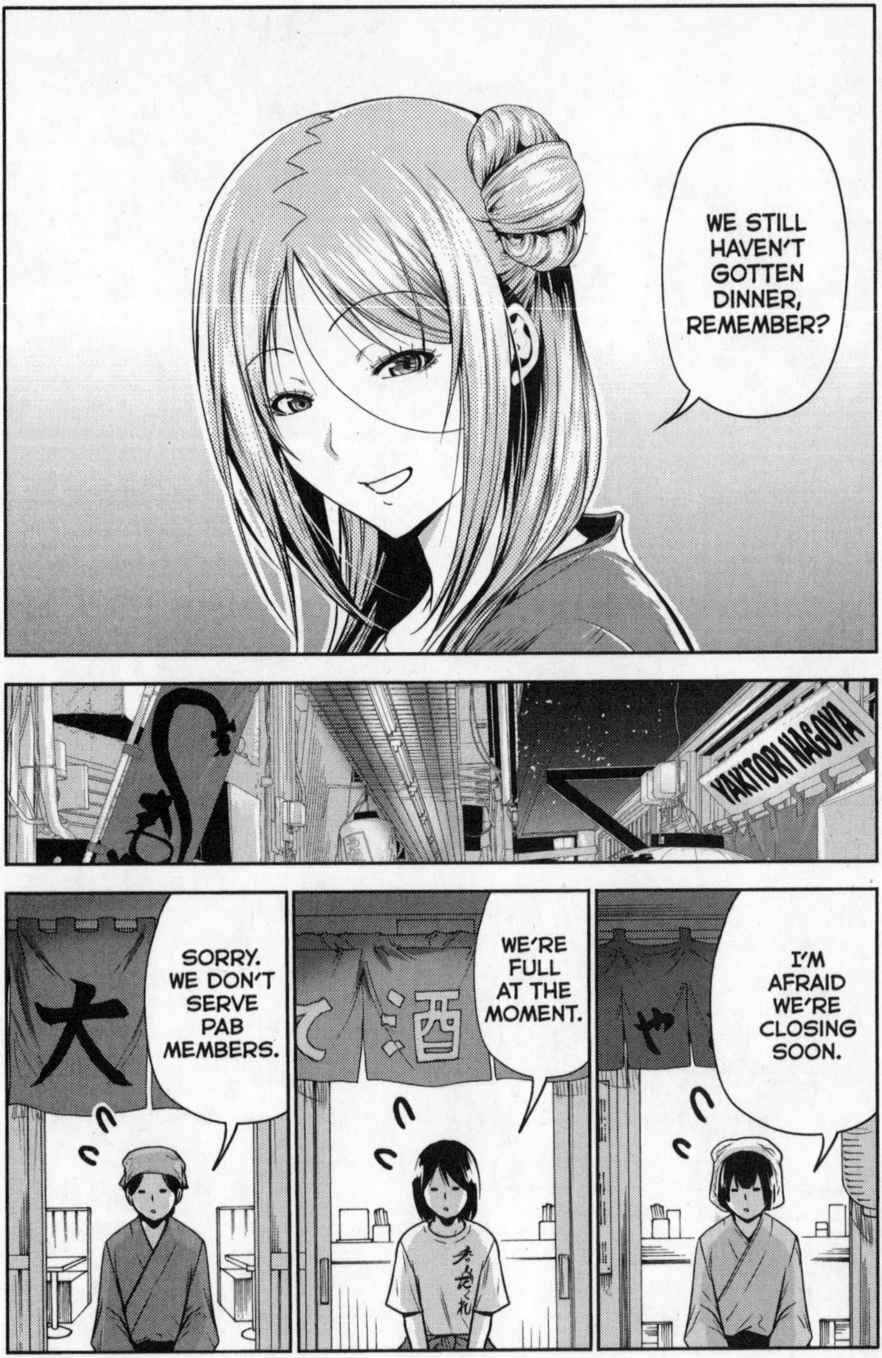
WE STILL HAVEN'T GOTTEN DINNER, REMEMBER?
YAKITORI NAGOYA
I'M AFRAID WE'RE CLOSING SOON.
WE'RE FULL AT THE MOMENT.
SORRY. WE DON'T SERVE PAB MEMBERS.

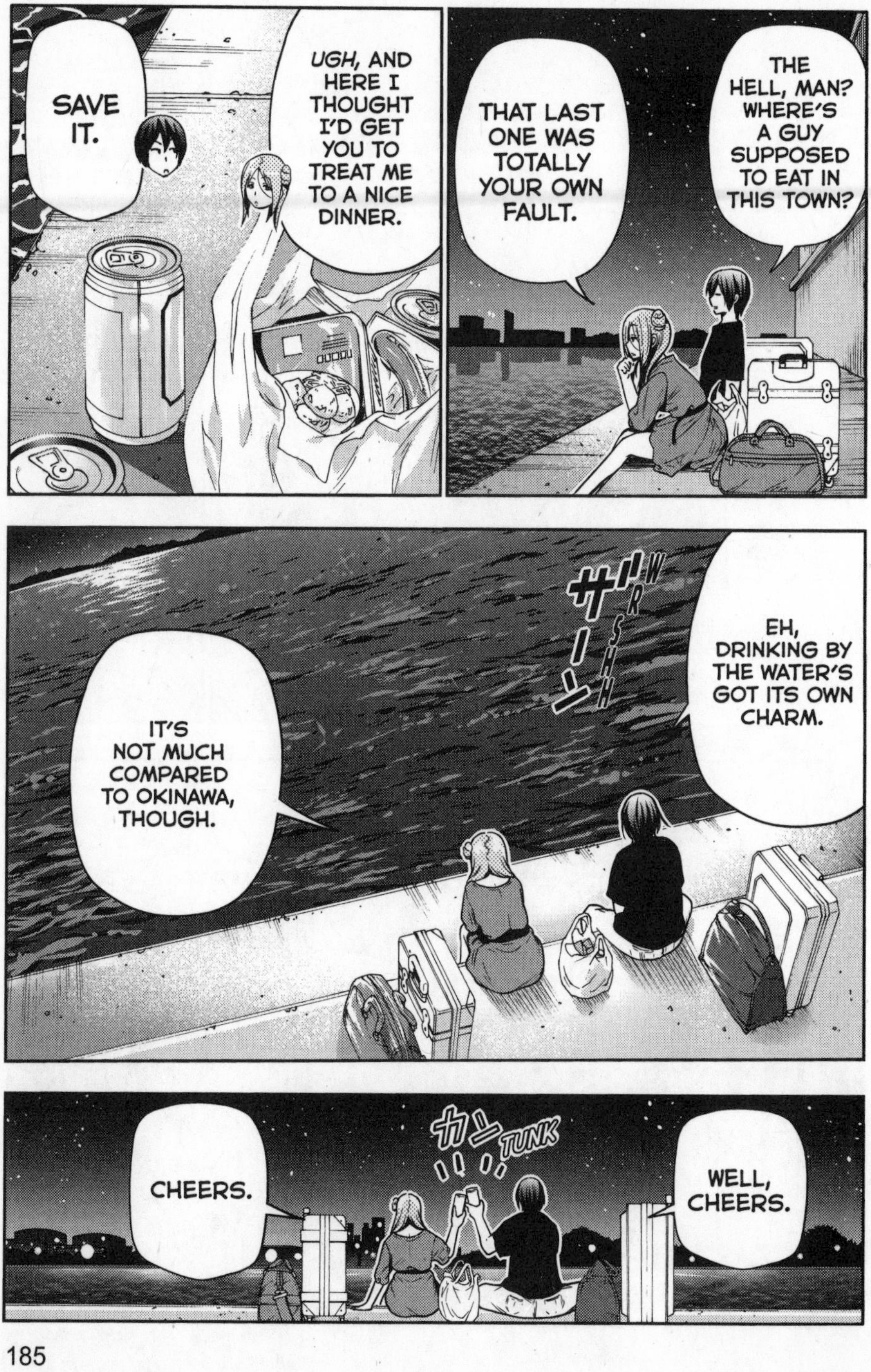
THE HELL, MAN? WHERE'S A GUY SUPPOSED TO EAT IN THIS TOWN?
THAT LAST ONE WAS TOTALLY YOUR OWN FAULT.
UGH, AND HERE I THOUGHT I'D GET YOU TO TREAT ME TO A NICE DINNER.
SAVE IT.
EH, DRINKING BY THE WATER'S GOT ITS OWN CHARM.
WRSHHH
IT'S NOT MUCH COMPARED TO OKINAWA, THOUGH.
WELL, CHEERS.
TUNK
CHEERS.

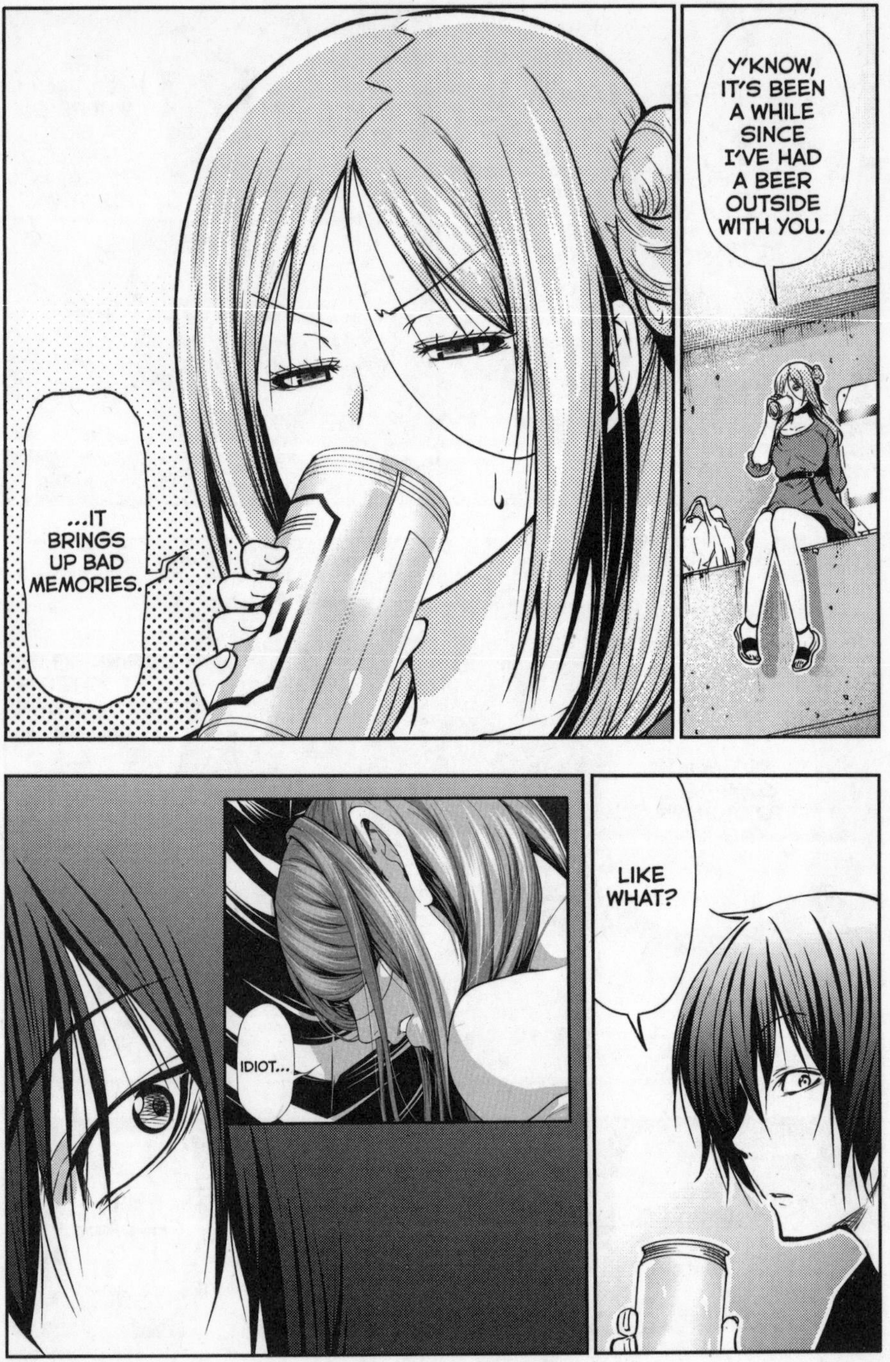
Y'KNOW, IT'S BEEN A WHILE SINCE I'VE HAD A BEER OUTSIDE WITH YOU.
...IT BRINGS UP BAD MEMORIES.
LIKE WHAT?
IDIOT...

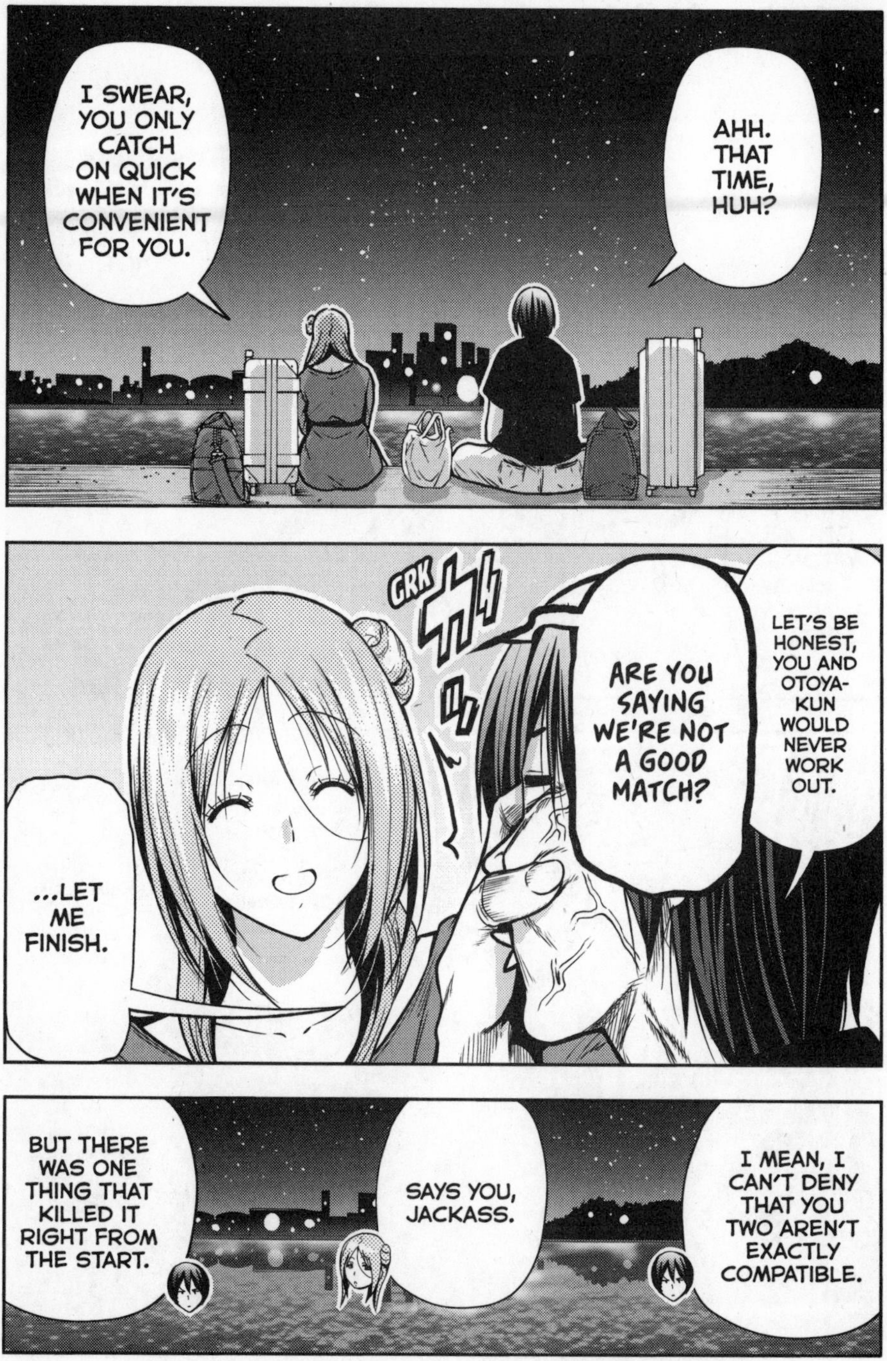
AHH. THAT TIME, HUH?
I SWEAR, YOU ONLY CATCH ON QUICK WHEN IT'S CONVENIENT FOR YOU.
LET'S BE HONEST, YOU AND OTOYA-KUN WOULD NEVER WORK OUT.
GRK
ARE YOU SAYING WE'RE NOT A GOOD MATCH?
...LET ME FINISH.
I MEAN, I CAN'T DENY THAT YOU TWO AREN'T EXACTLY COMPATIBLE.
SAYS YOU, JACKASS.
BUT THERE WAS ONE THING THAT KILLED IT RIGHT FROM THE START.

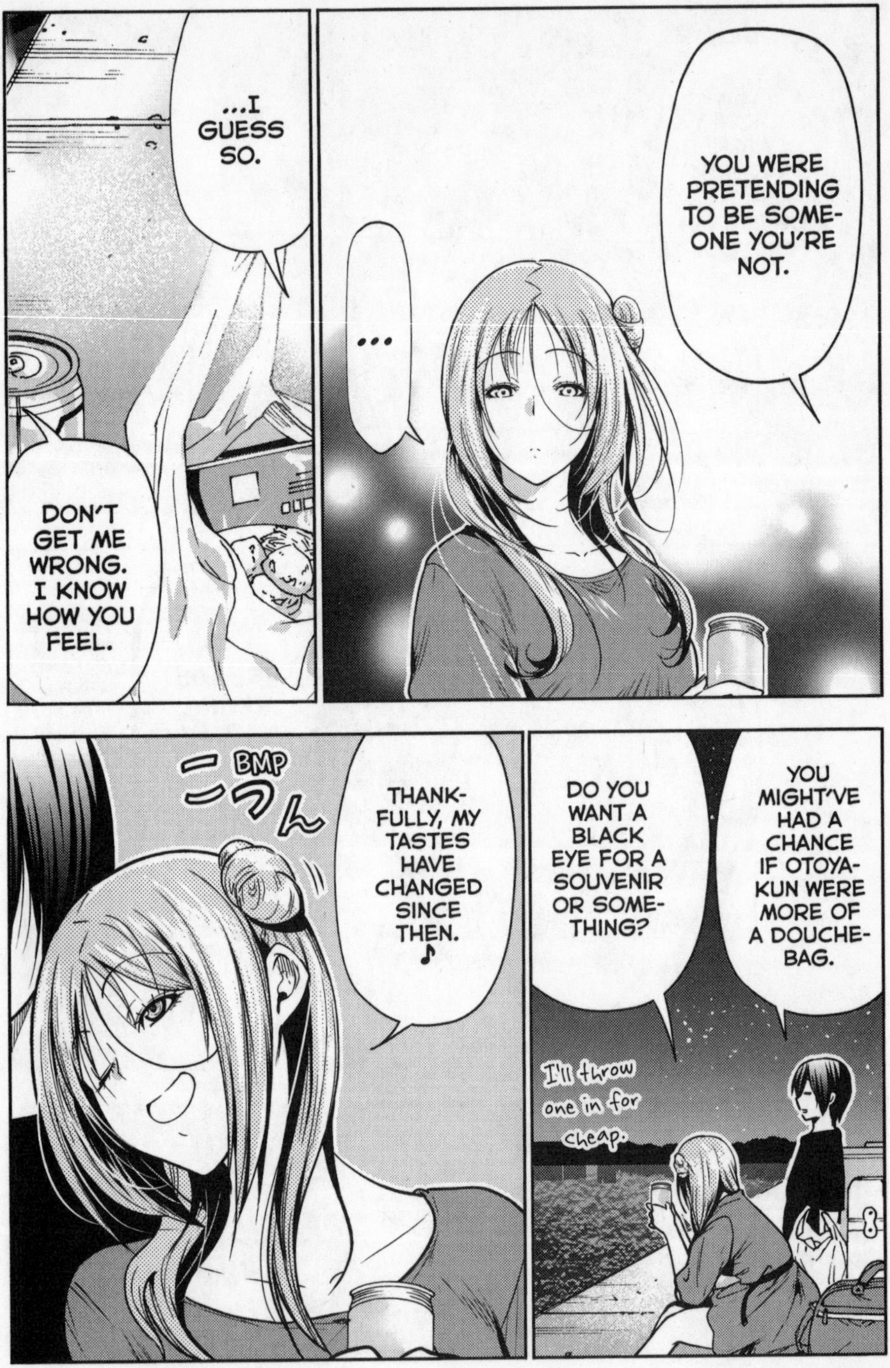

YOU WERE PRETENDING TO BE SOME-ONE YOU'RE NOT.
...
...I GUESS SO.
DON'T GET ME WRONG. I KNOW HOW YOU FEEL.
YOU MIGHT'VE HAD A CHANCE IF OTOYA-KUN WERE MORE OF A DOUCHE-BAG.
DO YOU WANT A BLACK EYE FOR A SOUVENIR OR SOME-THING?
I'll throw one in for cheap.
こつん BMP
THANK-FULLY, MY TASTES HAVE CHANGED SINCE THEN. ♪

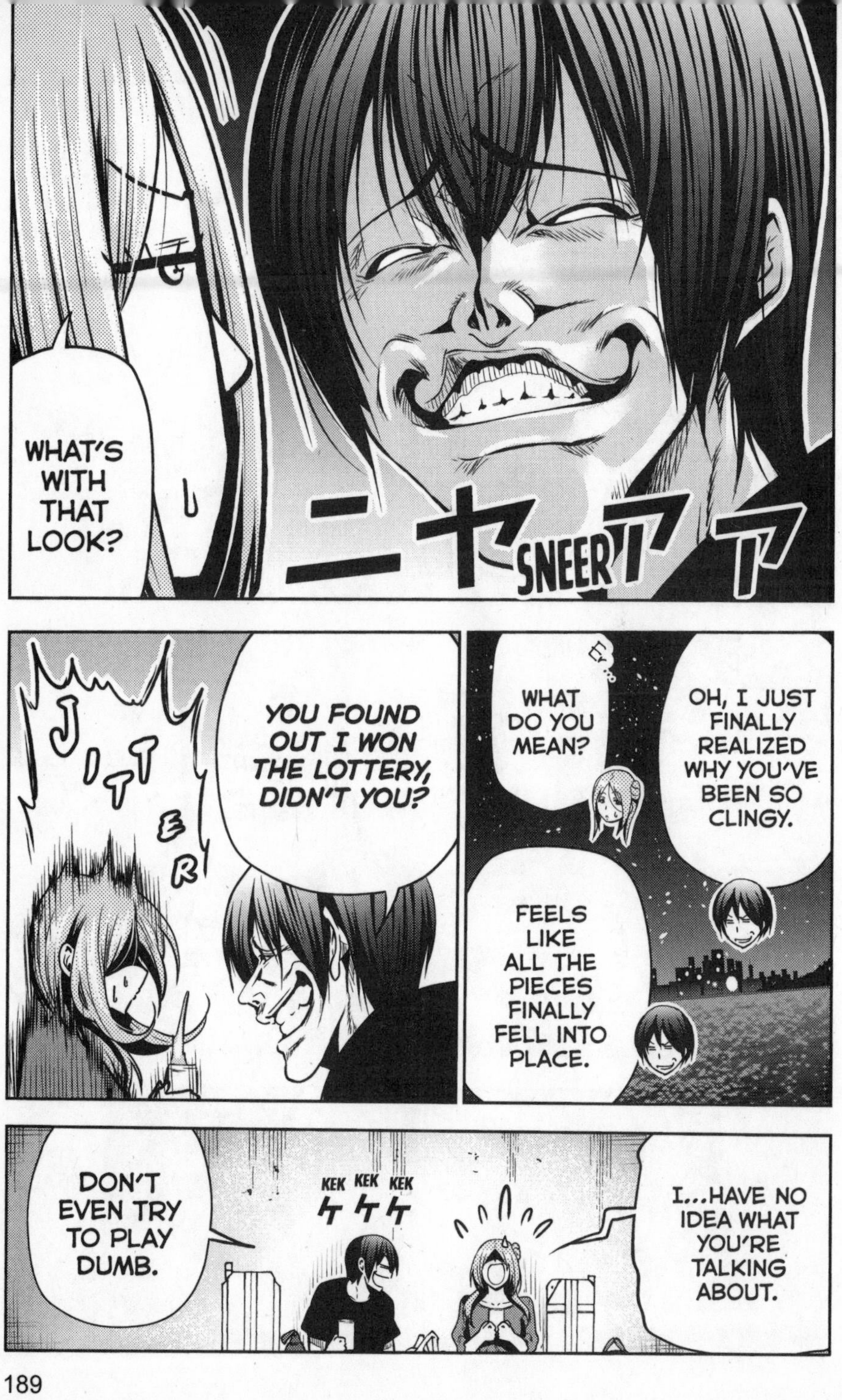
WHAT'S WITH THAT LOOK?
ニヤァァ
SNEER
OH, I JUST FINALLY REALIZED WHY YOU'VE BEEN SO CLINGY.
WHAT DO YOU MEAN?
FEELS LIKE ALL THE PIECES FINALLY FELL INTO PLACE.
YOU FOUND OUT I WON THE LOTTERY, DIDN'T YOU?
JITTER
I...HAVE NO IDEA WHAT YOU'RE TALKING ABOUT.
KEK KEK KEK
ケケケ
DON'T EVEN TRY TO PLAY DUMB.

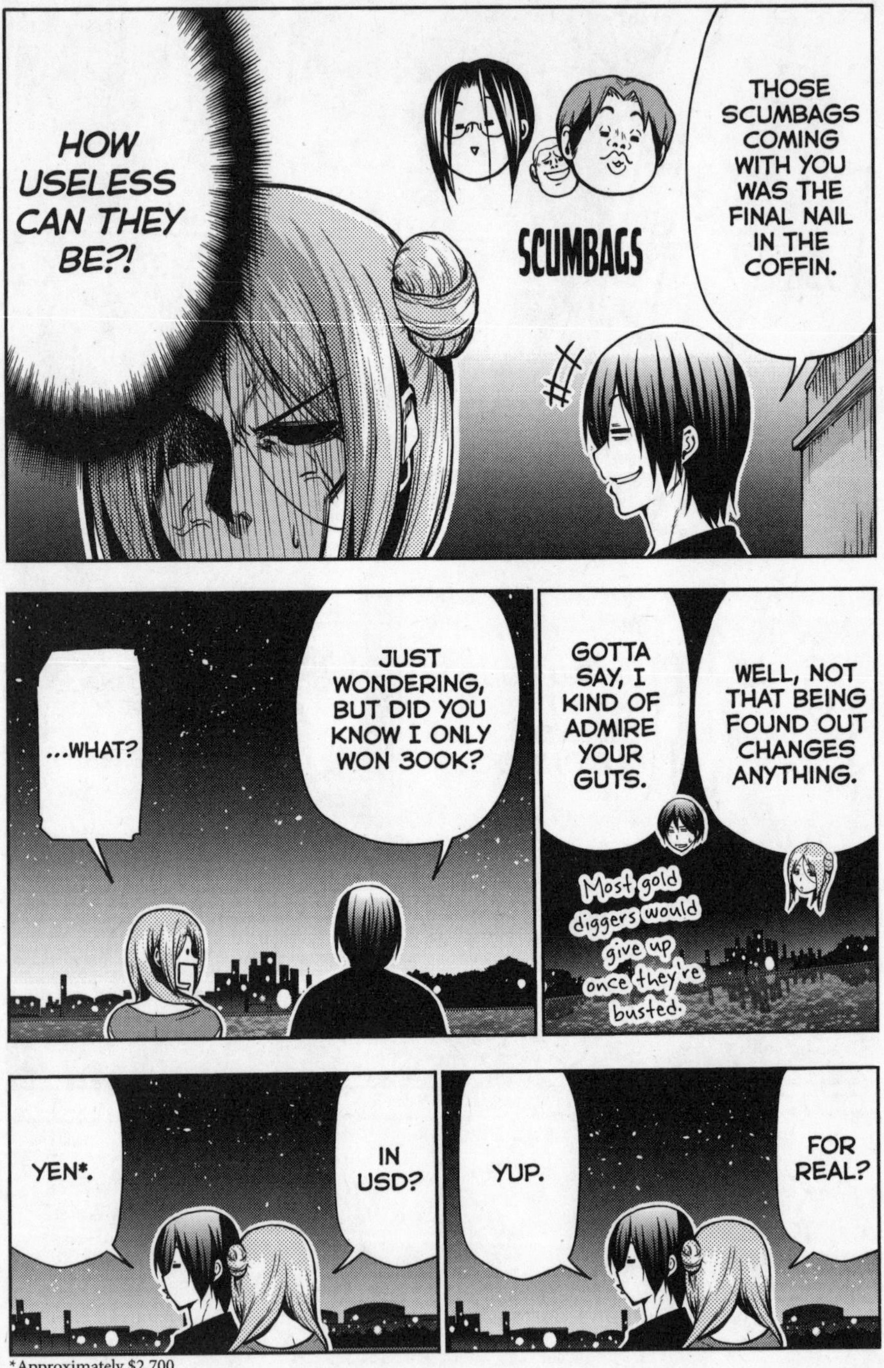
THOSE SCUMBAGS COMING WITH YOU WAS THE FINAL NAIL IN THE COFFIN.
SCUMBAGS
HOW USELESS CAN THEY BE?!
WELL, NOT THAT BEING FOUND OUT CHANGES ANYTHING.
GOTTA SAY, I KIND OF ADMIRE YOUR GUTS.
Most gold diggers would give up once they're busted.
JUST WONDERING, BUT DID YOU KNOW I ONLY WON 300K?
...WHAT?
FOR REAL?
YUP.
IN USD?
YEN*.

*Approximately $2,700.

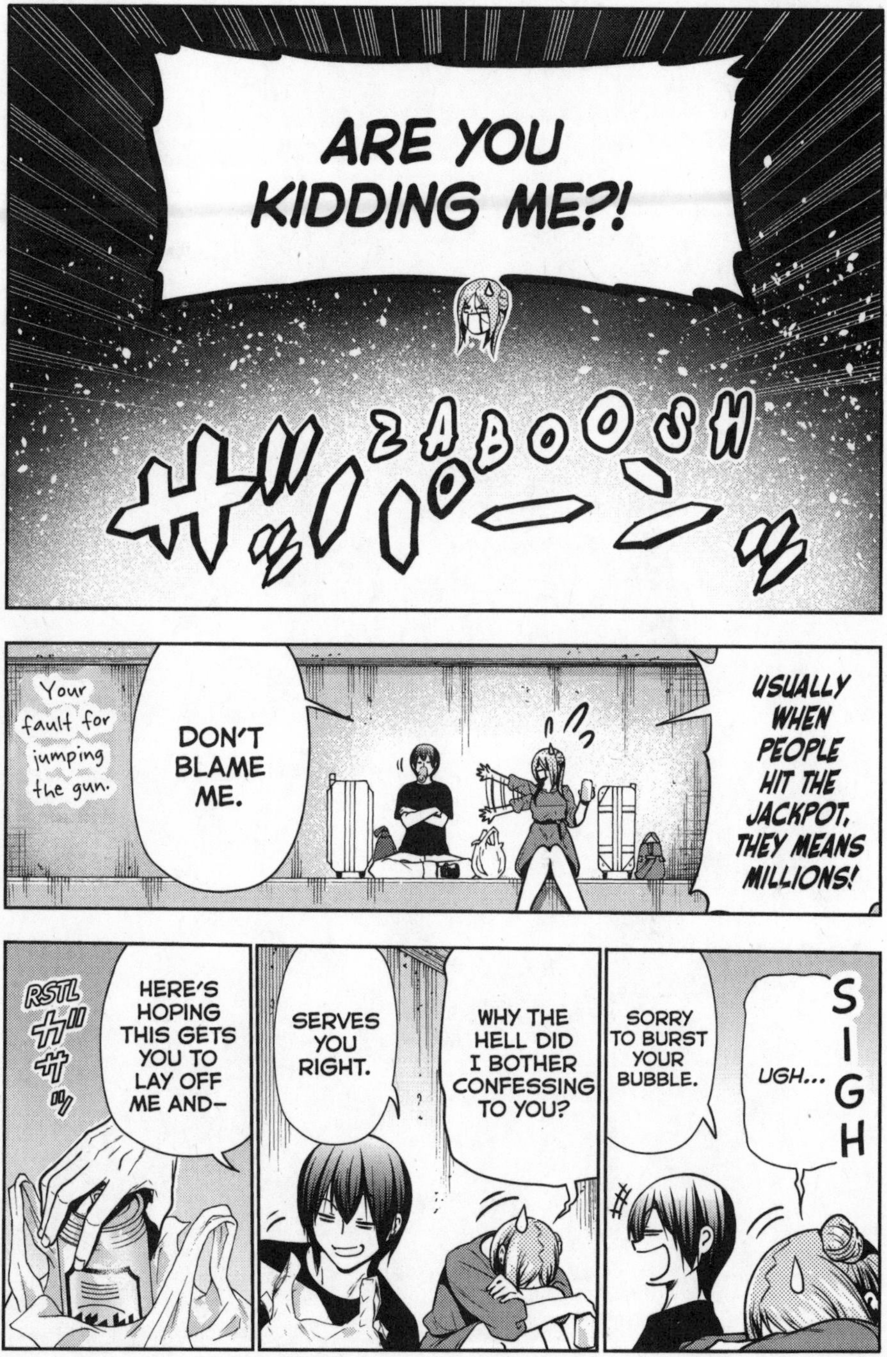
ARE YOU KIDDING ME?!
ZABOOSH
USUALLY WHEN PEOPLE HIT THE JACKPOT, THEY MEANS MILLIONS!
DON'T BLAME ME.
Your fault for jumping the gun.
SIGH
UGH...
SORRY TO BURST YOUR BUBBLE.
WHY THE HELL DID I BOTHER CONFESSING TO YOU?
SERVES YOU RIGHT.
HERE'S HOPING THIS GETS YOU TO LAY OFF ME AND–
RSTL

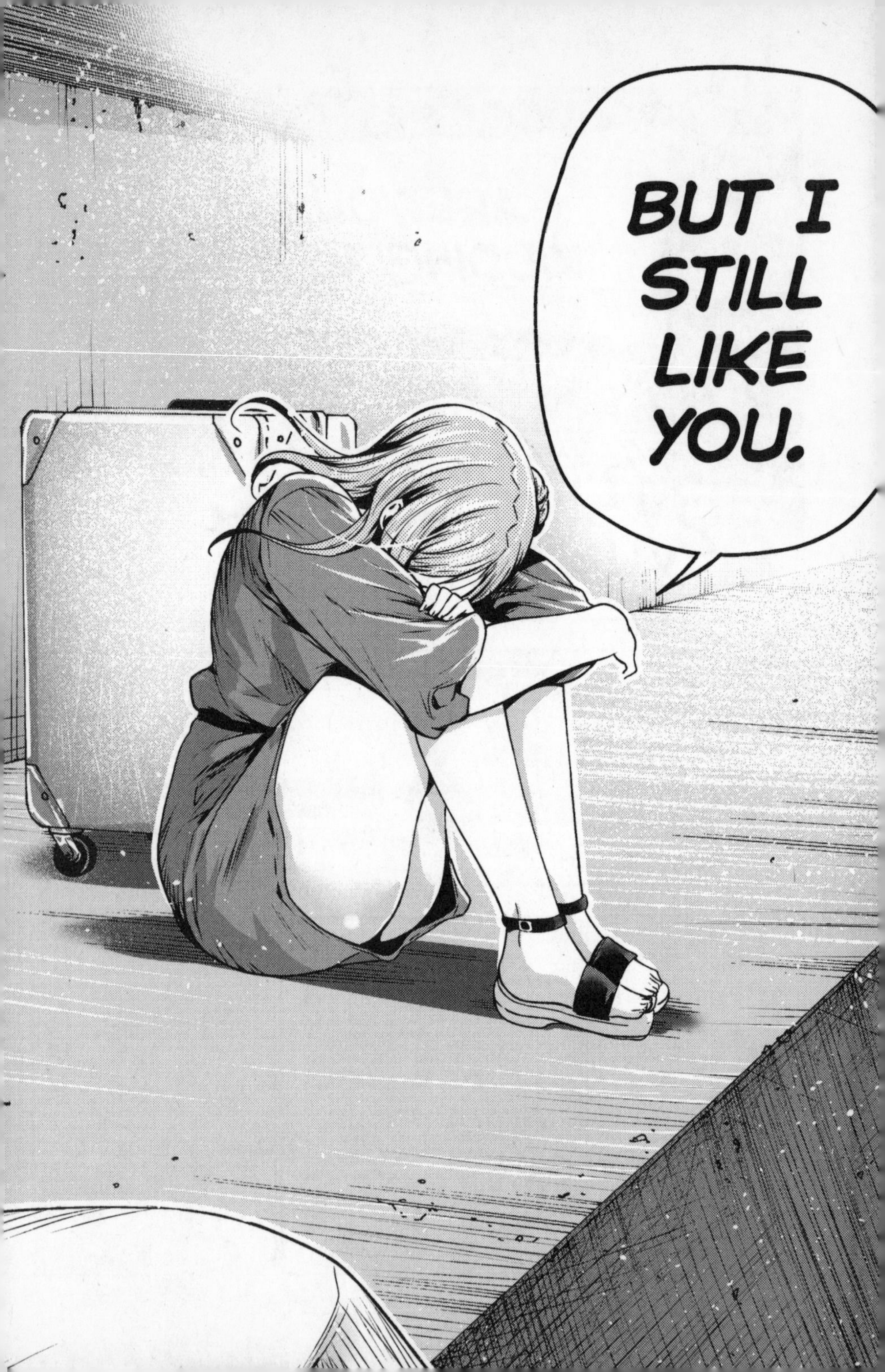
BUT I STILL LIKE YOU.

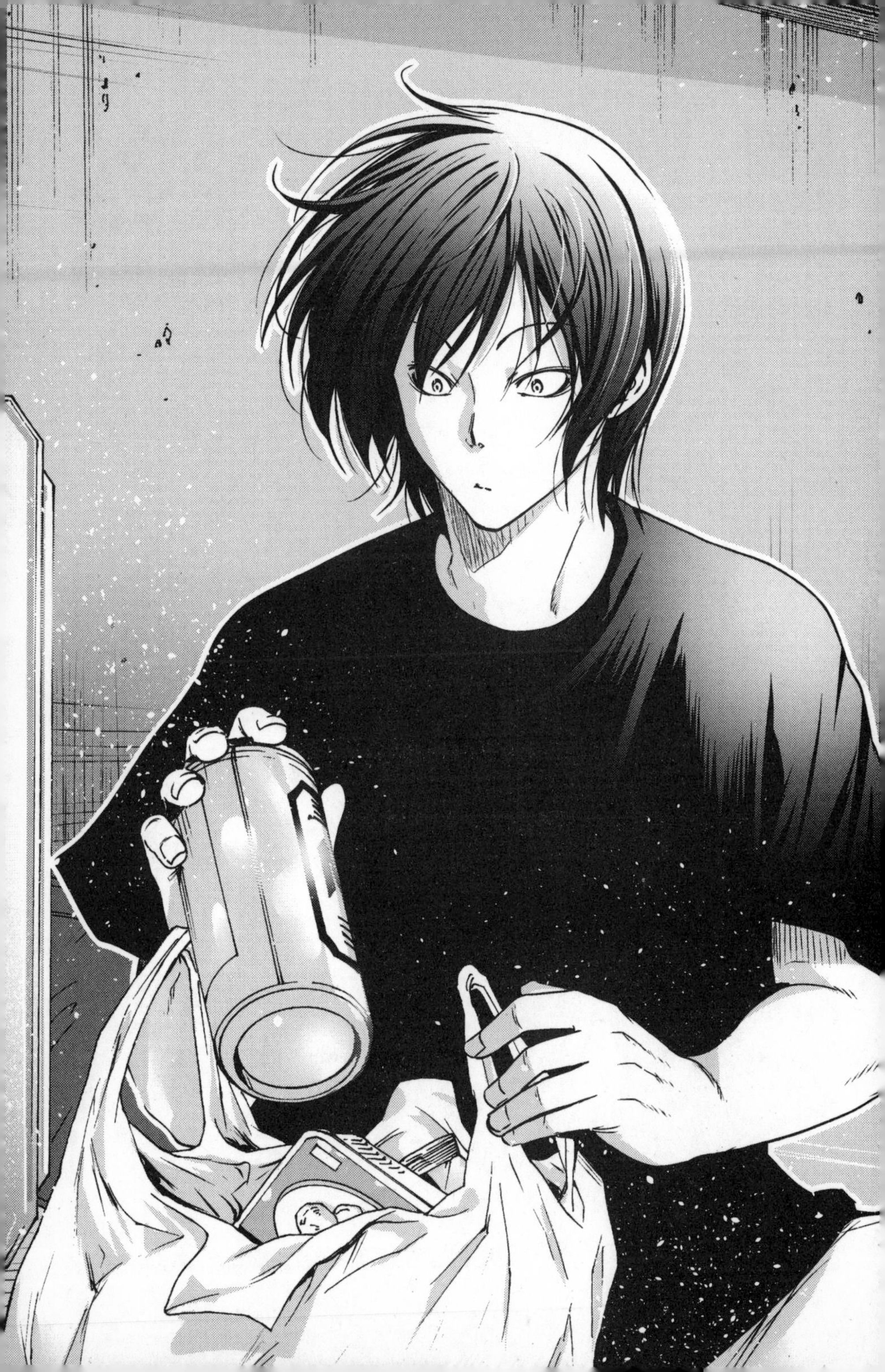

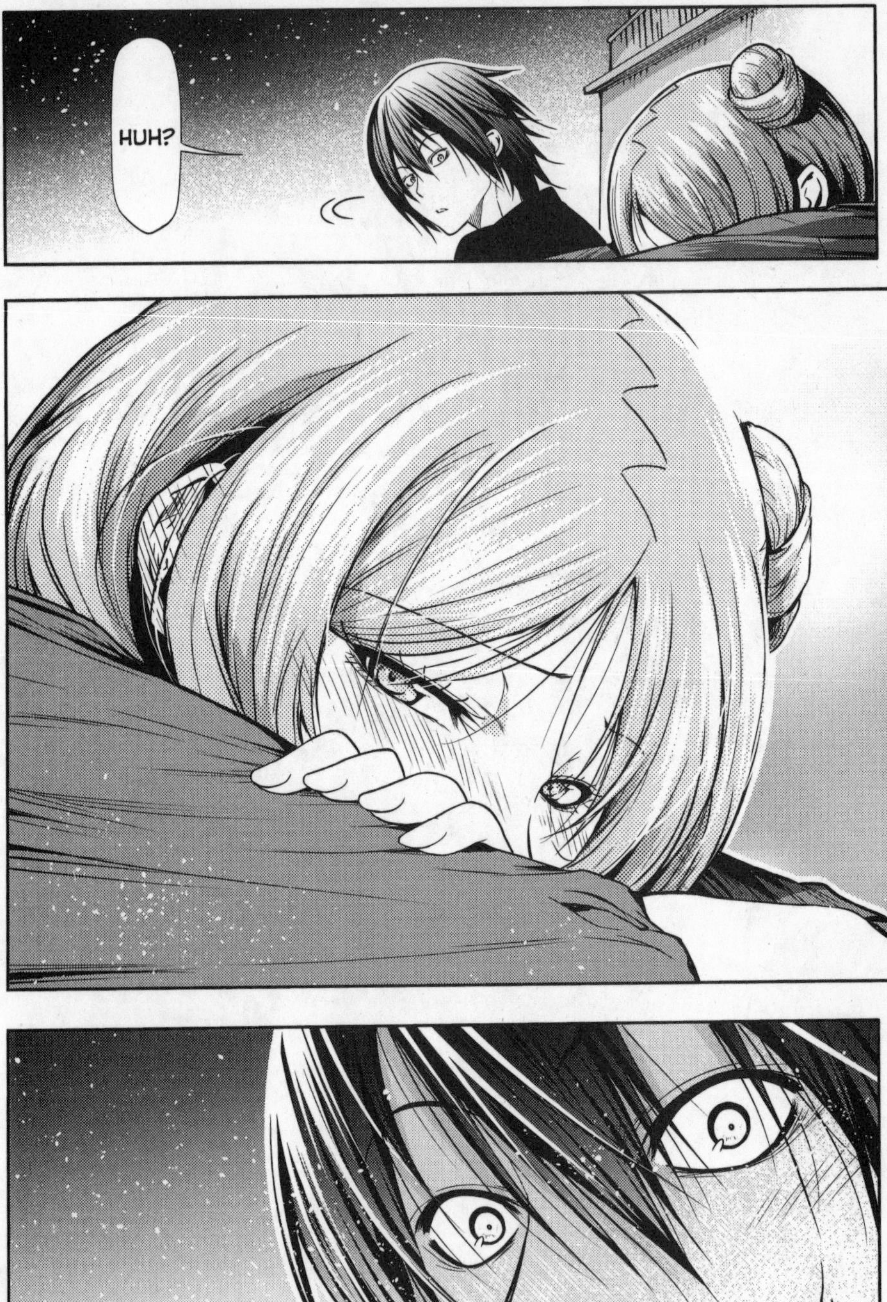
HUH?

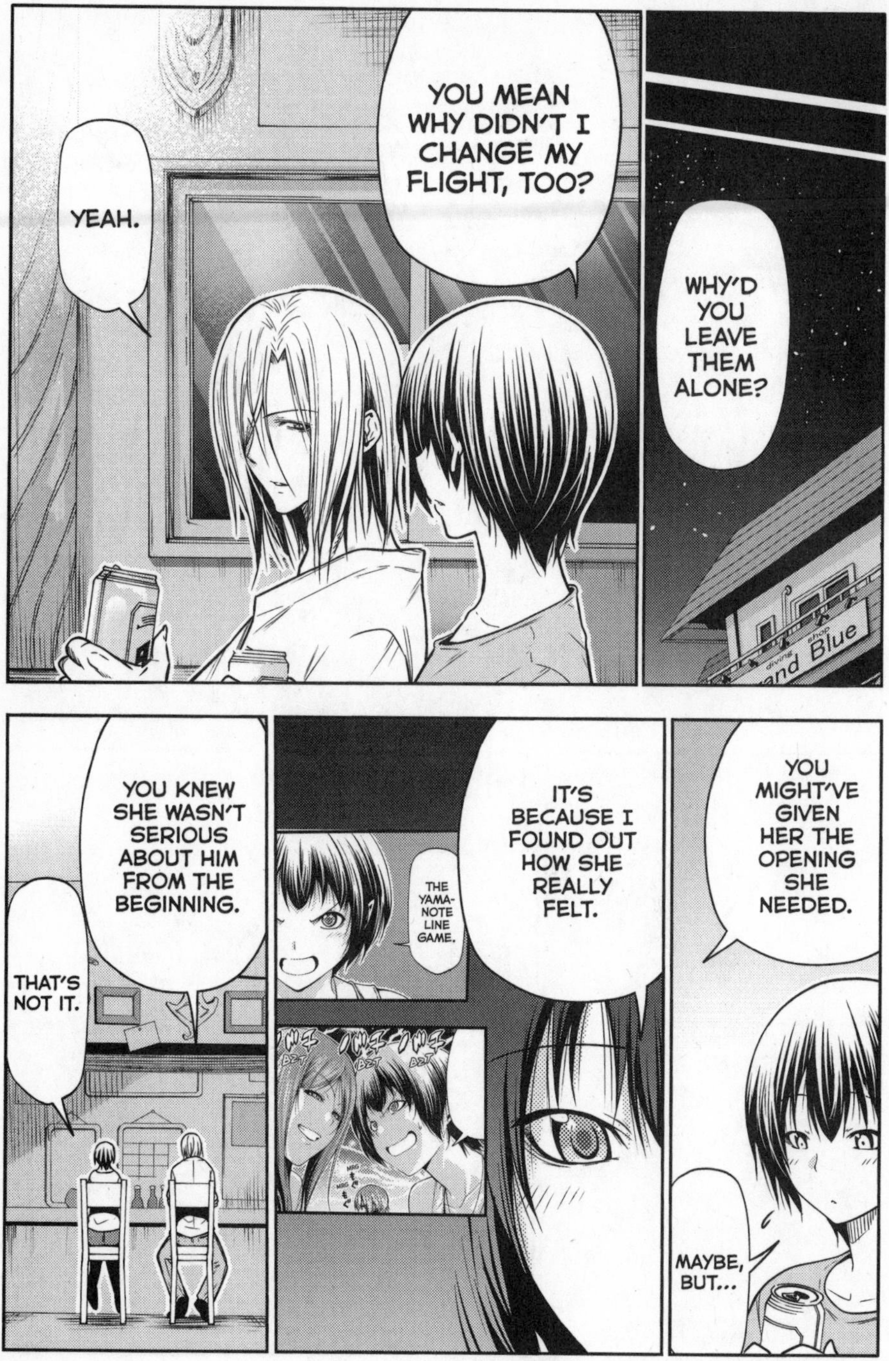
WHY'D YOU LEAVE THEM ALONE?
YOU MEAN WHY DIDN'T I CHANGE MY FLIGHT, TOO?
YEAH.
YOU MIGHT'VE GIVEN HER THE OPENING SHE NEEDED.
MAYBE, BUT...
IT'S BECAUSE I FOUND OUT HOW SHE REALLY FELT.
THE YAMA-NOTE LINE GAME.
YOU KNEW SHE WASN'T SERIOUS ABOUT HIM FROM THE BEGINNING.
THAT'S NOT IT.

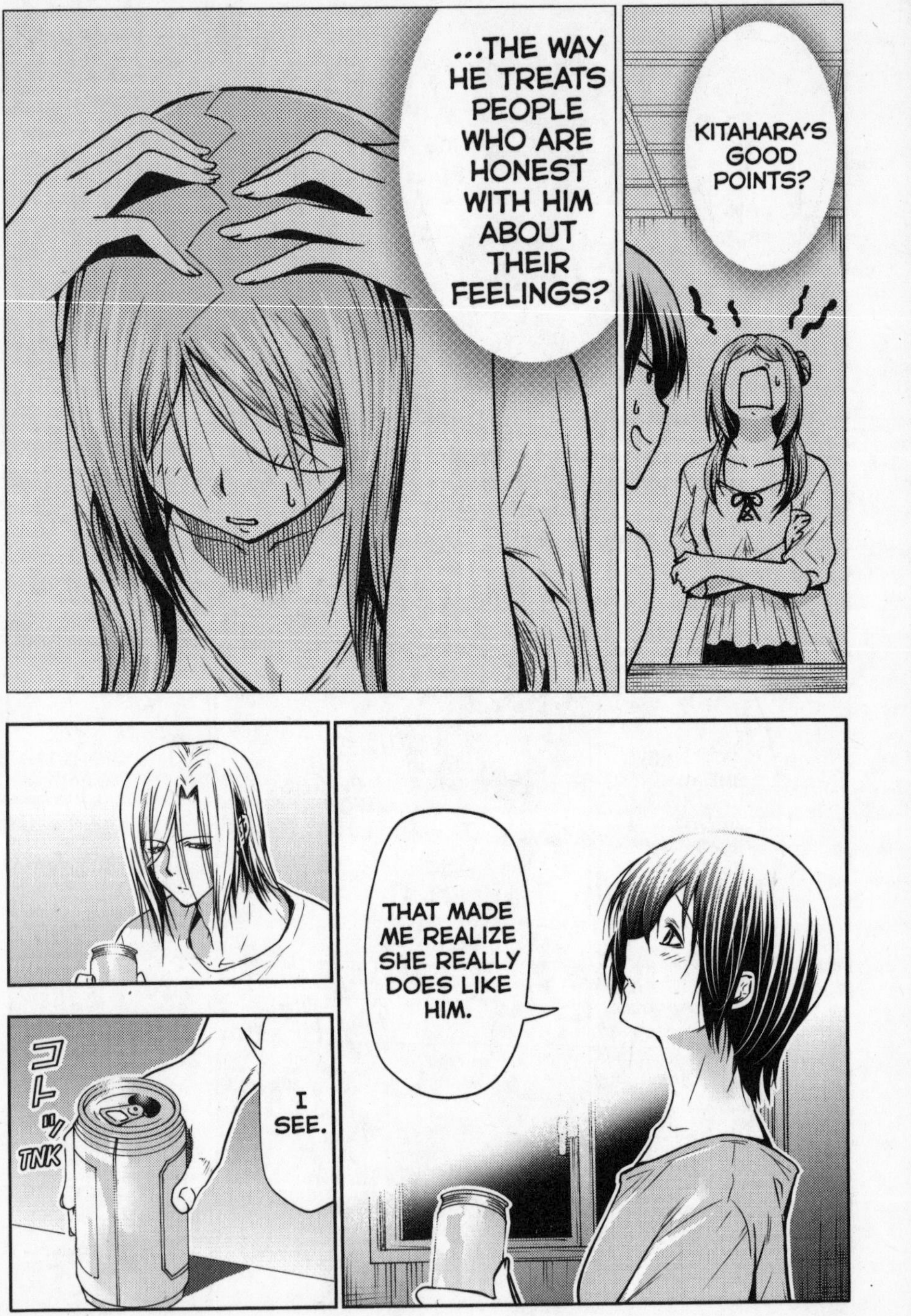
KITAHARA'S GOOD POINTS?
...THE WAY HE TREATS PEOPLE WHO ARE HONEST WITH HIM ABOUT THEIR FEELINGS?
THAT MADE ME REALIZE SHE REALLY DOES LIKE HIM.
コトッ
TNK
I SEE.

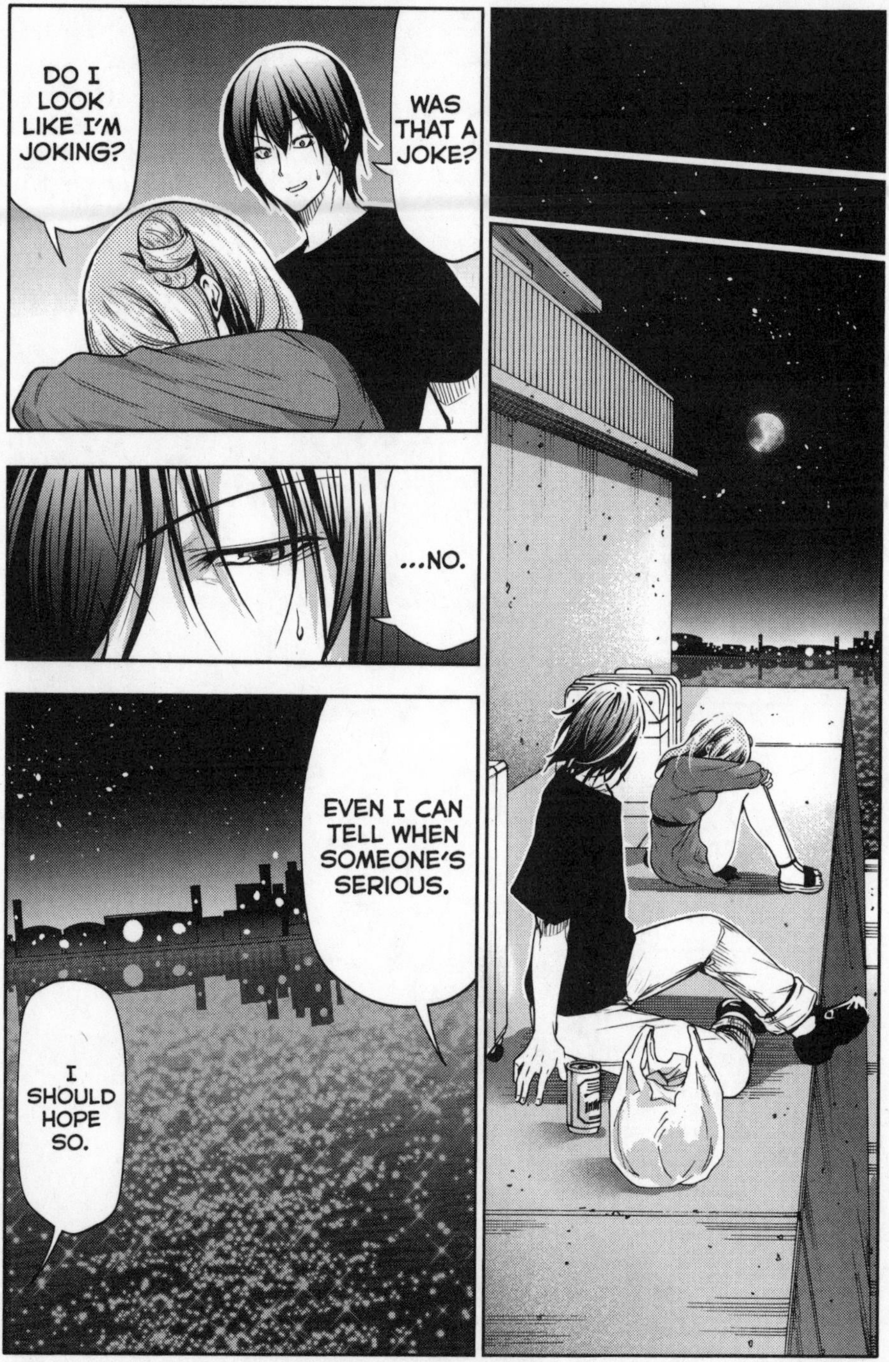
WAS THAT A JOKE?
DO I LOOK LIKE I'M JOKING?
...NO.
EVEN I CAN TELL WHEN SOMEONE'S SERIOUS.
I SHOULD HOPE SO.

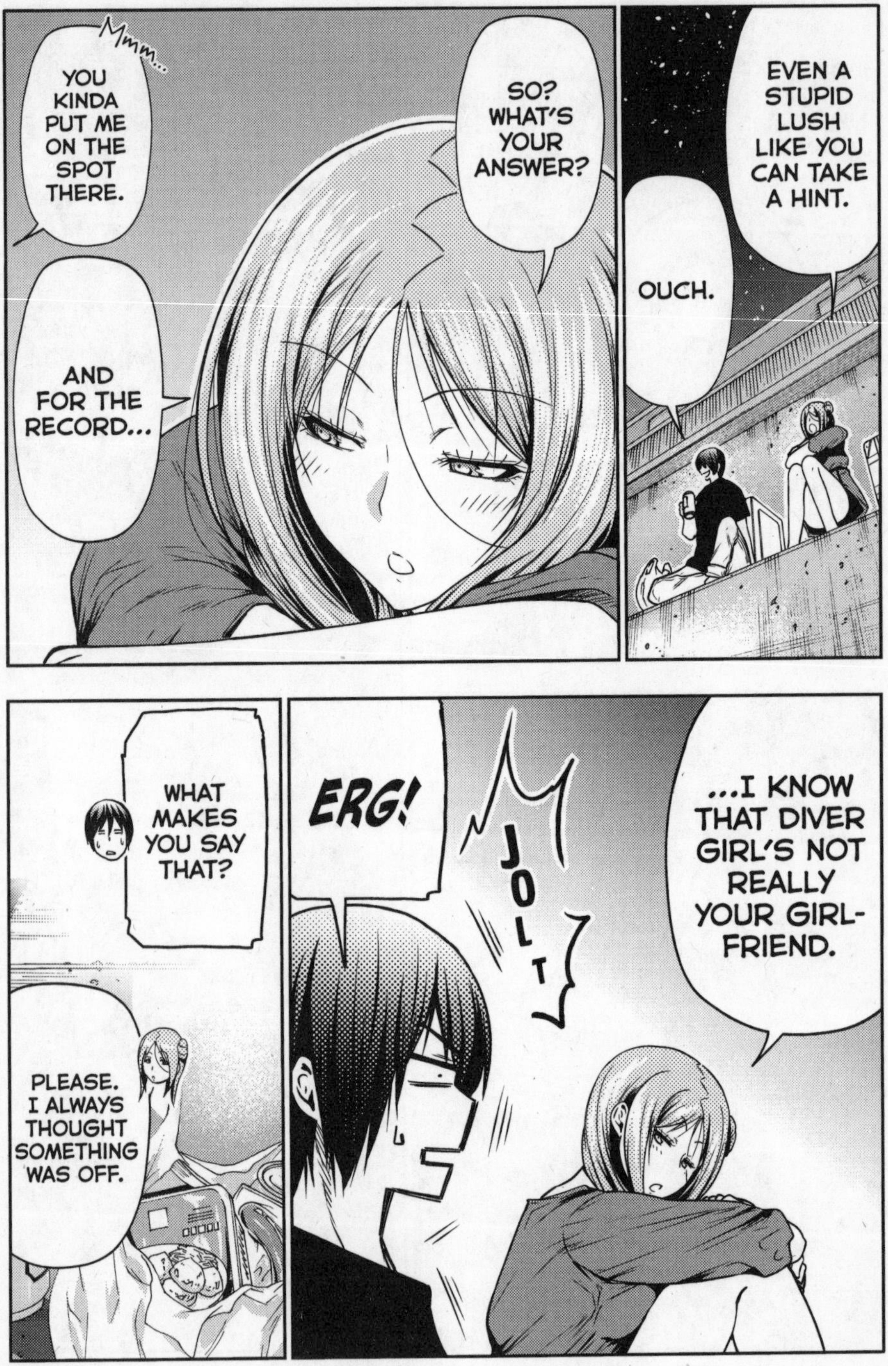
EVEN A STUPID LUSH LIKE YOU CAN TAKE A HINT.
OUCH.
SO? WHAT'S YOUR ANSWER?
Mmm...
YOU KINDA PUT ME ON THE SPOT THERE.
AND FOR THE RECORD...
...I KNOW THAT DIVER GIRL'S NOT REALLY YOUR GIRL-FRIEND.
JOLT
ERG!
WHAT MAKES YOU SAY THAT?
PLEASE. I ALWAYS THOUGHT SOMETHING WAS OFF.

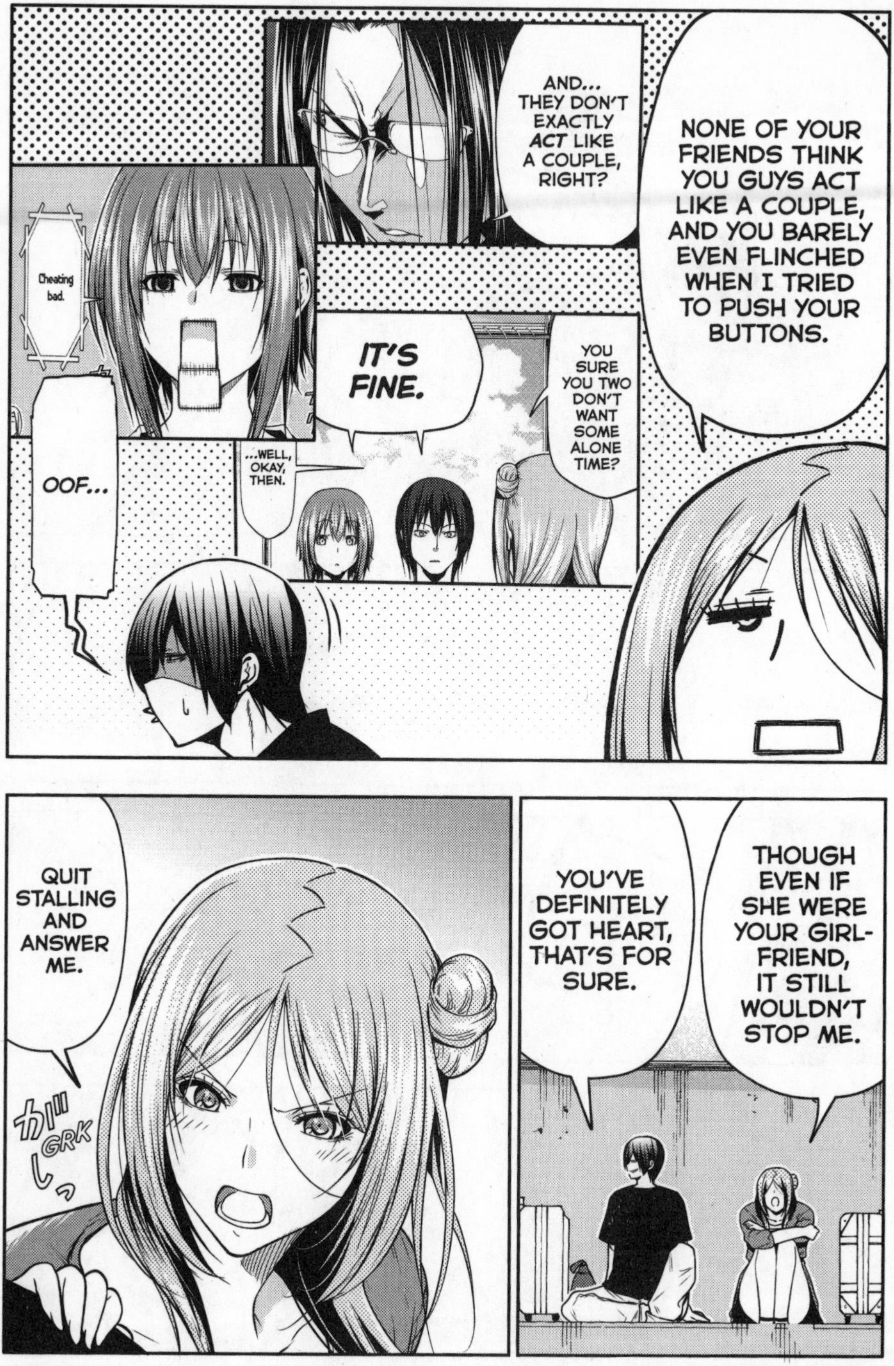
NONE OF YOUR FRIENDS THINK YOU GUYS ACT LIKE A COUPLE, AND YOU BARELY EVEN FLINCHED WHEN I TRIED TO PUSH YOUR BUTTONS.
AND... THEY DON'T EXACTLY ACT LIKE A COUPLE, RIGHT?
Cheating bad.
YOU SURE YOU TWO DON'T WANT SOME ALONE TIME?
IT'S FINE.
...WELL, OKAY, THEN.
OOF...
THOUGH EVEN IF SHE WERE YOUR GIRL-FRIEND, IT STILL WOULDN'T STOP ME.
YOU'VE DEFINITELY GOT HEART, THAT'S FOR SURE.
QUIT STALLING AND ANSWER ME.
がしっ
GRK

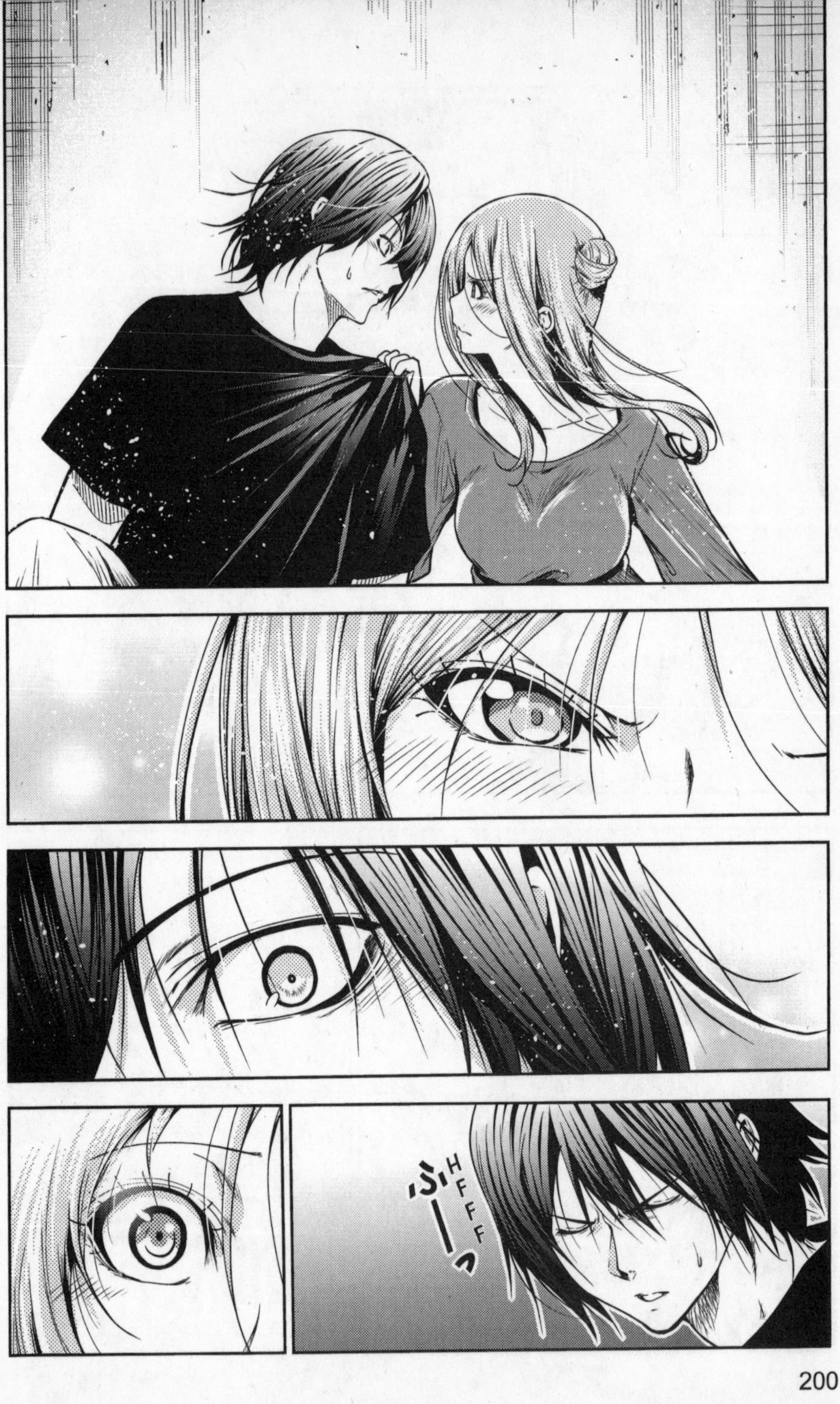
ふーっ
HFFFF

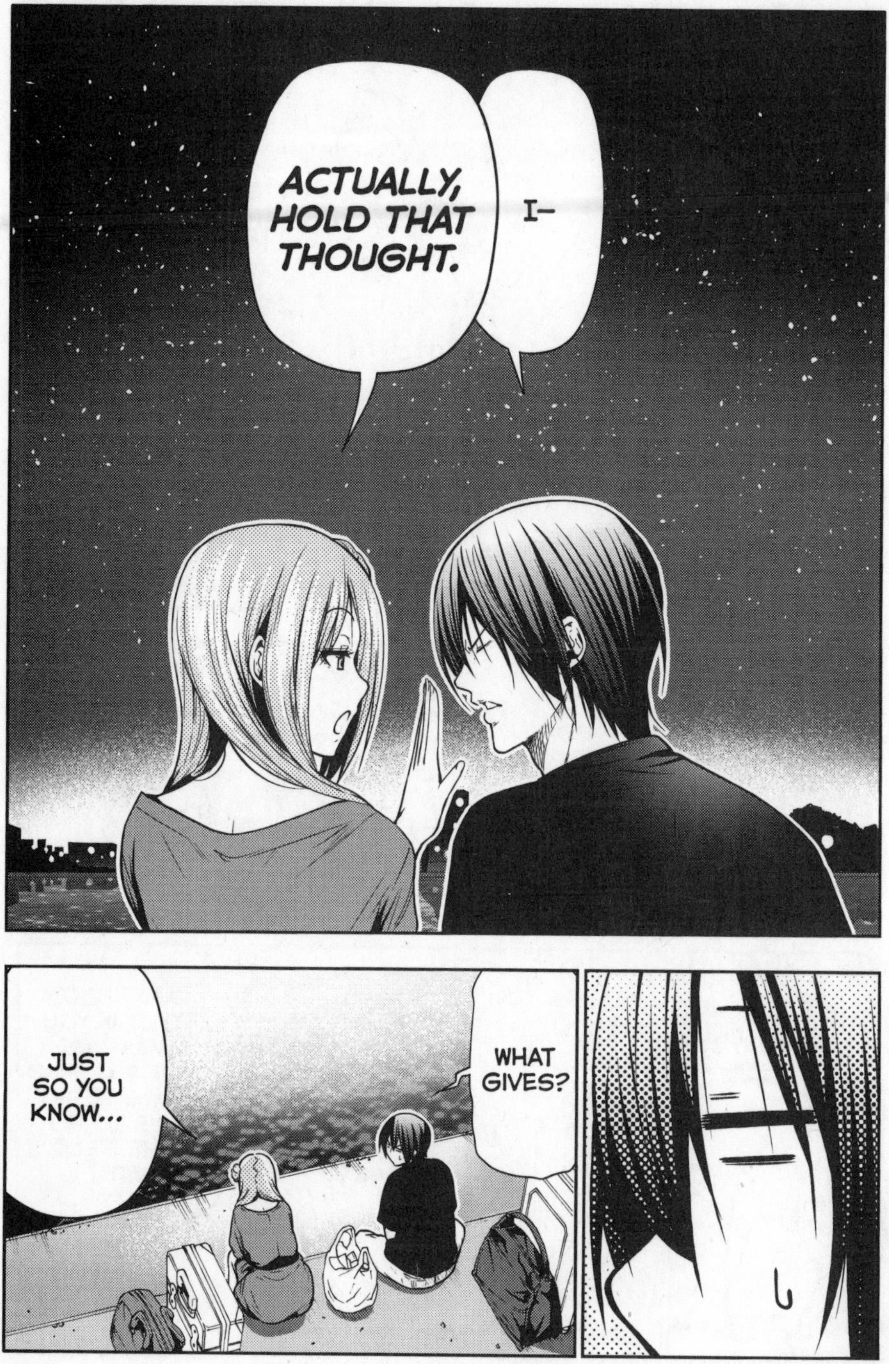
I—
ACTUALLY, HOLD THAT THOUGHT.
WHAT GIVES?
JUST SO YOU KNOW...

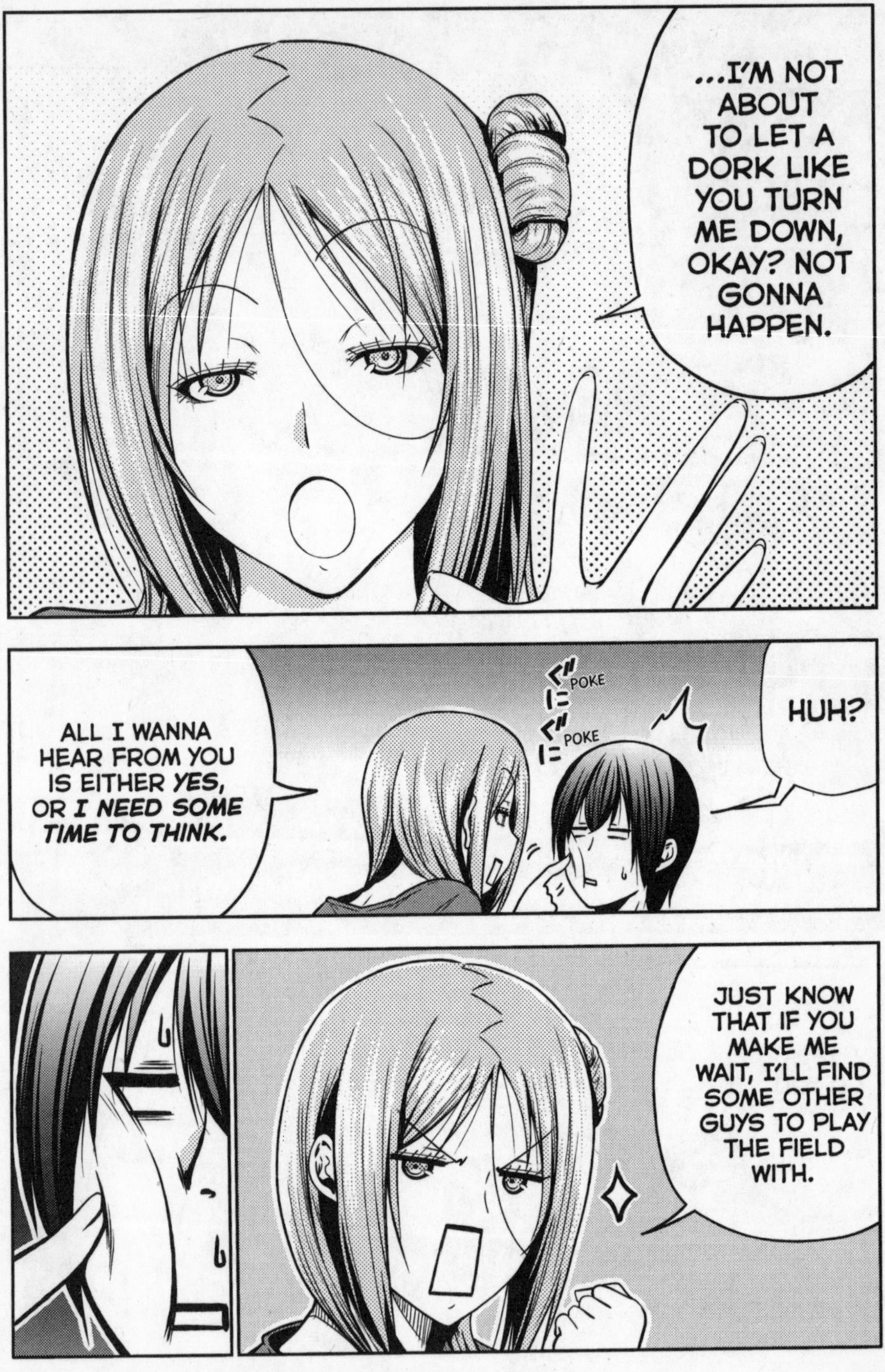
...I'M NOT ABOUT TO LET A DORK LIKE YOU TURN ME DOWN, OKAY? NOT GONNA HAPPEN.
HUH?
ぐに POKE
ぐに POKE
ALL I WANNA HEAR FROM YOU IS EITHER *YES*, OR *I NEED SOME TIME TO THINK.*
JUST KNOW THAT IF YOU MAKE ME WAIT, I'LL FIND SOME OTHER GUYS TO PLAY THE FIELD WITH.

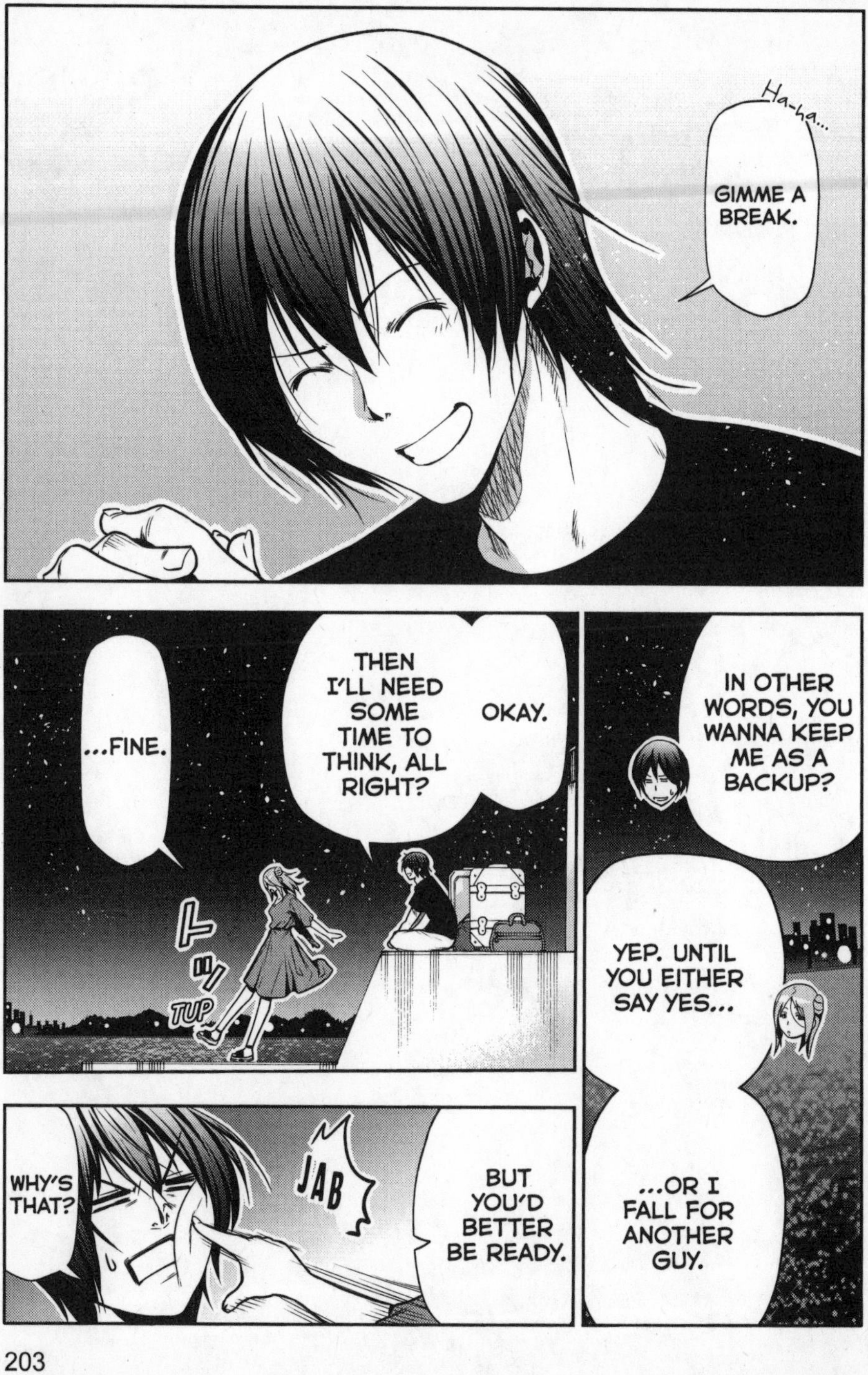
Ha-ha...
GIMME A BREAK.
IN OTHER WORDS, YOU WANNA KEEP ME AS A BACKUP?
YEP. UNTIL YOU EITHER SAY YES...
...OR I FALL FOR ANOTHER GUY.
OKAY.
THEN I'LL NEED SOME TIME TO THINK, ALL RIGHT?
...FINE.
TUP
BUT YOU'D BETTER BE READY.
JAB
WHY'S THAT?

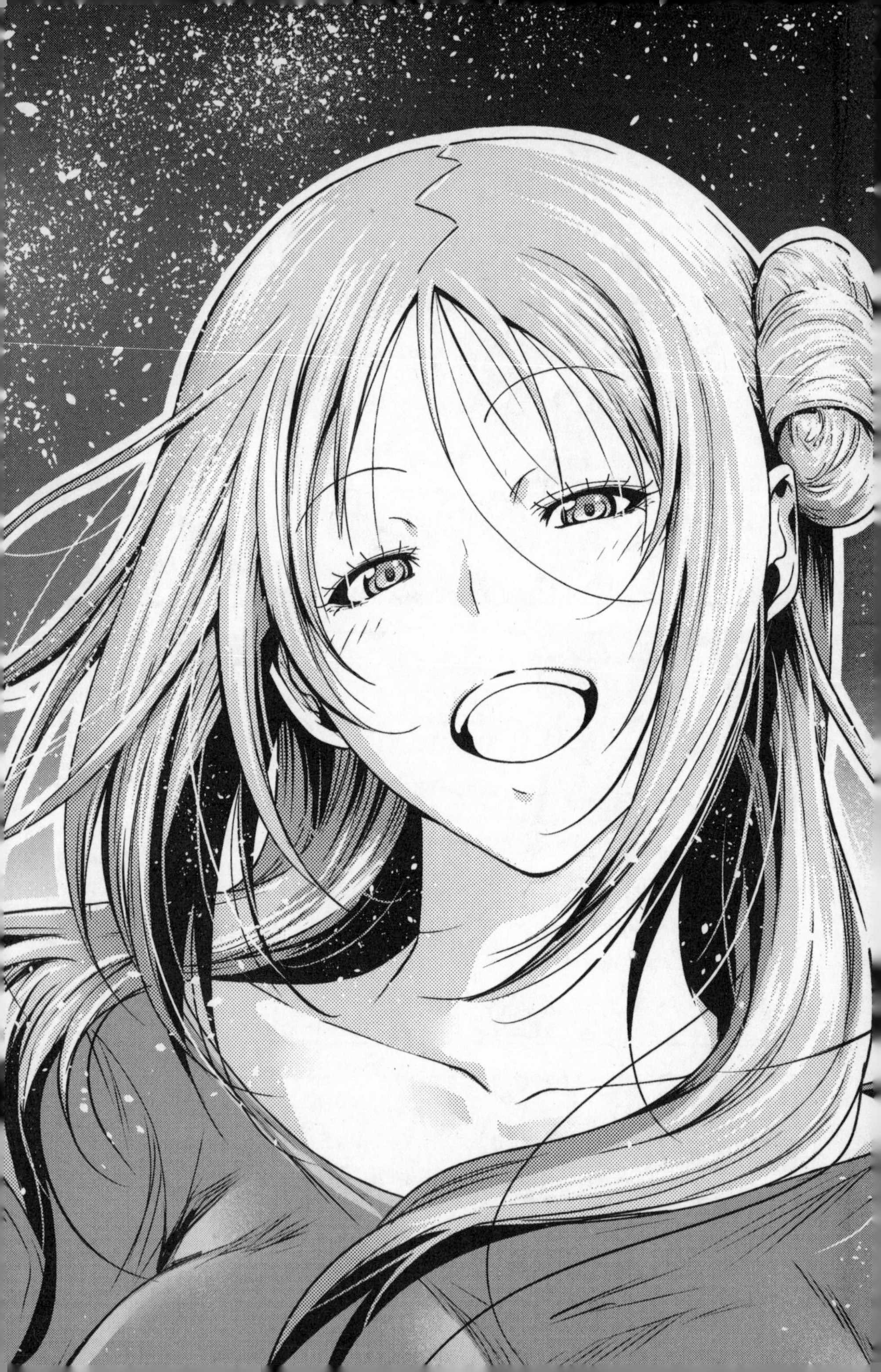

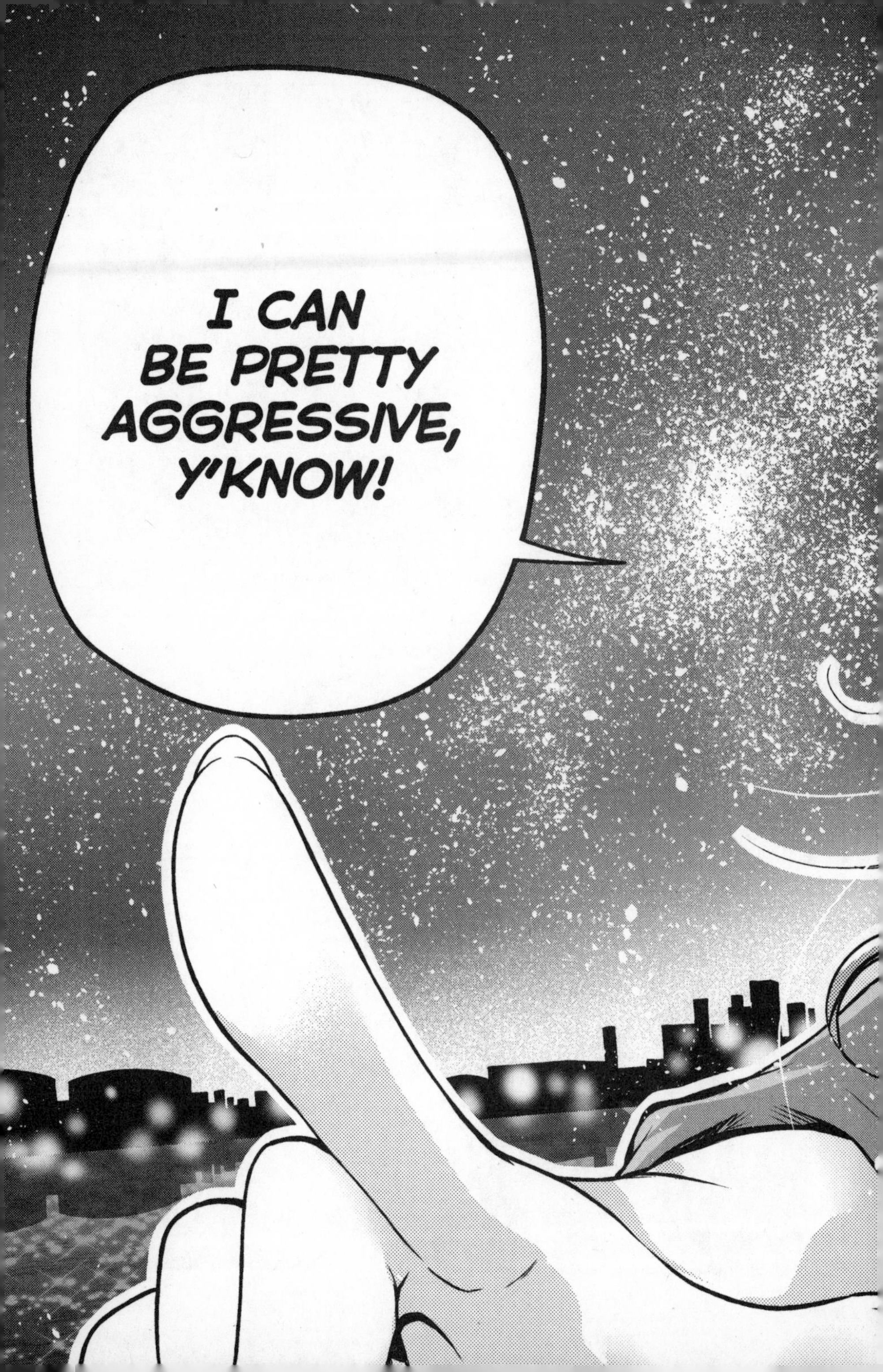
I CAN BE PRETTY AGGRESSIVE, Y'KNOW!

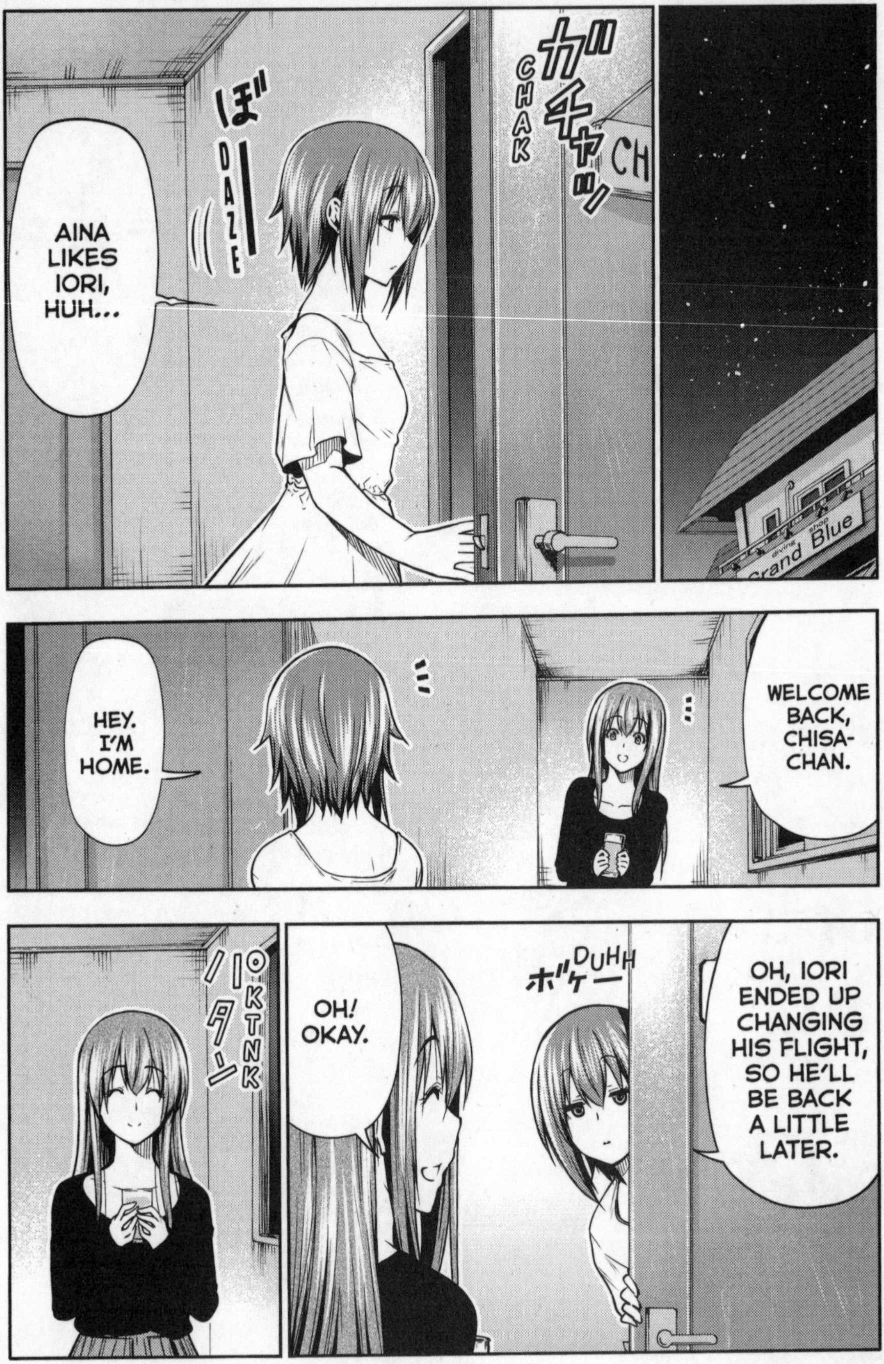

diving shop
Grand Blue
ガチャッ
CHAK
CH
ぼー
DAZE
AINA LIKES IORI, HUH...
WELCOME BACK, CHISA-CHAN.
...
HEY. I'M HOME.
OH, IORI ENDED UP CHANGING HIS FLIGHT, SO HE'LL BE BACK A LITTLE LATER.
ボケー
DUHH
OH! OKAY.
パタン
OKTNK

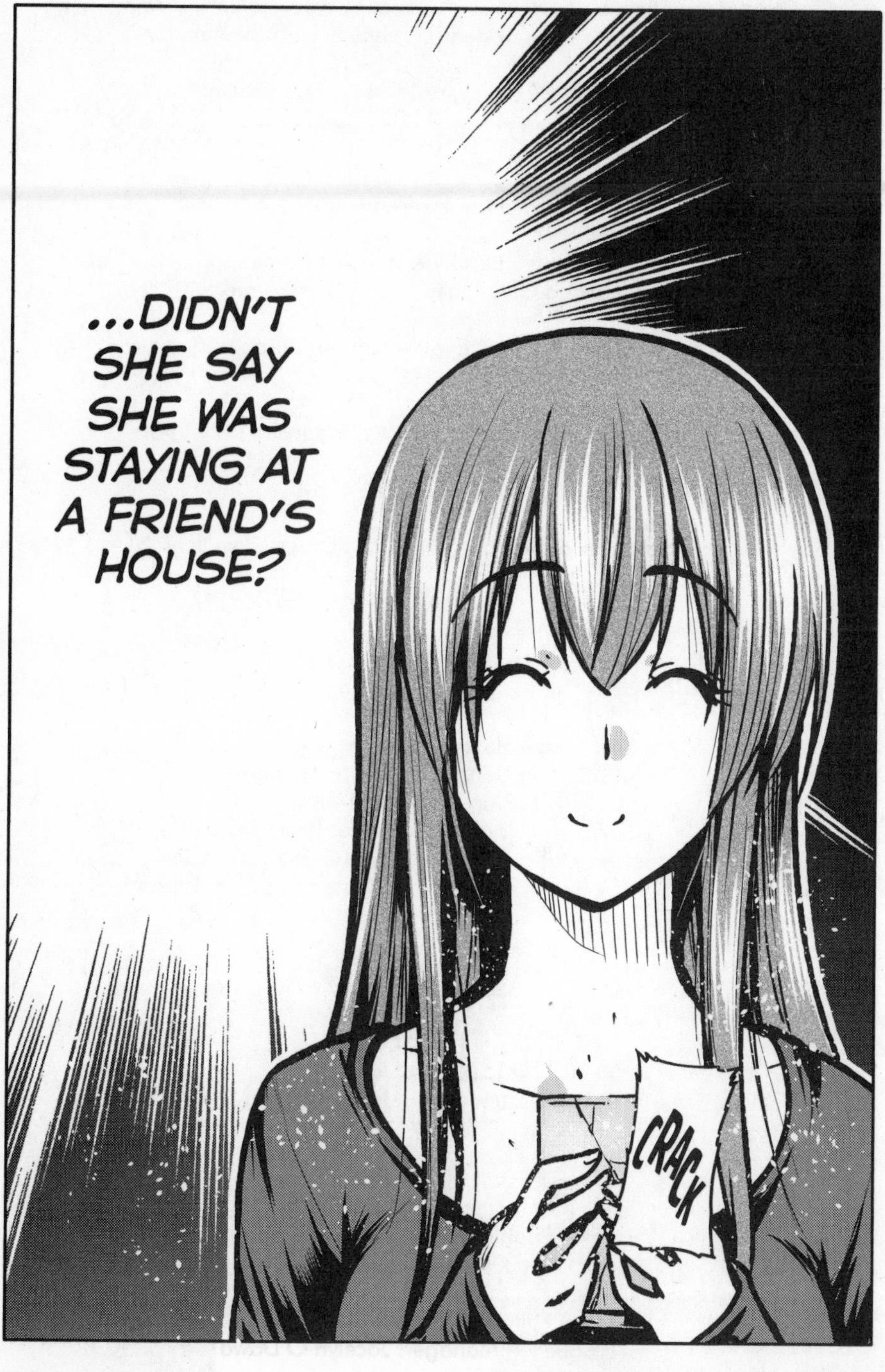
...DIDN'T SHE SAY SHE WAS STAYING AT A FRIEND'S HOUSE?
CRACK

A Kodansha Comics Trade Paperback Original
Grand Blue Dreaming 17 copyright © 2021 Kenji Inoue/Kimitake Yoshioka
English translation copyright © 2022 Kenji Inoue/Kimitake Yoshioka

Published in the United States by Kodansha Comics, an imprint of
Kodansha USA Publishing, LLC, New York.

Publication rights for this English edition arranged through
Kodansha Ltd., Tokyo.

First published in Japan in 2021 by Kodansha Ltd., Tokyo.

ISBN 978-1-64651-403-8

Original cover design by YUKI YOSHIDA (growerDESIGN)

Printed in the United States of America.

www.kodansha.us

9 8 7 6 5 4 3 2 1
Translation: Adam Hirsch
Lettering: Jan Lan Ivan Concepcion
Editing: Andres Oliver
Additional layout and lettering: Sara Linsley
Editorial Assistance: YKS Services LLC/SKY Japan, INC.
Kodansha Comics edition cover design by Phil Balsman

Publisher: Kiichiro Sugawara

Director of publishing services: Ben Applegate
Director of publishing operations: Dave Barrett
Associate director of publishing operations: Stephen Pakula
Publishing services managing editors: Alanna Ruse, Madison Salters, with Grace Chen
Production r